PHILOSOPHY AND CULTURE
Studies from Hungary

To Howard Parsons with personal sympathy and friendship
Montréal, 24. Aug. 1983.

PHILOSOPHY AND CULTURE

Studies from Hungary Published on the occasion of the 17th World Congress of Philosophy

Edited by

JÓZSEF LUKÁCS and FERENC TŐKEI

Associate Editors

ISTVÁN BALOGH, ELEMÉR KÉRI, JÁNOS KRISTÓF NYÍRI, JÁNOS SIPOS

AKADÉMIAI KIADÓ, BUDAPEST 1983

ISBN 963 05 3449 5

Printed in Hungary

LIST OF CONTRIBUTORS

ÁGH, Attila
    Hungarian Institute of International Relations,
    Budapest
ANCSEL, Éva
    Eötvös-Loránd-Universität, Budapest
BALOGH, István
    Institute of Social Sciences, Budapest
BALOGH, Tibor
    Université József Attila, Szeged
DÉRI, József
    Eötvös Loránd University, Budapest
FUKÁSZ, György
    Académie de la Musique Liszt Ferenc, Budapest
GEDŐ, András
    Politisches Institut der Ungarischen Akademie
    der Wissenschaften, Budapest
HERMANN, István
    Eötvös-Loránd-Universität, Budapest
HORVÁTH, József
    Eötvös-Loránd-Universität, Budapest
KELEMEN, János
    Eötvös Loránd University, Budapest
KÖPECZI, Béla
    Ministère de l'Instruction, Budapest
LENDVAI, L. Ferenc
    Université Eötvös Loránd, Budapest
LUKÁCS, József
    Philosophical Institute of the Hungarian Academy
    of Sciences, Budapest
MARTON, Imre
    Université Eötvös Loránd, Budapest
MARX, György
    Eötvös Loránd University, Budapest
MÁTRAI, László
    Hungarian Academy of Sciences, Budapest
NYÍRI, J. Kristóf
    Eötvös-Loránd-Universität, Budapest
SZIKLAI, László
    Georg-Lukács-Archiv, Budapest
SZÜCS, Ervin
    Eötvös Loránd University, Budapest
TŐKEI, Ferenc
    Institute of Linguistics of the Hungarian Academy
    of Sciences, Budapest
WIRTH, Ádám
    École des Hautes Études Politiques, Budapest
ZOLTAI, Dénes
    Institut des Recherches Philosophiques de l'Académie
    des Sciences de Hongrie, Budapest

PREFACE

J. LUKÁCS

In countries where the development of the <u>economic</u> and <u>political</u> spheres was able to take place only in a much too contradictory manner, in the form of some kind of <u>retarded evolution</u> - and Hungary may be counted as one of these countries - there was usually a keen interest in the best part of the last century toward the philosophical problems of culture, and within this toward the significance of art and science as begetters and vehicles of culture. And indeed: in the epoch up to the end of World War I there appeared in our country a number of outstanding thinkers who were to be influential also upon the future development of science abroad, and who examined - with rare exceptions - the basic questions of the world and the country principally from the angle of culture, - to mention only the names of Georg Lukács, Arnold Hauser, Charles de Tolnay, Béla Balázs and Karl Mannheim.

The universality and humanism of their outlook, however, came into conflict with the ideas prevailing in Hungary between the world wars. The representatives of the latter, with a measure of nationalist arrogance and bias, were eager to justify the professed superiority of Hungarian culture over that of the surrounding peoples. Then in the period following World War II the scientific analysis of the genuine values of national culture could be started simultaneously with the sudden renewal of interest in the general regularities of cultural changes. This latter tendency involved, as a matter of course, the claim to study the issues on a philosophical level, which - primarily owing to Georg Lukács's return from emigration - yielded important results in the fields of esthetics and the theory of art. Yet this did not imply a throwback to the conditions of half a century earlier: philosophical analysis was to take into consideration not only the consequences of vast social changes, but the new, culturally relevant questions posed by the social sciences - historical science, ethnology, economics, sociology, literary history, art history, linguistics and so forth - and, partly, by the natural sciences as well.

In this volume we try to give a sample from the writings principally dealing with the more universal issues of the theory of culture produced by Hungarian philosophical scholarship. Of course the attentive reader may perceive that these writings bear the marks of the development of philosophy in Hungary, not to mention the papers on an explicitly Hungarian theme. All these essays are impressed with the endeavor to preserve the significant essential values of culture, while they view with unconcealed anxiety those symptoms of crisis which are visible on the cultural face of mankind. The authors declare themselves Hungarians and Europeans, even if they do know that the cultural development of our epoch taking place on other continents not only complements the achievements of our continent but it also queries them in several respects. It is our conviction that the majority of the writers of these studies are aware that the preservation of the values of culture is possible only if we improve and enrich our interpretation of culture with answers given to the growing number of difficult questions our age raises, if we refine its theoretical and methodological bases. Meanwhile we are by no means in the delusion that our drafting is beyond censure: this would run counter to the theoretical stance, which most of the authors endorse, that life or culture itself is richer than the ideas through which we form a conception of it.

The authors of this collection of essays overtly profess to be adherents of modern Marxist thinking. However, this is not to say that they would consider the inspirations of other systems of ideas as irrelevant - on the contrary, they aspire to the critical acceptance of their rational gist. Nor does it imply that the views of the authors should be without divergences

and points of debate. These discrepancies are parthy accounted
for by historical causes, partly by the different approach toward the interpretation of Marxism produced by the point of de-
parture of the authors, and - quite naturally - partly by the
fact that Marxism as philosophy presupposes the constant recon-
sideration of its earlier stances. At the same time this diversi-
ty stemming from the plurality of ways of approach should not be
by any means the excuse for some kind of eclecticism. Moreover,
the requirement that this philosophical reflection consider all
forms of cognition and practice does not mean that this requirement - the combined claim for life-likeness and consistency of
principle - are being met by every one of our essays. And no
mention is made of what is common knowledge to the reader of any
collection of essays: the quality of the studies is also necessarily uneven.

The editors of this volume were aware of these problems and
of the fact that these cannot, and should not, be corrected by
means which are available to an editor. They had another goal
in mind: to give an overview - from the various areas of research - of the problems with which Hungarian philosophers-schol-
ars are concerned. In this volume one cand find studies on the
philosophy of history and society, on theoretical linguistics,
writings expounding the issues of the modern view of nature,
inquiries into the problems of esthetics and ethics, meditations
from today's vantage upon the motions of culture of the onetime
Austro-Hungarian Monarchy, analyses of the oeuvre of Georg Lukács and, of course, essays probing the methodological and theoretical questions of the research of culture.

It is hoped that the volume - the theme of which coincides
with the main topic of the 17th World Congress of Philosophy -
will elicit readers' attention as well as their critical reflections. In our world riddled with tensions and worries it appears
perhaps most important to get acquainted with the other's standpoint, to compare it with ours, and to carry on the dialogue
commanded by the vital interest of peace and humankind. What
could be in our epoch a more honorable duty for the philosophers

exploring culture than to phrase the questions and possible answers by dint of which they could contribute to the safeguard-
ing and proliferation of the objective and subjective values of
culture on the basis of a higher and at once a more action-minded
<u>humanitas</u>?

József LUKÁCS

CONTENTS

HISTORY AND CULTURE

Philosophy and Culture
J. Lukács and F. Tőkei eds.

ON THE COMMENSURABILITY OF CULTURAL SYSTEMS

J. LUKÁCS

In the debate in today's ethnology, anthropology and social philosophy concerning the commensurability and incommensurability of different cultures, these twin concepts are frequently employed uncritically. The major reason for this disadvantageous situation is that the starting point of the analysis is the existence of cultural identity or of cultural differences, and not the historical process of their genesis.
I assume that history, first of all the material reproduction of human life by similar or comparable means, creates a real continuity and a basis for commensurability between cultures and enables us to look at our own cultural standpoints in perspective where they can be compared and appraised without bias.
1.
    Comparison and differentiation are of course the basis and source of every elementary conceptual formation. At the dawn of history the divergences between groups of people are perceived, yet, as to the fact of otherness, the theoretical question of the content of culture and the question of translatability or commensurability of cultures is not propounded. The rudimentary nature of the means of comparison of cultures stems, on the one hand, from the relatively premature conceptual sphere and, on the other, from the low level of self-consciousness. In the background of these restricted circumstances the Marxist philosopher assumes to detect the undifferentiatedness and dimness of the relationship of man and nature, of man and man, the underdeveloped level of mediation, which is in accordance both with the blurred nature and inflexibility of the concepts.

In the societies of the ancient Near East this position is
modified so that religions integrating the cultures were already
vehicles of a highly advanced ethnic self-consciousness. These,
however, apart from important exceptions, constitute, so to say,
monadic, separate worlds and the theoretical problems of relations with other cultures continue to be missing. In a certain
aspect the situation is similar even in the ancient polis: the
Persian is not only an enemy, but also an inferior for the Greeks,
just as the Hebrew had been an intruding "new-comer" for the inhabitants of Canaan, and later, inversely, the settled Israeli
tribes considered the gojim - the other peoples - inferiors in
an ethnic-religious sense.

The awareness of difference, then, stands out in sharper relief. The apotheosis of self-consciousness is more and more
vigorously coupled with religious, and later with cultural-eth-
ical and quasi-political value-judgements. /In the Greco-Roman
world this links up with the aspiration towards hegemony, then
towards domination over other peoples./

Later Hellenistic and Roman cultural syncretism brought a
change by fusing almost all the significant cultures of the
ancient Mediterranean, the formerly disparate cultural unities.
Subjectively, in the consciousness of the identity - like in
some sort of a common denominator - the elements of earlier segregation and incommensurability all but wither away, but in a
way that the new identity comes to be identified essentially
with the predominant Hellenic then Roman culture, once again
sharply separating the new-born, yet inherently contradictory
unity from all that was left unintegrated outside or inside of
the Empires.

This process seems to be important because it has to do with
the genesis of Christian consciousness and, through it, with
that of modern European self-consciousness. If we are looking
for an ancient example of the clear consciousness of incommensurability, we could scarcely find a more unambiguous precedent
than the monotheism of ancient Israel with its awareness of
chosenness. Yahweh's chosen people, both in their defeats, as
well as in the yearned-for ultimate victory, sensed and conceived
themselves as being at the centre of history - for them the fate

4

of other peoples was only interesting as far as those, being God's instruments, hindered or promoted the deliverance of the Jews. Although here it is one single mythical act, the Covenant between Yahweh and his people that renders this people simply incommensurable with other peoples and therefore there is no need to examine the features of divergence and similarity either, the awareness of segregation in Jewish religious life has to date remained quite effective. Yet it is an instructive fact that this incommensurability was not a hindrance for the substantial elements of the religion /monotheism, messianism, the idea of the covenant, etc./ to become first hellenized, and later on, when Christianity posited them as its direct antecedents, to be incorporated into the new religion as well. What, then, had seemed incomparable for the separate cultures, proved in the actual process of historical changes to be not only commensurable but fusible as well and as such it again became the basis for a new kind of consciousness of incommensurability.

Ultimately, this did come to happen to Christianity as well which, as opposed to the Jewish ethnocentric particularism, had expressed and embodied the abstract claim to universalism, but which - after Nikaia legally as well as politically - tended to be linked with the Mediterranean cultures, emerging on the Hellenic-Roman ground, so much so that after a lapse of some centuries it was appropriate to speak of Roman and Greek Christianity.

The epithet "pagan" used by the Christians served to designate not only the religious but cultural and social incommensurability as well. European culture, therefore, appeared to be the universal model for all cultures and it was taken for granted that the measure of the judgement of other cultures should be none other than Christian, that is, European culture. To be sure, all this had not put an end to the conflicts between the Christian peoples, nor to the antagonism of the official churches and their heresies, but still the religious continuum of Christianity had survived in the history of mediaeval Europe.

Mediaeval Christianity had then become the precursor of that European-Christian consciousness which, following the discovery of the New World, then in the epoch of colonization, drove the

5

missionaries, once as the companions of the conquistadors, then as their rivals, to America, and later to Asia and Africa. Ever since Francis Xavier, this connection has been an urge to compare the cultures of the conquered continents with Christian European culture.

Although the great discoveries awakened the conquerors to striking ethnic divergences, yet, as Peter Strasser has pointed out in his recent article: "The savage cannot have been such a phenomenon who, taken the absolute paradigm of the Western cultural and value system as a basis, should have been permitted to transcend this system". /Archiv für Rechts- und Sozialphilosophie, 1980. No. 3, p. 308./

The eighteenth century saw the first attempt to question this awareness of Europe-centred continuity: the Age of Enlightenment posits the idealized morals and mentality of the then freshly discovered primitive and Eastern societies as a positive example against the patterns of Christian Europe and queries the universal validity of the latter. This attempt is made already on the ground of secularization - its adherents, however, transmit the fancied superiority of the "savage" over the Europeans with no less partiality and bias than their Christian adversaries profess their pre-eminence.

The positivistic and naturalistic evolutionism of the nineteenth century resumed in certain aspects the goals of the Enlightenment /insofar as it gave a non-religious model of social progress/, in a different sense, however it did precisely break with it, as it indirectly returned to the Europe-centred conception.

It is as though the main purpose of earlier events had been to further the evolvement of European culture disregarding in general that active impact which earlier history exercises over the subsequent one. So the continuity of evolution is frequently exaggerated, its contradictory and uneven strains and its features of discontinuity are not taken into account. Hegel and Marx seem never to have lived: the cultural identity, we might say, appears as the gradual unfolding of the same primordial historical and intellectual matter. And vice versa: those motifs which can hardly, or not at all, be inserted in the European-American model, are being played down as ephemeral or anomalous tendencies.

6

All this - we submit - is still the mirror image of that wide-flowing objective social process which might be called - after Marx and Engels - the genesis of world history. "The more the circles, which are in interaction, gain ground already now in the course of the development," we can read in The German Ideology, "the more the original isolation of every nationality is eliminated by virtue of the advanced mode of production and communication and by means of the division of labour effected between the different nations, theremore history becomes world history".

The history of historiography testifies from reverse to the unfolding of this process. In the beginning the ancient classics of historiography were naive to identify the history of their own town or people with history proper and until the end of the Middle Ages historical universality is conceived of in general only as "Heilsgeschichte", history of salvation. All this alludes to the fact that real human contact - from the sphere of economy to religion - must have been only limited and insular. Even Machiavel's range of thought is confined to the dimensions of Florence, and neither Luther nor Calvin could put forth a view of history transcending the European circumstances. The preconditions for the consolidation of a worldwide view could only be created by the emergence of the capitalist world market. Capitalist development ruthlessly crushed traditional boundaries; just as on the other hand the exodus of capital, the technological and mental "export" setting off from Europe and later from America, was conducive to the forging ahead of the Europe-centred world-continuum and the liberal idea of evolution.

However, we should not overlook the fact that this world-historical cultural identity-awareness has from the very outset implied grave contradictions and these are cropping up more and more vigorously as time passes. The global communication and the world market established by the bourgeoisie entailed also that the individuals were gradually coming under the sway of a universal power alien to them.

On the other hand this global communication presupposed the growth of the proletariat, "a class of a world-historical character". So in contrast with the bourgeois model of integration

the claim for and the reality of the socialist integration of
society has appeared in the twentieth century, the antagonism
has deepened between the ideas assessing the value and contents
of the particular national cultures, of European-American and
world culture. And, furthermore, the quickening process of the
liberation of colonies has produced and enhanced the discrepancy
between the cultural self-consciousness of the Third World countries and the Europe-centred notions of a bourgeois nature. All
this together has discredited the Europe- and America-centred
apologies, rendered their values declared as essential relative,
while holding up the possibility for divergent syntheses.

As was usual in the course of great changes earlier /let us
think of the militant and ideological exaggeration of the actual
differences between the English and French development early
in the modern era/, in this situation the reaction to the exaggeration of the idea of commensurability was again that the tendencies of discontinuity, the trends giving incommensurability
absolute validity, gained ground in the social consciousness.
This was manifest in the prominence of the prolet-cult avantgarde in the socialist cultural movements, even in the Soviet
Union, and was being expressed in the developing countries by
the spreading notions that the products of European culture,
be it Christianity, humanism or Marxism, are simply inapplicable
in the Third World. And the same inference was drawn by that
portion of the bourgeois intelligentsia condemning the oppression of colonies and rushing to defend the culture of the developing countries, - who now laid stress upon the incommensurability
of cultures and attacked in this way the earlier evolutionistic
historicism, the one-time ideological foundations of European
expansion.

The positivistic doctrine of progress was to receive the
sharpest censure from its own progeny: the post-positivists and
structuralists leaning towards methodical nominalism and relativism, who, at the same time - professing that the idea of historicity is uninterpretable - have, of course, on certain points,
come into conflict with Marxism. "History is a discontinuous
totality" asserts Claude Lévi-Strauss, "consisting of historical
spheres each of which is determined by the peculiar frequency

and divergent encoding of the Before and the After. Between the given qualities which make up every such entity, the transition is no more feasible than between the rational and irrational numbers." /La pensée savage/. Michel Foucault then tries to verify the idea of historical discontinuity in the field of ethnology, too. But-to the mistaken philosophical hypostases of commensurability which exaggerate the objective importance of the relationships of cultures, however, the response given by the hypostasis of discontinuity and incommensurability ignoring the real mediations and interactions of cultures seems not to be satisfactory.

2.

If we disregard those cultures in which the elements of interaction are negligible, we might say that every culture exists in a certain kind of continuum of the relations of production and communication, it incessantly interiorizes external impacts while being itself influential upon other cultures. Thus it is nothing surprising that, for instance, we come across legions of similar motifs - especially in the case of societies of a similar structure - in religion, in the arts and generally in social consciousness. For about two hundred years the discipline of comparative studies has been bringing home this fact, yet starting from the tacit presumption that these similarities are expressions of some kind of a common human essence, or perhaps some archaic, non-conscious mental content underlying the historically changing forms of consciousness.

With this, however, we cannot be contented. The various cultures actually do not display the same affinity towards external impacts, and they even tend to "select" from among them in a particular manner and acquire the received impact divergently, in compliance with their structural features. Thus the autochthonal character of each culture is not to be denied, nor its relative "incommensurability" with the others. Ultimately, every culture is to some extent adequate with those relations which provide the basis for it and it is inadequate with those of other cultures. This is meant to say that what is called cultural "incommensurability" is in some sense just as real as the commensurability of cultures. But this "incommensurability" implies no-

9

thing more than that every culture is the product and constituent of its own circumstances. This does not preclude but presupposes that cultures themselves shape their specific features by the reception and transformation of external impacts, just as they, too, exercise some kind of influence upon other cultures. Or expressed differently: the idiosyncrasies of cultures exist only in the process of inter-actions and just for this specific trait are they to be compared and measured to other cultures. Comparison is made possible by the fact that in reality the particular, the concrete carries in itself the general as a motif.

Let us adduce one single example - purposefully from the sphere of that culture the two stages of which Paul S. Feyerabend qualifies in a cognitive sense as incommensurable, as the paradigm of paradigm-change. The example is early Greek thought, one of the most relevant sources of our European cultures, particularly the myths of Homer and Hesiod.

With a slight overstatement we could say that the entire Greek mythology was "imported" to Greece from Asia by virtue of a cultural migration just as - perhaps apart from the Pelasgian people- the inhabitants of the peninsula and the archipelago had come en masse from Asia. It is not only that Hellenic consciousness ignored this continuity, - on the contrary: it emphasizes the discontinuity against the barbaric East /and against its own barbaric past/. In reality, however, as it is known, the rejection of Asian mythologies and Asian culture took place already in statu nascendi and in general behind this critical stance we can reveal semiconscious effects inspired by a new social structure, scarcely yet realizing its own potentialities, which influence the "logic" of cultural assimilation. This practice of assimilation is divergent from those of Eastern societies, notwithstanding the fact that this society, too, had evolved from those.

Reitzenstein has proved that almost all the important elements of the Kronos-story so essential to Hesoid are to be found in the Hittite and Hurrite myths. Kronos, who frustrates the coition of his parents, Uranos and Gaia, by castrating his father and taking their place on the throne is none other than the Greek counterpart of that Kumarbi who had also deprived his father Anu of his masculinity in order to supplant him. Kronos, just as

Kumbari, for fear of the repetition of his act, devours his children, until his son Zeus, with the aid of his mother, puts an end to this theophagy - the same fate as Kumbari suffers at the hands of his son Tesub in Hittite mythology.

At a cursory glance, therefore, these myths are the same. Yet we should repeat: the integration took place according to the specific logic of the Hellenic religious system. In the Asian myth Tesub would not sit on his father's throne, as Zeus did in the Olimpian realm, but restores the reign of his grandfather, Anu, that is he drives back the mythical cosmos to the original state of world thus completing the cyclic movement in the spirit of standstill represented by Anu. - In Greece, the purport of the myth is just the opposite: the three generations of gods succeed each other in a way that this process renders perceptible the distinct direction of time, the movement of history, which does not simply reconstruct the earlier state of affairs. So, here in this myth we can perceive the dynamic progression of history as opposed to the static principle of cyclic recurrence widely known in the East. Similarly, the consequences of the dethronement of the first generation of gods display also a marked difference. The chopped phallos of Kronos inseminates the sea just as that of Anu. But while in the Eastern myth it is Mot, the god of death and sterility, that springs to life from the sea, in the Greek version the very same act results in the birth of Aphrodite, the goddess of love, beauty and fertility. So the almost identical mythemes gave rise to two myths disparate as to their message: the Asian raw material was moulded by impulses rooted in the Hellenic ground according to different intentions.

Another example is the Hellenic mythic cosmogonies. As is known, they assume the form of theogony. But among the first generation of gods we can find the carriers of those primaeval principles which, from the 6th century BC onwards, the Ionian natural philosophers perceived to be physical arches in order to derive from them the multifold character of cosmos: Gaea is the goddess of the earth, Uranos is the god of the sky /the air-sky/, at the same time she is the Earth itself and he the Sky itself; and among Zeus' elder brothers we can see Poseidon, the god of the waters, and Hephaistos, guardian of fire, etc.

Later on philosophical thinking was to divest these formulas of its anthropomorphism, and this brought on a mutation, discontinuity in the development of thought. Yet this indicates at once that this philosophy could not have come into existence without the assimilation of its own mythic antecedents. The breaking off of continuity is due to the spreading of a new "logic" but the denial of the old comes to pass in a dialectical way: as a joint result of ceasing and transcending. The paradigm-change is not absolute.

In other words: the continuity of transmission is broken - still the material handed down has not been wasted. The message of the myths, we might say, has become "incommensurable", but this does not alter the fact of real historical reception, only the specific mechanism of the reception and acquisition has been modified. The incommensurability will not entirely disappear, but loses its absolute character and becomes relative. On the one hand discontinuity does not cover the whole of the cultural sphere, and on the other it also gains a historical explanation. Furthermore, continuity prevails in a way that external impacts come to be assimilated into divergent structures only if transformed in accordance with the structure of the system.

The original reason of the mingling, selection and elaboration of the effects can scarcely be sought in the "Greek spirit", if only because the "Greek spirit" is nothing else but the existing outcome of the linking of these effects. This selection and e-laboration of the effects is in the last analysis due to the impulses arising from the everyday conduct of life of people and this is determined primarily by the given shape and mode of social production. The ancient mode of production - in contrast with the Asiatic one - contains the tendencies of transcending and disrupting the given relations. And perhaps that is why it was favourable not to the myth-formation manifesting itself in the cyclic reproduction of the existing relations, but rather to one which embodies an unceasing change and a steady enlargement in reproduction and everyday life.
3.

As for the authentic figures of Marxism, primarily Marx himself, he was well aware of the significance of the problems just

12

outlined. In the famous Introduction to his Critique of Political Economy, he expounds in detail the dual character of scientific terms and concepts. These concepts - like the categories work, property, or money - are on the one hand vehicles of archaic, "antediluvian" contents and are expressions of a relevance valid to all social forms starting from as early as the rise of civilization or even earlier. But if the content of abstractness is examined, it will turn out that "even the most abstract categories, valid as they may be to every period just by dint of their abstract nature, are themselves in the determination of this abstractness the products of historical relations and have full validity only within these relations."

Or put differently: in our concepts are manifest both the common, comparable moments of historical reality and features specific to a given age /which have "full validity only within these relations"/, which constitute a unity without eliminating the differences.

I believe that all this is generally true not only of the relationships of different concepts, but also of those of the intellectual systems and cultures. Cultures are comparable and should be compared to one another, insofar as each culture is eventually the product of people reproducing their own existence as social beings under definite circumstances and at the same time it is an agent of this reproduction. This abstract "commensurability", however, cannot account for the profound differences between the types of culture, actually the logical schema does not exist independently of its historical base, of the historical determination of the above mentioned anthropological categories /the performance of work/, social existence, conscious activity etc/. The movement of history, which brings about both separation and identification between cultures, helps unfold and change primarily not the particular elements of the cultural systems /arts, philosophy, religion, morals, etc./, but the totality of the given systematic quality, its specific dynamic and static.

Therefore, with the mode of production grasped as the unity of the forces and relations of production, the socio-economic formations are comparable and can be measured to each other con-

cerning their historical stage of development and, from the angle
of universal history, constitute a progressive sequence. Even
those scholars who profess the incommensurability of cultural
types refrain from questioning the commensurability of specific
forms and elements of culture; they do deny mainly those cultural paradigms, those "logics" which arrange the elements. However, it is merely the logics that are connected to the historical structure of production, and indeed the possibility for the
comparison of social and cultural types is provided precisely
by the objective exploration of the structures of production laying the foundation of the whole culture and intertwining with
its historical development.

On an abstract level it remains true that there is a conceivable relationship between the historically developed socio-economic formations and their spiritual culture, and that, in general,
the identical modes of production are combined with a similar
cultural system, and divergent modes of production are accompanied
by different cultural systems. But all theory is grey and and the
golden three of life springs ever green. The crucial point is
how we interpret concrete history itself, how we describe its
regularities, its continuity and discontinuity, if the theoretical questions of cultural commensurability and incommensurability
are to be answered.

The question may be raised whether the recognition of social
laws operative in the whole of history is compatible with the
contradictions, with the unequal evolution, with the abrupt
changes? Are we not to give credit to Jürgen Habermas who insists
that the reconstruction of historical materialism is necessary
exactly because "neither linearity, nor necessity, neither continuity, nor the irreversibility of history" prevails in reality?
/Zur Rekonstruktion des historischen Materialismus. Frankfurt/M.,
1976. p. 154./

However, it would be futile to search for models of linear
progress in Marx. Instead we can read the following: "The so-
-called historical development actually rests upon the fact that
the latest form regards the bygone ones as stages leading to
itself and as it is able to censure itself only rarely and under
extremely fixed conditions ...it comprehends them always one-
-sidedly."

The famous Marxian criterion of historical progress, the Zurückdrängung der Naturschranken is the outcome prevailing over contradictions of the universal historical movement and not its formative principle gradually unfolding in every successive stage. For progress is not linear, so much so that in vast territories of the Globe the relations of production virtually did not change for thousands of years, while elsewhere profound social changes succeeded one another relatively rapidly.

In spite of this, the rising out of the natural may be finely grasped as a tendency, it is an apt gauge of progress in the context of progressive actions, in the advancing movement of the totality of culture during the entire history of mankind: the decrease of the working time necessary for reproduction, the shrinking of the natural element of the products of labour, the modification and gradual dwindling of the natural aspect of communities are all relatively certain criteria for the entire progress. This holds true even if in the course of the "prehistory" of humankind, the social connections coming into existence with the progressive formation of the relationship towards nature look back upon the people as alien forces, and even if the surmounting of this alienness is the precondition for the emergence of "human history proper".

This humanization of the natural - of which the most essential driving force is the development of the forces of production - is itself a process by no means harmonic but contradictory. As it was clearly perceived also by Marx, the production of wealth may at once undermine its own sources, the land and the health of the worker as well. Thus the purport of the realization of "history proper" is not confined to the fact that the direction of things should replace the direction of persons, but it must also warrant that in the course of the "direction" of nature the results of the process do not turn against the producer. Of course, this again is a tendency, and one which materializes in specific cases rather unevenly.

The law of harmony of the forces and relations of production - as every social law - has validity in concrete reality only as a tendency, which means that the comprehension of its real role does not preclude, but, on the contrary, presupposes the theoretical and empirical analysis of the actual or expected historical turns. So it is of crucial importance that the realization of the law, its actual strength of influence be explored. In a letter to J. Bloch, Engels observes accurately that it is "the interaction of political and legal forms, philosophical and religious ideas in which, through myriads of coincidences, the economic movement as a necessity will eventually prevail". This implies also that - as our recent history demonstrates - this law comes across by no means automatically, and that "decisions, accidents, initiatives, discoveries" /Foucault: Archéologie du savoir/ - indeed the activity of the subject - are not incompatible with the Marxist concept of laws in history. For here the role of the conscious element lies precisely in the decision to choose from the alternatives stemming from the developed objective possibilities and in the realization of that decision. On a certain point the alternatives do of necessity come forward, but eventually they "raise" the very question, whether to stay within the frameworks of the given social-economic relations, or - provided the given stage of social relations can offer us real possibilities - whether we should break this continuity and create a new scope for action. Of course, a mechanistic conception would dismiss the joint acceptance of the existence of alternatives, of the accident and of the necessities of the historical process, the emphasis on the importance of the social objectivity and the revolutionary significance of the subjectivity. A dialectical outlook - as it is borne out by the whole oeuvre of Marx or Lenin - would rather view these as substantial methodological principles without which history is a jumble of events and proper action will be beyond our grasp.

History proper, then - unlike the scheme of "Heilgeschichte"- will not comply with the notion of linear, steady, uninterrupted progress. Quite the contrary: the entire process of development up till now has been extremely spasmodic and unequal. There were flourishing cultures that perished, others are unable for thousands of years to step beyond the limits staked off by themselves, and still others soar high to sudden historical significance only to sink back again into irrelevance, or others still are for a long time capable of sustaining their prominent role and affect-

ing the universal development, the cultures unable to come near
to their level. Actually not a single society is known to have
passed all the progressive stages of the universal development
of mankind.

It is only from the abstract but real angle of universal human
development that the history of mankind appears to have moved
through every important historical stage - the Asiatic, the
ancient, the feudal and the bourgeois modes of production. /On
this plane, however, the sequence of these forms implies a colossal theoretical significance./ None of the societies of Europe
has passed all those stages and this indicates historical in-
equality. But, unlike the societies of Asia, Africa and America,
they did jointly pass these levels of development, and this provides the real basis for the apparent view that the European
course should be taken as a paradigm of the history of other
continents. Europe is rightly considered to be the classical and
typical vehicle of human development - yet it is a fallacy of
the Europe-centred view to infer from this, that, for instance,
Asia should have passed in a similar manner all those stages
that Europe has passed.True, some elements of the pristine, primordial culture will be transformed and surpassed in the course
of the acquisition of the European cultural impacts. Yet there
is a difference of type between the following: on the one hand
when, the impacts coming from a more advanced level, the less
developed cultures organically assimilate on their own basis
and with their own logic and go on improving themselves afterwards, and on the other, when another culture is being thrust
upon a less developed one, perhaps with the very intent of its
elimination. /Actually this antihuman effort succeeds in most
cases only incompletely: the elements of Aztec culture "beheaded"
by the Spanish conquerors were able to reawaken in 20th-century
Mexican painting./

The interaction has again a different character when a more
comprehensive culture absorbs the elements of more particular
cultures /e.g. the relationship of Jewish and Greek religion in
Hellenistic times, then their role in the formation of Christian-
ity/ without directly eliminating its own sources. And a separate
analysis ought to be devoted to that kind of interaction which

comes about between cultures of roughly identical level /Hellas and Rome/ where, owing to this, the problem of subordination and superordination does not even arise in the above mentioned sense.

Secondly: the historical-ontological and the logical - as opposed to Hegel's view - are not directly coinciding, even if the onto-logical /primarily borne by the activity of work/, is on basic levels underlying the logical, Engels' well-known aphorism, which claims that no single concrete social formation has ever been exactly corresponding to its own concept /with the possible exception of the 15-year-long artificial feudalism of the Templars in Jerusalem/, refers not only to the objective complexity of the systems and to the limits of our logical abstractions, but also to the fact that the description of history as a process obeying to abstract logical laws would be sheer anthropomorphic fabrication. All this has relevance to our theme because it makes us realize that the question of the objective commensurability of social processes must be distinguished from the issue of the incommensurability of our ideas.

Thirdly: the relationship of the given stage of social production and the achieved level of culture prevails again unevenly, or occasionally even in paradoxes. The courses of the development of culture are never determined by the economy in itself; what it does is to create a certain sphere of the actual cultural potentialities: while the realization of these potentialities depends on the interaction of so many non-economic /political, legal, moral, religious, philosophical, artistic, scientific/ forces and on the influence of this interaction on reproduction. Without the ancient type of Greek society Homeric epic could not have come into being, yet the Iliad and the Odyssey are not merely about the polis - and this partly accounts for the fact, why diverse possibilities of their historical acquisition, aesthetic pleasure and their cultural interpretation /at any rate within a defined cultural ambience/ were created.

Another example. Jewish monotheism could not have come into being without the still rather brisk and powerful tribal tradition on the one hand, and the weakness of monarchy unusual under the Asian circumstances on the other. Still its rise necessitated also political-historical events extraordinary and belonging to the sphere of contingency, whereas its impact - the vigorous integrating-unifying impact of the covenant with the sole god - went far beyond the horizon of the fertile crescent. The secret of the prolonged impact of the Bible is that while summarizing the norms of traditional social-moral behaviour, the experiences of everyday life - in other words: suggesting the idea of continuity - it expresses at the same time the conflicts between the fate of different ethnic groups and the general course of history, the conflicts of the individual and its community. In addition it spells out even potential solutions to them - as well as the problems of paradigm-change, preservation and renewal - and it does all this right at one of the most crucial turning points of history, at the borderline of the decline of the Asian empires and the ascendancy of the ancient mode of production.

Furthermore: unequalness turns up even within the sphere of culture as well. It is not only true that artistic and philosophical achievements regarded as practically "unattainable models" could also sprout on the base of relatively underdeveloped circumstances, and vice versa: some societies may reach a highly advanced economic level without a prominent literary, artistic, philosophical and political culture. It is also a fact that under certain conditions - for instance in the ancient polis - certain forms of culture - e.g. the myths - embody the raw material and precondition of other forms of culture - e.g. of the arts, whereas different conditions - e.g. those of advanced capitalism - will preclude this, viz., that the coincidence of different non-economic factors also varies in different situations.

I believe that - especially at seemingly unsolvable junctures of society - these developmental discrepancies, rooted in reality, are amplified by consciousness, to a degree that it converts the only historically commensurable into the theoretically incommensurable by eliminating the historical approach.

The paradigm-changes do not exclude the relative invariance of long-lasting cultural systems. That is why in the case of certain long-standing historical conditions /e.g. relatively advanced exchange of goods as the foundation of the universality of religion, a relatively developed individual etc./ it is possible to speak about Christianity in general, although we know that its ancient form is immensely different from mediaeval or modern Christianity.

The comparison of spiritual and cultural systems may lead to the quasi-mythic absolutization of their discontinuity, mainly when we fail to compare those systems of practical activity with which the cognitive structures share a symbiotic existence. The systems of Ptolemaios and Copernicus appear only contradictory as long as we ignore that in their epochs both fulfilled definite social, practical - mercantile, naigational etc. - requirements, and although these requirements changed in the modern era, the nature of this change would not be intelligible without the understanding of the objective course of history prior to the change.

The examination of this practice will answer the question what regularities are operative at a given period in shaping the inner structure of culture, when and why its certain forms - the arts or science etc. - become dominant or lag behind.

In order to grasp history in its contradictory essence, we should obviously transcend somehow the anthromorphic homogenization of history. In modern thought this pursuit has been present ever since Francis Bacon's idoles. This intellectual tendency has been vigorously bolstered by the alteration of the relation towards nature within the process of production. Yet it is a fact that simultaneously with this /as the complementary element of desanthropomorphization/ the overstressing of the importance of consciousness /experience, intellect, reason/ loomed large and with this the danger of a new kind of humanistic subject-ivism and subjectivistic historicism in the bourgeois conscious-ness. The newer developments in anthropology, ethnology and social psychology have endeavoured to correct this subjectivistic fallacy. Now, however, oddly enough as a result of the examina-tion of certain objective structures, the relativization of history and culture is once again impending, and precisely because in the investigations of some scholars the task of science is narrowed down to the analysis of structures theoret-ically regarded as incommensurable, they deny man any role in the shaping of history by claiming that the goal of science is generally the elimination of the human factor /and not the grasp-ing of the objective laws of human activity/.

Here again there arises a confrontation between a humanless objective structure-complex and a shoreless subjectivity not bound to structures.

The theoretical way out - we submit again - is to be found in the dialectic of the objective and the subjective, of the absolute and the relative, where the objective historical structure can be located in the systematic quality of the totality of subjective actions, where the relativity and dissimilarity of structures are not considered as independent of the universal and absolute tendency of the historical motion evolved from their interactions. Cultural difference and incommensurability can be dissolved only in the change of this process of historical-social practice. Nothing but this process can implant in consciousness a logic in which identity will not stay rigid and dead as it contains the element of dissimilarity, where cultural identity does not at all mean the predominance of some ideal-type but - as Hegel put it - the identity of identity plus non-identity. It may be true that magic or religion is able to receive and master the scientific argumentation only through its own logic. The question may be put, though, if there is behind these logics an objective continuity of social action which makes the social structures commensurable to one another and if there is an analyzable correlation between the logic of these structures and that of intellectual culture.

It would be the historical view and method, as has been referred to, that could measure the objective level of development of different systems. Although to demonstrate this would require a separate paper we might point out that this is no identification with any teleological evolutionist historicism. The systematic quality, as has been seen, does not obey to logical consistency. To understand its articulation helps us to have a peek at the construction of those vanished forms from the ruins of which it was built, the remnants of which may be, though "atrophied or travestied" /Marx/, detected in them. But in the other direction we cannot proceed: we cannot directly deduce the higher one from the inferior. Therefore the analysis of the cultural structure, reflecting on the past yet going beyond this reflection - the exploration of their historical dynamic period of cultural interactions in which we live, when the hitherto unsuspected divergences and similarities are taking shape. What is the significance of bourgeois culture for the <u>socialist</u> countries, and what is the importance of the culture of the socialist countries for bourgeois culture? In what does the relevant message of European culture consist for the developing countries and how can the contents of African or Asian cultures be described, which really influence the cultural life of the developed countries? These questions will only be answered in the future. But whatever these answers may be, we can be positive of two things. One is, that actual value, whatever mankind has ever produced, continues influencing the history of culture, and the other is that the products of our culture, our traditions are assimilated by every new culture by interpreting them according to its social logic.

Philosophy and Culture
J. Lukács and F. Tőkei eds.

LES CULTURES ET LEUR HISTOIRE.
BUTS ET MÉTHODES D'UNE HISTOIRE COMPARÉE DES CULTURES

B. KÖPECZI

Quand on veut étudier les relations entre les cultures, on se
heurte tout d'abord à la notion de la culture. Quand on parle
de culture primitive ou ancienne allant jusqu'au Moyen Age, on
pense à la culture intellectuelle tout aussi bien qu'à la culture matérielle, et le plus souvent au mode de vie aussi. Dès
la Renaissance, beaucoup d'historiens se contentent de décrire
l'histoire de la culture comme culture intellectuelle, c'est-à-
dire comme histoire des sciences, de la littérature et des arts,
ou bien des idées et des idéologies. Nous croyons qu'une telle
habitude s'explique d'une part par les difficultés qui surgissent
au moment ou la culture que nous étudions devient elle-même plus
différenciée et nos connaissances plus vastes, mais aussi par
le manque d'une base théorique, scientifiquement valable.

I.
CULTURE INTELLECTUELLE ET CULTURE MATÉRIELLE

Les théoriciens de la culture sont d'accord pour considérer
la culture comme un ensemble de biens intellectuels et matériels,
produits et diffusés par la société ou par une partie de la société et par ses institutions, un ensemble plus ou moins cohérent,
régi par un système d'idées, de croyances et de valeurs, qui est
déterminé par les besoins et les intérêts, mais qui influence
en même temps la vision du monde, le mode de vie et l'attitude
des groupes, couches et classes sociales, et des individus à un
moment donné de l'histoire /1/. C'est ce concept - interprété
de manières diverses - qui est appliqué par les historiens à
la culture des sociétés primitives et à celles des sociétés de
l'antiquité, et l'on peut bien dire que cette pratique a déjà
exercé une certaine influence sur l'étude de l'histoire de la
culture des autres époques.

Pour ce qui est de l'étude de la culture moderne, les historiens n'acceptent pas en général la notion d'une culture globale, à l'exception de l'École des _Annales_ qui a apporté un changement important avec l'histoire des mentalités. Toutefois on peut dire, avec Philippe Ariès /2/, qu'après 1945 l'histoire économique, démographique et sociale a été privilégiée par cette école aussi qui s'est penchée surtout sur les problèmes de l'histoire des mentalités dans ses relations avec celle de l'économie, de la société et de la population. Ces derniers temps, on s'intéresse de plus en plus à des catégories qui sont liées à l'existence biologique de l'homme, au fonctionnement de la société, aux vicissitudes historiques et à leurs influences sur l'homme, aux grands thèmes de la vie et de la mort, aux religions populaires et aux mythes. Une telle évolution implique nécessairement la coopération entre les diverses sciences sociales et humaines, en particulier entre l'histoire, la sociologie et l'ethnologie.

Dans l'historiographie marxiste, le besoin de s'occuper du fait culturel ne s'est manifesté qu'assez tard, surtout parce que la théorie marxiste a été interprétée pendant un certain temps dans un sens "économiste", bien que les changements radicaux de la société qui se sont produits dans cette partie de l'Europe aient été liés à des facteurs politiques et idéologiques et qu'on ait attribué un rôle important à la révolution culturelle dans l'édification de la nouvelle société. Outre cela, il faut reconnaître que les fondements théoriques de l'histoire culturelle n'ont pas été éclaircis.

Les discussions qui ont eu lieu dernierement en Hongrie au sujet de l'histoire de la culture montrent que, malgré leur unanimité à vouloir remettre à sa place cette discipline /3/, certains historiens considèrent l'histoire de la culture comme celle de la culture intellectuelle, et ils traitent de la technique dans le cadre de l'histoire économique, et du mode de vie dans celui de l'histoire sociale /4/. C'est un procédé traditionnel ou l'innovation réside dans l'établissement des relations entre cette culture et l'évolution sociale. D'autres veulent bien inclure dans la culture la culture matérielle aussi, mais ils ont des difficultés à réaliser un tel projet, surtout du point de vue méthodologique. Ces difficultés ne sont pas liées à une soi-disante incompatibilité du matérialisme dialectique et historique avec l'histoire de la culture matérielle, comme le pense un adepte de la "nouvelle histoire" J. M. Pesez. "La culture matérielle - écrit-il - se situe manifestement du côté des infrastructures: les pesanteurs matérielles ne peuvent être indifférentes au matérialisme historique qui cherche dans les infrastructures les motifs de l'évolution historique. Mais donner à l'histoire de la culture matérielle un statut indépendant comporte un risque, celui d'accorder aux faits qu'elle étudie un poids égal à celui du phénomène social; ou, ce qui serait plus grave encore, d'admettre qu'il puisse y avoir des faits historiques qui ne soient pas sociaux et d'expliquer les phénomènes extra-sociaux" /5/. Si nous cherchons la place de la culture matérielle dans l'histoire, ce n'est pas parce que nous nous intéressons à l'élaboration d'une théorie de l'évolution des sociétés et parce que nous considérons comme primaire dans cette évolution "le fait économico-social". Selon la théorie marxiste, la culture matérielle est bien composée - comme on le sait - de l'objet du travail /matières premières/, de la technique de production et de l'utilisation des produits matériels /consommation/. J'ajouterai les circonstances matérielles du mode de vie. Faut-il rappeler la fameuse définition selon laquelle le travail est "un processus entre l'homme et la nature ... par lequel l'homme médiatise, règle et contrôle sa propre activité"? /6/ La difficulté doit être recherchée dans la complexité du phénomène et dans ses multiples relations avec les autres activités humaines.

Faut-il lier la culture matérielle plutôt à la production, et par conséquent à l'économie, ou à l'évolution sociale dans son ensemble, ou la rapprocher de la culture intellectuelle? La culture constitue-t-elle une entité spéciale dans son ensemble, culture matérielle y comprise, et peut-elle être opposée à l'économique et au social selon les critères d'une analyse rigoureusement scientifique? Telles sont les véritables questions qui nous préoccupent. Pour y réponde, je crois qu'il faut remonter aux sources de la pensée marxiste, mais tenir compte aussi de certains nouveaux acquis théoriques. J'insisterai sur ces derniers.

a/ La théorie des formations sociales s'est enrichie de nouveaux résultats, dont nous devons tenir compte si nous voulons
définir la place de la culture dans l'évolution historique. L'é-
minent sinologue hongrois, F. Tőkei a démontré que chez Marx
la relation entre les forces productives et les rapports de production exprime la dialectique du contenu et de la forme, où
les rapports de la forme au sein du mode de production reflètent
les forces de production en tant que contenu. En ce qui concerne
la base et la superstructure, la distinction de Marx n'est que
l'application de la même dialectique du contenu et de la forme
aux "mouvements de la société" /7/. La superstructure comme forme
représente la production intellectuelle, et la base comme contenu
signifie la production matérielle qui se développe dans le cadre
de la première. Cette interprétation rejette la hiérarchie rigide
établie entre la base et la superstructure, et met en évidence
les rapports dialectiques qui existent entre elles.

Marx écrit dans Le 18 Brumaire de Louis Bonaparte à propos de
la superstructure: "Sur les différentes formes de propriété, sur
les conditions d'existence sociale s'élève toute une superstructure d'impressions, d'illusions, de façons de penser et de conceptions philosophiques particulières. La classe toute entière
les crée et les forme sur la base de ces conditions matérielles
et des rapports sociaux correspondants" /8/.

La superstructure se réduit ici aux impressions, aux illusions,
aux façons de penser et aux conceptions de vie /dans la traduc-
tion française on a conceptions philosophiques pour Lebensan-
schauungen/, et elle se base sur les fondements matériels et sur
les conditions sociales. Cette formule peut donner lieu à toutes
sortes de simplifications. Mais dans L'idéologie allemande, Marx
et Engels précisèrent leur pensée dans le cadre d'une conception
générale de l'histoire.

"Cette conception de l'histoire a donc pour base le développement du procès réel de la production... elle conçoit la forme
des relations humaines liée à ce mode de production et engendrée
par elle... comme étant le fondement de toute l'histoire, ce qui
consiste à la représenter dans son action en tant qu'Etat aussi
bien qu'à expliquer par elle l'ensemble des diverses productions
théoriques et des formes de la conscience, religion, philosophie,
morale, etc." /9/.

Ici, Marx et Engels entendent par base le mode de production, les forces et les rapports de production, mais ils parlent aussi de formes des "relations humaines", ou plutôt de "formes de communication", de "commerce" /en allemand: Verkehrsform/, relevant des rapports de production, mais aussi de la superstructure. Cette fonction transitionnelle de la "forme de communication" doit être prise en considération sous peine de simplifier les relations entre la base et la superstructure.

En ce qui concerne la superstructure, Marx distingue l'Etat des autres formes et produits de la conscience, ce qui est particulièrement important si l'on veut en avoir une idée différenciée.

Marx ne suppose pas des relations hiérarchiques rigides entre base et superstructure, comme le fait Plékhanov. Il admet une série de médiations entre les deux formes fondamentales, dont le rapport est bien hiérarchique, mais cette hiérarchie est interchangeable, c'est-à-dire qu'il y a des cas où la superstructure joue un rôle primordial /10/.

Si nous examinons la culture dans ses rapports ainsi conçus avec la base et la superstructure, nous ne pouvons pas la considérer uniquement comme le produit de la superstructure, ni surtout comme une partie seulement de cette superstructure. En effet, la base joue un rôle important dans sa formation, non seulement de façon indirecte, mais aussi directe, comme culture matérielle ayant ses rapports avec les forces de production, et en tant que culture intellectuelle liée aux rapports de production.

Dans l'histoire culturelle, nous devons étudier la culture matérielle avant tout du point de vue du rapport qui existe entre le niveau de la production et la culture: les idées relatives au travail, aux instruments du travail, à la répartition du travail, à la façon dont on utilise le temps de travail, aux relations entre le travail et le temps libre, et aux questions du mode de vie déterminé par les circonstances économiques et sociales.

b/ Au point de vue de l'objet et de la méthode de l'histoire de la culture, la question des relations entre le conscient et le non-conscient, entre la conscience quotidienne et les idéologies, entre l'idéologie et la culture, est d'une grande importance. György Lukács, dans La particularité de l'esthétique, distingue trois modes de connaissances: la connaissance quoti-

dienne, scientifique et artistique. Parmi les objectivations de
la conscience quotidienne, il met en relief le travail et la
langue, et du point de vue de ses caractéristiques, il établit
un rapport direct entre la théorie et la pratique, qui fonde
un matérialisme spontané, une façon de penser par analogies et
le désir d'avoir une conception totale de l'homme et du monde.
La conscience quotidienne influence non seulement la vie quotidienne, mais aussi les idéologies et les objectivations supéri-
eures telles que la science et les arts. Si du point de vue de
la philosophie cette approche est justifiée, nous ne pouvons né
pas tenir compte des enseignements qu'on peut en tirer relativement à la culture. Cela veut dire que la conscience et la culture
quotidienne doivent faire partie intégrante de la culture et que,
par conséquent, elles doivent être étudiées par l'histoire de la
culture.

c/ C'est un lieu commun de dire que la culture ne peut être
véritablement vivante que si nous l'assimilons, autrement dit,
si nous choisissons certains éléments d'une culture donnée. Ce
choix se réalise dans un contexte historique et social déterminé, et il implique l'existence d'un système de besoins, de valeurs et de normes accepté par une société ou par certains classes,
couches ou groupes de cette société. Ce système de besoins et
de valeurs est à la base des mentalités et des idéologies, il
influence l'activité des institutions et il détermine aussi, du
moins dans une certaine mesure, l'évolution des sciences et des
arts.

Gramsci exagère peut-être l'importance de la superstructure
quand il définit la notion de la culture, mais je pense qu'il
a raison quand il met en relief la fonction active de la culture
fondée sur une vision du monde déterminée. Voici sa définition:
"La culture, à ses différents degrés, unifie un plus ou moins
grand nombre d'individus disposés en couches nombreuses, dont
le contact, du point de vue de l'expression, est plus ou moins
efficace..." ..."On déduit de là l'importance que le "moment
culturel" a également dans l'activité pratique /collective/:
tout acte historique ne peut pas ne pas être accompli par "l'homme
collectif", c'est-à-dire qu'il suppose qu'a été atteinte une
unité "culturelle sociale" qui fait qu'un grand nombre de volon-

tés éparses, dont les buts sont hétérogènes, se soudent pour
atteindre une même fin, sur la base d'une même et commune conception du monde /générale et particulière, passagèrement agis-
sante - au moyen de l'émotion - ou permanente, qui fait que la
base intellectuelle est si bien enracinée, assimilée, vécue,
qu'elle peut devenir passion/" /11/.

Gramsci insiste sur le caractère actif d'une culture qui influence toutes les activités humaines et non seulement les objectivations artistiques ou scientifiques. De là nous déduisons
que le point de départ de toute histoire culturelle devrait être
l'examen des idées et des systèmes d'idées qui s'imposent à la
conscience quotidienne, scientifique et artistique. Cela évidem-
ment en tenant compte des caractéristiques des différentes formes
de conscience et de leurs objections, ainsi que des classes,
couches et groupes de la société qui les produisent.

d/ Une conception large de la culture rend sa valeur à la
superstructure autour de laquelle il y a eu tant de discussions
à l'intérieur et à l'extérieur du marxisme. Si nous acceptons
l'idée de L. Althusser, selon laquelle l'historiographie doit
étudier non seulement la reproduction des forces de production,
mais aussi celle des rapports de production, et que la reproduction de ces derniers se fait "pour une grande part" à l'aide de
la superstructure juridique, politique et idéologique, et des
appareils répressifs et idéologiques d'Etat, alors l'étude de
la superstructure revêt une importance particulière.

Bien qu'entre Gramsci et Althusser il y ait de grandes différences quant à l'interprétation de l'idéologie, leurs points de
vue ne diffèrent pas essentiellement en ce qui concerne la fonction de celle-ci. Je cite d'abord Gramsci: "Selon la philosophie
de la praxis /c'est-à-dire du marxisme/, la superstructure est
une réalité objective et fonctionnante... Cette philosophie déclare explicitement que les hommes réalisent d'une façon consciente leur situation et leurs tâches sur le terrain des idéologies, ce qui est une constatation de fait de grande importance; la philosophie de la praxis est elle-même une superstructure, c'est le domaine où des groupes sociaux déterminés prennent
conscience de leur existence sociale, de leurs forces, de leurs
tâches, de leur évolution" /12/.

Gramsci attribue donc le rôle de prise de conscience à l'idéologie, et cela non seulement dans le contexte d'une situation
donnée, mais également de celui de l'évolution de cette situation.

Pour Althusser, l'idéologie est la représentation que les individus se font de leurs rapports avec les conditions réelles.
Il met l'accent sur la notion de rapport, n'acceptant pas la
thèse selon laquelle l'idéologie serait le reflet des conditions
réelles. Nous n'avons pas l'intention d'entamer une discussion
à ce sujet, nous voulons seulement faire remarquer que la théorie
du reflet, telle qu'elle a été professée, par exemple, par Lukács, ne dit pas que l'idéologie est la photographie de la réalité, mais soutient qu'elle donne - par l'intermédiaire de
toutes sortes de médiations - une image plus ou moins déformée
de la réalité et qu'elle a une fonction active.

Althusser élargit la fonction de l'idéologie et fait décou-
ler de celle-ci les actes de l'individu tels qu'ils se manifestent dans la pratique et les rites matériels. En effet, ces
derniers sont, selon lui, déterminés par les appareils idéologiques. Il en résulte que l'idéologie revêt un caractère maté-
riel et qu'elle ne se manifeste pas seulement dans le domaine
de la conscience.

Quelle que soit l'approche que nous adoptons, qu'elle soit
"humaniste" ou "structurelle", il ne fait pas de doute que nous
devons examiner la superstructure non seulement du point de vue
des formes de la conscience, mais aussi de celui des institutions, de l'Etat, ce qui pour l'histoire de la culture implique
l'étude du système institutionnel de la diffusion de l'idéologie.

e/ A propos de la culture d'une période donnée, et plus généralement au sujet de l'évolution culturelle de l'humanité, la
question suivante se pose: doit-on étudier uniquement les grandes
valeurs, ou bien faut-il étendre l'analyse à tout ce que les
hommes ont considéré à une époque donnée comme appartenant à la
culture au sens large du mot? Si nous acceptons que la culture
quotidienne appartient également à la culture, nous devons étudier tout produit culturel d'une époque donnée. Tout cela ne
veut pas dire que le problème axiologique doit être éliminé.
Lukács en 1919 définit la culture de la façon suivante: "La notion de culture contient tous les produits et toutes les acti-

vités de valeur qui sont superflus au point de vue de la subsistance immédiate" /13/. Il va sans dire que nous ne sommes pas
d'accord avec cette définition trop étroite, peut-être trop aristocratique de la culture. Elle pose cependant le problème axiologique, et c'est pourquoi nous ne pouvons l'ignorer. Nous croyons
que sur ce plan, il faut tenir compte de deux approches possibles.
La première considère la valeur d'un point de vue général, par
exemple du point de vue du progrès de la société ou de la libération de l'homme. La deuxième envisage l'époque donnée et le jugement de valeur du public de l'époque. Je crois que l'historien
de la culture doit tenir compte de ces approches: connaître la
position axiologique de chaque époque, mais aussi celle de la
postérité, de la "longue durée". Une telle approche introduit
le point de vue de la réception dans l'histoire de la culture
qui, à notre avis, ne peut être négligé.

En dernière analyse, il s'agit de l'acceptation d'une notion
de la culture qui tient compte des relations étroites et inter-
changeables entre la base et la superstructure, entre la culture
matérielle et intellectuelle; qui part du système des valeurs
et par conséquent de la conception du monde; qui considère outre
les objectivations de la culture quotidienne, qui enfin étudie
non seulement la genèse, mais aussi la réception des produits
de la culture. Sur cette base, il y a quelques années, nous
avons proposé un schéma qui tient compte des facteurs permettant
une description de la culture au sens large du mot.

1/ Visions du monde, c'est-à-dire systèmes de valeurs et de
normes, liés aux besoins économiques, sociaux, politiques de la
société, leur influence sur la connaissance quotidienne, scientifique et artistique, sur les attitudes et les modes de vie;

2/ Conceptions de politique culturelle des différentes classes
et couches de la société, des divers mouvements et courants;

3/ Activités des institutions qui assurent la diffusion de
la culture matérielle et intellectuelle, telles que l'enseignement, l'édition, la presse, la radio, la télévision, les Eglises
et les organisations sociales, la langue comme moyen de communication;

4/ Rôle des intellectuels, leur fonction dans la diffusion de
la culture et la réalisation de cette fonction;

5/ Conditions d'existence, résultats et fonctions de la science dans la vie quotidienne, dans le développement de la société, de la conscience quotidienne et des idéologies;

6/ Conditions d'existence, résultats, fonction et influence de la littérature et des arts sur la conscience quotidienne, les idéologies, les attitudes et les modes de vie, image de la société et de l'homme dans leurs créations;

7/ Culture matérielle et intellectuelle de la vie quotidienne des diverses classes et couches sociales, et ses principales caractéristiques;

8/ Tradition et innovation culturelle d'une époque, valeurs qui se transmettent et qui disparaissent, position de la période examinée dans l'évolution générale d'un peuple donné et de l'humanité.

C'est un schéma approximatif et discutable, mais qui a peut-être l'avantage de regrouper les divers éléments en les hiérarchisant. En tout cas nous avons essayé d'appliquer cette méthode dans un livre intitulé Trente années de culture hongroise /paru en français et en allemand/ et dans des ouvrages portant sur l'histoire culturelle hongroise et européenne du XVIIe et du XVIIIe siècles.

II.

DIFFÉRENCES, RESSEMBLANCES, ÉVOLUTION

La "nouvelle histoire" salue avec joie le changement qui s'est opéré dans la conception de la modernité, et avec cela, l'idée de la différence des cultures. Philippe Ariès déclare dans son article déjà cité: "L'homme d'aujourd'hui n'est plus aussi convaincu ni de la supériorité de la modernité..., ni de celle de la culture qui semble avoir préparé la modernité... depuis l'époque de l'invention de l'écriture. Il voit des cultures différentes et également intéressantes, là où l'historien classique reconnaissait une civilisation et des barbaries. Ce dernier était donc plutôt tenté par les ressemblances avec un modèle universel. Aujourd'hui, la recherche des différences l'emporte au contraire sur celle des ressemblances" /14/. Nous devons nous féliciter de cette constatation, notamment parce que les cultures des pays de l'Europe Centrale et Orientale ont toujours été jugées par les historiens du monde occidental d'après les critères de la culture de l'Europe Occidentale considérée comme "modèle universel".

Si nous procédons à une étude descriptive de la culture de
la région culturelle de l'Europe Centrale et Orientale dans la
première moitié du XIXe siècle, nous constaterons qu'il y a non
seulement des différences, mais aussi des ressemblances avec
l'Europe Occidentale, ce qui s'explique par une évolution culturelle parallèle jusqu'à un certain moment de l'histoire. Qui plus
est, nous remarquons que la première essaye d'imiter la seconde,
tout simplement parce qu'elle la considère plus développée. Si
nous cherchons les raisons plus profondes d'une telle démarche,
nous voyons qu'elle ne s'explique pas uniquement par des facteurs
culturels: les motifs économiques et sociaux sont plus importants
encore. En effet, certaines couches sociales de cette région, unies
par des intérêts complexes mais évidents, trouvent qu'il faut
rattraper un retard historique qui est à la fois d'ordre économique, social et culturel. Les ressemblances sont donc non seulement de caractère génétique, mais reflètent aussi une certaine
conception de l'évolution.

A ce propos, nous devons parler du problème de l'évolution
inégale, de l'_ungleiche Entwicklung_, comme disait Marx, qui a
attiré l'attention sur les contradictions qui peuvent exister
entre le niveau de la littérature et les arts, et le développement économique et social, mais aussi entre les rapports de production et les rapports juridiques, entre le droit romain et la
production moderne, par exemple /15/. Selon sa conception, les
différentes inégalités n'infirment pas l'idée fondamentale qu'il
y a des rapports étroits entre les phénomènes, il s'agit seulement de trouver une interprétation adéquate des contradictions.

Les théoriciens marxistes ont pendant longtemps affirmé que
seules les idées qui rencontrent dans un pays donné une base
économique et sociale adéquate, peuvent y être implantées. Du
point de vue de la réalisation de ces idées, on a raison d'in-
sister sur l'existence des conditions nécessaires, cependant
l'évolution du XXe siècle nous offre des exemples éclatants
d'inégalité dans l'évolution de la base et de la superstructure,
et même de diverses variantes pour cette dernière. Il suffit de
penser aux changements radicaux survenus en Union Soviétique et
dans les autres pays de l'Europe Centrale et Orientale, et aux
contradictions qu'ils ont produites. On sait que, d'après Marx,

il aurait été souhaitable que le socialisme triomphe dans les pays les plus développés. Cela n'a pas empêché Lénine de réaliser la révolution socialiste dans un pays retardataire et de commencer l'édification de la nouvelle société dans des conditions économiques et culturelles défavorables. Nous sommes témoins aussi d'une évolution contradictoire des pays du tiers monde, où l'on trouve souvent une idéologie politique progressiste, ou même socialiste, dans le cadre d'une réalité économique et sociale arriérée, féodale et même esclavagiste.

A la lumière de ces faits, je pense que nous devons reconsidérer la théorie de l'histoire des relations entre les différentes cultures, et cela d'autant plus que nous commençons à nous libérer de l'eurocentrisme. Une approche plus complexe mettrait en évidence les contradictions et romprait nécessairement avec une conception de l'évolution qui voulait être linéaire, mais elle ne négligerait pas les relations dialectiques, les phénomènes vus à la lumière des grandes tendances de l'évolution.

Une philosophie néopositiviste de l'histoire entend attribuer au marxisme une conception mécanique et simpliste du progrès, et voudrait se contenter de la pure description des changements qui n'ont, selon elle, aucune finalité. Le "nouveau conservatisme" fait volontiers appel à cette philosophie pour nier toute possibilité de progrès et pour prêcher le retour à une société hiérarchisée qu'il considère comme plus proche de la nature humaine.

Dans son dernier ouvrage intitulé Ontologie de l'existence sociale, György Lukács a attiré l'attention non seulement sur l'expérience, mais aussi sur la nécessité ontologique de la reconnaissance des grandes tendances de l'évolution. En effet, l'évolution et même l'idée du progrès sont étroitement liées à l'essence du genre humain.

L'étude des relations entre les différentes cultures met donc en relief non seulement les différences, mais aussi leurs ressemblances, sur la base de la reconnaissance des grandes tendances de l'évolution de l'humanité.

Marx mentionne dans ses Manuscrits de 1857 la Kulturgeschichte du XIXe siècle, qu'il identifie avec la Religions- und Staatengeschichte. Il la qualifie de ideale Geschichtsschreibung /16/.

Nous croyons qu'en la nécessité d'une histoire réelle en général, et d'une histoire réelle de la culture en particulier. Et nous pensons qu'elle est faisable. Si nous acceptons une conception globale de la culture et une étude comparée des cultures.

NOTES

/1/ Sur la définition de la culture voir: A.L. Kroeber-G. Kluck-hohn: Culture, a critical review of concepts and definitions. New York, 1952, et The concept and dynamics of culture. Ed. B.Bernhardt, La Haye-Paris, 1977.

/2/ Philippe Ariès: La nouvelle histoire. Sous la direction de Jacques le Goff, Paris, 1978.

/3/ Voir: Béla Köpeczi: Objet et méthode de l'histoire de la culture. La Pensée, sept. 1978.

/4/ Ainsi par exemple l'un des meilleurs travaux hongrois portant sur la culture du XVIIIe siècle, le livre de D. Kosáry: Müvelődés a XVIII. századi Magyarországon, Budapest, 1980.

/5/ La nouvelle histoire, éd. citée, p. 68.

/6/ "ein Prozess zwischen Mensch und Natur... worin der Mensch seine eigene Tat vermittelt, regelt und kontrolliert". Marx-Engels Werke, Berlin, vol. 23. p. 192.

/7/ F. Tőkei: A társadalmi formák elméletéhez /Sur la théorie des formes sociales/.Budapest, 1968. pp. 63-64.

/8/ Karl Marx: Le 18 Brumaire de Louis Bonaparte. Editions Sociales, Paris, 1971. p. 47.

/9/ Karl Marx-Friedrich Engels: L'idéologie Allemande, Editions Sociales, Paris, 1971. p. 69. /Variante dans le manuscrit: "à expliquer la société civile à ses différents stades et dans son reflet pratique-idéaliste, l'Etat, de même que tous les produits différents et les formes de la conscience, religion, philosophie, morale, etc."/.

/10/ Cf. L. Althusser: Les appareils idéologiques d'Etat, La Pensée, n° 151. Juin 1970; partiellement repris in Positions. Editions Sociales, Paris, 1976. pp. 67 sq.

/11/ A. Gramsci: Il Materialismo storico e la Filosofia di Benedetto Croce, Torino, 1966, in Gramsci dans le texte. Editions Sociales, Paris, 1975. p. 173.

/12/ A. Gramsci: La dottrina delle ideologie politiche. Quaderni del carcere III, in: Il materialismo e la filosofia di Benedetto Croce. Einaudi, 1964. pp. 236-237.

/13/ Cf. Béla Köpeczi: Lukács en 1919. La Pensée, mars 1979.

/14/ O.c. 420-21.

/15/ K. Marx: Ökonomische Manuskripte 1857/58,MEGA, 1976. I. 44. "Das unegale Verhältniss der Entwicklung der materiellen Produktion z.B. zur künstlerischen. Überhaupt der Begriff des Fortschritts nicht in der gewöhnlichen Abstraktion zu fassen. Mit der Kunst etc. diese Disproportion noch nicht so wichtig und schwierig zu fassen, als innerhalb praktisch-

sozialer Verhältnisse selbst. Z.B. der Bildung- Verhältniss
der United States zu Europa. Der eigentlich schwierige Punkt
hier zu erörtern ist aber der, wie die Produktionsverhältnis-
se als Rechtsverhältnisse in ungleiche Ebtwicklung treten.
Also z.B. das Verhältnis des römischen Privatrechts /im Kri-
minalrecht und öffentlichen das weniger der Fall/ zur modernen Produktion". MEGA, ökonomische Manuskripte, 1857/58.
Dietz, 1976. I. 44.

/16/ Cf. ökonomische Manuskripte, MEGA, 1976. II/1.1.

Philosophy and Culture
J. Lukács and F. Tőkei eds.

POSTHISTOIRE?

A. GEDŐ

Der Gedanke eines nachgeschichtlichen Zustands - obwohl er immer
die Projektion einer je gegebenen Konstellation ist - umschrieb
schon in Tocquevilles Darstellung, Mitte der 30er Jahre des 19.
Jahrhunderts, die universelle Perspektive der bürgerlichen Gesellschaft: Tocquevilles Voraussage nach rufe die "Gleichheit"
eine Situation hervor, die "die Gesellschaft mehr stationär machen
werde, als sie in unserem Westen jemals war" /1/. Diese Prognose
wies auf seine Eindrücke von der Demokratie in Amerika hin, besonders auf seine Beobachtung, dass durch die ständige Erneuerung
des Sekundären, durch die bewegliche und wechselnde Oberfläche
nur in Wahrheit die Unantastbarkeit des Wesentlichen verhüllt
wird und hinter der grossen Mobilität menschlicher Handlungen
"die sonderbare Festigkeit gewisser Prinzipien" liegt. "Die Menschen bewegen sich rastlos, der menschliche Geist scheint aber
fast unbeweglich" /2/. Es zeigt die unbeabsichtigte Achtung des
liberalen Kritikers der Revolutionen - der zu jener Zeit noch
lebendigen bürgerlich-revolutionären Vergangenheit vom Ende des
18. Jahrhunderts und der schon geahnten, obschon als vermeidbar
betrachteten proletarisch-revolutionären Zukunft -, es zeigt die
Achtung vor diesen Revolutionen, dass Tocqueville das Zu-Ende-
Kommen der Geschichte deshalb für möglich hielt, weil ihm die
weiteren Revolutionen unmöglich /oder mindestens unwahrschein-
lich/ schienen. Diese Posthistoire-Perspektive war im Ambiguität
befangen, wie auch das Ganze von Tocquevilles Geschichtsanschauung
und Zeitdiagnose, aus dem sie folgte: Sie war Verheissung und
Trost, Hoffnung darauf, dass jene der die bürgerliche Gesellschaft bedrohenden neuen "grossen intellektuellen und politischen

4

Revolutionen" /3/ ausbleiben werden, und sie war zugleich Angst-
bild Vision des Vorherrschend-Werdens der fatalen "Gleichheit".
Die Verheissung und die Hoffnung konnten aber diese Vision nicht
kompensieren, da die Annahme, Revolutionen seien künftig unwahr-
scheinlich, vom Bewusstsein des unaufhaltbaren, schicksalshaften
Umsichgreifens der "Gleichheit" berrührte. Tocquevilles Impres-
sionen, die den Posthistoire-Gedanken authentisierten, gestalte-
ten sich auf Grund einer lückenhaften, in manchen Zügen eher skiz-
zenhaft als kohärent aufgebauten geschichtsphilosophischen Konzeption. Letzten Endes waren durch diese Konzeption sowohl die
Selektion und die Deutung seiner amerikanischen Beobachtungen,
das Mass und die Hierarchie ihrer Geltung bestimmt, als auch die
Prämissen des Posthisoire-Gedankens: die Missbilligung der an
"die individuelle Anstrengung der Vernunft" appellierenden Philosophie von Bacon und Descartes bis Voltaire, die Ansicht, derzufolge die Demokratie - die nivellierende "Gleichheit" - allgemeinen Ideen zustrebe, der Geschichte und der historischen Erkenntnis aber abgeneigt sei. Schon zur Zeit seiner Entstehung
galt der Posthistoire-Gedanke als "Kulturkritik" der Demokratie
/nur der Terminus der "Kulturkritik" ist späteren Datums, das
Phänomen trat bereits um die Wende des 18. und des 19. Jahrhunderts ins Dasein/, und dieser anfänglichen und rudimentären "Kulturkritik" waren auf implizite Weise schon Tendenzen des "negativen Denkens" /4/ immanent.

Bei Tocqueville blieb aber der Zusammenhang der Posthistoire-
Idee mit dem "negativen Denken", mit der Umwertung, dem Abbau und
dem Zerfall der Begriffe von Rationalität, Geschichte und Philosophie im Kontext des "negativen Denkens" noch fragmentarisch und
meistens latent, wie auch diese philosophischen Prämissen und Konsequenzen seiner Auffassung - ohne ausgeprägte Fragestellungen
und Durchführung - im Zwielicht des halb Geahnten, halb Konzipier-
ten schwebten.   In der Genesis des Positivismus und der Lebensphilosophie verflocht sich aber der Posthistoire-Gedanke mit der
Destruktion und der Umdeutung dieser Begriffe; eine solche Destruktion und Umdeutung enthielten - selbst wenn sie im Hintergrund der Auffassung verborgen waren - die Voraussetzungen eines
Abbruchs und Endes der Geschichte, der Restriktion und Ausschal-
tung der Geschichtlichkeit. In den Konzeptionen von Comte und

Nietzsche zeichneten sich die philosophischen Konturen des Posthistoire-Gedankens ab; dennoch war in seinen gesellschaftlichen
Beziehungen der Posthistoire-Gedanke hier weniger greifbar, war
er mehr in den Nebel der einer universellen Religiosität unter-
geordneten Wisssenschaftsfetischisierung bzw. des Mythisierens
eingehüllt, als in Tocquevilles Prognose. Das "positive" - "allein ganz normale" - Stadium gilt Comtes Auffassung zufolge als
"endgültige Einrichtung der menschlichen Vernunft", als "endgül-
tiger Zustand der rationalen Positivität" /5/, womit und wodurch
die Geschichte sich eigentlich abschliesst /6/. In Comtes Ver-
einigung von "Ordnung" und "Fortschritt" dominierte die unbe-
weglich-statische "Ordnung": "das positivistische Dogma setzt
überall eine strenge Unveränderlichkeit in der grundlegenden Ordnung voraus, deren spontane oder künstliche Veränderungen immer
sekundär und vorübergehend sind" /7/. Comte band diese unwandel-
bare und endgültige "Ordnung" an eine völlig ahistorisierte Vernunft /obschon seine frühen Schriften - von Saint-Simons Ideen
angeregt - sich gewissermassen für die Geschichtlichkeit der Erkenntnis interessierten/. Die Rationalität als Element des "positiven Glaubens" reduzierte sich auf das gedankliche Fixieren
"ständiger Relationen", die in der "Aufeinanderfolge und Ähnlich-
keit beobachtbarer Erscheinungen" zu konstatieren seien; das "me-
taphysische Stadium" überwindend verschloss sie sich programma-
tisch der Erforschung von Ursachen: Sie büsste ihre Universalität und ihre revolutionär-kritische Bestimmung ein /8/, dergestalt entleert und erstarrt wurde sie der "universellen Religion"
subsumiert. "Das grundlegende Dogma der universellen Religion besteht in der festgestellten Existenz einer unwandelbaren Ordnung,
der die Ereignisse aller Art unterworfen sind" /9/: die positivistische Philosophie - der gemeinsame Inbegriff der degradierten
Vernunft und des "subjektiven Prinzips", das den Primat des "Her-
zens" verkündete - repräsentierte an sich den nachgeschichtlichen
und aussergeschichtlichen Zustand, den sie in der Welt zu definieren bzw. eher herzustellen vermeinte.

In dieser Auffassung Comtes lebte mehr die Attitüde fort;
selbst sein Grundgedanke war nur zusammen mit Tocquevilles his-
torisch-soziologischer Prognose gepaart zu erneuern. Nietzsches
Posthistoire-Idee - mit und hinter ihr die Überwindung von Ge-

schichte und Geschichtlichkeit, die pragmatisch-instrumentalistische Deutung und Degradierung der wissenschaftlichen Rationalität, die lebensphilosophische Antiphilosophie - gilt als unmittelbarer Bezugspunkt des Ahistorismus im spätbürgerlichen Denken; diese Momente treten zutage oder reproduzieren sich auch in solchen Varianten der philosophischen Dekadenz, die Nietzsches Erbe nicht übernehmen. Der Posthistoire-Gedanke waltete als ständiges Motiv in Nietzsches Oeuvre: Seit der <u>Geburt der Tragödie</u> und den <u>Unzeitgemässen Betrachtungen</u> haben ihn die Wiederherstellung des tragischen Mythos, der Gedanke der unaufhebbaren Spannung zwischen Leben und Geschichte in ihrem Bann gehalten; er polemisierte gegen das "Übermass von Histoire", das "nicht mehr erlaubt, <u>unhistorisch</u> zu empfinden und zu handeln"; er war gewillt, "die Gegenmittel gegen das Historische", "<u>das Unhistorische und das Überhistorische</u>" aufzufinden /10/. In der Zarathustra-Vision wurde die Geschichte durch Gottes Tod, den Verfall des in den Abgrund stürzenden Menschen und das Prinzip der ewigen Wiederkehr des Gleichen gebannt; in seinem letzten Brief an Jacob Burckhardt schlug in den Paroxismus des Wahnsinns um - "dass im Grund jeder Name in der Geschichte ich bin" /11/ -, was früher die Illusion des Ichs gewesen war, das geglaubt hatte, die Geschichte seinem irrationalen Willen zu unterjochen, sie im tragischen Mythos zum Abschluss zu bringen und in einen tragischen Mythos zu verwandeln. In Nietzsches wechselnden und sich radikalisierenden Varianten des ständigen Posthistoire-Motivs nahmen die Empörung gegen die <u>Ratio</u> und die ersehnte Aufhebung der <u>Geschichte</u> die Form einer <u>Zivilisationskritik</u> an, es kam auch das ideologische Gebilde zum Vorschein, in dem auf der einen Seite "die <u>auflösenden</u> und <u>notwendig zur décadence treibenden Mittel</u> der Zivilisation" standen, auf der anderen die "Kultur" /12/, wobei die Ablehnung der wissenschaftlichen Rationalität sich mit dem <u>Antitechnizismus</u> verschränkte. Der Posthistoire-Gedanke kulminierte im philosophischen Setzen des <u>Nihilismus</u> und in der <u>nihilistischen Überwindung</u> dieses Nihilismus: Der Zwiespalt, in dem sich der Nihilismus zum absoluten Prinzip steigerte, war das Novum von Nietzsches philosophischer Einstellung. An diese Einstellung /und nicht unbedingt an die spezifischen Inhalte von Nietzsches Auffassung dieser Ambiguität/ lehnten sich - aus un-

terschiedlichen Beweggründen und mit divergierendem geistigem
Charakter - nicht nur Spengler und Ernst Jünger, Klages und Hei-
degger, sondern auch Adorno und Arnold Gehlen an, sie wird heut-
zutage in Daniel Bells oder Peter L. Bergers neokonservativer
Kritik an der "Moderne" und Deleuzes, Lyotards oder Foucaults
"poststrukturalistischer" Nietzsche-Renaissance heraufbeschworen.

Die ursprünglichen Varianten des Posthistoire-Gedankens, durch
Tocqueville, Comte und Nietzsche formuliert, stellten schon zu
ihrer Zeit Ansätze oder ausgeprägte Phänomene einer allgemeineren
Geistigkeit dar, die damals eher einen diffusen Ahistorismus bzw.
Antihistorismus vertrat, indem sie sich der positivistischen Geschichtsanschauung und Erkenntniskonzeption gegenüberstellte oder
sich mit ihr verflocht, in ihrem Schatten verbarg. Unter dem unmittelbaren oder vermittelten Einfluss von Tocqueville, Comte und
Nietzsche bzw. unabhängig von diesem schimmerte - oder. dämmerte -
die latente oder offen ausgesprochene Idee /oder das Ideenfrag-
ment/ eines Zu-Ende-Kommens der Geschichte, einer nachgeschichtlichen Situation, eines stationären Zustandes durch verschiedene
Abstufungen des Spektrums des bürgerlichen Denkens. Zu dieser
Zeit erschien die Revolution nicht nur in der Gedankenwelt der
Restauration, sondern auch im Bewusstsein mancher verspäteter Anhänger der bürgerlichen Revolution als Abbruch und Ende der Geschichte. Dieser ging infolge des Zerrinnens der Illusionen der
bürgerlichen Revolution, ihrer verblassten Nachblüte und ihres
neuerlichen Zerrinnens anhand der Erfahrungen der französischen
Revolutionen von 1830 und 1848 rasch in den anderen Schein über,
wonach selbst die Revolutionen die Konstanz der Geschichte kaum
verändern können /13/. Dieser zweifache Schein implizierte den
Gedanken des Zum-Stillstand-Kommens der Geschichte bzw. ihrer
Überwindung. In den 40er Jahren des 19. Jahrhunderts trat auch
der Terminus des Posthistoire /in Cournots geschichtsphiloso-
phischem Schema/ und der Begriff von einem stationären Wirtschafts-
zustand /in John Stuart Mills politischer Ökonomie/ in Erscheinung. Der zum Hegelschen Zentrum gerechnete Lorenz von Stein vermeinte 1850 zu konstatieren, was die Abarten der Posthistoire-
Idee ein Jahrhundert später für die neue differentia specifica
der derzeitigen nachgeschichtlichen Situation halten sollten:

"Ich glaube, dass die Zeit der sozialen Theoreme vorbei ist ...
Es ist möglich und wahrscheinlich, dass noch allerlei Systeme
entstehen; allein sie werden weder grosse innere Originalität
noch auch eine historische Bedeutung haben, die der, welche die
bisherigen Systeme hatten, auch nur annährend gleich kommt. Diese
Zeit ist vorbei" /14/. In dieser Vorstellung Lorenz von Steins
vereinigten sich das Adaptieren des damaligen französischen bürgerlichen Denkens und die Kritik an den sozialistischen und kommunistischen Doktrinen mit der den Schulen des Hegelianismus mehr
oder minder gemeinsamen Attitüde, dem Setzen eines Posthistoire
der mit Hegel abgeschlossenen <u>Philosophie</u>.

Lorenz von Steins Diagnose folgerte aber nicht notwendigerweise aus der Idee des Zu-Ende-Kommens der Philosophiegeschichte.
Cieszkowski und nach ihm die Jungehegelianer /besonders Moses
Hess/ zogen aus dem angenommenen Posthistoire-Zustand der Philosophie eine entgegengesetzte Konklusion: die Aktualität auf die
Zukunft hinzielender Taten, neuer politischer Ziele, Programme
und Auffassungen. Und das Erwägen von Aussichten des politischen
Handelns, das Suchen nach Richtungen einer solchen Tätigkeit konnte Ende der 30er, Anfang der 40er Jahre in Deutschland weder die
Auseinandersetzung mit der Geschichte der französischen Revolutionen und den Vergleich von französischer Vergangenheit und Möglichkeiten deutscher Zukunft /15/, noch die Kritik am Konserva-
tismus der "historischen Rechtsschule", ihrer "Opposition mit
der Geschichte gegen die Geschichte" vermeiden; "die Erkenntniss
der Geschichte ist aber sogleich selbst Philosophie und das Prinzip der Geschichte, die Entwickelung oder die lebendige Dialektik,
auch das Prinzip der Philosophie. Die Geschichte kann also wohl
von der Philosophie, die Philosophie aber nicht von der Geschichte sich trennen   ..." /16/. Trotz dem Illusorischen seiner Ansichten appellierte der Junghegelianismus, sich zur "Philosophie
der Tat" bekennend, mehr an ein idealistisch verstandenes histo-
risches Bewusstsein als an den Posthistoire-Gedanken. Zwar erwar-
tete Ruge von der philosophischen und politischen Tätigkeit der
Hegelschen Linke, dass die Rationalität sich geltend mache - "Der
Rationalismus aber und seine Methode wird sich durchsetzen, er
ist das Leben des Zeitgeistes selbst" /17/ -, doch ist die He-
gelsche Einheit von Vernunft, Geschichte und Philosophie auch

42

hier in Zerfall geraten:Schon Cieszkowski hat das Sich-Verschlies-
sen der Hegelschen   Philosophie vor der Zukunft so kritisiert,
die Zukunftsdimension der Geschichte ins philosophische "absolute
Erkennen" so eingeführt, dass er dem Prinzip des Willens den Vorrang zuschrieb. Er glaubte, dass "Hegels Freiheit noch mit der
Nothwendigkeit behaftet ist", dass auf der Stufe der "notwendigen
Freiheit" "die Vernunft das Leitende und das Objectiv-Wahre der
Geschichte" ist, dass der "notwendigen Freiheit" die "freie Freiheit" /18/, wo der Grundsatz des Tuns, des Willens vorherrscht,
übergeordnet wird, dass also "das Denken ein bloss integrales Moment des Willens" ist /19/ - und die politisch oppositionell ge-
ladene "Philosophie der Tat" des Moses Hess übernahm und entfaltete Cieszkowskis Idee. Diese historisch nicht unbegründete Kritik und Korrektion der Hegelschen Philosophie stellten aber
nicht nur subjektivistische, von Hegel schon überwundene Gedanken wieder her; war das Prinzip des Willens bei Cieszkowski und
der Hegelschen Linken weder in seinem philosophischen Gehalt noch
in seiner gesellschaftlichen Tendenz der /damals noch ohne Wider-
hall, im Dunkel der Unbekanntheit gebliebenen/ lebensphilosophischen Willenmetaphysik von Schopenhauer verwandt, so lag in jenem
Prinzip dennoch die Möglichkeit einer Fortsetzung auf die Lebensphilosophie hin /20/, eine Möglichkeit, die sich in Stirners geis-
tiger Laufbahn aktualisierte.

Auf die Trennung und Umgestaltung der Begriffe von Vernunft,
Geschichte und Philosophie weist auch das Geschick der Kategorie
Zivilisation nach der französischen Revolution von 1789 hin. Diese
Kategorie wurde in der zweiten Hälfte der 18. Jahrhunderts zu einem Knotenpunkt der Gedankenwelt der englischen und französischen
Aufklärung: In ihr manifestierten sich das Durchsetzen der Ratio,
der historische Fortschritt der universellen Menschheit, kam die
antifeudale Gesellschaftskritik zum Tragen, verschmolz sich der
erkenntnistheoretische Optimismus mit dem geschichtsphilosophischen /21/ /ohne in oder durch sich selbst die Spannung zwischen
der Idee der Geschichtlichkeit und dem Begriff der die Geschichte
vor sich zitierenden Vernunft, oder zwischen der als geschichtsphilosophische und erkenntnistheoretische Instanz verstandenen
Figur des "bon sauvage" und dem Gedanken des historischen Fortschritts aufzulösen/. Saint-Simon konfrontierte den wissenschaft-

lich-industriellen Aspekt der Zivilisationskategorie mit der bürgerlichen Gesellschaft konfrontiert, er berief sich auf die uneingelösten Versprechen des Fortschritts der Vernunft in der Kritik jener nachrevolutionären Realität, von der die Aufklärung die Verwirklichung der Ratio, die Vollendung des Fortschritts erhoffte. Hielt aber zeitweilig das nachrevolutionäre bürgerliche Denken mittels der Zivilisationskategorie den formalen Rahmen der früheren Einheit des Geschichts- und Vernunftsbegriffsaufrecht, bejahte es anhand dieser Kategorie den Kapitalismus, so haben sich die begrifflichen Inhalte innerhalb des verharrenden formalen Rahmens gewandelt - aufgelöst und entleert -, dass ihnen die kritische Spitze genommen wurde. In Guizots Vorlesungen über "die allgemeine Geschichte der europäischen Zivilisation", Ende der 20er Jahre war die Zivilisation mit dem "allgemeinen Los der Menschheit" identifiziert, galt Fortschritt als Grundidee der Zivilisation, deren Gliederung durch die Unterscheidung der "Produktion von Mitteln der Kraft und des Wohlstands in der Gesellschaft", der "sozialen Verhältnisse" und des "individuellen Lebens", des "inneren Lebens" des Menschen bestimmt wurde; der Fortschritt hat sich aber hier schon zur "Perfektionierung des bürgerlichen Lebens /vie civile/" verharmlost. Nur konzipiert, aber nicht beantwortet hat Guizot die Frage, "auf die man am Ende der Zivilisation stösst; schöpft sich die Geschichte der Zivilisation aus, kann sie schon über das wirkliche Leben nichts sagen, dann stellt sich der Mensch unvermeidlich die Frage, ob alles ausgeschöpft, ob er am Ende von allem ist" /22/. Guizot nahm aber die Posthistoire-These nicht nur mit diesem Gedanken vorweg, sondern auch - und noch eher - mit seiner Auffassung, die die nachrevolutionären bürgerlichen Zustände als Realisierung von Gerechtigkeit, Legalität, Öffentlichkeit und Freiheit betrachtete und welcher der Kapitalismus als unüberwindbares Ergebnis der Geschichte der Zivilisation erschien.

Diese Betrachtung hat Fouriers Polemik entzündet /die auch der Theorie Saint-Simons galt/: "die Zivilisation" sei "das Idol aller philosophischen Richtungen", "in ihr glaubt man die höchste Vollendung zu erblicken", obwohl sie tatsächlich einen vorübergehenden Zustand, eine Verirrung darstellt, indem "das Industriesystem eine verkehrte Welt ist" /23/. Fouriers Urteil über die

Zivilisation beinhaltete eine direkte Kritik am Vernunftbegriff, die Überwindung der Zivilisation, die Hoffnung auf eine neue Gesellschaftsordnung konnten sich aber auf den Vernunftbegriff berufen. Die allgemein gesetzte Einheit von Geschichte und Ratio zerfiel, indem sich die Möglichkeit des Gedankens von der Geschichtlichkeit des Kapitalismus, einer über die bürgerliche Gesellschaft hinausgehenden Geschichte eröffnete; Fourier stellte von der Rationalität einer imaginär-kommenden Geschichte - bzw. der aus der Geschichte ausscheidenden Utopie - her die Spaltung zwischen Ratio und bisheriger Geschichte fest. Die Auflösung der früheren, im klassischen bürgerlichen Denken hergestellten Verbindung von Rationalität, Geschichte und Philosophie und das Bestreben, sie, wenn auch nur partiell und provisorisch, aufs neue zu verknüpfen, begleitete den Wandel der vormarxschen sozialistischen und kommunistischen Lehren in der ersten Hälfte des 19. Jahrhunderts. Selbst der französische /und deutsche/ "Arbeiterkommunismus" war bestrebt, in dem der klassischen bürgerlichen Philosophie entlehnten - und dann modifizierten - Vernunftbegriff /24/, im Gedanken eines rationalen Zustandes Halt zu finden.

Die Entstehung und Gestaltung der materialistischen Dialektik fiel im grossen und ganzen mit der Genesis der Posthistoire-Idee zusammen. Was sich im bürgerlichen Denken als Beschränkung und/oder Relativierung der Geschichte, als Verbreitung des Ahistorismus und Antihistorismus, als Absage an die Kategorie der Rationalität und/oder ihr positivistisches Verwelken widerspiegelte und sich in der Posthistoire-These, letztlich im Verkünden oder Implizieren des philosophischen Nihilismus und der nihilistischen Philosophie niederschlug, war in der historischen Realität die Wende der Bourgeoisie, ihr Rollenwechsel, das unwiderrufliche, in den sozialen Auseinandersetzungen entscheidende In-Erscheinung-Treten des Proletariats. Auf dieselbe Realität reflektierte der Marxismus vom Klassenstandpunkt des Proletariats durch die dialektisch-materialistischen Erneuerung von Geschichtsbegriff, Rationalitätsidee und Philosophiekonzeption. Diese dialektisch-materialistische Erneuerung hielt die Einheit, in die das klassische bürgerliche Denken jene Begriffe unter dem Primat der Rationalitäts-

45

idee verknüpfte, nicht aufrecht/der Primat des Vernunftsbegriffs
verlieh dem Geschichtsbegriff und der Philosophiekonzeption sowie
ihrer Einheit mit der Rationalitätsidee selbst in materialistischen Auffassungen eine idealistische Färbung/. Marx' und Engels'
Kritik an Hegel begegnete in dieser Hinsicht ihrer Auseinandersetzung mit der klassischen bürgerlichen Ökonomie, besonders Ricardos Theorie. Hegel stoss im rationalen Begreifen der Geschichte
und der Historisierung der Ratio bis zur äussersten Grenze der
Möglichkeiten der bürgerlichen Philosophie vor, die idealistische
Dialektik von Vernunft, Geschichte und Philosophie beruhte dennoch auf dem absoluten Primat der Vernunft; die ahistorische Anschauung des Kapitalismus war in Ricardos politischer Ökonomie
durch die abstrakte Rationalität des homo oeconomicus vermittelt,
der sie die Geschichte subsumierte. Die nietzscheanischen und
heideggerianischen Interpretationen, die Marx zum Denker des Posthistoire umstilisieren möchten, unterstellen Marx einen den Lehren von Saint-Simon und Hegel entnommenen Begriff der allmächti-
gen Vernunft /25/ oder erklären die dialektisch-materialistische
Umgestaltung und Ausdehnung der Idee der Geschichtlichkeit, den
Gedanken einer über den Kapitalismus hinausgehenden Geschichte
- die Aufhebung sowohl des klassischen bürgerlichen Historismus
als auch des Utopismus - zum Posthistoire: Die "revolutionäre
Veränderung der Klassen-Gesellschaft" bedeute bei Marx das Ende
der Geschichte. "Die Notwendigkeit dieses Endes aus der Eigenart
des Kapitals und seiner Krisen zu beweisen, ist die Hauptabsicht
der marxischen Wissenschaft. Es ist das Ende der Geschichte..."
/26/.
    Die materialistische Dialektik stellt dem klassischen bürger-
lichen Denken nicht die Subjektivierung oder Mythisierung des Ge-
schichtsbegriffs /bzw. seiner Entwertung zugunsten des aussergeschichtlichen Mythos/, nicht den Abbau und die Enthöhlung der
Rationalitätsidee, nicht den Lehrsatz vom Ende der Philosophiegeschichte entgegen. Die Kategorien von Rationalität, Geschichte
und Philosophie liegen im Marxismus nicht als membra disjecta
nebeneinander, die als Begriffstrümmer den Posthistoire verkünden, das Kommen eines historischen und geistigen Nihil suggerie-
ren. In dem ihr eigenen neuen Kontext wandelt die materialistische Dialektik diese Kategorien um, gestaltet sie ihre neue

Einheit. In dieser Einheit gibt das Begreifen der Geschichte,
vor allem der Materialität der Geschichte der Gesellschaft und
der Natur als bestimmend wird die Rationalität in der Dialektik
des historischen Prozesses der Realität /die Praxis mitinbegrif-
fen/ und der Geschichte der Widerspiegelung, der geistigen Aneignung dieser Realität aufgefasst, versteht sich die Philosophie
weder als Symptom und Argument eines kulturellen Relativismus
noch als philosophia perennis, sondern als Moment der Geschichtlichkeit, als wissenschaftliche Erkenntnis sui generis.

ANMERKUNGEN

Aus einer grösseren Abhandlung zum Thema "Rationalität, Geschichtlichkeit, Philosophie. Zur Posthistoire-These"

/1/   A. de Tocqueville: De la démocratie en Amérique, T. III.
      Paris, 1868. p. 419.

/2/   Ebd. pp. 417 ff.

/3/   "Wenn die Geschichte sich jemals in der Welt allgemein und
      permanent befestigt, dann werden die grossen intellektuel-
      len und politischen Revolutionen recht schwierig und selte-
      ner als man es vermutet"./Ebd. p. 428./

/4/   Der Terminus des "negativen Denkens" kennzeichnete früher
      den philosophischen Prozess von Nietzsche bzw. von Kierke-
      gaard bis Adorno /vgl. z.B. Lyotards Reflexion. In: Nietz-
      sche aujourd'hui? T. I. Paris, 1973. p. 179./, später
      schloss er im gewissen Sinne auch die positivistische Tra-
      dition und Max Webers Auffassung ein /vgl. unter anderem
      M. Cacciari: Krisis. Saggio sul pensiero negativo da Nietz-
      sche a Wittgenstein. Milano, 1976. - M. Cacciari: Pensiero
      negativo e razionalizzazione. Venezia, 1977./.

/5/   A. Comte: Discours sur l'esprit positif. In: A. Comte: La
      science sociale. Ed. par A. Kremer-Marietti. Paris, 1972.
      pp. 219 ff. Vgl. auch A. Comte: Système de politique posi-
      tive ou Traité de sociologie, instituant la Religion de
      l'Humanité. T. I. Paris, 1890. p. 33.

/6/   "Comte dachte..., dass in der industriellen Menschheitsge-
      sellschaft das 'Ende der Geschichte' erreicht werde. ...Die
      Geschichte wird in der Geschichte beendet. Die industrielle
      Gesellschaft wird die erste 'geschichtslose Gesellschaft'
      sein". /J. Moltmann: Der Mensch. Christliche Anthropologie
      in den Konflikten der Gegenwart. Stuttgart—/West/Berlin,
      1971. pp. 48 f./ - Moltmanns Kritik am Posthistoire-Gedanken
      des Comteschen Positivismus gründet auf die "Theologie der
      Hoffnung", die nicht weniger, nur auf andere Weise ahisto-
      risch ist als der Positivismus.

/7/   A. Comte: Système de politique positive... T. I. p. 54.

/8/ "Die empörerischen Gewohnheiten der modernen Vernunft geben noch keine Ermächtigung, ihr einen revolutionären Charakter zu unterstellen, wenn schon ihre legitimen Forderungen reichlich befriedigt wurden". /Ebd. p. 20./

/9/ A. Comte: Catéchisme positiviste. Paris, 1966. p. 66.

/10/ F. Nietzsche: Werke. Hrsg. von K. Schlechta. München, 1969. Bd. I. pp. 276 ff.

/11/ Ebd. Bd. III. p. 1351.

/12/ Ebd. p. 810. - Nietzsches Kulturbegriff nahm später antinomische Inhalte auf; er verwickelte sich in den Zwiespalt der Kritik an der Dekadenz und ihrer Vertretung, der Überwindung der Philosophie und ihrer Fetischisierung, des lebensphilosophischen Ästhetisierens und Biologisierens, wobei der Antihistorismus nicht aufgehoben, sondern an die grundlegenden Momente des "negativen Denkens" gebunden, und auf solche Weise intensiviert wurde. In seinem späten Nietzsche-Aufsatz /Nietzsches Philosophie im Lichte unserer Erfahrung/ konstatierte Thomas Mann, Nietzsche hat "eigentlich sein Leben lang nur einen überall gegenwärtigen Gedanken variiert, ausgebaut, eingeprägt", den Gedanken, "Kultur, das ist die Vornehmheit des Lebens,... während als Totfeinde und Zerstörer von Kultur und Leben Bewusstsein und Erkenntnis, die Wissenschaft und endlich die Moral figurieren..." /Th. Mann: Gesammelte Werke. Bd. IX. Frankfurt am Main, 1960. p. 685./

/13/ Nach Lorenz von Stein "ist die letzte Revolution eine sociale gewesen. Sie hat in der Gesellschaft nichts geändert; sie hat die Klassen derselben nicht gestürzt; sie hat keine gesellschaftliche Unabhängigkeit erzeugt; sie hat Niemand reicher, Tausende ärmer gemacht..." /L. Stein: Geschichte der socialen Bewegung in Frankreich. Bd. I. Der Begriff der Gesellschaft und die sociale Geschichte der französischen Revolution. Leipzig, 1850. p. VI./

/14/ Ebd. p. III.

/15/ Vgl. unter anderem M. Hess: Philosophische und sozialistische Schriften, 1837-1850. Eine Auswahl. Hrsg. von W. Mönke. Berlin, 1980. pp. 150 ff.

/16/ A. Ruge's sämmtliche Werke. Bd. II. Mannheim, 1847. p. 103.

/17/ Ebd. Bd. IV. Mannheim, 1847. p. 33.

/18/ A. von Cieszkowski: Prolegomena zur Historiosophie. Berlin, 1838. pp. 95 ff., 120 ff.

/19/ Ebd. p. 124. - Cieszkowskis "Philosophie der Praxis" hat die Universalität der Vernunft, den Gedanken der Verbundenheit von Geschichte und Ratio, sowie die Einheit der die Geschichte begreifenden Philosophie preisgegeben: Sie ordnete der Idee eines über die Geschichte Recht sprechenden Gottes den fichteisierenden Kult der Tat unter. So wich sie in dieser Hinsicht von Hegel und Fichte zum Vorrang des theologischen Prinzips, zu Augustin und Bossuet zurück: "Wie die Weltgeschichte das Weltgericht ist, so wieder Gott der Richter der Weltgeschichte..." /Ebd. p. 69./

/20/ Landgrebe verabsolutiert diese Möglichkeit, indem er die Hervorkehrung des Willens an den Gedanken der "restlosen Emanzipation" des Menschen knüpft, um eine Kontinuität zwischen der Hegel-Kritik der Junghegelianer, Feuerbachs und Marx' einerseits und dem "deutschen Irrationalismus" und dem Nihilismus zu stiften. /Vgl. L. Landgrebe: Zur Überwindung des europäischen Nihilismus. In: Der Nihilismus als Phänomen der Geistesgeschichte in der wissenschaftlichen Diskussion unseres Jahrhunderts. Hrsg. von D. Arendt. Darmstadt, 1974. pp. 31 f./ In dieser Auffassung wird der Nihilismus mit dem Verlust des religiösen Glaubens gleichgesetzt, erscheint das Selbstvertrauen der Vernunft als "ein Ersatz für den verlorengegangenen religiösen Glauben" ebd. p. 30./; dieser Konzeption zufolge beging das neuzeitliche Denken die Stationen des Nihilismus. Landgrebe behauptet, dass "die neuzeitliche Emanzipation des Menschen in ihrem Endergebnis eine Befreiung in das Nichts ist". /p. 32./

/21/ In diesem Zivilisationsbegriff trat "nicht nur die historische Auffassung der Gesellschaft" zutage, sondern "manifestierte sich auch die optimistische und ausgeprägt nicht-theologische Deutung ihrer Entwicklung". /E. Benveniste: Civilisation: Contribution a l'histoire du mot. In: Éventail de l'histoire vivante. Hommage à Lucien Febre. Vol. I. Paris, 1953. p. 51./ - Zum Schicksal von Terminus und Begriff der Zivilisation vgl. auch L. Febvre: Pour une Histoire à part entière. Paris, 1962. pp. 481 ff. - G. Gusdorf: Les sciences humaines et la pensée occidentale. Vol. IV. Les principes de la pensée au Siècle des Lumières. Paris, 1971. pp. 333 ff. - Zum Historischen Verhältnis von Begriffen der Zivilisation und der Kultur vgl. H. P. Thurn: Kultursoziologie - Zur Begriffsgeschichte der Disziplin. In: Kölner Zeitschrift für Soziologie und Sozialpsychologie. Heft 3, 1979.

/22/ Guizot: Histoire générale de la civilisation en Europe, depuis la chute de l'Empire Romain jusqu'à la Révolution Française. Bruxelles/Livourne/Leipzig, 1854. p. 24.

/23/ Ch. Fourier: Ökonomisch-philosophische Schriften. Eine Textauswahl. Hrsg. von L. Zahn. Berlin, 1980. pp. 9, 15 ff., 62 ff.

/24/ "Aus dem bürgerlichen Rock schlüpft die Vernunft in die proletarische Bluse, und vor dem Richterstuhl dieser proletarischen Vernunft müssen nunmehr alle gesellschaftlichen Verhältnisse und Einrichtungen ihre Daseinsberechtigung verteidigen. Wie die proletarische Bedürfnisse und Bestrebungen als die naturgemässen schlechthin, so erscheinen sie auch als die einzig vernünftigen". /J. Höppner/W. Seidel-Höppner: Von Babeuf bis Blanqui. Bd. I. Leipzig, 1975. p. 411./

/25/ Vgl. H. Lefebvre: Une pensée devenue monde. Faut-il abandonner Marx? Paris, 1980. pp. 33 f., 112 ff.

/26/ H. Boeder: Topologie der Metaphysik. Freiburg/München, 1980. p. 694.

Philosophy and Culture
J. Lukács and F. Tőkei eds.

UN ASPECT DIALECTIQUE DE LA CULTURE: PARTICULARISME ET INTERNATIONALISATION

Á. WIRTH

Si l'on veut aborder les questions historiques et sociales im-
pliquant les notions de "culture" et de "civilisation", on se
heurte d'emblée à une grosse difficulté. A. L. Kroeber et Clyde
Klukhohn ont recueilli 161 définitions de la culture, Armand Cu-
villier dans son "Manuel de sociologie" énumère au moins 20 si-
gnifications du mot "civilisation". L'histoire, l'anthropologie,
la sociologie utilisent ces notions dans des sens très variés;
dans les diverses langues leur signification est souvent diver-
gente. L'ambiguité de ces notions, la multiplicité terminologique
impliquent et expriment des divergences plus profondes, situées
au niveau de la philosophie de l'histoire, de l'interprétation
de la société et de l'individu, de l'appréciation des formes historiques des communautés humaines, de la conception du progrès
social.

Le sens et l'emploi des mots "civilisation" et "culture" se
sont établis dans un contexte déterminé et ont changé historiquement /comme Lucien Febvre l'a brillamment démontré à propos de la
notion de "civilisation"/ /1/. Au cours du développement de la
société et de la pensée bourgeoises, le sens de ces termes s'est
progressivement modifié. Lors de leurs premières apparitions et
diffusions au Siècle des Lumières, la pensée bourgeoise a mis l'accent dans ces notions sur les différences entre société humaine
et Nature: la "civilisation" était opposée à la "barbarie", la
civilisation et la culture représentaient une valeur absolue, valable pour tous les peuples et pour tous les pays. Cette conception exprimait à la fois l'opposition radicale de la bourgeoisie
au féodalisme barbare, et l'illusion selon laquelle la société

bourgeoise, répondant aux exigences de la Raison, devait être un
état stable, éternel de l'humanité, le seul mode d'existence qui
convienne à l'Homme. Cette interprétation de la civilisation com-
portait un certain historisme /elle considérait le passage à la
civilisation comme un progrès historique et se montrait optimiste
quant à la possibilité d'un perfectionnement sans fin de la civi-
lisation/. Mais d'autre part, elle attribuait à la civilisation
un caractère statique, en enfermant ce développement dans les
cadres de la société bourgeoise. La complexité du processus historique et des transformations économiques, sociales et politiques qu'il entraînait, la grande diversité des facteurs stimulant et freinant ce processus, l'aggravation des contradictions
internes, propres à la société bourgeoise, ont contribué à la naissance dans la philosophie de l'histoire chez Herder, et surtout
chez Hegel, d'une forme spécifique de l'historisme: l'historisme
dialectique. Et cependant, c'est l'historisme évolutionniste, et
non cet historisme dialectique, qui domine la pensée bourgeoise
du XIXe siècle. A la fin de l'époque des révolutions bourgeoises,   dans la notion de civilisation l'accent se modifie une
fois de plus: la justification de la société bourgeoise, récemment consolidée passe au premier plan, et parallèlement, nous
assistons à la dégradation de l'historisme en un simple relati-
visme.

  La notion de la culture ou de la civilisation soulève inévi-
tablement la question des rapports de l'universel et du particulier dans l'histoire. Dans ses écrits sur l'histoire de la civilisation en Europe, Guizot avait déjà remarqué: "Une certaine
unité éclate dans la civilisation des divers Etats de l'Europe",
"elle découle de faits à peu près semblables malgré de grandes
diversités de temps, de lieux, de circonstances"; "si elle a de
l'unité, sa variété n'en est pas moins prodigieuse" /2/. Bien
entendu, cette compréhension de l'unité et de la diversité de la
civilisation européenne n'exclut pas l'interprétation nationa-
liste de cette unité: Guizot lui-même n'a-t-il pas attribué une
place privilégiée à la nation française dans la civilisation européenne? Comment peut-on appliquer cette idée de l'unité et de
la diversité de la civilisation à notre époque, à l'époque où
s'opère "l'internationalisation" la plus large de la civilisa-

tion, qui dépasse de loin les cadres de la civilisation européenne? Le passage de la civilisation, au singulier, aux civilisations, au pluriel, ne signifie-t-il pas le triomphe de la particularité, la négation de l'universel dans l'histoire? Ou au contraire: l'internationalisation de la civilisation signifierait-elle la tragédie des civilisations, au pluriel, leur uniformisation plus ou moins complète?

Dans la multiplicité et la diversité des réponses, deux tendances extrêmes et philosophiquement typiques se dessinent. D'une part, un universalisme abstrait qui met unilatéralement l'accent sur le caractère général et universel du processus historique. Cette tendance cherche à fonder l'unité trans-historique de la civilisation, de la culture sur divers arguments philosophiques, sur l'esprit du monde de Hegel ou l'essence générique de l'homme, ou encore sur une conception positiviste de type scientiste et techniciste. Aujourd'hui, cette tendance cherche sa justification sociologique dans la théorie de la société industrielle et post-industrielle, elle trouve sa forme d'expression adéquate dans l'idée de la supranationalité. De ce point de vue, les nations contemporaines, les éléments nationaux de la vie et du développement de la société ne sont qu'un atavisme historique, qu'un obstacle à la réalisation de l'unité de l'humanité, alors que l'internationalisation de la culture apparaît comme un processus rectiligne, une simple croissance, le prolongement mécanique de l'unité de la civilisation européenne. Dans cette conception, il n'est pas difficile de découvrir la justification et l'idéalisation de la civilisation capitaliste occidentale.

L'antipode de l'universalisme abstrait est un certain particularisme relativiste: il tend à absolutiser l'unicité des processus historiques, à nier ou relativiser leur contenu général. Du point de vue philosophique, cette position se fonde avant tout sur la philosophie néokantienne de l'histoire, sur l'irrationalisme de la philosophie de la vie, sur l'empirisme positiviste. La théorie cyclique des "cultures", élaborée et formulée par Spengler et Toynbee, est reprise de nos jours; elle insiste sur l'autonomie, sur les divergences essentielles des différentes cultures. Les adeptes de cette tendance considèrent l'internationalisation de la culture comme un processus purement superfi-

ciel qui ne peut dépasser les différences originelles et essentielles des systèmes de valeurs particuliers. Dans cet esprit,
on parle de la renaissance des nations et du nationalisme comme
du trait le plus caractéristique de notre époque. Les uns, se référant à la renaissance du nationalisme, construisent un nouveau
mythe de la particularité; d'autres y voient un indice de décadence, la preuve que tous les "projets universalistes" aboutissent à une impasse finale. Cette conclusion est formulée, parmi
d'autres, dans les livres récents de Raymond Aron, dont les ti-
tres mêmes sont très expressifs: "Les désillusions du progrès",
"Plaidoyer pour l'Europe décadente".

L'universalisme abstrait et le particularisme relativiste dé-
coulent à certains égards d'une source commune: de la séparation
et de l'opposition métaphysique de l'universel et du particulier
dans l'histoire. Dans les deux cas, l'élément "international" et
le moment "national" sont traités comme s'ils n'étaient pas les
aspects d'un développement historique unique, en action réciproque
constante, comme s'ils n'étaient pas un produit de l'histoire,
dont le contenu, les rapports mutuels, le rôle concret se transforment nécessairement dans le mouvement historique. L'universalisme abstrait et le particularisme relativiste comprennent chacun de ces aspects comme quelque chose d'absolu: le premier, comme
la manifestation de "l'esprit du monde", de "la nature humaine
éternelle", de "l'essence générique de l'homme"; le second, comme
l'incarnation de "l'esprit du peuple", du "caractère national",
des valeurs inchangées de la particularité, de l'inégalité des
ethnies biologiquement et génétiquement déterminées. Ils font
donc de chacun de ces aspects, isolés l'un de l'autre, un absolu
qui précède et dépasse l'histoire, qui plane par-dessus l'histoire.

Les vulgarisateurs et les critiques du marxisme identifient
faussement le matérialisme historique à un schéma philosophique,
totalement abstrait, qui contiendrait, à leur dire, dans une
forme achevée, les lois universelles de l'histoire, également
valables pour tous les peuples et toutes les époques historiques,
et qui rendrait superflue l'étude concrète du processus historique concret. Marx fut le premier à refuser avec force une telle
interprétation du matérialisme historique. Il protestait contre

la tentative de transformer son esquisse historique de la genèse
du capitalisme en Europe occidentale "en une théorie historico-
philosophique de la marche générale, fatalement imposée à tous
les peuples, quelles que soient les circonstances historiques où
ils se trouvent placés" /3/. Une théorie "passe-partout", comme
il le remarquait, serait totalement impuissante à rendre compte
de la disparité des évolutions historiques concrètes. On sait que
le vieil Engels avait lui aussi jugé nécessaire de se démarquer
de ceux qui avaient transformé le matérialisme historique en phrases vides /on peut, disait-il, tout transformer en phrases/, de
ceux pour qui la conception matérialiste de l'histoire servait
de "prétexte pour ne pas étudier l'histoire". "Or, notre conception de l'histoire, soulignait Engels, est avant tout une direc-
tive pour l'étude et non un levier servant à des constructions
à la manière des hégéliens. Il faut réétudier toute l'histoire,
il faut soumettre à une investigation détaillée les conditions
d'existence des diverses formations sociales..." /4/. La nécessité d'une étude détaillée et concrète de l'histoire dont Engels
parlait, suppose la mise au jour de l'unité dialectique de l'universel et du particulier dans le processus historique donné. Cette
étude doit viser à saisir non pas une universalité abstraite, mais
l'universel concret, comme l'entendait Hegel: "l'universel qui
englobe en soi la richesse du particulier, de l'individuel, du
singulier".

Les éléments nationaux du développement de la société /la formation des nations et leur rôle dans les processus historiques/,
de même que l'internationalisation de la vie sociale, ne représentent nullement des facteurs supra-historiques immuables: bien
au contraire, ils sont des produits historiques. Les nations, au
sens moderne, se sont formées à un stade précis du développement
social, sur une base économique déterminée. En Europe, ce processus a coïncidé avec la formation du capitalisme. Le même processus qui a produit les nations a mis également en marche l'internationalisation de la vie sociale. "L'histoire mondiale" n'a
pas existé toujours, l'histoire considérée comme histoire universelle est un résultat, elle a été véritablement créée par la
grande industrie et le marché mondial. L'histoire devient l'histoire de l'humanité à mesure que les forces productives et les

rapports sociaux grandissent: "Il se forme une connexité dans l'histoire des hommes, qui est d'autant plus l'histoire de l'humanité, que les forces productives et en conséquence leurs rapports sociaux ont grandi" /5/. Avec l'internationalisation de la vie et du développement de la société, quand, dans l'histoire, "à la place de l'ancien isolement des provinces et des nations se suffisant à elles-mêmes se développent des relations universelles, une interdépendance universelle des nations" /6/ une forme qualitativement nouvelle de l'unité de l'universel et du particulier a commencé à se créer.

Le développement des nations et l'internationalisation de la vie de la société à notre époque représentent deux tendances historiques liées l'une à l'autre, progressant en une interaction dialectique. Sans elles, on ne peut comprendre la dialectique de l'universel et du particulier de nos jours. Naturellement, l'unité dialectique du développement national et de l'internationalisation ne signifie pas qu'il n'y ait pas de contradictions, que des contradictions ne puissent exister au sein de cette unité. Le progrès à cet égard se fait également par et à travers des contradictions, par la formation de tendances contraires qui se heurtent et se pénètrent réciproquement. Comme Lénine le notait en lisant Hegel: "La dialectique est la théorie de la façon dont les contraires peuvent être et sont habituellement /dont ils deviennent/ identiques; des conditions dans lesquelles ils sont identiques en se changeant l'un en l'autre; des raisons pour quoi l'esprit humain ne doit pas prendre ces contraires pour morts, figés, mais pour vivants, conditionnés, mobiles, se changeant l'un en l'autre" /7/. L'unité du national et de l'international comporte des contradictions, des conflits, mais aussi la transformation mutuelle des contraires. On ne peut comprendre pleinement les contradictions et les conflits du national et de l'international qu'en les considérant dans le contexte historique concret de notre époque.

Il nous semble entièrement justifié d'appliquer à notre époque cette réflexion de Hegel: "Il n'est pas difficile de voir que notre temps est un temps de gestation et de transition à une nouvelle période" /8/. Il est naturel et légitime que chaque philosophie répond à sa manière au défi de notre temps, qu'elle réfléchisse de nouveau sur ses problèmes, qu'elle repense ses propres questions et réponses à partir de sa position fondamentale. Pour la conscience bourgeoise, les contradictions de notre monde, l'aggravation de la crise de la société bourgeoise, les douleurs de la gestation et de la transition apparaissent comme la crise de la culture universelle, comme la séparation et la collision tragique de la culture et de la civilisation. Cette même situation historique signifie pour la classe révolutionnaire la possibilité de l'action révolutionnaire, la promesse d'une nouvelle société, la transition révolutionnaire à un nouveau monde. Mais, selon l'expression de Hegel, "ce nouveau monde a aussi peur d'une réalité effective parfaite que l'enfant qui vient de naître, et il est essentiel de ne pas négliger ce point". Dans les discussions philosophiques on peut nier et refuser, ou au contraire accepter et soutenir ce monde nouveau qui n'a pas encore "une réalité effective parfaite"; on peut contester et discuter ses valeurs, mais on ne peut plus ne pas en tenir compte, que ce soit dans la réflexion sur les questions philosophiques essentielles touchant la culture et la civilisation.

NOTES

/1/ Voir L. Febvre: Civilisation: le mot et l'idée, Centre international de Synthèse, Paris, 1930.

/2/ Guizot: Histoire générale de la civilisation en Europe, Bruxelles, 1834.

/3/ Sur les sociétés pré-capitalistes, Textes choisis de Marx, Engels, Lénine, Editions Sociales, 1970. p. 351.

/4/ Marx-Engels: Etudes philosophiques, Editions Sociales, 1968. p. 153.

/5/ Marx-Engels: Oeuvres choisies, Editions du Progrès, 1975. p. 690.

/6/ Op. cit. p. 35.

/7/ V. Lénine: Cahiers philosophiques, p. 107.

/8/ Hegel: La phénoménologie de l'esprit, tome I, ed. Montaigne, p. 12.

Philosophy and Culture
J. Lukács and F. Tőkei eds.

CULTURE AND THE SOCIAL NATURE OF LANGUAGE

J. KELEMEN

1. It is a remarkable fact that the first modern formulations
of the basic problems of cultural philosophy were connected with
problems of linguistic philosophy. This connection is a heritage
of the late Enlightenment and the Eastern European national movements, especially the German one.

The neologistic movements of the first decades of the 19th
century started from the principle that nation, culture and language are intimately interconnected. We are still living in a
world in which these three notions are inseparable. In order to
give reason for their endeavour, the German, the Czech, the Hungarian or the Russian linguistic reformers referred to the arguments, formulated among others by Herder, according to which the
national communities are to be taken for peculiar and single in-
dividualities. In this framework the National Spirit, defined
as the totality of the individual features of a given historical
community, manifests itself mainly in the Genius of a language.
Within the system of culture it was the literature which gave
the national movements of Eastern Europe the most adequate means
of expressing themselves. As a consequence of this, the linguistic
reform, too, asserted itself primarily as a literary movement.
And yet, following Rousseau, many people did profess that language,
forms of government and morals exercise mutual influence. Following Leibniz, Herder and Hegel they accepted similarly that the
development of the sciences depends, to a large extent, on linguistic conditions and the presupposition of a philosophy that
won't hold water is to be found in the national language, shaped

according to the principles of its own genius. It became nearly a commonplace that the genius of language determines a particular way of thinking or world view.

After these antecedents the problem of the relationship between culture and language has been explored from the most different points of view in the fields of human sciences and philosophy. /It will suffice to recall the theories of linguistic relativism, the problems that emerged in the course of describing American aboriginal languages or the structural anthropology of Lévi-Strauss/. In this place there is no possibility to deal with the concrete problems concerning the relationship of culture and language. There is, however, one basic question which has to be answered in order to get a conceptual framework in dealing with any aspect of this subject. This is the question of the sociality of language. It is no mere chance that the tradition of linguistic philosophy which was the background of the nascent cultural philosophy emphasized the unity of language and thought and formulated the idea of the social nature of language. /The thesis according to which the bearer of a language is the nation and not the individual is one way of conceptualizing the social character of language/.

The concept of the social and that of culture, as opposed to the concept of nature, are coextensive. It is evident that in the case of deriving language from the individual or taking it a biological endowment we have to face the problem of language and culture quite differently from the case of accepting the sociality of language. In the following, therefore, I should like to deal with the basic notion of the social character of language.

2. It is hard to imagine a more exemplary commonplace than the statement that language is a social institution. However, the discussion about the social nature of language has not lost its attraction. Among the causes of the current importance of this discussion we may note the following:

    a/ It is always sensible to ask the question whether language should not rather be considered as a biological or individual-psychological fact.

b/ The arguments in favour of the possibility of a private language have not been outdated even after Wittgenstein.

c/ It is by no means simple to expound what is meant by saying that language is a social phenomenon.

Let me observe that by accepting the statement about the social nature of language one is committed to reject the possibility of a private language and the strong versions of innatism. This is, of course, not an empirical thesis; so I could have expressed this point perhaps by saying that I am using the notion of the social character of language in a sense which excludes the possibility of a private language and innatism /at least its strong versions/.

This interpretation of the social character of language follows the great tradition in the framework of which Herder, Hegel, Humboldt, Marx or Wittgenstein, in view of certain basic problems, can be regarded as representatives of very similar ideas. This tradition has evolved through breaking with classical rationalism and empiricism and rests on the supposition, formulated in different ways, that the concepts capturing collective phenomena are primary in relation to the concepts expressing individual ones. Such collective concepts are the concept of spirit /Geist/, of popular spirit or spirit of nation /Volksgeist/, of life /Leben/, of social consciousness /Gesellschaftsbewusstsein/, of forms of life /Lebensformen/, and so on. It is part of this supposition that the isolated individual /such as the animated statue of Condillac or Diderot/ is unthinkable not only on a factual but on a conceptual level too. Human consciousness and awareness cannot have emerged on the basis of the sensuous experience belonging merely to an individual biography. The individual person can become what he is only by appropriating the conditions of his community and by participating in the different forms of the common spirit. Therefore, language cannot be a device of connecting subsequently the separate individuals or of expressing and communicating ulteriorly the thoughts which were born in the private and independent sphere of the mind. Language is essentially a social phenomenon and not only with respect to the contingent circumstances of its functioning.

In this tradition the philosophy of language obtains great importance. The essentially social character of language becomes the main reason for taking every kind of individuality to be of a social disposition and for taking the very individual mind to be a social entity. It is worthwhile comparing a few characteristic quotations. Fr. von Schlegel says that "even when we are alone, or we believe ourselves to be alone, in our thinking we have to be, actually, in two, and our most intimate and deepest being has to be recognized as essentially dramatic". /"... dass wir selbst dann, wenn wir allein sind, oder allein zu seyn glauben, immer eigentlich /noch/ zu Zweyen /denken und diess auch so/ in unserem Denken finden, und unser innerstes tiefstes Seyn als ein wesentliches drammatisches anerkennen müssen" /1/. W. v. Humboldt expounds this idea in a similar way: "Without taking into consideration the communication among men language is a necessary condition of the thinking of an individual in closed isolation". /"Ohne daher irgend auf die Mittheilung zwischen Menschen und Menschen zu sehn, ist das Sprechen eine nothwendige Bedingung des Denkens des Einzelnen in abgeschlossener Einsamkeit" /2/. And I believe the similarity of Marx's formulation is quite striking: "Even if I pursue a scientific activity, an activity I seldom pursue jointly with others, I am acting in a social way because I am acting as a human being. Not only the medium of my activity -- such as language itself in which the thinker works -- is given me as a social product, my own existence is a social activity...". /"Allein auch wenn ich wissenschaftlich etc. tätig bin, eine Tätigkeit, die ich selten in unmittelbarer Gemeinschaft mit andern ausführen kann, so bin ich gesellschaftlich, weil als Mensch tätig. Nicht nur das Material meiner Tätigkeit ist mir -- wie selbst die Sprache, in der der Denker tätig ist -- als gesellschaftliches Produkt gegeben, mein eignes Dasein ist gesellschaftliche Tätigkeit ..." /3//. Another characteristic statement of Humboldt is that "in man thinking is essentially bound to his social being". /"Im Menschen aber ist das Denken wesentlich an gesellschaftliches Daseyn gebunden" /4/ /. Note by the way that Humboldt already used the category of "gesellschaftliches Sein"!

3. Even if it may seem to be astonishing I think it is true
that analytical philosophy has repeated the development which
led from classical empiricism through Kant to Hegel and the ro-
mantic movement. In a fairly interesting book Richard J. Bernstein has the following to say: "The stages in contemporary e-
pistemological investigations which have moved from phenomenalism
with its foundation in 'sense data' to the emphasis on a 'thing
language' as an epistemological foundation, to the realization
of the importance of 'theoretical constructs' and finally the
'new' concern with total 'conceptual frameworks' or 'language
games' closely parallels the development that Hegel sketches for
us in the opening sections of the Phenomenology" /5/. Bernstein's
statement can be supported by the fact that in opposition to the
early stage of analytical philosophy in the last two decades the
problem of action has risen into prominence. The concept of action has come to play an important part for analytical philosophers just as the concept of praxis has come to be one of the basic
notions for Marxist thinkers. I am not proposing to deal with
this striking parallel or its possible consequences, I am going
to touch upon its linguistic aspects.

Its is evident that there is an intimate connection between
the popularity of speech act theory and the general interest in
the problem of action. Austin accomplished a real revolution, as
he could subsume language under a new category, the category of
action, the introduction of which into linguistic investigations
seemed to have no precedent and was contrary to the usual way of
accounting for language in terms of sign systems. This revolution,
however, amounts to restore /willy-nilly/ the tradition I characterized with the names of Herder, Schlegel, Humboldt or Marx. The
foundation of Humboldt's philosophy of language is to be found
in the idea that language is primarily an action and it is only
its secondary feature that it can be taken for a system of signs,
structure, means of expression, and so on. It is indeed conspicu-
ous that the notions in terms of which Humboldt characterizes
language as a phenomenon of social life are activity /Handlung/
and labour /Arbeit/. He says e.g.: "Language is no work /Ergon/,
but an activity /.../. It is a for ever recurring labour of the
Spirit /Energeia/". /"Sie selbst ist kein Werk /Ergon/, sondern

eine Thätigkeit /Energeia/ /.../. Sie ist nemlich die sich ewig
wiederholende Arbeit des Geistes" /6/.

It is small wonder that the appreciation of language as an
essentially social phenomenon and its consideration as a form
of activity were so intimately interwoven in the tradition discussed above. I believe this contingent historical fact throws
light upon a conceptual connection too. It is a part of the thesis
of the social character of language that language is a form of
activity and its all other functions, including the descriptive
one, are submitted to this feature. This conceptual connection
is described in Marxism in the form of reducing language to labour. As is well known, the explanation of language in terms of
labour is, according to Engels, the only correct account /7/.
Engels' relevant statements seem to refer only to a genetic tie
between language and labour but it is fully intelligible to suppose that labour has a prominent role not only in the genesis of
language but also in framing its immanent structure. So far, Marxism has not taken much advantage of its theoretical possibilities
in this field but what is to be regarded as a starting-point for
a Marxist theory in examining the nature of language was explicitly formulated by G. Lukács: "in the dynamic structure of ordinary
language the most general features of human praxis are expressed".
/"In dieser dynamischen Struktur der Sprache des Alltags drückt
sich /die! allgemeine Wesensart /.../ der menschlichen Praxis
aus /.../" /8/.

4. The most dangerous rival conception to explaining language in
terms of praxis, to subsuming it under the category of action and,
in general, to the idea of the social determination of language
is to be found in the theory in which the linguistic power of man
is accounted for in biological terms. If the view of holding language to be part of the inherited biological programme is accepted then the reflections related to labour and to the forms of social actions will become irrelevant.

It is well known that Chomsky worked out his innatism in controversy with the behaviourist conceptions /which are a matter of
secondary importance for our discussion here/. Moreover, the arguments in favour of his own conception owe their strength to
having been born in this context.

Let us recall that the argument which has been considered the most powerful one rests upon the assumption that in the process of language learning the child is confronted with a finite number of data from adult language. On the basis of a finite number of data he succeeds, however, in constructing a grammar which enables him to generate an infinite number of sentences. This fact counts as evidence both for the creativity and the innateness of the human language faculty. It is worth noticing that this argument seems to be strong also because the scientific paradigm prevailing in the given situation, the behaviourist learning theory, was not able to account for the relation between the available data and the grammar possessed by the child.

Is this argument as strong as it appears to be? In the first place, its premise is false. It is not the case that the child is confronted with data from adult language. We get a better picture if we take into consideration that, while talking to children, adults are using a reduced language adapted to the level of the children. In other words, the conversation of adults between them can be truly described in accordance with the picture given by Chomsky, but in the light of a common experience and of current research we have to suppose the existence of a particular strategy applied by adults in the verbal interaction with children. This strategy rests upon a principle of gradual growth. It is only to a small degree that in its formal and semantic aspects the speech of adults can be more complicated than the actual language of children is. In the verbal interaction with adults the child is not "exposed" to a chaotic conglomerate of data.

How is it possible to overlook such a simple fact? The answer, in my opinion, is to be found in Chomsky's philosophy of science, namely, in the way in which he extends the explanatory models of physics to linguistics. Conforming to Chomsky's picture the child is /subconsciously/ a little scientist. He observes the speech of adults as the scientist observes the behaviour of physical bodies, and on the basis of the available data he constructs and controls hypotheses as the scientist does in the light of his own data. /Needless to say: the child performs these acts of scientific observation without being aware of what he is doing/. According to this picture the child has the role of an observer.

Contrary to this, during the period of language learning the child does not _observe_ anything. He communicates and takes part in interactions.

At this stage Chomsky could work out a defense in the following way. It makes no difference what kind of language is used by the adults. What counts alone is the fact that the child constructs a grammar relying upon a finite number of observational data. Quite apart from the nature of data he is gaining experience and his experience is sufficient for actualizing the underlying innate principles. This, in essence, amounts to a Kantian solution in itself and though, in general, it is not to be rejected, it does not work here. The counter-argument is still founded upon the assumption that the child does observe the linguistic facts of his environment. However, observing the linguistic facts and taking part in communicative interactions are two fully different things. We have to make a sharp conceptual distinction between them. There is evidence that the child who is exposed to a number of linguistic stimuli but lacks the possibility of taking part in a mutual communication does not learn to speak in a normal way /9/. /Such a situation arises in the case of a child who may watch television but is not talked to/. Relying on these findings there is much to be said for the thesis according to which language learning does not follow the pattern underlying learning strategies in the field of other kinds of knowledge. Language learning cannot be described in terms of theoretical generalizations on the basis of observational data; it is to be described in terms of interaction and controlled communication. Communication is action and, as has been pointed out by Habermas /10/ as well, it is not experience.

5. If language capacity is innate then, evidently, what is to be taken into consideration in explaining its nature is only its structure. There cannot be any essential connection between its structure and its use. So there cannot be any interesting connection between structure and speech acts, between structure and communication. Chomsky himself emphasizes that "language is essentially a system for expression of thoughts" /11/, and, therefore, language cannot be accounted for in terms of communication.

"Communication is only one function of language, and by no means an essential one" /12/. /The quotations are taken from Chomsky's book of 1975 but as far as I can see his standpoint, in this respect, did not change substantially /13/. As a matter of fact, it is the standpoint which is compatible with innatism/.

Searle, on the other hand, has convincing arguments for assuming that meaning and speech acts, linguistic structure and communication are interdependent /14/. The debate of Chomsky and Searle is going on in terms of structure and function, but it is only one form, the modern form, of the debate on the more general question whether language is essentially or only contingently a social phenomenon.

The notion of action refers to the specific human behaviour all forms of which presuppose an explicit or implicit social context. It is, by the way, one of the main reasons for the descriptions of action to be dualistic, and that is why it is impossible to eliminate from them the intention terms which cannot be translated into physical ones. What has been said holds true of linguistic actions too. If we take into consideration these characteristics of the notion of action the following conclusion is to be drawn from the assumed innateness of linguistic structures: The structure, already given on the biological level, anticipates those contingent social contexts in which our actions are performed and are to be taken for actions at all. Since every kind of social context emerged through history, such a conclusion, in my opinion, is both unacceptable and senseless.

The danger of having to draw such a conclusion is evoked in Katz's proposal to combine speech act theory with generative grammar /15/. Katz's endeavour leads to a grammatical monism which makes all linguistic facts appear as a grammatical fact. This can be seen from the thesis that all information about the illocutionary force of a sentence is incorporated into the grammatical structure of that sentence. The thesis is ambiguous. On the one hand, it would follow that language has a social nature also in the sense that all information about the essential types of social situations and actions are somehow coded in its historically developed structure. On the other hand, the above mentioned unacceptable conclusion can follow from it as well.

According to this, provided the linguistic structure is inherited, language anticipates the essential types of social situations and actions. If one succeeded, as in my opinion Katz did not, in constructing a theory in the framework of which the speech acts and the illocutionary meanings can be completely represented on a grammatical level I would commit myself to the former conclusion.

6. Finally, I would like to touch upon one more question in connection with the social character of language. Some time ago Marxists were discussing whether language belonged to the basis or to the superstructure of the society. As is known, since the memorable debate Marxists have accepted the view that language belongs to neither. In the light of this it seems to be striking that in an important place in <u>The German Ideology</u> Marx speaks about a "bourgeois language". With respect to certain words /"propriété", "Eigentum" and "Eigenschaft"; "Property", "Eigentum" and "Eigentümlichkeit" and so on/ Marx analyzes the interesting semantic feature of their being used both in mercantile and individual-psychological sense /16/. He noticed that the language governed by such semantic rules is a product of the bourgeoisie. According to Lukács's interpretation this remark refers to the effects of reification upon language. The structures of reification penetrate into the linguistic structure as such. Lukács added: "A philological study from the standpoint of historical materialism could profitably begin here" /17/. I believe, following the quoted remarks, it could be systematically demonstrated that the concrete social structures and ideologies also have an effect upon the formal structure of language. The writers /18/ who suppose there being such a phenomenon as linguistic alienation may be right. Such phenomena call attention to a new dimension of the social character of language.

Those, however, who limit the social character of language to this dimension or are trying to build upon it a global linguistic theory, relevant from the point of view of social theory too, are on the wrong track. One has to make a careful distinction between what is to be taken for universal categories of a general social and linguistic theory and in what terms the connections of historically given social and linguistic structures are to be described. It is on this latter level that Marx's problem is to be located and questions concerning the relationship of culture and language arise. It is on this level that language can be treated as part and bearer of a given culture and the efforts to compare the relative value of particular languages, in terms of their suitability for certain functions /their fitness for philosophizing, for poetic achievements and so on/, do not lack a certain kind of intelligibility. The principles of the equivalence of languages and the universal expressability certainly hold but it is not accidental that in certain epochs and cultures people sensed the need of a linguistic reform and, indeed, they did carry out such a reform. These principles, accordingly, are to be interpreted as expressing a universal possibility which has to be actualized, sometimes by means of a conscious effort, in particular cultural conditions.

In a given state of language the two kinds of determinations are interwoven, they form the different strata of a unique code. A linguistic theory which aims at elucidating the social nature of language has to establish a connection between the fundamental strata of the code and the basic structures of the social life as such. It will afterwards be possible to show the way in which the social-historically and culturally more specific strata or subcodes are related to this basis and in which they are organized into a functional whole in a given state of language. Although in the functioning of language these different factors cannot be separated and the consciousness of a given speaker is determined by the network of specific subcodes language presupposes nothing else but the social as such. That could be put in this way too: The real language games are related to this or that form of life, but there is an ultimate ground of language games which is the manifestation of the social as such. It is on this ultimate level that the sources of such principles as the universal expressability can be identified.

NOTES

/1/ Friedrich v. Schlegel, <u>Philosophische Vorlesungen insbeson-</u>
     <u>dere über Philosophie der Sprache und des Wortes</u> /1830/.
     F. v. Schlegel, <u>Philosophie des Lebens, Philosophie der</u>
     <u>Sprache und des Wortes</u>, Kritische Friedrich-Schlegel-Ausgabe,
     Herausgegeben von E. Behler, München-Padeborn-Wien: Verl.
     F. Schöningh, Thomas-Verl., 1969. p. 352.

/2/ Wilhelm v. Humboldt, <u>Über die Verschiedenheiten des men-</u>
     <u>schlichen Sprachbaues</u>. W. v. Humboldt, <u>Schriften zur Sprach-</u>
     <u>philosophie</u>, Werke III., Stuttgart: Cotta, 1969. pp. 195-
     196.

/3/ Marx, <u>Ökonomische-philosophische Manuskripte /1844/</u>. Karl
     Marx/Friedrich Engels, Werke, Berlin: Dietz Verlag, 1956-
     1968, Ergänzungsband I., p. 538.

/4/ W. v. Humboldt, <u>Über die Verschiedenheiten des menschlichen</u>
     <u>Sprachbaues</u>, p. 201.

/5/ Richard J. Bernstein, <u>Praxis and Action</u>, Philadelphia: Uni-
     versity of Pennsylvania Press, 1971. p. 24.

/6/ W. v. Humboldt, <u>Über die Verschiedenheiten des menschlichen</u>
     <u>Sprachbaues</u>, p. 418.

/7/ "Dass diese Erklärung der Entstehung der Sprache aus und
     mit der Arbeit die einzig richtige ist, beweist der Vergleich
     mit den Tieren". Engels, <u>Dialektik der Natur</u>. Cf. Marx/Engels,
     <u>Über Sprache, Stil und Übersetzung</u>, Berlin: Dietz Verlag,
     1974. p. 49.

/8/ Georg Lukács, <u>Die Eigenart des Asthetischen</u>, Georg Lukács
     Werke, Neuwied am Rhein, Berlin Spandau: Luchterhand, 1963.
     Band 11, p. 61.

/9/ Jean Berko Gleason's conference in Budapest, April 1981.
     Verbal communication.

/10/ Jürgen Habermas, <u>Was heisst Universalpragmatik?</u> K-O. Apel
     /Ed./, <u>Sprachpragmatik und Philosophie</u>, Frankfurt am Main:
     Suhrkamp, 1976. p. 203.

/11/ Noam Chomsky, <u>Reflections on Language</u>, New York: Pantheon
     Books, 1975. p. 57.

/12/ Ibidem, p. 69.

/13/ In <u>Rules and Representations</u> /New York: Columbia University
     Press, 1980/ Chomsky holds the somewhat different view that
     language has no basic function. I do not think it should be
     taken, in the relevant respect, for an essential revision
     of his views about language.

/14/ John Searle, "Chomsky's Revolution in Linguistics". Gilbert
     Harman /Ed./, <u>On Noam Chomsky</u>, New York: Anchor Books, 1974.
     pp. 2-34.; Cf. Searle, <u>Expression and Meaning</u>. <u>Studies in</u>
     <u>the theory of speech acts</u>, Cambridge: Cambridge University
     Press, 1979.

/15/ Jerrold J. Katz, <u>Propositional structure and illocutionary force. A study of the contribution of sentence meaning to speech acts</u>, New York: Thomas Y. Crovell, 1977.

/16/ Marx/Engels, <u>Über Sprache, Stil und Übersetzung</u>, p. 123.

/17/ Georg Lukács, <u>History and Class Consciousness</u>, Cambridge Massachusetts: The MIT Press, 1971. p. 209.

/18/ E. g. Rossi-Landi. Cf. Ferruccio Rossi-Landi, <u>Linguistics and Economics</u>, The Hague-Paris: Mouton, 1975.

CULTURE AND THE DEVELOPING COUNTRIES

Philosophy and Culture
J. Lukács and F. Tőkei eds.

THE CONFLICT OF NATIONAL AND WESTERN CULTURES IN THE THIRD WORLD

A. ÁGH

1. THE CONCEPT OF A EUROPEANIZED WORLD CULTURE

The emergence of a European World Economy led to an aggressive diffusion of European Culture and generated the concept of World Culture as the general culture of all peoples but practically tantamount to European Culture spread all over the world /1/.

At the end of the last century, the scientific status of anthropology also provided a scientific foundation for the general theory of World Culture as well as "local" cultures. All precapitalist-preindustrial societies were summarized in the term of traditional societies producing in this way the negative ideal-type of modern/ized/ societies. According to the theory of traditional society,

/i/ traditional society generates only a traditional - or "primitive" - culture which can attract the interest of science at the very most with its exotic character but which is certainly unable to enrich World Culture with its particular content;

/ii/ the specific varieties of traditional cultures - as well as the traditional societies - can be parallelled with the former stages of the European development. At the same time their particular character diverging from the European forms is not to be taken for ways of development, quite to the contrary, as ways leading to different blind alleys in cultural history;

/iii/ thus traditional cultures formulate the spiritual programmes of passivity and stagnation and should be destroyed in

the process of modernization and replaced by the European culture. Thus by the destruction of the <u>main internal obstacle of
development</u> the modern, universal Europeanized World Culture
emerges /2/.

This "optimistic" theory meant that from the end of the last
century on, European thinking in the spirit of unilinear evolutionism unequivocally opted for the forceful destruction of
local cultures and the aggressive diffusion of Europeanized
World Culture. The former European theories of World Culture
were "pessimistic" and pluralistic and in spite of the rapid
diffusion of European World Economy they acknowledged the independent spirituality of other World Cultures. They featured them
in an eternal dualism and extreme contradiction with European
Culture, i.e. an unbridgeable gulf was supposed between the different World Cultures excluding the possibility of a universal
World Culture. The controversy of universalist and pluralist approaches to World Culture continues in this century as well but
dominated by the universalist approach offering a programme for
the aggressive diffusion of Europeanized World Culture, while
the pluralist approach is confined to the mere survival programmes
of Third World cultures.
The dominance of unilinear evolutionism in the concept of
World Culture, as we have seen above, has not meant a solution
for the extremities of universalism and pluralism but produced
their special mixture. Namely in anthropology, functioning as
scientific as well as ideological system for the concepts of
culture, the dualism of "internalism" and "externalism" seems to
be unsurmountable /3/. In anthropological studies, the subject-
-matter of research may be presented either as an individual culture with its ethnical and regional unity in certain isolation
from the others - the atomistic, nominalist approach - or the
diffusion process of a particular individual culture - the universalist approach. That is, cultures may change in their isolation /internalism/ or totally under the influence of the external forces /externalism/ but never in their mutual interdependence which is contrary to this "anthropological view", the
essence of culture and the cultural intercourse of different
peoples proves to be the main factor in forming history. Cul-

ture, we think, as a social sub-system is the most important in-
termediary sphere in the contacts among different societies being
that sub-system of society which reacts to the internal and external challenges in the most dynamic way and which is able to
translate the external changes and impacts into the internal code
of behaviour and thinking, mediating them thus to all members of
the society. This synthesis-model, however, was rejected and remained alien to the concept of Europeanized World Culture because
the real history of European conquest and colonization knew only
the alternative of complete destruction and subjugation /in the
New World/ or the preservation of the intact internal relations
/isolation with some external contacts: in Asian civilization for
centuries/. As a consequence of the aggressive expansion of world
capitalism the "normal" model of mutual interdependence of cultures was ruled out or it occurred only as a secondary trend in
the process of the emergence of Europeanized World Culture. The
European colonizers were concerned above all with the destruction
of local, traditional culture-atoms by the violent expansion of
their own European-type national culture. This is why the notion
of acculturation has got a priority in anthropology covering all
forms of universal diffusion of Europeanized World Culture and
the destruction of local cultures. Acculturation means in this
conception also the process of a particular re-socialization of
"traditional personalities" as their re-education in the spirit
of European values and their mobilization for the European-type
modernization.

The general offensive of European World Culture against the
local cultures was launched throughout the periphery of world
capitalism in the late 19th century. By the challenge of Europeanized World Culture the intelligentsia of dependent or colonized
countries was faced with the absurd and threatening alternative
of either completely giving up their own traditional cultures or
preserving it but in that way giving up the chances of development and modernization totally. In this conflict many representatives of the local intelligentsia chose the way of the European-
ization of traditional culture, sometimes giving it up completely,
while others, on the contrary, used the traditional culture as
a shield protecting themselves against the European economic-po-

litical and cultural challenge /4/. But this conflict proved to be a pseudo-conflict and in both ways almost equally false: they fell between two societies in any case, on the one side the effort to Europeanize did not lead to their personal "acculturation" since they were rejected by the metropolitan societies and did not lead to the successful modernization of their respective societies either. On the other hand even those strata which opted for preserving the traditions at any price were forced to accept the everyday realities of modern societies and this compromise provoked among them the need for compensative actions because of the permanent compromisés with the alien culture.

The period until after the Second World War can be characterized by the defense of local cultures against the European World Culture and by the cultural ambivalence and deep embarassment of the intelligentsia of dependent and colonial countries. Since Europeanized World Culture appeared as the programme of the aggression against local cultures the national independence movements also appeared, against the cultural aggression and for a long time, in their most strikingly marked forms as <u>cultural</u> resistance movements. The events of political struggle for independence overshadowed the cultural resistance for a short time but in the long run it was the dominating form of resistance which changed after the Second World War from defensive into offensive. In the period of rapid national development the programme for nation-building was prepared by these cultural resistance movements in the whole periphery of world capitalism, thus everywhere <u>local</u>, traditional cultures were transformed into <u>national</u> cultures. The claim for national identity and cultural independence ushered in the establishment of an independent national state and economy and became the main form of mobilization of masses for the national development strategies. So it is not by chance that also a lot of theories emerged claiming priority for cultural resistance and national identity in the whole process, sometimes in a very extreme way and polemizing one against another as e.g. the concepts of Senghor, Fanon and Cabral in Black Africa. In these very fertile but also very contradictory theories characteristically manifested itself the progressive and mobilizing role of national identity as well as its compensative role for the latecomers in the modernization process. In this way the formal criticism of the above mentioned theories misses the point, since this criticism is usually unable to grasp the essence of cultural-national identity in the national development of Third World countries /5/.

In the new situation after the Second World War, when the more indirect forms of dependence came to the fore in the period of neocolonialism, the struggle in the sphere of culture has continuously been growing on both sides. From the center of the world capitalism the theories of modernization represent the main form of cultural aggression against the national cultures of periphery claiming their independence. The modernization theories have proved to be the new form of the diffusion of Europeanized World Culture implying that the only way for development and modernization leads through the unconditional acceptance of westernized values and attitudes, even in the newly independent countries. This is why these theories of cultural subjugation seem to be the optimal form of the preservation of its previous domination of the center of world capitalism with new means. For the same reason the modernization theories came to the fore in the late fifties since they showed the Western model and value structure of modernization as generally compulsory, cosmopolitan and socio-politically neutral. The modernization theories, therefore, are aimed at the so-called modernizing elite of the newly independent countries to initiate a socio-cultural change imitating the westernized value structure of "modern society" and "modern man". The demonstrative effect of the Western way of life plays in itself a great role in the formation of the "homo consumens universalis" and in the cultural offensive against the national cultures with indirect means and forms. It is not a "theological" question to raise any longer, as it was in the 16th century, whether we may consider an Indian a human being at all, if he or she is not baptized, i.e. not a member of the /Spanish or Portuguese/ Catholic Church. Nowadays the question is, e.g. whether we may consider a Black African a cultured or educated human being if he or she does not lead an American way of life? /6/

But the essence of these approaches has remained the same through the centuries of world capitalism: culture as the generic

definition of man is formulated here in a very narrow national
form and this particular national form is forced onto the whole
mankind and all human existence as universal. Consequently, the
creative force of cultural variety and the interdepending national cultures disappear totally and instead of the catalytic influence of cultural contacts the cultural unity of mankind and the
universality of World Culture appear as a dictate to accept Europeanized World Culture, nowadays with an American face. The significance of cultural offensive, partly in the form of modernization theories, partly through the mass media as cultural imperialism has grown in the seventies because of the failure of
economic growth or political development strategies advertized
largely by these modernization theories. It is true that not only
the motives of cultural offensive have increased in this period
but the motives of "technological culture" and "political culture" have gained momentum, too. Thus in the last decade a slowly growing process of internal decomposition of bourgeois modernization theories and the emergence of an internal criticism a-
gainst their monolythic character may be noticed. It is getting
clearer and clearer even in the framework of these theories that
modernization and development cannot be optimal with the uncritical acceptance and imitation of Western models. Quite to the contrary, the optimalization is but a result of the re-application
of general models by their creative adaptation to the national
development. This approach has gradually become dominant in the
programmes and development strategies of the big international
organizations and, without any doubt, this approach will dominate
in the 1980s, in the third development decade of the UN.

2. THE DYNAMISM OF NON-EUROPEAN NATIONAL CULTURES

The struggle between the core and the periphery of world capitalism for the determination of the trend of development of World
Culture has intensified in the last decade. In the efforts concentrated on the creation of a genuine universal World Culture
the socialist countries also play a significant role but in our
present study we deal exclusively with the development of national
cultures in Third World countries. In this respect we have to

point out two conflicting tendencies, one being the emergence of
the national cultures of the Third World as the rebirth of the
local historical cultures after the centuries of Pax Britannica
and the decades of Pax Americana, the second one being the appearance of transnationalization tending to suppress even those
independent cultural forms which have succeeded in establishing
themselves in the Third World nations so far. The raison d'etre
of the nations as economico-political units in the Third World
is not questioned by anybody even in this period, although they
are dependent and secondary units. But the question is raised
seriously concerning national cultures: is there any real meaning or possibility for an independent cultural development in
the Third World in the age of cultural imperialism which is the
"domination of socialization and mass media means" over the culturally subjugated nations? /7/ Our answer is unequivocally positive: there is a real possibility for an independent national
culture to develop even in the age of cultural imperialism, what
is more, this is the only way and sine qua non precondition for
the socio-economic development, too. That is, there is no viable
development strategy without a really independent national culture and national identity which are a blueprint for the future
and at the same time engine of all kinds of present-day national
development. The establishment of these national cultures at the
world level, i.e. in all Third World countries may be the only
guarantee for a genuinely universal World Culture as a synthesis
of all national cultures and against the permanent reappearence
of Europeanized World Culture.

The conflict between the capitalist World Culture and national
cultures is very often discussed in the Third World literature.
In S. Amin's Class and Nation modern universal culture is treated
as the characteristic ideology of world capitalism. According to
Amin there is a tendency to homogenization in world capitalism
with the material basis of the continual extension of markets
which also gradually envelops all aspects of social life. Therefore, the homogenization of use values through their domination
by generalized exchange values - he emphasizes - must tend to
homogenize culture itself but, on the other side, this tendency
is held in check by the effects of unequal accumulation. So the

imperialist development accelerates real homogenization in the
center while blocking it in the periphery, where only a minority
of the people can become modern consumers. Amin describes the
conflicting tendencies generated by the homogenization effort
of world capitalism as the claim of world capitalism to spread
Europeanized World Culture in its practical, use-value forms of
way of life with its hidden ideological motives. He also depicts
the failure of the diffusion of this way of life due to the unequal accumulation blocking the development of peripheral nations
and provoking their cultural resistance against homogenization.

As Amin shows, the tendency to homogenization under capitalism
is stronger in some areas than in others. In the area of industrial production techniques, in the realm of modes of consumption,
"lifestyles", Amin says, its force is virtually irresistible. It
is somewhat weaker in the domain of ideology and politics. And,
finally, when it comes to the use of language, its impact is very
weak. Furthermore Amin emphasizes that there is no technological
determination of the homogenization of world culture due to the
diffusion of modern forces of production. Capitalist World Culture has no real universal character and its pseudo-universality
plays the ideological function suggesting that the development
of modern material culture directly and automatically determines
the development of non-material culture, namely in the direction
of westernized modernization. Amin does not conclude, however,
at the central significance of cultural resistance of Third World
nations against this tendency of the homogenization of pseudo-
-universal capitalist World Culture and, therefore, he is not
able to point out the significance of the development of national
culture and identity in the general development of non-European
nations /8/.

We find an even more markedly formulated thesis on the tendency
of the aggressive expansion of Europeanized World Culture in the study
of O. Sunkel and E. Fuenzalida, "The Transnationalization of Capitalism and National Development". The authors raise very sharply
the question whether an independent national development of Third
World countries is possible at all and they initiate a deep and
thorough investigation in economic, political and cultural aspects. Sunkel and Fuenzalida consider the tendency of transnation-

alization to be the major and dominating tendency of the latest decades. During these decades capitalist system has changed from an international system to a supra-national one and in this process of transnationalization capitalist national societies have also passed through important changes in both developed and underdeveloped countries. The authors envisage three phases of transnationalization, starting with transnational integration which generates in the second phase the appearance of national desintegration and provokes in the third phase a national reintegration. The result, however, is a certain ambivalence between the re-affirmation of national and subnational ideas and values and emergence of a transnational community integrated at the world level, although its members live in geographically and politically separated places.

In this conflict of national and transnational community Sunkel and Fuenzalida consider the latter one as dominating and producing a transnational culture. The last three decades have seen an enormous expansion of the capitalist economic activity and this has led to the establishment of social, cultural and political institutions in the Third World countries adequate to this capitalist expansion, and, at the same time, to the emergence of transnational culture there with its values, norms, ideas, symbols and ideologies. The authors re-emphasize the significance of national reintegration as a possible solution of this conflict of transnational and national cultures and suggest that the new way of life and consumer behaviour in developing countries should be harmonized with the satisfaction of basic needs and built upon a particular national culture of their own in each country /9/.

In the Third World literature I. Wallerstein tries in the most consistent way to outline a general concept of the world system approach according to which the world system is based on world economy connected by the worldwide system of division of labour and articulated by the political systems and cultural heterogeneity of its national units. Wallerstein also sees the tendency of cultural homgenization in the world system but in its different parts - core, semiperiphery and periphery - with totally different results. What is more, Wallerstein sets the cultural heterogeneity of the world system against its predominant economic homogeneity, that is, he thinks that in the cultural process, heterogeneity and in the economic one, homogeneity has become the predominant tendency in the capitalist world system. The member-states of this world system are culturally heterogeneous units making big efforts for an internal cultural homogenization. The bearer of this tendency, i.e. the national state is not only the political representative of the local-national economic interest but also creates a particular system of symbols expressing the cultural traditions of an "ethno-nation" as an auto-representation of self-manifestation of its ruling classes. Consequently, Wallerstein overexaggerates both poles in the world system: on the one hand, the complete unity or homogeneity of world economy and, on the other, the total individuality or heterogeneity of national culture. It is true that in this framework of the absolute extremities he describes realistically that process in which developing countries after their political independence have created their own national cultures with particular cultural symbols, national language and other forms of expression. Thus the culture as one of the social sub-systems turns out to be the unique expression of national individuality and identity opposed to the economic and political sub-systems in which the general character of transformation in the world history is reflected in a more direct way.

Wallerstein indicates the real process in which national culture has become the bearer of the particular-individual character of a nation and by that it mobilizes and motivates masses for modernization. The national consciousness or identity appears, however, as an automatic result of the world system development without the counter-acting tendencies in Wallerstein's studies. When he deals with world economy in a proper way, he neglects the antagonisms in the development of the national cultures, and, in return, when he deals with these antagonisms he neglects the worldwide economic tendencies. So, in his research proposals prepared for the Fernand Braudel Center and written with T. Hopkins "Patterns of Development of the Modern World System" the cultural sub-system as the third aspect of the world system appears only per tangentem. This time, we think, not the World Culture proves to be heterogeneous but its description given by Wallerstein.

The only certain feature he mentions about World Culture is that its fundamental laws of motion differ essentially from those of economy and politics although, as he states finally, we know only little about it in a systematic way /10/.

The three concepts outlined by us very briefly above show well the conceptual framework in which the Third World literature theorizes the conflicting tendencies of World Culture and National Cultures. It shows, at the same time, the manifest limitations of this research-topic as well: we know much less the interdependency-system of World Culture and National Culture than that of world economy and national economies or world politics and national state politics although it is about the equally important processes and conflicts. The ideological character and sensitivity of these three aspects, of course, significantly diverge, the research of world economy takes place in the framework of the allegedly completely objective scientific theories; in the theories of world politics the objectivity-centered political research is largely mixed with the openly ideological self-estimations of national political systems; and finally, the research of national cultures is faced with artistically formulated national myths based on self-evidence of the historical traditions and very rarely meets the scientific criteria of historical or international comparisons. This is not only so in the Third World countries but in the industrially advanced countries too, the only difference being that they have more chances to have their own national evidences internationally accepted or, at least, tolerated while the Third World countries generally reject one another's overexaggerated national consciousnesses. The low profile and scientific prestige of comparative research of national cultures is highly regrettable, not only because it excludes the cancellation of the paradigm of Europeanized World Culture in social sciences but also because it isolates the Third World national cultures among themselves /11/.

In the Western modernization literature of the sixties there are some tendencies towards the recognition of the particularity--individuality in the national process of modernization. Eisenstadt clearly realized the contradictions coming from the identification of modernization and westernization, namely that the latter is not only a particular and restricted form of the former but may be an obstacle to the expansion and carrying out of the former. Eisenstadt expressed his views in Modernization, Protest and Change /1966/, suggesting that the relation of modernization and westernization can have vital significance for the start of self-sustained development. Thus the crucial problem of modernization is: until what extent can the non-European countries develop the features of modernity without becoming westernized in the cultural respect, that is, without uncritically imitating those special cultural forms, values and institutions under the influence of which the Western societies had been modernized.

Our conclusion is quite clear: the Western modernization concept has proved to be false since it claimed that a breakthrough towards modernization demands the complete destruction of the special local culture as a break with continuity of traditions and presupposes its replacement with the Europeanized World Culture which has been advertized as the only way to development and modernization. This was one of the greatest European myths of our age which declared the non-European national cultures to be the major obstacle to progress and went to the defamation and ridiculization of all non-European cultural norms and values. It is not only Japan that has shown strikingly the "efficiency" of the traditional national culture in industrialization and modernization but also a series of other "latecomer" countries have proved that the particular national culture could and should be the engine of social progress. The monolythic and westernized concept of modern man with an American face presented by McClelland and Inkeles has nothing to do with the real human features of modern man in the Third World countries.

So we may summarize that:

/i/ the consequences of the total destruction of traditional cultural values are disfunctional for modernization, whereas if the development is taking place in the framework of the local national culture it is not only the continuity that is secured but also the special, creative application of modernization to the local circumstances, i.e. the transformation of universality to particularity, to a national way of development;

86

/ii/ the special national programme of modernization instead of the mechanically applied westernized foreign model at the same time increases very much the efficiency of development strategy, since the national culture is able to play its proper role of mobilization and motivation for the national goals and helps to overcome the conflicts in the modernization process with the individuals being actively involved in this process and realizing the completion of their national goals in the development process;

/iii/ the particular national culture may be classified as the main form and fundamental means of development and modernization, i.e. in the nation-building process of the Third World countries culture as a secondary social sub-system gets primary role and function, namely cultural development and national identity are the main preconditions and promoters of socio-economic development and modernization /12/.

3. NATIONAL CULTURE AND DEVELOPMENT

The development crisis which broke out in the poorest countries of the Third World in the seventies manifested not only the failure of development strategies and modernization programmes but also the crisis of the westernized, universalist ideology of modernization and the absurdity of westernization=modernization. The theoretical and ideological conclusions of the development crisis are manifested in the following:

/i/ the unilateral economic growth and/or political development strategies have been blocked by their own internal limitations. The unilateral economic growth strategy does not generate economic growth because it undermines its own preconditions, i.e. the establishment and enlargement of an independent national economy and market, and the unilateral political development strategy does not generate political development because the introduction of the Westminster-type democracy in developing countries was incompatible with the internal political instability and the "political culture" of the masses. In such a way even the westernized modernization concepts were forced to change their options and open towards the complex programmes and strategies involving

the active role of local attitudes and values and accepting the
significance of national culture in modernization /13/.

/ii/ Those development programmes and strategies which have
been present in the modernization literature as votum separatum
or minority views since they favourized the human investment,
human capital or rural development-centered breakthrough towards
modernization against the physical capital and industrial development-centered "push" in the modernization process, have gained
momentum in the late 1970s. The enclaves created by the Western-
-type industrial development have generally remained inorganic
parts in the national economies of the Third World countries not
producing any linkages and not generating a complex development
of the national economy. It is the same with the westernized programmes of education which have served only the preservation and
enlargement of the European culture of the urban population and,
by blocking the formation of the particular national culture,
the westernized local elite culture has not promoted but distorted the modernization process itself /14/.

/iii/ In the 1970s the need of a genuinely national and efficient education really involving the largest masses of population in the modernization process by preparing them for the social changes with a personal adaptivity has met the need of the
satisfaction of the other Basic Needs of the population. By the
end of the 1970s a new development strategy emerged which was
based on these Basic Needs and generally accepted by the big international organizations and agencies. In this new development
strategy the formation of the particular national cultures was
thrown in the cast of main promoter of socio-economic modernization.

The Basic Needs Development Strategy has become central and
vital by the sharpening of the development crisis. The increase
of the GNP in the great majority of developing countries has
slowed down or even fallen back, therefore, the catching up with
the industrially advanced countries has lost all its validity
for the next future. The new strategy has been necessitated by
the new situation in which the satisfaction of the Basic Needs
of the population has come to the fore instead of the economic

growth at any price. These developing countries have not given up the economic growth as such at all but have changed the approach and means: they are going to reach development by transforming the fundamental structure of production and consumption. This strategy presumably will not meet its own internal limitation but the "external" obstacles to development institutionalized in the political structure of the given societies and the solution of this conflict may decide the evolution or devolution of the great potentials incorporated in the Basic Needs Development Strategy. Anyway, the role of the national culture is also of great importance in fighting out this conflict /15/.

As a final word about the unique role and primary importance of national culture in the socio-economic development and modernization we quote the summary of the D. Seer's views:

"The 'oil crisis' of the 1970s really shook the conventional paradigm... The time is ripe for another critical look at the meaning of development... The essential element to add - as is being widely recognized - is self-reliance... This would involve changing consumption patterns as well as increasing the relevant productive capacity. Redistribution of income would help, but policies would also be needed to change living styles... There are other implications as well, especially in cultural policy. These are more country-specific, but as a general rule, let us say that 'development' now implies, _inter alia_, reducing cultural dependence on one or more of the great powers - i.e. increasing the use of national languages in schools, allotting more television time to programmes produced locally /or in neighbouring countries/, raising the proportion of higher degrees obtained home, etc." /16/

NOTES

/1/   The terms of world history, world literature and world culture came into use in the late 18th century.

/2/   Many Western modernization theories consider nationalism as such or the development of national culture as the internal obstacle to modernization, see J. H. Kautsky, An Essay in the Politics of Development, in: Kautsky /ed/ Political Change in Underdeveloped Countries, Nationalism and Communism, Wiley, New York, 1962. pp. 57-69. This principle has gone through the modernization theories starting from Parsons and, presumably, by the mediation of M. J. Levy's Modernization and the Structure of Society /1966/. In J. Röpke's Primitive Wirtschaft, Kulturwandel und die Diffusion von Neuerungen /Mohr, Tübingen, 1970. pp. 129-142, 177. etc./ the theory of cultural change is elaborated in the optimistic spirit of the modernization literature of the 1960s and in the terms of Schumpeter's innovation model.

/3/ The concepts of internalism and externalism are treated by B. S. Turner's Marx and the End of Orientalism /George Allen and Unwin, London, 1978. pp. 10-13./. In the Third World literature the modernization theories represent mostly the Weberian, internalist concepts and Wallerstein, Amin and other radical thinkers the externalist ones.

/4/ We may refer to the concept of Afghani, islam reformer of the last century or to the discussions of the same period in India between "anglicists" and "traditionalists" etc. This conflict was very characteristic also in the debates of slavophils and modernizers in Russia. R. Lowenthal deals extensively with these debates in his Model or Ally? Communist Powers and the Developing Countries /Oxford University Press, 1977. pp. 24-25, 338, 356 etc./ concentrating on the cultural ambivalence of the Third World intelligentsia and ending with a declaration about the universality of Western cultural values.

/5/ See Imre Marton Contribution a une Critique des Interpretations des Spécificités du Tiers Monde /Institut D'Économie Mondiale de l'Académie des Sciences de Hongrie, Budapest, 1978/.

/6/ The revival of local-national culture led to a vivid criticism of anthropology and its Euro-centric culture-concept, see the study of Ikenna Nzimiro, Nigerian Professor, Anthropologists and Their Terminologies or the study of Wanda Avila Toward a Theory of American Culture in Bernardi /ed/ The Concepts and Dynamics of Culture, Mouton Publishers, The Hague-Paris, 1977.

/7/ About the theories of cultural or communication imperialism see the studies of D. Senghaas Elemente Einer Theorie des peripheren Kapitalismus, in: D. Senghaas /ed/ Peripherer Kapitalismus, Frankfurt am Main, Suhrkamp Verlag, 1974. pp. 7-34, or J. Galtung, A Structural Theory of Imperialism, Journal of Peace Research, Vol. 8, No. 2. 1971. pp. 81-118.

/8/ See S. Amin Class and Nation, Historically and in the Current Crisis, Heinemann, London, 1980. pp. 31-33.

/9/ O. Sunkel, E. Fuenzalida The Transnationalization of Capitalism and National Development, IDS, Reprint, March 1977.

/10/ I. Wallerstein, The Capitalist World Economy, Cambridge University Press, 1980. pp. 5, 23, 228 and T. Hopkins and I. Wallerstein, Patterns of Development of the Modern World-System /1977/.

/11/ The compensative character of the national consciousness
is increasing with the level of underdevelopment as it may
be noticed even in Eastern Europe where nationalism is i-
dentified traditionally with the development of national
consciousness.

/12/ Hungarian sociologists have shown that even in the modernization of the Hungarian society after the Second World War
the continuity of the traditional values of national traditions was of great importance.

/13/ About the crisis of the former development strategies and
theories see the studies published in D. Lehmann /ed/ Development Theory, Frank Cass, London, 1979.

/14/ W. A. Lewis, The Evolution of the International Economic
Order /Princeton University Press, 1978/, T. W. Schultz,
Investment in Human Capital /The F ˀ Press, New York, 1971/
and M. P. Todaro, Economics for a Devel ˀinˀ World /Longman,
London, 1977/.

/15/ The World Development Report, 1980 /Published for the World
Bank, Oxford University Press, 1980/ deals extensively with
the Basic Needs Development Strategy.

/16/ D. Seers, The Meaning of Development, in: D. Lehmann /ed/,
Op. Cit. pp. 27-28. For further readings about the Basic
Needs Development Strategy see A. Singh, The "basic needs"
approach to development vs the new international economic
order: the significance of Third World industrialization,
World Development vol. 7, No. 6, 1979. pp. 585-606 and S.
J. Burki, Meeting basic needs: an overview, World Develop-
ment vol. 9, No. 2, 1981. pp. 167-182. Our concept of Basic
Needs was formulated in our study, A. Ágh, Human Nature and
the Concept of Basic Needs, Dialectics and Humanism /Warsaw/
Vol. VIII, No. 3, Summer 1981. pp. 81-94.

Philosophy and Culture
J. Lukács and F. Tőkei eds.

MYTHOLOGIE ET DEVENIR HISTORIQUE
DE LA RECHERCHE DE L'IDENTITÉ NATIONALE

I. MARTON

1./ De nos jours, la recherche de l'identité peut être assimilée à une entreprise aventureuse vers un avenir qui fuit comme l'horizon devant le voyageur, ou à une fouille archéologique décelant les strates d'un passé de plus en plus lointain.

Le ciel de l'identité est balayé par les phares du narcissisme, de l'agressivité vis-à-vis de l'Autre, de l'identification passionnelle avec l'Autre, des déchéances et des renaissances nationales.

La recherche de l'identité est un feu d'artifice et en même temps le foyer de la renaissance nationale. Elle est perpétuellement soumise à l'attraction d'un passé dépassé par l'histoire et d'un futur inabordable, car c'est avec le présent qu'il est le plus déroutant aux humains de s'identifier.

Cette recherche de l'identité est comparable au cycle de la vie et de la mort. Héraclite commentant l'incantation à Osiris dans le Livre des morts note: "Il vit sa mort et meurt sa vie". L'identité est l'unité toujours éclatée et recomposée, toujours renouvelée et enrichie de la présence vivante des morts et de l'éclosion d'un monde futur qui germe en son sein.

2./ La notion d'identité nationale échappe à la définition, mais s'impose comme évidence dans la vie sociale, culturelle, dans les motivations qui président au mode de pensée et d'action des groupes sociaux et des individus se réclamant ou provenant d'une même communauté nationale.

Il faut distinguer l'aspect objectif et l'aspect subjectif de l'identité nationale.

L'identité renvoie à l'objectivation des activités matérielles et spirituelles des générations successives des communautés humaines qui se sont constituées en nation au cours de l'histoire. En somme l'identité nationale serait l'ensemble des strates des réponses spécifiques aux défis auxquels la communauté nationale a été confrontée. C'est la somme des alternatives choisies, des initiatives, des recréations des libertés conquises dans l'étau des contraintes naturelles et historiques.

La réalité objective de l'identité nationale est le devenir historique de la spécificité d'une communauté nationale. Cette spécificité s'élabore et se forge au cours de l'émergence de la nation dans le cadre d'une mondialisation soumise à la dialectique de l'intégration et de la désintégration internationale et nationale. L'identité nationale est la localisation des processus économiques, politiques, culturels mondiaux, et la mondialisation des processus locaux. Ainsi l'identité nationale est permanence et changement, homogénéité et diversité, altérité et altération.

L'identité nationale est une limite qui sépare et met en contact les communautés humaines.

Le devenir historique de l'identité nationale recoupe la problématique des rapports entre la tradition et la modernité, de la dialectique de l'universel et du particulier.

L'identité nationale est l'histoire de la dialectique de l'universel et du singulier, de la spécification nationale de l'universalité et de l'universalisation de la spécificité.

L'identité nationale est un centre de médiation privilégié entre cohésion nationale et différenciation sociale.

L'aspect subjectif est le vécu de l'identité nationale au niveau de la conscience quotidienne et de la conscience historique de l'individu, de la classe sociale, de la nation et de la communauté mondiale.

C'est une certitude, une évidence qui s'effrite et s'embrouille quand on tente de la préciser. C'est une prise de conscience de ce qui différencie notre "moi" face aux autres "moi", et de la façon dont les autres "moi" m'identifient. Sur le plan du vécu, c'est ce qui se conserve et est conservé dans la mémoire collective à un moment donné. C'est l'ensemble des valeurs et des faits

du passé que l'on réactive et réanime en fonction des contradictions, des espoirs, des illusions et des désillusions, des projets et des aspirations actuels. On observe une non-adéquation
entre la signification originelle d'une valeur, d'un événement,
et la signification actualisée. L'originel devient symbolique.
Il n'a pas de relecture innocente du passé. "Lorsque le symbole
est utilisé dans un rapport de force, il ajoute sa propre force
à ce rapport de force" /Bourdieu/. Selon l'usage que l'on en
fait, il reçoit un sens supplémentaire, mais altéré.

L'identité nationale renvoie à un devenir historique, à un
imaginaire, à une fuite vers le passé, face aux instabilités et
décrépitudes du présent, ou à un dépassement des limitations du
présent, vers un rêve ou projet anticipateur avec lesquels on
s'identifie, vers la recherche d'une harmonisation de la renaissance nationale et du renouveau de la mondialité.

L'identité nationale peut être comparée à un drame qui "continue de mettre en scène résurrection, déguisements, costumes,
erreurs fécondes, exactitudes catastrophiques" /Harold Rosenberg/.

L'identité nationale est un héritage historico-culturel et
le remodelage continu de cet héritage.

3./ Dans les sociétés dominées par l'économie d'auto-subsistance, la dialectique de l'universel et du particulier est ré-
gie d'une part par l'humanisation de la nature /maîtrise des
forces naturelles/, d'autre part par la socialisation de l'homme
soumis aux solidarités biologiques, linguistiques, morales, religieuses, culturelles d'une communauté s'opposant aux autres
communautés. L'histoire universelle n'est pas encore un processus totalisant, intégrateur, mais plutôt une démultiplication
d'histoires locales sans rapports de réciprocité endogènes.

4./ Lorsque les rapports marchands, la loi de la valeur deviennent dominants, lorsque les rapports capital-travail affectent
à des degrés divers, à travers des médiations multiples, alors
toutes les sociétés, "toute l'histoire de l'homme n'est que l'histoire de la marchandise" /Horkheimer/. La dialectique de l'universel et du particulier se manifeste dans l'interdépendance et
la confrontation entre mondialisation et communautés nationales.

A partir du XVIe siècle, la dialectique négative de l'intégration internationale et de la désintégration nationale se manifeste le plus intensément dans les zones du sous-développement
européen et extra-européen.

La colonisation est une des résultantes de l'internationalisation des rapports de production capitalistes, de l'expansion
universelle du Capital. Celle-ci propulse à l'échelle de notre
planète les échanges des biens, des valeurs culturelles et scientifiques, et favorise le brassage des populations. Toutefois,
cette mondialisation comporte des aires endeuillées et ensoleil-
lées. L'initiative historique, la culture, le capital, la technique se diffusent à partir du Centre qui est l'étalon-or. Les
territoires colonisés, la périphérie deviennent des aires ré-
ceptives et de mimétisme.

"Le monde était divisé en deux camps: le camp des hauts-par-
leurs et le camp des bouches closes. Le dialogue n'a jamais été
du goût de ceux qui ont pris, depuis des générations, l'habitude
de monologuer à tue-tête et à tout vent" /Jacques Rabemanannja-
ra/.

L'assimilation culturelle entreprise et imposée par la métropole va de pair avec la discrimination. Le mondial disqualifie
le national. L'assimilation induisant la discrimination va devenir un nouveau ferment de la recherche de l'identité et induire
des réactions ambigües. Elle pourra susciter, par effet de retour, un refus de l'autre poussé à l'extrême, dans un repliement
obstiné sur l'ancestral, un cloisonnement, une traditionalisa-
tion de la tradition. Cette assimilation-discrimination est
la source de complexes d'infériorité, de mépris de l'autre et
de mépris de soi-même, de survalorisation de soi-même, du ré-
trécissement du champ historique dans lequel se déploie le devenir de l'identité nationale.

Sartre, dans sa merveilleuse étude sur le mouvement de la négritude, "Orphée noir", avait montré que la lutte contre la discrimination raciale pratiquée par les colons pouvait et devait
déboucher inéluctablement - dans un premier temps - sur un ra-
cisme anti-raciste, en raison de la non-correspondance et de
l'articulation entre le vécu de la situation coloniale et les
facteurs objectifs régissant le système colonial à l'échelle lo-

cale et mondiale. Il a fourni les raisons pour lesquelles la
conscience raciale précède la conscience de classe. Ce chemine-
ment dialectique aurait pour forme d'expression privilégiée la
littérature, avant tout la poésie.

Le colonisé ressent sa situation de subordination, de sous-
-homme, dans sa condition raciale, ethnique. Il s'identifie avec
fierté à ce qui est l'objet de mépris de la part du colon. Il
est en exil dans sa propre patrie, dans sa propre peau, dans
sa propre langue, dans sa propre religion. D'où le retour au
pays natal, au legs de ses ancêtres, dans la pigmentation de sa
peau.

"Le nègre comme le travailleur blanc, est victime de la structure capitaliste de notre société... Mais, si l'oppression est
une, elle se circonstancie selon l'histoire et les conditions
géographiques: le noir en est la victime, en tant que noir, à
titre d'indigène... Et puisqu'on l'opprime dans sa race et à
cause d'elle, c'est d'abord de sa race qu'il lui faut prendre
conscience... Ainsi est-il acculé à l'authenticité: insulté,
asservi, il se redresse, il ramasse le mot de "nègre" qu'on lui
a jeté comme une pierre, il se revendique comme noir, en face
du blanc, dans la fierté... Etrange et décisif virage: la race
s'est transmuée en historicité, le Présent noir explose et se
temporalise, la Négritude s'insère avec son passé et son avenir
dans l'Histoire universelle, ce n'est plus un état, ni même une
attitude existentielle, c'est un devenir... Ainsi la Négritude
est pour se détruire, elle est passage et non aboutissement,
moyen et non fin dernière... Il /l'homme de couleur/ est celui
qui marche sur une crête entre le particularisme passé qu'il
vient de gravir et l'universalisme futur qui sera le crépuscule
de sa négritude." /Situations III, Gallimard 1949, pp. 229-286/

Bien que Sartre ne précise pas les médiations et les modalités
à travers lesquelles s'effectue le passage de la conscience raciale à la conscience de classe, maints révolutionnaires afri-
cains, comme Nkrumah, Sékou Touré, Cabral ont, dans leur pratique et leurs oeuvres théoriques, tiré les enseignements dé-
coulant de la prise de conscience des similitudes et des différences de l'exploitation du prolétariat de la métropole et de
l'exploitation des Noirs dans les colonies. Ils ont accordé une

place de choix aux facteurs subjectifs et culturels, dans les
mouvements de libération nationale.

Cabral a choisi la région peuplée par les Balantes pour dé-
clencher l'insurrection armée, bien que les Balantes constitu-
assent le groupement ethnique économiquement et socialement le
plus arriéré, ne connaissant ni les rapports de subordination
de type précapitaliste, ni ceux de type capitaliste. Les Balantes
seront plus facilement sensibilisés par les militants du PAIGC,
car ils ont à défendre leur identité ethnique, religieuse, lin-
guistique, culturelle minée, perturbée, menacée par les Portu-
gais et leurs intermédiaires, les chefs de canton foulahs re-
crutés dans les milieux islamisés. Face aux exactions, les Balantes constituent un front de refus pour préserver leurs institutions, leur mode de vie, leurs traditions. En défendant,
les armes à la main, la tradition communautaire sous la conduite
du PAIGC, ils aideront à transformer leur mode d'existence sociale qu'ils voulaient conserver intact, et seront entraînés
dans une dynamique sociale favorisant l'harmonisation de l'universel et du particulier.

5./ Si dans la période coloniale, la dialectique de la mondialisation et de la désintégration nationale s'exprime dans les
mouvements de libération nationale, dans l'amalgame de la conscience raciale, de la conscience nationale et de la conscience
de classe, elle se manifeste entre autres, après la conquête de
l'indépendance, dans la dimension ethnique de la formation des
classes et des luttes de classes, et dans la dimension de classe
des rivalités et des conflits régionaux ethniques, religieux.
Ces interférences marquent de leurs empreintes la recherche de
l'identité nationale, expliquent les distorsions de l'interprétation des liens organiques entre l'universel et la spécificité.

Ces phénomènes sont liés à deux séries de causes: l'une au
blocage, à la perturbation du processus de formation de la nation à la suite de l'intégration des sociétés précapitalistes
dans le système mondial du capitalisme; l'autre à une urbanisation accélérée, sans support économique adéquat, engendrant un
nouveau bloc social intermédiaire: le sous-prolétariat, dont la
survie, le champ social est délimité par le secteur dit informel.

Sous certains aspects, la colonisation et la lutte anti-coloniale ont accéléré la formation de la nation. L'administration a mis en place un système politico-juridique englobant tout le territoire. Les rapports marchands et monétaires, en se diversifiant, créent des embryons de marché national. L'exploitation économique des colonies entraîne le brassage des populations. Une stratification de type non précapitaliste se dessine.

La résistance au colonialisme passe du niveau tribal au niveau national.

Le colonialisme freine et déforme le processus de la formation des nations en découpant les mêmes ethnies entre différents empires coloniaux, en faisant éclater des Etats centralisés, en accentuant les disparités régionales. L'identité d'une communauté ethnique est restructurée et destructurée par l'apport des valeurs dominantes dans les différents types de colonisation /française, anglaise, portugaise, espagnole etc./. Cette balkanisation des groupements ethniques, par exemple en Afrique, a eu un effet destabilisateur sur les Etats nationaux qui se sont constitués lors des indépendances: tensions entre les Etats limitrophes à la suite des tentatives de réunification des ethnies divisées lors du partage du monde entre les puissances impérialistes, tensions entre les ethnies au sein d'un même Etat national, en raison du développement inégal entre les régions /régions côtières et la brousse/.

Les ethnies sont portées à lutter entre elles pour la répartition du budget, des projets de développement, de l'implantation des infrastructures routières, culturelles, scolaires, sociales. Les plans de développement sont jugés à partir de critères régionalistes, religieux, ethniques. La représentativité dans les organismes de décision, au niveau du pouvoir politique, est conçue non en fonction des options politiques et idéologiques, mais à partir de l'appartenance à une ethnie.

Ainsi, dans une société pluristructurelle et pluriethnique s'entrelacent les solidarités archaïques et les solidarités modernes. La solidarité ethnique masque les différenciations sociales au sein de l'ethnie. Les solidarités de classe sont occultées par les solidarités ethniques.

Cette stratification des solidarités a pour corrolaire la stratification de l'identité: strates de l'identité familiale, villageoise, tribale, régionale, de castes, de classe, du national, du mondial.

L'identité devient un système à composantes hétérogènes comprenant des cloisonnements, des voies de passage, des passerelles, des rapports d'incompatibilité et d'affinité, des osmoses et des verrouillages, des greffes et des lésions.

6./ Quel est le destin de la pluristructuralité dans la période post-coloniale? Est-ce que la combinaison de l'économie naturelle et de l'économie marchande, du secteur traditionnel et du secteur moderne, du développement extraverti et introverti, exogène et endogène se perpétue nécessairement? Ou bien peut-on assurer le passage, la traversée des étapes allant de l'accumulation primitive du capital au capitalisme industriel? Les rapports de production capitalistes peuvent-ils devenir hégémoniques dans toutes les sphères de la vie sociale? Avec le temps, la pluristructuralité est-elle appelée à disparaître, ou se maintient-elle dans le cadre du capitalisme dépendant?

Ces dernières décennies, on observe une urbanisation rapide sur la base d'une croissance économique lente, voire même d'une croissance bloquée.

Le gonflement de la population urbaine dans le Tiers monde n'est pas induite, comme en Europe à l'époque de la révolution industrielle, par la reproduction élargie du capital. Il est, en grande partie, la conséquence d'un capitalisme dépendant qui sous-prolétarise davantage qu'il ne prolétarise, qui clochardise plutôt qu'il n'urbanise. Le dualisme entre ville et campagne, entre le secteur moderne et le secteur traditionnel, se reproduit en tant que bidonvillisation et urbanisation. En 1976, la population urbaine se chiffre à 400 millions dans la Périphérie, soit près des deux tiers de celle du Centre. Selon une étude publiée par l'ONU, "Les villes dans les pays en voie de développement", la population urbaine passera de 37,3 millions à 103,2 millions au Mexique, de 65,1 millions à 161 millions au Brésil, de 17,8 à 42,7 millions en Egypte, de 11,4 à 41 millions au Nigéria, de 132,4 à 354,9 millions en Inde, de 207,5 à 478 millions en Chine.

De 1950 à 2000, la population de la ville de Mexico doit passer de 2,9 à 31,5 millions, celle de Saõ Paolo de 2,5 à 26 millions, celle de Lagos de 0,3 à 9,4 millions, de Djakarta de 1,6 à 17,8 millions, de Bombay de 2,9 à 19,8 millions.

Phénomène angoissant: une proportion de plus en plus importante de la population urbaine, avant tout les jeunes, sont marginalisés. Ils subissent une excommunication sociale, car il semble qu'ils ne seront jamais intégrés dans les couches sociales cristallisées, dérivant du système de production dominant.

Il se constitue un bloc intermédiaire de type nouveau, se situant entre une paysannerie traditionnelle en dissolution et une classe ouvrière en malformation. Il s'agit d'une configuration sociale aux frontières floues, aux composantes multiples, ayant sa dynamique, sa mobilité sociale, sa structuration hiérarchique, sa propre pluristructuralité.

Il s'agit d'un sous-prolétariat à qui on refuse le statut de producteur, à qui le système refuse même la situation de prolétaire. Le sous-prolétariat est l'expression la plus crue des limites internes, sociales de l'universalisme du capitalisme. Cette marginalisation, cette paupérisation, cette cour de miracle du système capitaliste, ce monde concentrationnaire de la "modernisation" sont induits par l'exportation des capitaux, par la division internationale du travail mis en place par l'impérialisme. Les effectifs et les composantes de ce bloc social varient selon les pays et les phases de la restructuration de la division internationale du travail et les fluctuations du cycle économique.

Quelles sont les strates et les catégories sociales de ce sous-prolétariat?
- L'exode rural draine vers les centres urbains les jeunes, avant tout les scolarisés. Le voltaïque Ki-Zerbo écrit: "Les zones rurales font les frais de l'éducation pour subir finalement une perte de substance qui abaisse leur capacité de progresser et même de survivre. Or dans les villes, ces gens /les jeunes scolarisés/ deviennent des épaves. Ils sont déracinés sans être plantés ailleurs, ils sont littéralement coupés et descendent au fil d'un fleuve qui n'a pas de port..."
- La croissance démographique des citadins. De nos jours près de 50 % de l'accroissement de la population urbaine sont fournis par les urbanisés,

- des paysans sans terre, des saisonniers, des travailleurs migrants;
- des petits artisans, des petits commerçants menant une existence précaire, misérable, s'aggrippant à leurs outils, à leur savoir-faire comme à un fétu de paille sur une mer démontée;
- des apprentis que l'on accueille par gratitude, pour répondre aux sollicitations des solidarités archaïques.
- des chomeurs temporaires;
- des femmes, des enfants délaissés;
- les hors-la-loi, les jeunes se regroupant en bandes, les vagabonds;
- les handicapés, les clochards qui vont à la dérive;
- Les enfants, les mineurs au travail. Le Bureau International du Travail estimait en 1977 que 54,5 millions d'enfants de moins de 15 ans, et notamment 30,5 millions en Asie méridionale, 9,9 millions en Asie Sud-Est, faisaient partie de la population active. A Calcutta et dans bien d'autres grandes villes, des milliers de gosses ont pour "mission" de passer au peigne fin les immenses tas d'ordures, car tout est à récupérer.

Comment ce sous-prolétariat assure sa survie? Le secteur informel est l'espace économique et social de ce bloc social.

Le secteur informel, notion utilisée par la Banque Mondiale pour désigner les activités économiques comprises entre l'économie d'auto-subsistance et le secteur capitalistique, est une notion qui masque les réalités dramatiques de l'espace vital du sous-prolétariat, susceptible de devenir l'espace de l'agonie à des centaines de millions de jeunes. Le secteur informel est l'enfer de la modernisation. Il est la résultante de l'urbanisation d'une société qui n'a pas les moyens de s'urbaniser.

Le gonflement de la population urbaine et la large gamme des situations sociales, des revenus, du pouvoir d'achat, des modes de consommation engendrent des activités multiples.

Les prestations de services sont fournies dans le cadre de relations familiales ou mi-salariales. Il s'agit d'employés de maison, de cireurs, de gardiens, de porteurs.

102

Une partie importante des masses flottantes est engagée dans la transformation des produits récupérés à partir des tas d'ordure, des déchets du secteur moderne. On utilise le sous-prolétariat comme colporteurs, comme intermédiaires, comme vendeurs au compte-goutte, aux transports non mécanisés. Le préprolétariat survit en grande partie grâce aux solidarités familiales, claniques, religieuses.

L'étude du sous-prolétariat est appelée à mieux cerner la mouvance sociale, l'entrelacement des structures capitalistiques et précapitalistiques, l'hybridité des blocs et des couches sociales, les dimensions non classistes des classes sociales, la dimension religieuse de la politique, la combinaison originale des éléments idéologiques d'inspiration diverse, la situation gélatineuse de la société civile et de la société politique, les mouvements de pendule de la vie politique.

Le secteur informel est un réseau de médiations entre couches sociales, entre styles de vie, entre classes et ethnies, entre citadins ruralisés, ruraux urbanisés et citadins déruralisés, entre le préprolétariat, le prolétariat et les couches petites-bourgeoises, entre les tenants de l'appareil d'Etat et l'aristocratie villageoise, entre l'économie d'auto-subsistance, l'économie petite marchande et l'économie capitaliste.

Le secteur informel est le cycle infernal des tensions, des contradictions entre la ville et la campagne, entre la tradition et la modernité, entre la déchéance et la renaissance nationale.

Le secteur informel, le nouveau type de bloc social intermédiaire a une influence de plus en plus déterminante sur la dynamique politique et idéologique, sur la recherche de l'identité nationale, sur la stratification de cette identité.

La mouvance de ce bloc social permet de mieux comprendre comment sont réactivés, réanimés des illusions, des préjugés, des espoirs, des fiertés enfouis dans la mémoire collective, comment ceux-ci réapparaissent dans la recherche de l'identité en fonction des préoccupations et des blocages du présent. Ce phénomène doit nous inciter à nous préoccuper de l'archéologie de l'identité nationale, des mécanismes de réapparition et de réinterprétation de valeurs anciennes dans la conscience quotidienne des masses, car ce processus de revalorisation explique les motivations qui président au mode de pensée et de comportement des agents, des acteurs de la scène politique.

7./ L'analyse du devenir historique de l'identité nationale dans les sociétés européennes et non-européennes marquées par le sous-développement et le blocage de la formation de la nation ou du renouveau national, doit s'interroger sur le rôle extra--littéraire de la littérature.

Existe-t-il une corrélation entre, d'une part, le rôle privilégié de la littérature dans les mouvements de libération nationale, et d'autre part, le sous-développement, l'hybridité des rapports de production précapitalistes et capitalistes, le mûrissement-pourrissement de la crise entre un ancien qui se perpétue en se désintégrant et un nouveau qui n'arrive pas à devenir hégémonique? Les distorsions et les inégalités des structures économico-sociales font que les différentes formes des activités intellectuelles ne se développent pas en se complétant et en se stimulant mutuellement. On observe un développement inégal entre la pensée philosophique, politique, sociologique, économique, et la littérature.

L'universalisme, le progrès historique et social universel est pris en charge par la littérature qui l'exprime unilatéralement et partiellement. La littérature transgresse ses frontières et devient le bassin de la politique, de l'éthique et de la philosophie.

Les fonctions extra-littéraires de la littérature présentent certaines affinités avec la religion qui est le complément d'un monde à l'envers, exprime les détresses matérielles et morales de l'homme, et est en même temps une protestation contre les conditions inhumaines. La littérature exprime, complète une réalité contre laquelle on s'insurge.

Existe-t-il une corrélation entre la présence d'une base sociale fragile de l'émancipation nationale et sociale, et le rôle privilégié de la littérature? Dans les conditions du sous-développement, la science serait encore incapable d'exprimer l'universalité, de motiver l'initiative historique. C'est à la littérature qu'incomberait la tâche de remplir les fonctions de la religion, de la science, de la politique, de l'éthique.

J'insiste. Je ne soutiens pas la thèse que le rôle privilégié de la littérature est alimenté exclusivement par le sous-développement et que ce dernier ne permet pas d'accéder à des formes de conscience sociale plus théoriques pour exprimer la dialectique de l'universel et du particulier. Je formule simplement l'hypothèse que le sous-développement induit un développement inégal entre les formes de la conscience sociale, et que, dans certaines conditions historiques, la littérature a un rôle privilégié, se fait le porte-parole des aspirations nationales.

Ce développement inégal entre la littérature et les sciences sociales s'affirme à des degrés divers dans des contextes différents du sous-développement.

A la fin du XVIIIe et au début du XIXe siècle, en Allemagne, la philosophie et la littérature culminent simultanément /Kant, Fichte, Hegel, Goethe, Heine, Novalis, Hölderlin/.

En Russie, au XIXe siècle, la littérature et l'esthétique s'enrichissent mutuellement et atteignent des cimes remarquables /de Radichtchev à Tolstoï et Dostoïevski, de Herzen à Biélinski/.

En Hongrie, du XIXe siècle à nos jours, la littérature marque profondément la recherche de l'identité nationale, la vie politique, les sciences sociales. C'est l'embarras de la richesse qui m'étreint. Un seul nom: Endre Ady. A la fin du XIXe siècle, lorsque la crise d'un régime mi-féodal, mi-capitaliste oblige des centaines de milliers de paysans hongrois à s'expatrier, lorsque l'aristocratie étouffe la vie intellectuelle, le poète Ady se fait le chantre de la renaissance nationale. Il refuse une identité qui s'accroche à un passé mystifié, reposant sur des solidarités et affinités biologiques, raciales et s'enferme dans un provincialisme desséchant. Ady veut que la Hongrie s'ouvre au monde, que la culture hongroise s'universalise, en intégrant dans sa spécificité ce qui est le plus progressif, le plus dynamisant dans cet universel. Il magnifie les apôtres du renouveau:

"Ce sont des êtres merveilleux, des saints, et bien que miséreux, combien riches ces hommes qui, en Hongrie, ont une âme neuve et des aspirations nouvelles. Chacun est un Christ dans son âme attristée. Ils ont à entreprendre, à partir de presque rien, l'édification d'une Hongrie européenne... Leurs chants annoncent comme les mouettes l'orage sacré et merveilleux. Dans la

société, dans la politique, ce ne sont encore que les gémissements de l'inquiétude. Mais dans la littérature, dans l'art,
dans la science luisent déjà les éclairs du renouveau".

Aimé Césaire, dans son intervention au 2e Congrès International des Ecrivains et Artistes noirs /Rome 1959/: "L'homme de
la culture et ses responsabilités", déclare:

"Oui, en définitive, c'est aux poètes, aux artistes, aux écrivains, aux hommes de culture, qu'il appartient, brassant, dans
la quotidienneté des souffrances et des dénis de justice, les
souvenirs comme les espérances, de constituer ces grandes réserves de foi, ces grands silos de force où les peuples dans
les moments critiques puisent le courage de s'assumer eux-mêmes
et de forcer l'avenir. Certains ont pu dire que l'écrivain est
un ingénieur des âmes. Nous, dans la conjoncture, où nous sommes,
nous sommes des propagateurs d'âmes, des multiplicateurs d'âmes
et à la limite des inventeurs d'âmes".

Ce rôle extra-littéraire de la littérature, dans un monde ti-
raillé par des forces contraires, régies par les contraintes du
sous-développement, s'exprime dans le chef d'oeuvre de Khalil
Gibran, "Le prophète", en conformité avec maintes spécificités
du croissant oriental du bassin méditerrannéen. Dans cette aire
qui, des millénaires durant, a été le berceau de tant de civilisation qui se sont mutuellement fécondées, qui ont vu naître des
mythologies et des religions qui ont fertilisé la sensibilité
et la spiritualité des habitants de ces régions comme les crues
successives du Nil, le Liban se situe à la croisée des chemins
de ces courants de pensée. Il semble que ce soit là une terre
de prédilection pour les envoyés des dieux, pour les prophètes
venus apporter aux hommes la sagesse divine. Le Prophète de Gibran se situe dans la lignée des prophètes vivant dans la mémoire collective de ces peuples.

Dans les enseignements du Prophète de Gibran, il y a désa-
cralisation de la sensibilité, de l'imagination, des valeurs
morales pour que la sensibilité, l'imagination, le bien et le
beau deviennent puissances humaines dans la vie quotidienne.
La loi divine est la condition humaine devenue humaine. C'est
un traité poétique de l'art de vivre. "Votre vie quotidienne
est votre temple et votre religion", écrit-il. Le Prophète, dans

les réponses qu'il donne aux questions posées par les habitants,
incite les hommes à une autoréalisation, à une purification, à
une élevation de l'homme vers les cimes du bien et du beau, à
la plénitude de l'entrelacement du physique et du spirituel. Le
véritable amour, c'est "connaître la douleur de trop de tendres-
se... Emplissez chacun la coupe de l'autre, mais ne buvez pas à
la même coupe".

Le Prophète est l'oeuvre d'un poète qui, dans sa sensibilité,
harmonise et spécifie les poèmes de Baudelaire, les Nourritures
terrestres de Gide, les versets du Coran, les paroles de l'Evan-
gile et les aspirations de l'homme moderne.

La dimension extra-littéraire de la littérature soulève dans
cet ordre d'idées un problème bien ardu, mais passionnant. Pour
saisir et décrire la dialectique de la totalité, de l'objectif
et du subjectif, de la raison et de l'émotion, de l'universel et
du particulier, doit-on, devrait-on trouver des formes d'expression qui se situent aux limites, aux confins, aux frontières de
la philosophie et de la littérature, du concret et de l'abstrait,
de la parole et du chant?

8./ La pensée marxiste est également confrontée au devenir
historique de l'identité nationale. Quel est l'impact de la dialectique de l'universel et du particulier sur le devenir de
l'identité de la pensée marxiste en conséquence de son déploiement
dans le temps et de son expansion dans l'espace, de sa reproduction élargie?

La théorie et la méthode marxistes, dont les fondements ont
été élaborés en Europe en tenant compte de l'évolution historique,
sociale, culturelle universelle, ne peuvent s'enraciner dans le
Tiers monde, leur assimilation ne peut féconder les sciences politiques et sociales dans les contrées qui ont connu une évolution historique présentant des différences notables par rapport
à celles de l'Europe et imprégner la conscience des masses, qui
si cette appropriation ne se fait pas comme celle d'un texte é-
tranger que l'on apprend par coeur ou que l'on traduit mot à mot.

L'appropriation de la pensée marxiste signifie qu'elle doit
être cet outil permettant de mener à bien cette tâche définie
par Anouar Abdel Malek:

107

"Le marxisme travaillera dans les pays arabes, de concert avec les autres groupes politiques et écoles de pensée, à redonner vie au fond national culturel et à la civilisation autochtone... à susciter et à animer par dessus- tout une renaissance nationale qui soit celle des classes populaires... c'est en étant pleinement soi-même, non l'image d'autrui, fût-il privilégié entre tous, qu'on rejoindra la communauté internationale des autres 'moi'." /La pensée politique arabe contemporaine. Edition du Seuil. 3e édition, Paris, 1980./

Long est le chemin qui va de la diffusion des idées marxistes jusqu'à leur appropriation, leur utilisation créatrice. Il ne s'agit pas d'une relecture africaine de Marx, d'une africanisation de la pensée marxiste, comme Senghor le préconise. La pensée marxiste doit puiser aux sources d'une culture donnée, trouver des précurseurs. Elle est appelée à interpréter les spécificités de l'histoire, des structures sociales et politiques, des mentalités, des systèmes de valeurs qui caractérisent une société. Elle doit prendre en charge la dialectique du général et du particulier, contribuer à ce qu'un peuple apprenne à avoir une connaissance plus vraie, plus totale de son propre devenir historique et culturel. Sans la particularisation, la concrétisation de l'universel, l'universel n'a pas de devenir. En somme est valable dans cette sphère également ce qu'Attila József, ce grand poète hongrois, chantre du prolétariat, écrivait:

"Si une classe n'est pas capable d'exprimer son rapport au monde sur le plan social, et donc dans le domaine de l'art aussi, elle ne peut pas prétendre, faute d'une vigueur suffisante, occuper, au nom de toute l'humanité, l'avant-scène de l'histoire."

CONCLUSIONS HYPOTHETIQUES

1./ Depuis le XVIe siècle, la problématique de l'identité est intimement liée dans toutes les sphères de la vie sociale à la dialectique du mondial et du national.

La mondialité n'affaiblit pas, mais exaspère la recherche de l'identité nationale dans un mouvement d'autodéfense, de refus de devenir Autre. Le mondial, en accumulant conflits, distorsions, inégalités, fait refluer l'identité vers l'ancestral, vers l'âge d'or dont les falaises n'auraient pas encore été corrodées, ébranlées, disloquées par les vagues du monde extérieur.

Le national, par contre, s'ouvre sur le mondial, s'universalise, veut s'affirmer dans la mondialité, devient un réseau d'interférences et d'interdépendances. L'identité nationale, soumise à la loi de la négativité, exige un effort de recréation de soi-même et de fraternisation des renaissances nationales. "L'homme, disait mon Père, c'est d'abord celui qui crée. Et seuls sont frères les hommes qui collaborent." /Saint-Exupéry/

2./ L'identité nationale n'est ni permanence dans le changement, ni homogénéité face à la diversité. Elle est récréation du passé en fonction des exigences du dépassement du présent. "Du foyer des ancêtres transmettons non la cendre, mais la flamme." /Jean Jaurès/

3./ Les différentes strates, composantes de l'identité nationale, s'éteignent ou se réaniment en fonction de l'identification politique et idéologique des groupes sociaux face aux conflits et aux aspirations de la conjoncture.

L'identité nationale telle qu'elle est vécue est une médiation fondamentale entre la dynamique de la stratification sociale et la mouvance de la vie politique, idéologique. Cette médiation explique en partie le décalage entre le vécu et la situation objective, entre la pensée et l'action, entre les intérêts immédiats et à long terme des classes, des couches sociales et de la nation.

L'identité nationale est une composante essentielle et de l'universalité et de la spécificité. Le devenir de l'identité nationale est en corrélation avec la spécification de l'universel et l'universalisation de la spécificité.

La dialectique ascendante, progressive de l'universel et du particulier est appelée à déboucher sur le double mouvement de la renaissance nationale et du renouveau de la mondialité, d'une renaissance nationale et d'un renouveau de la mondialité au diapason de l'émancipation nationale et de l'émancipation sociale.

Une identité nationale qui s'approprie, intériorise une riche diversité, court moins le risque de se laisser subjuguer par une

et exclusive idée-force, passion. Grâce à une assimilation di-
versifiée, l'identité nationale se maintiendra dans une finitude
s'enrichissant infiniment. Grâce à ces implantations et trans-
plantations successives, l'identité nationale, tout comme l'homme,
croît en même temps que ses blés et ses rizières.

FROM A NATURAL SCIENTIFIC POINT OF VIEW

IS INTELLIGENCE GEOCENTRIC?

Gy. MARX

> Wenn ich zum Augenblicke sage:
> Verweile noch! Du bist so schön! -
> Dann magst Du mich in Fesseln schlagen,
> dann will ich gern zugrunde gehn!
> Dann mag die Totenglocke schallen,
> dann bist Du deines Dienstes frei,
> die Uhr mag stehn, die Zeiger fallen,
> es sei die Zeit für mich vorbei!
>
> Fausts Teufelspakt /Goethe/

CHALLENGE AND CONVERGENCE

Human cultures never were able to develop in isolation for a long period. The decadence of the imperial Roman Empire was broken by the fresh impulse of the Northern barbarians. The revolution of the Italian Renaissance took over the Hellenic ideas from the Arabs. In the New Age of history the infusion of the geographic discoveries catalyzed the progress of the European civilization. The powerful Mexican fine arts profited from Indian influence, the American jazz from African folklore, the music of Bartók from Hungarian folk songs. Evolution is a consequence of challenges caused by the changing environment, a consequence of frontiers in an open world. This is a fundamental biological law, which is valid also for human culture.

Another law of evolution is that of convergence. If an efficient contact has been realized among the individuals, they will conform to each other. From the symbiosis of similar entities a higher organism will be created, which behaves as a more developed unity. This is how multicellular organism was created from monocel algae, how packs were formed from predatory animals, how tribes and nations were made of human individuals. This higher organism has a larger survival value in the competition with its challengers.

A beautiful result of the scientific revolution is that in the mind of our children the place of one's birth is taken to be the globe. Telecommunication makes us ear- and eye-witnesses of

113

anything relevant, wherever it happens on the Earth. Scientists discuss the new observations and ideas by mail and phone. We are going to exploit the confrontation of different ideas by calling conventions, forming discussion groups. The outcome is progress and convergence of ideas. In this way the formation of a universal human culture will be accelerated, spreading all over the Earth. This unified culture becomes more powerful than any of the earlier organizations.

The price we are about to pay for this totality is the loss of frontiers. The surface of a sphere does not have any boundaries, but its surface is finite. This is valid for Earth, too.

What picture will our children have of the world when each spot on Earth will be explored and exploited by man, when the folklore of each nation will be merged in a unified culture? In their mind a closed world will take the place of the open universe of pioneers. Will the feeling of closedness stay with us forever? Will the loving contact of two individuals be replaced by masturbation? How long can a lonely organism remain capable of evolution? Or at least of survival?

Navigare necesse est, vivere non est necesse. The open minds will always look for new physical and cultural frontiers. There will be people who are depressed by the finiteness of the globe. Like Leif Ericson and Christopher Columbus, they will yearn for new worlds. There will be people who will not be willing to give up the pioneer spirit characteristic of the Homo Sapiens and of life in general. These people consider the contact with extra-terrestrial intelligence to be a necessity.

GAIA

The Galaxy is 10 billion years old, the Solar System was formed 5 billion years ago. Here on Earth life started from a single strand of a molecule, which became capable of reproduction about 4 billion years ago. The blue-green algae have been living in the oceans for billions of years, gradually enriching the atmosphere with oxygen. For the last one billion years, life took hold on our tiny planet. Combustible woods, coal and oil fields wrapped in oxygen clouds - this has become a tense, chemically unstable situation, which does not have a counterpart anywhere in the Solar System. New, aggressive parasites appeared, the animals, to exploit this chemical tension. Environmentalists consider the present ecosystem to be a single organism, which regulates its components, even the atmosphere. This entity is called Gaia, according to the name of the ancient Greek goddess, who was born as the granddaughter of Chaos.

The zoological evolution produced several successful species. The arthropoda and the vertebrata appeared half a billion years ago. Protected by its shell the scorpion survived for five hundred million years without significant change. Millions of shark generations followed each other in secure conformity. These champions of survival and conservativism did not pay much attention to the passing of time.

But biological experimentation went on. New variants amplified certain properties, which lay dormant in the fish as hidden possibilities. The amphibians left the comfortable luke-warm ocean, to take the challenges of changing weather. The drakes of the Mezozoicum realized the extremes of size and force, but they were deadly slow in locomotion and in mind. With the birds the mobility reached its maximum, but the energy hunger of the wing did not leave food enough for thinking.

The mammals succeeded in evading these dead ends. The tiny mongoose is weaker than the cobra, but it wins in the life and death struggle of nerves. Mammals have spread over the continents in the Kainozoicum and they adapted to diverse environments. Some of them, the opportunistic dolphins went back to the comfortable luke-warm sea and these playboys live now merrily like fish in the water. But others, like man, adapted to the changing climate with a plastic brain. The Homo Sapiens, this "badweather animal", is much younger than a million years, but in the last thousand years it started spreading fast. The human population is doubling now in 40 years; it hoped to have made itself independent of the physical environment and took its fate into his own hands. But in the seventies the exponential increase of the population number reached a turning point. This inflexion of the population curve calls our attention to the finiteness of the globe.

The quietly stupid sharks survived hundreds of millions of
years in the invariable ocean. The revolutionary man is happy
with the accelerated progress, it transforms the surface of
Earth in deacdes. What will be the decision of Cosmic History:
which of them turns out to be right in the long run?

The laws of motion for a pendulum can be learned from repeated
experiments. But there is only one single civilization in the
whole Solar System. We are interested in learning to know about
our destiny, but experimenting with Mankind is a dangerous game.
If one experiment goes wrong, it may kill Gaia.

There is one escape. In a gas, the time average of the behaviour of a single molecule equals the simultaneous set average
of several molecules. One can look around in the Universe, to
search for other civilizations. A contact with them may teach us
about the general laws of cultural evolution. We may learn to
know our own fate.

NUMBER OF CIVILIZATIONS

The laws of motions for atoms are the same everywhere and
everytime in the Universe. Science has clarified an impressive
number of steps on the road leading from the primordial hydrogen
cloud to the emergence of intelligence. We consider ourselves to
be natural descendants of more simple forms of matter. If this
is true, life, intelligence and culture must have emerged at different parts of the Galaxy, where the physical conditions had
been favourable.

Let N_* be the number of stars in the Galaxy. A fraction q_*
of these stars has a structure appropriate to bear life in its
neighbourhood. A fraction q_p of these stars has a system of or-
biting bodies around it. n_p is the average number of planets,
which are capable to carry life. q_1 is the probability for the
emergence of life, if the necessary conditions are fulfilled.
q_i is the probability for the emergence of intelligence if life
exists. q_t is the chance that an intelligent species will develop
a technological civilization. From these quantities one can find
expected N_c number of civilizations in cur Galaxy. Independent
probabilities are multiplicative, so one arrives at the celebrated

seven factor formula of Drake:

$$N_c = N_* \, q_* \, q_p \, n_p \, q_l \, q_i \, q_t \; . \qquad\qquad /1/$$

The formula calls for numerical values.

The first factors can be obtained from astronomers, who are ready to supply us with rather accurate answers. The stars in our Galaxy can be stated as follows: $N_* = 10^{11}$. Only those have to be taken into account which are luminous enough to warm up a considerable environment and which radiate steadily enough to offer time not only for the emergence but also for the evolution of life. Bright stars waste their energy very fast, so the two conditions work against each other. Only modestly shining stars like the Sun have to be taken into account: $q_* = 10\%$. A spinning cloud cannot condense itself into a single star, it has to leave its angular momentum outside. So most stars must be parts of an association of several objects, which orbit around each other. This orbital motion is the carrier of the initial angular momentum of the cloud. The astronomical evidence confirms this conclusion: q_p is near 100%. The number of planets fit for life is a bit trickier question. Neither the stars of a double system nor a planet of the size of Mercury or Jupiter are good candidates for the cradle of life. In our Solar System we have the Earth, $n_p = 1$, but in order to remain on the safe side, let us write $n_p = 0.01$. I think the astronomers are ready to agree that we do not make order of magnitude errors with these estimations. If so, $N_* \, q_* \, q_p \, n_p = 10^8$. Maybe ten times more or ten times less, but about hundred million planets wait for the birth of life in the Galaxy.

The other factors are rather uncertain because there is no empirical evidence of statistical value available. We know only about one life, that on Earth, which is based on the right handed double helix of DNA, on a very special genetic code and on proteins composed of L-amino acids. But there is a geological evidence that life appeared immediately within 0.1 billion years, after the formation of terrestrial oceans about 4 billion years ago. So we may put $q_l = 100\%$. If life exists and diversifies, intelligence certainly offers a higher survival value; let us

9

write q_i = 100%. Not all intelligent beings started hard technology: not the dolphins, not the people of ancient India or Mexico, but it is difficult to imagine that no one starts science and engineering. The assertiveness of Western civilization encourages us to assume q_t = 100%. These numbers say that a planet fit for life will bring up a technological civilization with the necessity of Darwinian evolution. We are far from certain in the latter numbers, but the obtained value $N_c = 10^8$ may serve as first orientation. It may happen that N_c is somewhat smaller, not a billion /optimistic estimation/, but a million /pessimistic value/.

The average distance of stars is about $d_* = 10$ light-years or smaller in our galactic vicinity. The average distance between civilizations is $d_c = d_* /N_*/N_c/^{1/3}$, i.e. it may be within 100 light-years. The nearest candidate is the Sun-like Tau Ceti, just beyond 10 light-years.

The favorite idea of science-fiction novels is the space travel between stars with rockets or flying saucers. But such trips are limited by the strict conservation laws of Nature /conservation of energy, momentum, baryonic charge/. These conservation laws prevent the stars and planets from exploding, from frittering away, but also limit the range of human explorers. The energy supply of mankind does not allow journeys beyond a very few light--years within the life span of a man. We are pretty safe against invasion from outside and we are not allowed to conquer other people by space armies.

MESSAGE THROUGH SPACE

Our space probes need months to reach the nearest planets of the Solar System, but the radio signals return in minutes. A space probe would be on its way to another habitable planetary system for thousands or hundreds of thousands of years, but a radio signal can get there in years. A real opportunity for contact is offered by telecommunication.

By using a highly directional aerial, a narrow band receiver, a low noise detector, our present technology is able to receive signals from a distance of 100, even 1000 light-years, if the faraway transmitter works with a power comparable to our most powerful ones. There are scores of habitable planets within the reach of our telecommunication technology. As a matter of fact, attempts to receive and send messages were made both in the USA and the USSR.

Let us notice that this limitation of opportunities is in many ways beneficent. An invasion of superintelligent beings would certainly destroy any adolescent civilization, as the Spaniards destroyed the Aztec empire. If not biologically, certainly culturally. But telecommunication assumes technological maturity on both sides. The most valuable outcome of such contact is the gaining of information, which needs no space fleet, only a radio or laser beam.

/If contact is established by telecommunication, a slight possibility will be opened for personal contact also. One cannot use rocket propulsion, which wastes most of the fuel for the kinetic energy of exhausted gases, as a consequence of momentum conservation. But the space ship can be accelerated by the push of an Earth-based laser beam. In this case the recoil is absorbed by the body of the Earth, which prevents the energy loss. Evidently we can accelerate only a departing ship. Upon arrival it has to be decelerated by the other civilization in the same way. A personal visit is possible only if the host is willing to cooperate in arranging the meeting/.

A radio contact assumes somebody who is speaking and somebody else who is listening. The two partners have to find the corresponding direction, wave length and timing. Ingenious strategies have been invented to catch any intelligent signal from the sea of stars and from the sea of all wave length values. Ambitious projects have been designed to watch even the local television broadcasting of the Tau Ceti People. This problem can be solved if the necessary amount of effort and money is devoted to the undertaking.

The main question is the simultaneity of the interest in the contact.

The Galaxy has a history of T_g = 10 billion years. It is made up of $N_* = 10^{11}$ stars. A new star is born on an average every T_g/N_* = 0.1 years. One star in a thousand may be fit for bearing life. Thus a new civilization may arise every one hundred years.

One civilization here /we are just born, because our interstellar telecommunication ability is only a few years old/, the next one on the other side of the Galaxy, several thousand light-years away, maybe a hundred years from now. Will they find each other in the vastness of galactic spacetime?

Let us denote the life span of the scientific interest for a technologically active civilization by T_a. In this case the number of simultaneous civilizations in the Galaxy turns out to be

$$N_s = N_c \frac{T_a}{T_g}. \qquad\qquad /\,2\,/$$

We are willing to substitute numbers, but T_a is a major unknown. So, using the values given earlier, one gets

$$N_s = \frac{T_a}{100 \text{ years}}.$$

This is a surprisingly disappointing result. If the period during which a civilization pays attention to the Universe, and is risking effort and money on space exploration is less than a century, it may find itself alone in the Galaxy. A rich society of people, living comfortably in splendid cosmic isolation, is dead from the galactic point of view. The curious young civilizations may not overlap in time! Even more interesting is the average distance d_s between simultaneous civilizations:

$$d_s = d_* \, (N_*/N_s)^{1/3}.$$

Making use of the former numbers,

$$d_s = 1000 \text{ light-years} \times \left(\frac{10 \text{ million years}}{T_a}\right)^{1/3}.$$

So, the necessary condition for the existence of a simultaneous civilization in the reach of our radio telescope is that the longevity of the scientific curiosity and technological interest should exceed million years! It is true that the Sun will shine

120

for several billion years. But today we are much less confident
in the longevity of scientific activity, having witnessed the
Moon exploration period having ended after a decade! Poets and
politicians are uncertain if one asks them about the next decade.

MESSAGE THROUGH TIME

There is a real chance that intelligent life has emerged in
the space-time volume called Galaxy, but the civilizations which
are not separated from each other by unbridgeable space, miss
each other in time. This conclusion raises a new question: what
are the means for an advanced self-expressive civilization to
send messages to its partner through time? Through millions
/maybe, billions/ of years?

The most advertised idea is that of Bracewell's. A space
probe can be sent to the vicinity of another star. The journey
may take a thousand or a hundred thousand years, never mind.
On arrival the probe goes automatically into a parking orbit
around the star or around the promising planet. This probe sleeps
on this orbit for aeons, until it is activated by the first radio
signals, which indicate that on this planet a technological civilization emerged and utilizes radio waves for local communication. In this event the space probe calls attention by sending
radio signals, and transfers the message of the advanced Early
People. A faint possibility of the existence of such a probe or-
biting around the Earth was discussed recently /Lunan, Lawton,
1972-1974/. The economy of such a communication system is not
inferior to radio search. The main question is whether the elec-
tronics can survive long enough to bridge the time gap.

There may be other ways to send corrosion-free letters through
time. One possibility is to use an artificial isotopic composition in a piece of alloy for coding a few thousand bits of information. This is a heat and cold resisting letter indeed. The main
difficulty is that such a mute letter may be lost easily. A richer information can be written in the nucleotid sequence of a
DNA-type macromolecule, but in this case the problem of corrosion
is added to the former ones.

Spontaneous generation of life does not occur on Earth now-adays. According to the most accepted hypothesis life was born on Earth just after the formation of the crust and the ocean. There is a strong empirical indication, however, that the first living beings appeared already in the first 0.1 billion years, which is a surprisingly short time for the spontaneous creation of life. An alternative explanation is offered by the panspermia hypothesis /Arrhenius 1908/, namely that the Earth was infected from outside. Radiation, however, would destroy any free spores floating in the outer space. The arrival of a meteorite on Earth from another planetary system is most unlikely to happen. Seeing these difficulties, Crick and Orgel suggested the idea of direct-ed panspermia /1973/. Earth might have been infected by intention by an advanced civilization, which flourished billions of years ago!

The formation of the Solar System was probably triggered by a nearby supernova explosion. The supernova abundancy was the same or even higher in the earlier era of the Galaxy, so life and intelligence might have been born on several planets before us. When the very first advanced civilization saturated its own solar system, it searched the Galaxy for intelligence, but in vain. At this point a psychological urge arose to spread life all over the Galaxy. The technologically most simple and bio-logically most promising way is to send deep-frozen microorgan-isms in tiny space probes to other planetary systems. These could be the seeds from which the whole tree of life emerged according to the law of evolution and adaptation. This idea is psychologic-ally well-founded, technologically realizable and scientifically acceptable. It could explain a number of biochemical puzzles con-cerning terrestrial life /universality of the Genetic Code, es-sential biological role of the rare Molybdenum, some apparently teleological aspects in terrestrial organisms, like the preadapt-ed eye or brain/.

If the hunch of Crick and Orgel is supported by firmer indica-tion, we shall be faced by the evident question: is the possi-bility of life the only content of the message, sent to us by the First People?

The microorganism, sent to the stars may be one which evolved under natural conditions and was collected from a puddle of that planet faraway in space and time. But the DNA could be also an artifact of genetic engineering, planned by computers to be a-daptive to conditions on foreign planets. In the latter case the DNA may have an artificial structure. The information content of the DNA is comparable to that of a small library. The majority of this information is needed to direct the synthesis of enzymes, which create an appropriate chemical environment for replication. But there is a temptation to speculate that the DNA /its biologic-ally unutilized part/ may contain an intellectual message. This message could have been sent to their descendents by the First People because they were convinced of the Law of Evolution. They hoped that once upon a time intelligence will emerge from the seeds they scattered far and wide in the Galaxy and the intelli-gent offsprings will read the message written in their own genes. These could be the ways and means of a biological and cultural continuity in space-time.

In this hunch the weak point is that the statistical mutations work for the Evolution and, at the same time, the genetic drift destroys the information content in the inactive part of DNA. /It is not clear whether the very conservative chapters of DNA are defended against mutations by specific repair enzymes or by selection pressure/. There is, however, a very rigid system in the genetic machinery, that is the Genetic Code. The slightest change in the Code would inactivate millions of enzymes in the metabolic network, so any variant code is eliminated by the natu-ral selection immediately. The Genetic Code is the same for man and mould, it has not changed for billions of years. As Orgel mentioned, this could be an appropriate place to write a message, if terrestrial life was designed by the biological architects of the First People.

Up to now nobody has succeeded in deciphering any other mes-sage from the Genetic Code than that it is a mixture of logical chemistry and historical accident.

VIRGIN GALAXY

If an active civilization, fertilized by science, has got enough time, its engineers will perform any task which has been formulated by the society.

This was the initial assumption of Dyson when he tried to imagine the advanced state of a civilization. One idea is to cover the energy consumption by making use of the full power of the central star. The maximum Lebensraum will be available, if the society builds a spherical shell around the star. /Dyson proved that the metals available in the planets were enough to perform this undertaking/. According to Dyson an advanced civilization could not be expected near brilliant stars but at faint infrared spots. This means that the stars shining in the evening sky indicate the absence of any mature civilization. The Galaxy has a natural look, like a jungle never touched by man.

Looking from the Cosmos, people seem to be nonexistent, if they are introverted, if they are not interested in communication, if they do not leave the print of their fingers on their environment. From the outside one cannot tell the difference between the silence of a desert, the silence of a cemetery or the silence of consolidation. Only active societies can be accepted as members of the Galactic Club.

If life, civilization and humanized cosmic environment could not be discovered in the Galaxy, that indicated that in the formulae /1/ and /2/ at least one of the factors was very small.

There were speculations about this problem. Evidently the most uncertain data are questioned. How about the probability of the origin of life in the primordial soup? How about the thermal stability of the planetary atmosphere through the billions of years required for evolution, in spite of shifts in stellar luminosity and atmospheric composition? How about the formation of a multicellular animal organism in an atmosphere polluted by oxygen? How about the emergence of consciousness in the brain of evolved animals? How about the beginning of the restless curiosity and engineering activity, so characteristic of our twentieth century? Or the longevity of this active interest in understanding and shaping the Universe? Some of these questions are directed to the biological sciences, but the last ones pertain to the field of social science and human psychology. The duration of T_a of technological activity may be limited by several dangers.

The scientific evolution created the A=bomb. In a few decades so many bombs were accumulated which are more than enough to de-

stroy any developed life form on Earth. The survivors of a full
scale Third World War may be the anthropoda, the scorpions. They
can tolerate 1000 times higher radioactive level than man.

The chemical fall-out of the scientific revolution pollutes
the water, air and soil. "Limits to growth" are predicted by
several learned scholars.

The scientific revolution makes luxuries available to wide
layers of society. Will satisfaction and surfeit spread instead
of discovering curiosity and revolutionary impatience? By chemical tranquilizers, by stiffening police or by conformizing school
the Homo Sapiens may change his living habit. Will he stop sending expeditions to the Moon, will he stop supporting construction
of radio telescopes and high energy accelerators?

Or will the tension created by the scientific revolution be
cured by a biological mutation? Will a new, quiet Homo Stabilis
show more surviving power than the restless Homo Sapiens? Looking back from the distant future, will the Homo Sapiens turn out
to be a dead end, like the drake, compared to the higher surviving
power of the conservative scorpion and shark?

There is, however, also another edge of the dilemma. If we
succeed in realizing contact with other civilizations, it is
rather certain that it will be a very advanced one, because they
have learned to know how to avoid the menace of a nuclear holo-
caust, the density of environmental self-contamination and the
temptation of the luxurious spleen. They have discovered the
secret of eternal youth and they may be ready to teach us how
to follow their path.

The nine-factor formula /2/ is based on the multiplication
law of independent probabilities. We have become interested to
find out the value of N_s empirically, because it can inform us
about the expected life time T_a of a civilization. But the search
for extraterrestrial civilization is a challenge, which may keep
us active and help us in enlarging our own value of T_a. In this
way an interest in the value of N_s will result in an increase
of N_s. This hidden feed-back of the nine-factor formula /2/ creates a new turn in the whole story.

At the conclusion let me quote a heretical Franciscan monk,
Francis Bacon, from the 13th century: "The Universe is not to

be narrowed down to the limits of understanding, as has been man's practice up till now, but rather the understanding must be stretched and enlarged, to take in the image of the Universe as it is discovered".

REFERENCES FOR-DETAILED LITERATURE

G. Marx: Why go to the Moon? Scientific World 13 /1969/ 14-17

G. Marx: Über die Energieprobleme der interstelleren Raumfahrt. Acta Astronautica 6 /1960/ 367-372

G. Marx: The Mechanical Efficiency of Interstellar Vehicles. Acta Astronautica 9 /1963/ 132-139

G. Marx: Interstellar Vehicles Propelled by Terrestrial Laser Beam. Nature 211 /1966/ 21-22

G. Marx: Message through Time. Acta Astronautica 6 /1979/ 221-223

G. Marx: Questions about the Thermal History of the Terrestrial Atmosphere. Acta Astronautica 5 /1978/ 601-603

G. Marx: The Question of Simultaneity. Proc. Int. Conf. on Search for Extraterrestrial Intelligence. Academy of USSR, Tallin /1981/

G. Marx: The CO_2 Greenhouse Effect and the Thermal History of the Atmosphere. Advances of Space Research 1 /1981/ 5

Philosophy and Culture
J. Lukács and F. Tőkei eds.

TECHNICS, CULTURE, EDUCATION

J. DÉRI - E. SZÜCS

The scientific-technical revolution we see today is not only a
revolution in science and production but also a revolution of
the "cultural ideal".

It must be emphasized that it is not only the substance of
general culture that is in question. That substance changes constantly /it is not only expanding but gets also modified/, in
the wake of the evolution of the human environment, of mankind,
society and the forms of social consciousness which mirror the
real world. It would be meaningless to speak of a general culture of eternal validity divorced from space and time.

At present, however, more than this is at stake: in our age
the very concept of culture must be reinterpreted. We must be
aware that an educated person today is not one who possesses
lexical knowledge only, but one who is able to store his knowledge systematically, to keep it up-to-date and, what is most
important, to use it effectively.

1/ THE INTERPRETATION OF GENERAL CULTURE

We do not intend to provide an all-embracing definition of
scientific validity for general culture. However, it appears
necessary to elucidate the features considered by us most important, which permit the definition of the place and role of
technical culture.

In our opinion, culture is the systematized sum total of such
knowledge and purposeful behaviour that enables a person
- to orient in his environment /in space and time/;

127

- to adapt himself /actively/ to his environment;
- to protect and develop his environment /in other words: to exploit the potentials inherent in the environment in a way so as to produce an "optimum" result from the viewpoint of present and future society/;
- and, finally, to develop himself, to enrich his knowledge and to improve his behaviour.

Thus, culture does not only involve knowledge but also a form of behaviour, an active relationship to one's environment.

Even without a detailed analysis of cultured behaviour it must be fairly obvious that culture cannot be imagined without an education in literature and art, in history and social sciences. We consider a person uneducated if he does not know, e.g., the basic rules of his native language. It is well-known that the "mass of the uncultured" includes illiterate persons, those who do not know the purpose and ways of hygiene, those incapable of establishing human relations and, as it were, poison the atmosphere of their environment by antisocial behaviour. But the question arises, whether one has to regard as uncultured those who do not know, e.g. the basic rules of road traffic. Should we extend the term "uncultured" to those who are technologically ignorant and have no idea of the practical use of everyday technical devices, who are unable to establish contact with useful and "intelligent" machines or cause heavy damage by using them in the wrong way or by misunderstanding them?

It is no accident that we defined the features of both the "humanistic" and the "realistic" behaviour in similar terms. We wished to emphasize that the so-called humanistic and realistic knowledge are inseparable parts of culture.

To this observation, however, it must at once be added that in the foregoing culture was interpreted as general culture. The use of the word without the adjective may be misleading, particularly when the interpretation of professional and general knowledge are mixed. True, they are closely connected with each other, and it would be certainly strange to qualify a person generally educated if he is uneducated in his own profession, or to qualify somebody as professionally educated if he has no general knowledge. /This latter type is often called in Hungarian a "specialist-barbarian", i.e. a specialist concerned exclusively with his own field of knowledge, but we are convinced that such a person would be no less barbarian where his own profession is concerned/. All the same, it is necessary to distinguish clearly between the two concepts which are different but not antagonistic. To put it briefly, /or in first approximation/, general knowledge means something comprehensive, broad and horizontal, while profession-al knowledge refers to something special, deep and vertical. Ob-viously, a good specialist is someone who has a sound profession-al knowledge, knows his field at an adequate level and his pro-fessional skill enables him to carry on creative activity. The special character of professional knowledge means that it is re-lated to a narrower field of human knowledge and activity, and thus it has differing contents in each given group of persons. On the other hand, the substance of general education refers /in principle/ to everybody. This substance is constantly changing and expanding historically and geographically, in the sphere of both general and professional knowledge, and the number of edu-cated people is constantly increasing.

From the foregoing it follows that the environment is a funda-mental concept in the interpretation of culture. Historically, nature was the first environment of man. Or, to be more exact, nature existed before man. The existence and history of man /man-kind/ cannot be separated from the interaction with the natural environment. In the course of this interaction, man had to learn the art of active adaptation to the environment. He had to learn how to reduce harmful environmental effects and strengthen the useful ones. The survival of mankind was made possible by two parallel processes:
- the development of society, and
- the development of tools.
Human society is the second environment of man. Of course, man did not /and cannot/ exist prior to, or outside of, human society. It would be a grave mistake to conclude from the fore-going that there was a time when individuals were surrounded only by the "first environment". Nor can the development of tools be imagined outside of human society. It must be emphasized that what we are speaking of is the development of tools and not simply

their use. There are examples for the latter even in the animal
kingdom. But only man is capable of recognizing the imperfection
of the tool he uses and to shape and modify it to the form best
suited to his preconceived purpose. The process of developing
tools is of paramount importance: on the one hand, it affects
man's biological development /it brings into motion and changes
every part of the human body, from the limbs to the brains/; on
the other hand, the individual tools give rise to a whole system
of devices, facilities and their use, i.e. to technics.

2/ TECHNOLOGY AS ENVIRONMENT

The interpretation of technics has considerably changed in
the course of history. For thousands of years it meant the sum
of knowledge gathered from practical experience, and in that
sense it is as old as mankind. Man was created by productive
work. He rose out of the animal kingdom because he did not only
use objects found in nature /as tools/, but also transformed
them to suit his purpose. Man, therefore, is a "tool-developing
animal". The tool and its use, in turn, transform man: they develop in man knowledge, routine and skill, in other words: the
art (τεχνη) of using tools. Using natural materials and energy,
man builds between himself and nature a filter letting through,
and possibly strengthening, the natural effects favourable for
himself and separating the harmful ones.

With the spread of literacy practical knowledge and the traditions of various trades got more and more separated from the
sphere of "higher knowledge". A long period followed in which
nobody was dealing with the theoretical questions of production
and with the scientific generalization of practical experience.
The separation between theory and practice had adverse effects
on the development of both science and production. From the 11th
century onwards, however, an increasing number of new /or renewed/
technological achievements appeared and, following them /starting
with Roger Bacon/, science too began dealing with the "craftsmanship experience". A radical change, however, came only with the
industrial revolution, and afterwards with the development of
capitalist society. A qualitative change took place in the re-

lationship between technology and society, and between technics and science. Technics impressed its mark more and more strongly on the whole of society. The interaction between science and technique intensified, and the inheritance and development of craftsmanship experiences within families was gradually replaced by a scientific examination of the problems raised by technology and by the technical application of the achievements of science.

Owing to the accumulation of practical experience and to the development of sciences, man became able to bring nature under his power in broader and broader fields. He was no longer at the mercy of every effect of nature; a whole system of "filters" was constructed, and man's artificial environment came into being. Along with this, also the character of the environment changed gradually. Man was no longer surrounded only by a natural and a social world but also by a technical one. Technics in this period was already more than an "art" or a sum of "purposefully actuated forces, processes and materials". In essence, technics became a new, "artificial /man-made/ nature", a so-called "third environment".

This of course does not mean that the three environments /nature, society and technics/ might exist sharply separated from each other in space and time. The three surround /and always have surrounded/ man simultaneously and in interaction with each other. But the connections between the "parts" of the environment and man, as well as the "weight" of the effect exerted on man by various environmental phenomena and processes changed from time to time.

At the beginning, the phenomena of nature were predominant in the environment of man. Man had to orient himself in their sphere, and to adapt himself to them. From the viewpoint of survival, the greatest danger came from breaking or abusing the laws of nature. Purposeful human behaviour was made possible by the knowledge of the effects of nature /by their understanding and the accumulation of practical experience/.

Later on, particularly after the emergence of class societies, the impacts of the social environment grew increasingly intense. /A slave, e.g., had more reason to fear a violation of the social rules than a thunderbolt/. This does not mean that the ef-

131

fects of the natural environment disappeared, only that together with them and in a "commensurable way", the weight of the social environment increased. Purposeful behaviour required a thorough consideration of these effects.

Owing to the rapid development of technology, in our century the technical environment /and its knowledge/ is of equal importance with the other two environments. /It is perhaps sufficient to refer to the fact that in Hungary hundreds of people die of electric shock or gas poisoning every year, and about two thousand are killed in traffic accidents. The decisive cause of this is not technology itself, but much more human factors: ignorance, the lack of adaptability, i.e. wrong human behaviour/. Such a transformation of the environment is a fact that simply cannot be ignored. "Worse than the deaf are those who are not willing to hear", said Lenin. We must take notice of the transformation of the surrounding world and draw the conclusions that

- a person who is disinterested and indifferent to the operation and correct use of the equipment and devices employed cannot adapt himself actively to his environment;
- a person who does not know the consequences of his handling technological devices /e.g., the environment pollution caused by revving a car engine or littering plastics/ cannot protect and develop his environment;
- a person who refuses to use the up-to-date /technological/ devices of information handling cannot acquire new knowledge /or at least obtain the most important up-to-date knowledge required in his own activity/.

From all this it follows that nowadays a person cannot be qualified as educated unless he is in possession of a technical education as well, i.e. of the sum of the knowledge and purposeful behaviour that make one able

- to orientate in the technical environment,
- to adapt himself actively to the natural, social and technical environment,
- to protect and develop his environment /by means of technics/,
- to develop his knowledge and behaviour.

In other words: in our times technical knowledge is an organic part of general culture, and without it no general culture is possible.

3/ ANTI-TECHNICAL VIEWS

Nobody calls it into doubt that persons having a technological profession /i.e. a profession in engineering/ and those preparing for such professions must have a technical knowledge and education. But there are numerous people who think that for those having careers other than engineering, and for those interested in arts, a technological knowledge is a superfluous burden, and it hinders the unfolding of their personality. The essence of this view is that technical knowledge belongs in the sphere of professional education, while general culture contains purely humanistic elements /or at best "some traces" of natural sciences/.

Can such a view be maintained in an age when it is generally recognized that "knowledge has become a direct productive force"? This means among other things that the existence and development of society, and of the individual within it, cannot be imagined without science and the techniques applying the results of science.

In our age there are fashionable trends of thinking bitterly condemning technology, identifying it with inhuman mechanization. They blame technology for everything from changes in weather conditions, to the spread of cancerous diseases and the pollution of water. Proclamations and literary works are written against "dehumanizing technology". They try to revive the slogan "back to nature", hold lengthy conferences on the dangers, the curse and dehumanizing role of technology and science.

These anti-technical manifestations, heart-stirring as they are, cannot conceal that their advocates misunderstand the essence of technics.

First: Man was made man by work, by the use and development of tools. There can be no art without technics, and no human way of life is possible either.

Second: The technical environment is an objective reality. Lamenting over its certain harmful effects is as senseless as grieving over the harmful effects /hail, storm, earth-quake/ of the natural environment while doing nothing against them. Of course, the crucial difference is that natural effects are in-dependent of man, whereas the effects of the technical environ-ment are man-made. Therefore, deliberate human activity, taking also the secondary effects into account, has a much greater role in weakening - and in certain cases eliminating - the adverse effects of technology. Man cannot do away with his environment, and it only shows his lack of knowledge if, instead of trying to live in it and with it, he begins to be afraid of it /asking mystical forces to help/ or wants to get rid of the environment.

There is only one kind of relationship that a cultured man can have with his environment /including the man-made environ-ment/: to study and classify the phenomena, to recognize their essence and laws, then, in possession of this knowledge, to strive to strengthen the advantageous effects and to reduce the harmful ones.

Third: The threat to mankind does not consist in technology /and its instruments/ but in its inhuman use. Even in the capital-ist world more and more people recognize that the technical de-velopment if subordinated completely to profit-making, exerts a destructive effect on human relations, culture, and the living world, i.e. on both the social and the natural environment.

We must emphasize that it is technics not itself but its u-tilization that may be dangerous and inhuman. There is no such thing as a capitalist or a socialist technology only technology subordinated either to capitalist or to socialist interests, and there are technical views, goals of development and using tech-nics, determined by political attitudes. One of the basic princi-ples /one might say the credo/ of our ideology is inherent in the statement that our ideal is not "technicized man" but an anthropocentric technology; that the level of technology is de-termined not only /and not primarily/ by the technical perfec-tion of the devices, but by the objectives and direction of their use and by their effect on the development and welfare of the whole of society, of mankind.

4/ TECHNOCRATIC VIEWS

The formation of a socially sound picture of general culture is hampered not only by anti-technical views but also by a blind worship of technology, by the technocratic view putting technology before and above everything else.

The achievements of modern technology, the speed, performance, controllability, aesthetic forms, the accomplishment of goals undreamed before /or only found in science fiction/ has filled many people /especially the young/ with such uncritical admiration that they are becoming slaves to technology. We do not only mean, and not in the first place either that they are longing for the most up-to-date gadgets /this is bad only if it makes them forget the beauties of nature and social life and the pleasures offered by art while the content of their life is restricted to technology, and parallel with enjoying technology, they destroy the natural environment and social relations/. This becomes really dangerous when a sort of "technocratic" attitude develops with the idea that the whole human society /arts and sciences, politics and economy/ ought to be subordinated to the demands and requirements of technology /or even governed by it/.

The views glorifying technics, however "technicistic" they may seem, cannot conceal that their propagators fail to understand the essence and role of technics.

First: Even the most sophisticated machinery is nothing but a senseless mass of devices without man /without human control, human goals/. Man does not exist for machines, but machines exist for man. Shallow, empty lives cannot be made human even by the most perfect machine.

Second: Society is the environment and precondition system not only for the individual but also for technics itself. Without society /or outside of it/ neither man nor technics can exist. /As Aristotle wrote in his Politika: "A being that could live outside society may be a wild beast or a god, but in no way could it be a man"/.

Third: The specialist who is ignorant of the laws of the development of science and art /and in general of the spheres other than his profession/, and wants to subordinate all these to his goals, does not only hamper the development of all these spheres but endangers also the future of his own profession. /This, however, is true not only of the technical professions, but also of the so-called "humanistic" professions.

5/ THE SYSTEM OF TECHNICAL KNOWLEDGE

In our opinion the Greek word (τεχνη) art, craft, trick, skill from which the terms "technics" and "technology" derive meant essentially the manner in which man entered /and enters/ into interaction with his environment. Thus one may say that the technics is equal to an interaction between man and his environment. This interaction, however, grew increasingly complex in time from handicraft technics through simple machines, then through engines and machine units to logic machines and to systems requiring high-level technology, and to more and more complicated structures. This technics became an organic part of the environment surrounding man, thoroughly changing the original picture of the natural environment. This fact demonstrates what we know from experience: technics not only changed, and is changing at present too, our natural and social environment, but became /and is becoming/ incorporated in it; our environment of today and tomorrow is a natural-social-technical environment. Modern man can no more live without technology than without nature and society. We must be aware of this, and act accordingly. It requires not only a novel interpretation of culture, but has a profound effect also upon the contents of general education, upon the substance of pedagogical work in schools.

From the foregoing it follows that technical, natural and social knowledge are inseparable components of culture, complementing each other. The laws of technics cannot be understood without the aid of natural and social sciences. Without a knowledge of natural sciences one might get the impression that technics is "capable of anything", that its development knows no limits. Without an awareness of the laws of nature even the cleverest

136

technological idea may become an impracticable dream, and its originator may go the way of alchimists and the inventors of the perpetuum mobile.

Technics, however, is not simply the user of natural and social sciences, but it synthesizes the knowledge revealed by these sciences in order to produce an object of determined function. This does not mean that technics absorbs or subordinates the other sciences. Among sciences there can be no supremacy or subordinacy. Each discipline deals with the same objective world; each are models of the world /or of a part of it/; they are mirror images of the world according to differing viewpoints. The special branches of science are separated by their peculiar viewpoints /or system of viewpoints/. They are distinguished from each other not by the object to be reflected but - in the first place - by the manner in which they reflect it. Investigation according to narrow viewpoints makes it possible to acquire deep knowledge. Technics uses **this** knowledge but - owing to the great complexity of producing a new construction - it cannot delve into every detail. Its activity is governed by its own autonomous principles and methods.

These autonomous principles follow mainly from the fact that technical knowledge concerns primarily the man-made environment, the new product, the development of the existing object, and construction and maintenance. Physics, chemistry, history, political economy, etc., are descriptive, analytical sciences aimed at clarifying the interrelations of cause and effect connected largely with existing phenomena. Of course, this does not mean that they · deal exclusively with existing things, just as technics does not only synthesize knowledge connected with the production of new things.

Of the special principles /and methods/ of technics the most important are:
- goal-orientation /"why" and "what"/
- purposefulness /"what" and "how"/
- economy /"how" and "for how much"/
- organization /"for how much" and "by whom"/, and finally:
- a systems approach synthesizing all these.

The first principle is: goal-orientation. Each product intro-
duces some change in the relationship between man and environment. While natural sciences generally examine the behaviour of
some object, the relationship between input and output and the
laws of behaviour, technics strives primarily to find the means
for a prescribed objective, e.g., an object that ensures a /pre-
scribed, desirable or necessary/ behaviour, a transforming action
or an anticipated input-output relationship. The former can be
termed a direct or identification-type task, and the latter an
indirect task. The determination of indirect tasks starts with
an unambiguous definition of the goal, in other words, by the
description of the intended state. From all that has been said
so far about technical culture it follows that the determination
of the goal cannot be limited to a consideration of narrow interests or viewpoints only. It must be ensured that the' change to
be achieved is useful for the whole environment, and that it does
not have any harmful consequences for the future /even in centuries or millennia/. /There are many examples for harmful effects
occurring later on or at a greater distance: e.g. the consequences
of the draining of the Small Balaton - a part of the Hungarian
lake Balaton, the upsetting of the ecological balance, pollution
of the sea water, etc./. From all this must be evident that technics has a functional approach. This means that it does not look
for the internal character of materials and equipment but for
the measure to which they satisfy its objectives. E.g.:
  - In the case of a type of material the main question is not
    its composition, but how it can be shaped, loaded and what
    other materials can be replaced by it.
  - Familiarity with radio or TV does not require a knowledge
    of the laws of electrodynamics and solid-state physics
    /this belongs to the sphere of specialist knowledge/, but
    one must be able to operate the set and understand its role
    in communication and its expectable development.
The number of examples is endless, but this ought to be sufficient to understand what is meant by a functional, goal-orient-
ed approach.

The second principle is purposefulness. When the "why" and
"what" have been decided one must also determine "how". A simple

description of the goal, a clear-cut characterization of the intended state, still only tells us where we have to arrive. To get there, however, it is necessary to plan
- the means satisfying the objective, i.e. the "product";
- the way leading to the achievement of the goal /to the realization of the product/, i.e. the process of "production".

Taken in a strict sense, planning precedes the determination of the goal. The first step is the analysis of the situation, which equals a survey of the existing state. In the course of the state analysis the contradiction between the existing needs and possibilities is recognized and/or concretized. The determination of the goal marks out that point in the field of possible states which must be reached in order to eliminate the tensions of the present state. In this regard it must be made clear that "task" and "problem" are not synonyms. What they have in common is that in both cases one must arrive from an existing situation /state/ to a desired /pre-determined/ situation /state/. The desired state or situation is produced by the solution of the task or problem. However, in the case of a task there is a known /one might say algorithmized/ way which alone leads to the right solution. On the other hand, a problem must first be recognized. The recognition of a problem is a complex intellectual activity. One must start from an analysis of the existing condition and realize that the known /or expectable/ demands cannot be satisfied by the existing /or expectable/ potentials. A man sensitive to problems does not search for "something new" in general but for something that will eliminate the contradiction between the demands and the possibilities; he is no utopian /who, ignoring the possibilities, builds castles in Spain/ and no anarchist /one who denies all existing order and rules/ either. He is a realist who does not accept existing things as "perfect" but strives to continuous development, and whose motto is "to change while preserving". The direct opposite of this type is the conformist whose motto is: "Don't leave the beaten path". For a conformist everything is all right as it is; he is content with imitation, with keeping strictly to the rules he has learned. /A conformist will never be an innovator or an inventor/.

139

The difficulties of problem-solving are as follows:
- the desired state can be reached in several ways, and
  the person wanting to solve the problem has to select
  one from among several alternatives, i.e., he has to
  decide on the basis of some viewpoint ensuring that he
  not only reaches the desired state, but - according to
  the selected viewpoint - reaches it in the best possible
  way;
- very often none of the ways leading to the desired state
  is known; thus research is needed to explore the possible
  ways of changing the state;
- not all the /essential/ characteristics of the desired
  state /or condition/ are known, i.e. the description of
  the complex situation is not unambiguous. /It is a general
  truth, but in this case especially valid, that it is not
  only impossible to solve a problem but also to define it
  without the cooperation of specialists /and special branches
  of science/ examining and analyzing the objective world
  from differing points of view/.

All this, instead of diminishing it, increases the importance
of planning and of the use of methods carefully thought out in
advance. When the problem is clearly defined and known, the possible ways of the solution can be planned and the possible methods
can be selected.

When planning the alternatives to solving the problem, we must
be aware of the fact that each problem is part of a greater problem. Thus one must take into consideration in advance the viewpoints of selecting /deciding on/ one of the alternative solutions. One has to consider not only the human, economic and aesthetic viewpoints, but also social ones, i.e. viewpoints determined by a system higher at least by one hierarchy level than
the problem in question.

The third principle is economy. In simple terms, after the
"why, what and how", the most important question is "for how
much". The measure is not always money since very often an optimum determined according to different values /e.g. environment
protection, public health, etc./ has to be achieved. In other
words, on the basis of some scale of values, one has to select

140

one of the possible solutions, and for this purpose, make comparisons between the variants. The viewpoint of the comparison
/and of the decision/ is economic efficiency, which means that
the available sources of raw material and energy must be utilized
reasonably.

If a scalar function can be assigned to each of the variants,
then the decision can be made simply by mathematics. This, however, is not always possible, since a state cannot always be
quantified; it has qualitative parameters, too. The future development of science will be very likely to permit the consideration of an increasing number of decision parameters and conditions, which will be built into the mathematical model of the
decision-making. Nevertheless, there will always remain some
non-numerifiable parameters that cannot be handled mathematically
in an exact form; thus, decision-making will always be a human
activity, and the responsibility of the decision-maker will remain unchanged.

The fourth principle is organization. Even the best decision
will remain on paper if its execution is not organized. The solution of a problem is always some kind of activity. Only seldom
is a single individual, independent of other persons, capable
of this activity, but even in such a case he must organize his
own activity. In the overwhelming majority of technical problems,
however, this activity is collective: it requires the joint work
of smaller or larger groups, coordinated in detail. Therefore
the organization of the execution demands that we know the characteristics of human relations as well as the methods of the division and coordination of work. In this respect it is especially
important to understand and employ the cooperation of individuals
and groups /factories, enterprises, economic branches, nations/.
Selection of the participants, awakening their interest /and keeping it alive during the work/, and, in general, organization and
management are inseparable parts of technology.

Finally, perhaps the most important characteristic of technology is the systems approach. To avoid any misunderstanding: the
systems approach is a characteristic feature not only of technics
but of any up-to-date field of science. And vice versa: not everybody concerned with technics has a systems approach. But without

such an approach the above four principles of technics fall into parts and lead to effects contrary to those expected.

In contrast to natural systems, the function of technical systems is not a spontaneous change of state but a controlled modification of state. As to their structure, technical systems are combinations of part systems corresponding to and mutually supposing each other, and in their process they are transfers of matter /mass and energy/ and information. From this it follows that the five basic categories of technics are material, energy, information, system and model.

/Classifying energy into a separate category is not a philosophical aberration, but indicates the peculiarly important role of this remaining material attribute in technics/.

It is on this basis that the curriculum of the subject "Technics" is built up, on the level of both general and higher education.

6/ THE SUBJECT "TECHNICS"

The technical education lasting for 10 /or 12/ years in the primary and secondary schools is aimed at teaching every member of the future generations, irrespective of his profession,

a/ to know the basic laws of society, nature and technics as well as the relations and combinations of the laws and the processes determined by them;

b/ to be able to handle purposefully the technical devices in his environment;

c/ to be able to form his environment purposefully and methodically;

d/ to be able to evaluate technical systems rationally and in a socialist way;

e/ to be capable of organized human activity and of solving problems in a straightforward manner;

f/ to know and esteem the various sorts of productive work, and to choose his profession accordingly.

Based on all this, the subject "Technics" not only contributes to the education of extensively cultured people, but helps also in choosing careers and, if necessary, also to change careers later on.

Philosophy and Culture
J. Lukács and F. Tőkei eds.

NATURWISSENSCHAFT UND KULTUR

J. HORVÁTH

Noch nie wurde von der Kultur so viel gesprochen wie heutigentags
- schrieb der namhafter sowjetische Ästhet Mihail Lifschiz im
Jahre 1958 /1/. Diese Tatsache hat während den vergangenen Jahren
nicht geändert. Sowohl in der bürgerlichen als auch in der sozialistischen Literatur steht die Frage der Kultur im Vordergrund.
Wir können noch hinzufügen, dass die Gleichheit der bei der einen
und der anderen auftauchenden Probleme augenfällig ist. Davon
zeugt die Auseinandersetzung, die sich über die beiden Kulturen
in den 60er Jahren entfaltete /2/. Die in den damaligen Polemiken
aufgeworfenen Probleme haben an ihrer Aktualität auch heute nichts
verloren. <u>Die Stelle und Rolle der Naturwissenschaft, der naturwissenschaftlichen Bildung</u> sind auch heute wichtige kulturolo-
gische und, fügen wir hinzu, praktische Fragen. Summarisch aus-
wertend könnten wir sagen, dass das alles gesetzmässig ist, denn
es handelt sich um eine Folge der wissenschaftlich-technischen
Revolution. Dieser kulturelle Dualismus ist nichts anderes als
eines der globalen Probleme unserer Zeit, das durch die wissenschaftlich-technische Revolution hervorgerufen wurde. Unserer
Beurteilung nach ist die Lage nicht so einfach. Im weiteren versuchen wir es klarzulegen. Natürlich müssen wir uns darüber im
klaren sein, dass die verschiedenen Kulturauffassungen, irgendeine Annahme der Widersprüche der Kultur schon ökonomisch-so-
zial, politisch-ideologisch motivierte Deutungen der wirklichen
Lage sind,in denen sich schon eine Art Auswertung widerspiegelt.
Demgemäss ist die Aufgabe zweifältig - ausser dem Vergleich der
verschiedenen Ansichten müssen darüber hinaus auch die gesamt-

gesellschaftlich-wirtschaftlichen, politischen, ideologischen
und geschichtlichen Grundlagen der vorhandenen Wertordnungen
aufgeschlossen werden.

DIE EINHEIT UND VIELFALTIGKEIT DER KULTUR,
DIE EINORDNUNG DER NATURWISSENSCHAFT

Die Einordnung der Naturwissenschaft ist nicht nur und auch
nicht in erster Linie ein kulturologisches Problem. Die Utopie
und die Illusionen sind auch hier nur dann zu vermeiden, wenn
wir die Probleme an den Wurzeln fassen, diejenigen wirtschaftlichen und gesellschaftlichen Voraussetzungen aufschliessen,
unter und auf Grund welcher sich die Naturwissenschaft entwickelt,
existiert und funktioniert /3/.
Die Wurzel der beiden, in der heutigen bürgerlichen Gesellschaft auftauchenden Kultur-Dilemmas liegen geschichtlich bei
der Entstehung dieser wirtschaftlich-gesellschaftlichen Formation. Auf dem Gebiet der Naturumbildung, der Zurückdrängung der
Naturschranken des menschlichen Daseins, der Entwicklung der
Technik und der Naturwissenschaft bringt diese wirtschaftlich-
-gesellschaftliche Einrichtung den grössten Fortschritt in der
Geschichte bis zu dieser Zeit. Das alles ist aber nicht mit einer
ähnlichen Entfaltung der gesellschaftlichen Befreiung verbunden.
Im Gegenteil, die bürgerliche Gesellschaft bereitet auf diesem
Gebiet wegen ihren gesellschaftlichen Grundlagen neuere Schranken, Hindernisse. Diese Gesellschaft kann diesen Widerspruch im
Laufe ihrer ganzen Entwicklung nicht lösen. Die moderne bürgerliche Gesellschaft - wie István Hermann zutreffend schreibt -
ist in den meisten entwickelten kapitalistischen Ländern fähig,
die alte Form der Entfremdung, die Entfremdung des Elends zu
beseitigen, gleichzeitig schafft sie aber eine neue Form der
Entfremdung - der Entfremdung des Luxus /4/. Infolge dessen entsteht in der bürgerlichen Gesellschaft die Kulturlosigkeit, entstehen die "Schulden der Kultur", zerfällt die Einheit der Kultur. Diese Verhältnisse führen nicht nur in der Verwirklichung
der gesellschaftlichen Funktionen der Technik und der Naturwissenschaft zu unversöhnlichen Widersprüchen /ist die Technik ein Fluch
oder ein Segen, spielt die wissenschaftlich-technische Revolution

eine vernichtende oder erhebende Rolle?/. Im Falle der Naturwissenschaft begegnen wir neben den funktionellen Deformationen
/d.h. der Charakter, die Weise, die Wertordnung der Anwendung/
auch inneren, den Inhalt, das erkenntnistheoretische Wertsystem
der Naturwissenschaft betreffenden Deformationen. Mit dramatischen
Besorgnissen schreibt darüber der bürgerliche Philosoph Abel Rey
schon im Jahre 1907. Die Wissenschaften der Physik und der Chemie
- schreibt er - die in der Geschichte eigentlich eine emanzipatorische Rolle gespielt haben, scheitern in einer Krise, die ihnen
nur den Wert nützlicher technischer Rezepte hinterlässt, aber
ihnen ihre ganze Bedeutung hinsichtlich der Erkenntnis der Natur
nimmt, dann muss das in der Geschichte der Logik und der Ideen
ein vollkommenes Durcheinander hervorrufen /5/. In dieser Auffassung verliert die Naturwissenschaft gerade ihren inneren kulturellen Charakter - ihre emanzipatorische Rolle, ihren Erziehungs-
wert. Der Verfasser spricht hier über die bürgerlich-philosophi-
sche, konkret gesagt positivistische Wertung der Krise der Physik
am Anfang des Jahrhunderts. Das weist auch schon darauf hin, dass
der Pluralismus der aus einem bürgerlich-gesellschaftlichen Boden
entsprungenen philosophischen, weltanschaulichen Tendenzen dem
Prozess des Zerfalls der Kultur nur noch mehr beiträgt. Eine der
Grundthesen der szientistischen, pragmatischen Wissenschaftsauf-
fassungen unserer Zeit ist schliesslich die These, dass die Wissenschaft kein wirkliches Wissen, sondern nur praktische Rezepte geben kann. Die Naturwissenschaft wird ohne inhaltsreiche Ideenwer-
te antihumanistisch, sie verliert ihre Verbindung mit den positiven moralischen Werten, sie gerät in Konflikt mit der Literatur
und der Kunst, die diese Lage ausdrücken möchten. Es muss aber
auch über weitere Seiten des Dualismus der bürgerlichen Kultur
gesprochen werden. Schon Rey weist darauf hin, dass man, wenn
die Wissenschaft kein wirkliches Wissen gibt, die Erkenntnis der
Wirklichkeit mit anderen Methoden suchen soll. Man soll der subjektiven Intuition, dem mystischen Wirklichkeitsgefühl, dem Rätsel-
haften all das wiedererstatten, wovon wir gedacht haben, dass es
ihnen die Wissenschaft entrissen hat. Die die inneren, kulturellen
Werte der Wissenschaft beschränkende wirtschaftliche und ideologische Situation bringt wirklich den Anspruch für die Mystik hervor und schafft die Formen für die Befriedigung dieser Ansprüche.

Es ist die Erklärung dafür, dass z.B. die Pseudowissenschaft
mit dem Kult der Wissenschaft gut auskommt und sich erfolgreich
verbreiten kann, neben dem Kult der Wissenschaft finden wir auch
den Kult der Mystik.

Hinsichtlich "der beiden Kulturen" geht es also nicht nur um
den Widerspruch zwischen der Physik und der Literatur, oder im
weiteren Sinne zwischen der Naturwissenschaft und der Kunst, der
Naturwissenschaft und der Moral, sondern man soll auch das Komple-
ment der Wissenschaft und der Mystik aufwerfen. Sehr oft werden
gerade die Literatur, die Kunst zum Träger und Vermittler der
subjektiven Intuition, des geheimnisvollen, mystischen Wirklich-
keitsgefühls. Ihre tiefste Quelle ist die aus den bürgerlichen
Gesellschaftsverhältnissen notwendigerweise folgende idealistische Gesellschafts- und Menschenauffassung. Im Grunde wird der
Dualismus der naturwissenschaftlichen und der humanen Bildung,
der Naturwissenschaften und der Gesellschaftswissenschaften dadurch determiniert. Die Gesellschaftswissenschaften /die politische Ökonomie, die Geschichtswissenschaft, die Soziologie usw./
sind - mit Lenins Worten - parteiische Wissenschaften, d.h. sie
drücken aus und vertreten Klasseninteressen. Deshalb kann die
Einheit dieser zwei grossen Gebiete der Kultur, der Naturwissenschaften und der Gesellschaftswissenschaften auf dem Boden der
kapitalistischen Gesellschaft, des Imperialismus nicht verwirklicht werden.

Die wissenschaftlich-technische Revolution und die sich immer
weiter ausbreitenden wirtschaftlichen, kulturellen Beziehungen
zwischen den Ländern von verschiedenen gesellschaftlichen Syste-
men werfen auch in der bürgerlichen Gesellschaft den Anspruch
für die Einheit der Natur- und Gesellschaftwissenschaften mit
einer neuen Notwendigkeit auf. Dieser Anspruch wird aber auf
dem Boden der allgemeinen Krise der bürgerlichen Gesellschaft
gestellt, wenn sich die kulturelle Verelendung in dem Luxus er-
höht, die Schulden der Kultur zunehmen und immer tragischer
werden. Der Zerfall der bürgerlichen Kultur ist unaufhaltbar.
Wie kann diese Situation richtig gewertet werden? Nur auf dem
Wege der Aufschliessung ihrer realen Widersprüchlichkeit. Der
Anspruch für die Einheit dieser beiden Kulturen - und damit die
Möglichkeit der Entfaltung des wirklichen kulturellen Gehalts

146

und Funktionen der Naturwissenschaft - werden durch die sprung-
hafte Veränderung in der Entwicklung der Produktionskräfte hervorgerufen, die aber zur gleichen Zeit auch die bürgerlich wirtschaftliche Form dieser Entwicklung in Frage stellt. Der Anspruch
für die Einheit der beiden Kulturen wird also in den meisten entwickelten Ländern des Kapitalismus auf dem Boden eines allgemeinen kulturellen Niederganges formuliert, andererseits drückt er
das hohe Niveau der technischen und kulturellen Entwicklung aus.
In den Ländern des Sozialismus ist die Lage bedeutend anders.
Das Problem "der beiden Kulturen" taucht - in den 60er Jahren -
auf dem Boden des kulturellen Aufstieges auf, es hängt zwar mit
der wissenschaftlich-technischen Revolution zusammen, aber auf
einem weniger entwickelten Niveau der Produktionskräfte.

DIE SOZIALISTISCHE KULTURREVOLUTION
 UND DIE NATURWISSENSCHAFT

   Die Kulturrevolution ist ein unentbehrliches Element bei dem
Bau des Sozialismus, bei der Gestaltung der neuen, kommunistischen gesellschaftlichen Formation, eine allgemeine Gesetzmässig-
keit im Bau des Sozialismus /6/. Ein von Illusionen und Utopien
freies Verstehen des Inhalts und der Zielsetzungen der in dem
realen Sozialismus zustandekommenden Kulturrevolution fordert
eine konkrete geschichtliche Analyse. Vor allem die Berücksichtigung der Lage, dass die sozialistische Revolution infolge der
ungleichmässigen geschichtlichen Entwicklung zuerst in den mit-
telmässig entwickelten, technisch und wirtschaftlich verhältnis-
mässig zurückgebliebenen Ländern gesiegt hat. Daraus ergibt sich,
dass der Kulturrevolution auch die Aufhebung der Rückständigkeit
zur Aufgabe gestellt wird. Es geht um diese Obliegenheiten, wenn
Lenin im Zusammenhang mit der Staatsverwaltung, der Arbeitsdiszi-
plin, der Bildung der Genossenschaften die Notwendigkeit der
Erhöhung der kulturellen Ebene schildert. Der Sozialismus als
die erste Entwicklungsphase des Kommunismus, ist im Prozess der
gesamtgesellschaftlichen Entwicklung eine neue, höhere, die kapitalistische gesellschaftliche Formation übersteigende Phase.
In diesem Zusammenhang ist die sozialistische Kulturrevolution,
wie es Gorki formuliert hat, der Beginn einer grossen, neuen

Renaissance, die nicht mehr ausschliesslich eine nationale Renaissance wird, sondern die Wiedergeburt der ganzen Welt /7/.
Die Einheit der unmittelbaren, konkreten, sowie der perspekti-
vischen weltgeschichtlichen Inhalte und Ziele der sozialistischen Kulturrevolution kann so formuliert werden, dass das Wert-
vollste, die unbestreitbaren Werte der durch die ganze Entwicklung der Menschheit geschaffenen Kultur angeeignet werden müssen,
wobei sie weiterentwickelt, mit neueren Werten bereichert, auf
eine höhere Ebene gehoben werden müssen.

Die wirtschaftlich-technische Zurückgebliebenheit der Umstände
vor der sozialistischen Revolution, so die Verhältnisse in Ungarn
vor 1945 - mit einer unmittelbaren Auswirkung auf die Lage und
Rolle der Naturwissenschaft - haben die Widersprüchlichkeit und
Krisenmerkmale der bürgerlichen Kultur auf eine eigenartige Weise
ausgedrückt. Die Wertordnung der bürgerlichen Kultur wurde durch
die zurückgebliebenen Spuren der Wertordnung der feudalen Gesellschaft sogar in mehreren Beziehungen belastet. Stärker war der
Einfluss der idealistischen, sogar ausdrücklich religiösen Weltanschauung /die kirchliche und die staatliche Ausbildung waren
nicht getrennt/. Ein ganz eingeengter Kulturbegriff wurde zu
einer festen, allgemeinen ideologischen Konzeption und ebenso
zu einer konventionellen Grundlage der Wertordnung des Alltags.
Die idealistische Deutung beschränkt den Begriff der Kultur ohne-
hin auf das geistige Gebiet. Wegen den dargelegten Gründen erfolgt hier auch noch eine weitere Einschränkung. Jene Deutung
der Kultur wird allgemein, die die Ästhetik in den Mittelpunkt
stellt, der Begriff der Kultur bezieht sich auf die künstlerische, vor allem auf die literarische Sphäre.

Für die Veränderung dieser Lage waren solche fundamentale
wirtschaftliche und soziale Umwälzungen nötig, deren Bedingungen
nur die sozialistische Revolution geschaffen hat. Der kulturelle
Fortschritt, die Aufhebung der Rückständigkeit, die Entstehung
der neuen Wertordnung konnten sich nur auf der Grundlage der gesellschaftlichen Veränderungen, stufenmässig vollziehen, das ist
ein auch heute noch dauernder Prozess. Die in dem realen Sozialismus stattfindende Kulturrevolution ist also ihren Inhalt be-
treffend ein sehr zusammengesetzter und komplizierter Prozess.
Die Übernahme der Werte der bürgerlichen Kultur soll mit der

148

Aufhebung der Unkultiviertheit, mit der Beseitigung der "Schulden der Kultur", mit der wirklichen Schaffung der Einheit der Kultur verbunden werden.

Auf Grund von geschichtlichen Erfahrungen sind drei Phasen des kulturellen Aufstieges zu unterscheiden.

Das grundlegende Merkmal der ersten Phase ist - als Folge der unmittelbaren revolutionären Aufgaben - ein krasses Gegenüberstehen der bürgerlichen und der sozialistischen Kultur. Die zugespitzten Zusammenstösse sind durch den unversöhnlichen Gegensatz der ideellen und ideologischen Grundlagen der sozialistischen Kultur hervorgerufen. Das alte Institutionssystem soll umorganisiert, die reaktionären, retrograden Kräfte sollen aus der Leitung, der Lenkung verdrängt werden.

In der zweiten Phase, nachdem das kulturelle Leben und die Volksbildung unter die Leitung des sozialistischen Staates gekommen sind, bahnt die Kulturpolitik der führenden kommunistischen Partei einen weiten Weg zum Zusammentreffen der Kultur und der Massen. Das ist mit einem ausserordentlich grossen quantitativen und qualitativen Aufstieg verbunden. Ein neues Bildungs- und Volksbildungssystem wird ausgebaut. Mit der Entwicklung der Hochschulbildung und der Forschungsinstitute beginnt die Beseitigung des technischen und naturwissenschaftlichen Rückstandes/8/. Die im Jahre 1958 formulierten bildungspolitischen Richtlinien der USAP stellen die weiteren Aufgaben nach dem Abschluss einer schweren Periode voll von Widersprüchen /9/.

Die Ergebnisse der extensiven Entwicklung bereiten die Bedingungen für den Übergang zu der neuen, intensiven Etappe vor. Die dritte Phase des kulturellen Aufstieges entfaltet sich in den 60er Jahren. Die erzielten Resultate der industriellen und landwirtschaftlichen Produktion, die mit dem wissenschaftlich-technischen Fortschritt verknüpften Anforderungen, die Erhöhung des Lebensstandardes, die Erweiterung der sozialistischen Demokratie machten die Weiterführung der Kulturrevolution nicht nur möglich, sondern auch notwendig. Die Erhöhung der Qualität der Bildung und der Volksbildung erlangt eine grundlegende Bedeutung. Den ersten Platz nimmt die Frage der Verwirklichung der Fachausbildung auf einem guten Niveau ein. Die Wissenschaft bekommt eine zentrale Stelle, die naturwissenschaftliche und technische Ausbildung spie-

11   149

len eine besonders grosse Rolle /10/. Die vertiefte und sich
differenzierende Fachausbildung ruft unter den gegebenen Bedingungen der Arbeitsverteilung diejenigen kulturellen Spannungen
ins Leben, unter denen das Dilemma der "beiden Kulturen" auch
bei uns viel Anklang findet. Zum richtigen Verstehen der Spannungen, Widersprüchlichkeiten unserer kulturellen Entwicklung
ist die Analyse der konkreten gesellschaftlichen Bedingungen
und ihrer Auswirkungen unentbehrlich. Unter ihnen sind die Spaltung der geistigen und der physischen Arbeit, das Problem der
Warenproduktion, der wirtschaftlichen Entwicklung, die bestehenden Klassen- und Schichtenunterschiede besonders hervorzuheben.
Diese sind in erster Linie die objektiven Ursachen derjenigen,
im Prozess der sozialistischen Kulturrevolution bestehenden Widersprüche, die bei der allseitigen Entfaltung der Einheit der
Kultur vorübergehende Grenzen bedeuten.

Die wirtschaftlich-gesellschaftlichen Bedingungen des entwickelten Sozialismus, die Möglichkeiten und die Bedürfnisse der
die Ergebnisse der wissenschaftlich-technischen Revolution maxi-
mal ausschöpfenden intensiven Entwicklung führen zu einer neuen
Etappe der Kulturrevolution. Die jetzt auszuarbeitenden perspek-
tivischen Pläne für die Bildung, Forschung und Volksbildung enthalten solche Züge, die sehr günstige und in vielen Beziehungen
qualitativ neue Möglichkeiten für die weitere Entfaltung der
einheitlichen sozialistischen Kultur schaffen. Aus dem Gesichtspunkt der Verwirklichung der Einheit der Kultur ist die Verwirklichung der Einheit der Fachausbildung und der Ausbildung der
Intelligenz von einer grundlegenden Bedeutung. Mit anderen Worten: Eine solche Ausbildung der Fachleute, die die aus der Spe-
zialisierung stammenden Einseitigkeiten aufhebt, eine allgemeine
Bildungsbasis gibt, zu einer gesamtgesellschaftlichen und univer-
salen weltanschaulichen Betrachtungsweise, sowie zu einer allseitigen gesellschaftlichen Aktivität anspornt. Es zu verwirklichen ist nur die sozialistische Kultur fähig.

Der revolutionäre Kern der sozialistischen Kultur ist der
Marxismus. Die allgemeine ideelle Grundlage der Einheit der sozialistischen Kultur ist die Philosophie des Marxismus, die materialistische monistische Weltanschauung. Eine der grossen Ent-
deckungen von Marx ist die materialistische Auffassung der Ge-

150

sellschaft. Der Marxismus hat damit eine der grundlegenden prin-
zipiellen Beschränkungen der bürgerlichen Ideologie und Kultur,
die Spaltung der naturwissenschaftlichen und der gesellschaft-
wissenschaftlichen Auffassung überschritten. Marx schreibt bereits 1844 darüber, dass "die Naturwissenschaft wird später eben-
sowohl die Wissenschaft von dem Menschen, wie die Wissenschaft
von dem Menschen die Naturwissenschaft, unter sich subsumieren:
es wird eine Wissenschaft sein" /11/. Das grundlegende Interesse
der sozialistischen Gesellschaft ist - stellt die Programmerklärung der USAP fest - die wissenschaftliche Aufschliessung, die
praktische Anwendung der Gesetzmässigkeiten der Natur und der
Gesellschaft /12/. Infolge der Entfaltung der entwickelten sozialistischen gesellschaftlichen Verhältnisse verflechten sich
die verschiedenen Zweige der gesellschaftlichen Tätigkeit immer
enger, allmählich kommen die Möglichkeiten der einheitlichen
Regelung der gesellschaftlichen und Naturprozesse zustande. Das
bildet die objektive Grundlage, auf der sich die wirkliche Einheit der Kultur realisieren kann. In dieser einheitlichen sozialistischen Kultur können sich die kulturellen Werte und Funktionen der Naturwissenschaften widerspruchlos und ohne Beschränkungen entfalten.

NATURWISSENSCHAFT UND NATURWISSENSCHAFTLICHE KULTUR

Das Verstehen der Sachlage und Eigenartigkeiten der wissenschaftlichen Kultur setzt die Aufschliessung des wirklichen gesellschaftlichen Wesens und Funktionen der Wissenschaft voraus.
Die Wissenschaft kann nicht auf ein eigenartiges System der I-
deen beschränkt werden. Auch sein Institutionsnetz in Betracht
gezogen bekommen wir kein vollkommenes Bild darüber. Die Wissenschaft ist eine komplexe gesellschaftliche Erscheinung. Die unmittelbare Grundlage und der determinierende Faktor ihrer ideel-
len-inhaltlichen Momente ist die gesamtgesellschaftliche praktische Tätigkeit der Menschheit. Die Wissenschaft ist eine menschliche Tätigkeit, die im Falle der Naturwissenschaft auch die
sensorisch-erfahrungsmässige, experimentell-praktische Tätigkeit
in sich begreift. Nur die Analyse der Wissenschaft als einer
menschlichen Tätigkeit führt zum Verstehen ihres kulturellen

Inhalts und Funktionen. Im weiteren beschäftigen wir uns nur
mit der Naturwissenschaft, viele unserer Feststellungen werden
aber auch für die Wissenschaft im allgemeinen gültig sein.

Am Anfang wurde mit dem Begriff der Kultur die Bestellung der
Natur bezeichnet. Die Bebauung, die Kultur ist also vor allem
mit der praktischen menschlichen Aneignung der Natur verknüpft.
Aus dieser Tätigkeit wächst die Naturwissenschaft als die empi-
risch-experimentelle und geistig-theoretische Aneignung der Natur hervor. Die geschichtliche Analyse führt uns zu der grundlegenden kulturellen Funktion der Naturwissenschaft, zu dem
wichtigsten inhaltlichen Moment der naturwissenschaftlichen Kultur - zu der Rolle der Emanzipation. Aus dem Stoffwechsel zwischen dem Menschen und der Natur, aus dem praktischen Verhältnis
des Menschen zu der Natur, aus der praktischen Aneignung der Natur wächst die Naturwissenschaft hervor und erscheint und funktioniert als die sich geschichtlich entfaltende substantielle
Kraft des Menschen.

Die emanzipatorische Rolle der Naturwissenschaft ist vielseitig und zusammengesetzt, ihr Inhalt verändert sich geschichtlich. Geschichtlich, aber auch prinzipiell muss vor allem über
die kulturelle Rolle gesprochen werden, die die Naturwissenschaft
bei der Zurückdrängung der äusseren natürlichen Grenzen des
menschlichen Daseins und Tätigkeit spielt. Hier knüpft sich die
emanzipatorische Rolle der Naturwissenschaft an die Produktions-
praxis und als Produktionskraft dient sie dem Aufstieg des Menschen. Die Resultate der wissenschaftlich-technischen Revolution
unserer Epoche zeigen die Entfaltung dieser Rolle auf einem hohen
Niveau. Die gesellschaftlichen Bedingungen der allseitigen und
harmonischen Entfaltung dieser Funktion kann nur die weitere
Entwicklung des Sozialismus verwirklichen, im Laufe deren die
Wesenseinheit des Menschen und der Natur verwirklicht wird. Die
emanzipatorische Rolle der naturwissenschaftlichen Kultur kommt
weiterhin bei dem Bewusstwerden der substantiellen Kräfte des
Menschen zur Geltung. Das trug und trägt der geistigen Befreiung
des Menschen von der Macht der Religion bei. Damit sind wir aber
schon bei einer weiteren grundlegenden kulturellen Funktion der
Naturwissenschaft - bei ihrer Erziehungsrolle angekommen.

Hier gibt es keine Möglichkeit für die vielseitige Analyse der kulturellen-erzieherischen Rolle der Naturwissenschaft, wir können z.B. ihre Persönlichkeit formenden Aspekte nicht erörtern. In gesamtgesellschaftlicher Beziehung entfaltet es sich in vollem Masse bei der Bewusstmachung der Stelle der Menschheit in dem Weltall, in dem naturwissenschaftlichen Weltbild.

Die naturwissenschaftliche Kultur drückt zur selben Zeit auch den Grad des Bewusstwerden der naturwissenschaftlichen Entwicklung, die innere Wertordnung der Naturwissenschaft aus. Mit einem Wort kommt die naturwissenschaftliche Kultur in der gegebenen Weise der Kultivierung der Naturwissenschaft zum Ausdruck. All das steht mit den allgemeinen weltanschaulichen Grundlagen der naturwissenschaftlichen Forschung in einem untrennbaren Zusammenhang. Die Gestaltung der Wissenschaft der Wissenschaften im 20. Jahrhundert, die in den Vordergrund tretenden wissenschaftlichen Forschungen haben der Entwicklung der inneren Kultur der Wissenschaft, der wissenschaftlichen Forschung im grossen Masse beigetragen, sie haben einer neuen Etappe dieser Entwicklung den Anstoss gegeben. Die Deutung der Wissenschaft, der Naturwissenschaft als einer komplexen gesellschaftlichen Erscheinung, ihre Betrachtung als ein geschichtlicher Prozess haben so einen Selbstreflexionsprozess in Gang gesetzt, der zur selben Zeit ganz neue Möglichkeiten für die Entfaltung der kulturellen Funktion der Naturwissenschaft auf einer höheren Ebene, für die gesamtgesellschaftlich bewusste, organisierte und planmässige Verwirklichung dieser Funktionen schaffen.

Die bisher Gesagten zusammenfassend können wir sagen, dass die Kulturwerte und Kulturfunktionen der Naturwissenschaft drei Knotenpunkte haben:

a/ Die Naturwissenschaft als die Erkenntnis der Natur gibt ein wahres Wissen und auf dieser Grundlage erfüllt sie eine erzieherische Funktion;

b/ Als eine geistige Produktionskraft spielt sie eine emanzipatorische Rolle, trägt der Verwirklichung der tatsächlichen Einheit zwischen der Natur und des Menschen, der bewussten und planmässigen Lenkung der Natur- und gesellschaftlichen Prozesse, der allseitigen Entwicklung der substantiellen Kräfte der Menschen bei;

c/ Die Naturwissenschaft funktioniert infolge ihrer theoretischen und methodischen Synthesen, ihrer Weltbildschaffung als
ein die Weltanschauung fundierender, die weltanschauliche Richtung
beeinflussender Faktor.

Die geschilderten Funktionen der Naturwissenschaft verkörpern
die naturwissenschaftliche Kultur nur im Falle ihrer Einheit.

Die bürgerliche Ideologie trennt diese voneinander untrennbaren Seiten der naturwissenschaftlichen Kultur, besonders in
der Etappe ihrer retrograden, rückgängigen Veränderung, voneinander, sie bricht die Einheit der naturwissenschaftlichen Kultur, sie verdreht ihren Wesensinhalt /13/.

Zu Grunde der immer erfolgreicheren Entfaltung der Einheit
der naturwissenschaftlichen Kultur liegen die Praxis des Sozialismus und die Theorie der marxistischen Philosophie.

Die Philosophie des Marxismus - im Besitz der materialistischen Auffassung der Gesellschaft, sowie mit der Anwendung der
bewussten dialektischen Denkart - legt nicht nur die Grundlagen
für die naturwissenschaftliche Kultur, sondern sie entwickelt
sie auch erfolgreich /14/.

ANMERKUNGEN

/1/ Mihail Lifschiz: Ausgewählte ästhetische Schriften /Váloga-
tott esztétikai irások/. Budapest, 1973. p. 574.

/2/ C. P. Snow: Public Affairs. London, 1971. - The Two Cultures
and the Scientific Revolution. The Two Cultures and a Second
Look. Wissenschaft und Kunst /Tudomány és müvészet/ von
György Kulin, György Marx, Alfréd Rényi, Oszkár Szimán. In:
Valóság H. 3 /1963/. Mihály Sükösd: Nachwort zu einer Studie
/zur Studie von Snow/ /Utószó egy tanulmányhoz /Snow tanul-
mányához/ . Kortárs H. 1 /1964/.

/3/ György Lukács weist auf die Wichtigkeit dieser von Lenin so
konsequent durchgeführten Annäherungsweise hin. Die Methode
des historischen Materialismus für die Fragen der Kultur und
seine konkreten Antworten auf die konkreten Probleme der Geschichte. György Lukács: Lenin und die Fragen der Kultur
/Lenin és a kultura kérdései/. "Sozialistische Volksbildung".
Textsammlung. Budapest, 1980. pp. 328-329.

/4/ István Hermann: Die Probleme der heutigen Kultur /A mai kultura problémái/. Budapest, 1974. p. 6.

/5/ A. Rey: La théorie de la physique chez les physiciens con-
temporains /Die physikalische Theorie bei den Physikern der
Gegenwart/. Paris, 1907. V., p. 19.

154

/6/ Miklós Óvári: <u>Drei Jahrzehnte unserer Kulturrevolution</u> /Kulturális forradalmunk három évtizede/. "Sozialistische Volksbildung". Textsammlung. Budapest, 1980. p. 354.

/7/ M. Gorki: <u>Die wirkliche Kultur</u> /Az igazi kultura/. Budapest, 1950. p. 260.

/8/ Béla Köpeczi gibt über die Ergebnisse eine sich auf konkrete Angaben stützende, umfassende theoretische Analyse. Siehe: Béla Köpeczi: <u>30 Jahre der ungarischen Kultur /1945-1975/</u> /A magyar kultura harminc éve /1945-1975/ /. Budapest, 1977.

/9/ <u>Die Richtlinien der Bildungspolitik der USAP /25.Juli 1958/</u>. Beschlüsse und Dokumente der Ungarischen Sozialistischen Arbeiterpartei, 1956-1962 /Az MSZMP müvelődési politikájának irányelvei /1958. julius 25./. A Magyar Szocialista Munkáspárt határozatai és dokumentumai. 1956-1962/. Budapest, 1964. pp. 231-260.

/10/ Im Jahre 1969 fassen diese Aufgaben die wissenschaftspolitischen Richtlinien der Partei zusammen. Siehe: <u>Die wissenschaftspolitischen Richtlinien des Zentralkomitees der USAP /27. Juni 1969/</u>. Beschlüsse und Dokumente der Ungarischen Sozialistischen Arbeiterpartei. 1967-1970 /Az MSZMP Központi Bizottságának tudománypolitikai irányelvei /1969. junius 27./. A Magyar Szocialista Munkáspárt határozatai és dokumentumai. 1967-1970/. Budapest, 1974. pp. 335-367.

/11/ K. Marx: <u>Ökonomisch-Philosophische Manuskripte aus dem Jahre 1844</u>. Marx Engels Werke, Ergänzungsband I.T. Berlin, 1968. p. 544.

/12/ <u>Die Programmerklärung der USAP /21 März 1975/</u>. Beschlüsse und Dokumente der Ungarischen Sozialistischen Arbeiterpartei. 1971-1975 /Az MSZMP programmnyilatkozata /1975. március 21./. A Magyar Szocialista Munkáspárt határozatai és dokumentumai. 1971-1975/. Budapest, 1979. pp. 967-970.

/13/ Diesbezüglich weist auf zahlreiche Relationen László Mátrai in seinen Arbeiten: <u>Philosophie und Fachwissenschaften</u> /Filozófia és szaktudományok/; <u>Zivilisation und Kultur</u> /Civilizáció és kultura/; <u>Praxis, Kenntnis, Wissenschaft</u> /Gyakorlat, tudás, tudomány/ hin. Siehe: László Mátrai: <u>Die Geschichtlichkeit der Kultur</u> /A kultura történetisége/. Budapest, 1977.

/14/ Wir bringen dafür zwei Beispiele an. Erfolgreich erörtert József Szigeti, im Gegensatz zu der auf Grund des Positivismus verbreiteten Auffassung, die wesentlichen Kriterien der Wissenschaftlichkeit auf der Basis des dialektischen und historischen Materialismus. Siehe: József Szigeti: <u>Die Philosophie und die Natur der fachwissenschaftlichen Erkenntnis - die wesentlichen Kriterien der Wissenschaftlichkeit</u> /A filozófia és a szaktudományos megismerés természete - a tudományosság lényegi kritériumai/. "Philosophie und Fachwissenschaften". Budapest, 1981. Physiker Imre Fényes erklärt, indem er die Grenzen der Anwendbarkeit der formalen Logik sowie der axiomatischen Methode umreisst, die Bedeutung und Rolle der Dialektik, der dialektischen Logik in der Geschichte der Physik und in der Physik des 20. Jahrhunderts. Siehe: Imre Fényes: <u>Der Ursprung der Physik</u> /A fizika eredete/. Budapest, 1980.

Philosophy and Culture
J. Lukács and F. Tőkei eds.

LOISIRS ET CULTURE EN HONGRIE

Gy. FUKÁSZ

Partout dans le monde, l'élaboration d'une politique des loisirs pose des problèmes. C'est ce qu'a souligné Joffre Dumazedier dans son exposé sur la nécessité et les caractéristiques fondamentales de la politique des loisirs, lors du premier congrès international des loisirs, qui s'est tenu à Bruxelles en avril 1973 /1/. De même, l'importance grandissante que prennent les loisirs dans la vie des Hongrois fait apparaître la nécessité,dans ce pays aussi, de mettre au point et d'appliquer une politique concertée des loisirs.

L'augmentation des loisirs est un élément qui doit particulièrement être pris en considération lors de l'élaboration de la politique culturelle, étant donné que la structure des loisirs détermine sous bien des rapports la formation culturelle d'importantes couches sociales, même si la culture trouve également un terrain vital dans le travail et la vie professionnelle /2/. La compréhension de ce dernier point est d'ailleurs à l'origine de la place croissante que tient dans la planification culturelle l'analyse des aspects culturels de la vie professionnelle.

L'importance attribuée aux rapports entre culture et loisirs est attestée par le grand nombre de documents relatifs à la politique de formation culturelle publiée ces derniers temps, dont un plan culturel à long terme portant sur quinze ans, élaboré par le groupe de travail de planification culturelle de la Commission à la Main-d'oeuvre et au Niveau de vie /3/.

En Hongrie, l'analyse des rapports entre loisirs et culture est devenue,au cours de ces dernieres années, de plus en plus urgent, notamment parce qu'on a réduit en 1969 le travail hebdo-

157

madaire à 44 heures, et introduit à partir de 1982 la semaine
de 5 jours, qui représente actuellement 42 heures. Cette réduction générale des heures de travail constitue déjà en soi un motif suffisant pour que la planification culturelle s'attache en
premier lieu à la structuration des activités de fin de semaine
et aux changements qui accompagnent l'amélioration du mode de
vie. La réduction de la durée du travail a ouvert des possibilités réelles permettant à la population de consacrer ces loisirs
supplémentaires à la culture. Bien entendu, le temps libre ne
suffit pas en soi. Il s'agit également de mettre en place des
formes modernes, des bases matérielles et des techniques nouvelles pour la culture, et d'assurer aux travailleurs des revenus qui leur permettent d'avoir accès à toutes les réalisations
culturelles. Il est néanmoins indiscutable que la culture demande beaucoup de temps. Si les loisirs sont insuffisants, toutes
les voies qui mènent à la culture se trouvent automatiquement
fermées. Avoir du temps à sa disposition est une condition sine
qua non pour se cultiver, et c'est seulement ensuite qu'entrent
en scène toutes les autres conditions qui, ensemble, permettent
à l'individu d'employer son temps libre de façon intelligente et
féconde. Mais même cela ne suffit pas: il faut que les gens comprennent la valeur des possibilités qui s'offrent à eux pour l'u-
tilisation de leurs loisirs, et qu'ils s'efforcent, en connaissance de cause, de les employer raisonnablement. C'est seulement
ainsi que le temps libre assuré par la réduction de la durée du
travail a valeur de loisirs. En effet, si ces conditions ne sont
pas réunies, ce temps peut très facilement se transformer en temps
perdu et mériter le nom de temps gaspillé plutôt que celui de loisirs.

Il faut également tenir compte, lors de l'utilisation du temps
libre à des fins culturelles, de différents facteurs propres à
la société socialiste. Tout d'abord, la révolution socialiste et
la révolution culturelle léninienne ont mis fin au monopole culturel des anciennes classes dirigeantes et ont permis de faire accéder les masses aux valeurs de la culture. Ces principes ont trouvé
une base solide dans le système scolaire socialiste, qui apprend
aux jeunes, dès leur plus jeune âge, à utiliser leur temps libre
de manière fructueuse. Enfin, la création d'une culture socialiste

s'appuyant sur les traditions progressistes de la culture internationale a ouvert de nouvelles perspectives à une utilisation culturelle des loisirs. Naturellement, l'emploi des loisirs se situe dans le contexte de processus sociaux complexes, dont la réduction du temps de travail n'est qu'un des éléments. Les possibilités créées par le développement socialiste - par l'utilisation socialiste de la technique par exemple - jouent un rôle fondamental dans l'évolution de la structure des loisirs et suscitent des exigences culturelles nouvelles, tout en assurant le développement de la culture.

Grâce aux efforts considérables entrepris dans ce domaine par la société socialiste, la Hongrie est actuellement pourvue d'un réseau culturel offrant un vaste choix à ceux qui désirent se cultiver. Sous ce rapport, les institutions culturelles /centres et maisons de la culture, etc./ revêtent une importance particulière.

Les statistiques permettent de se faire une idée du développement multiforme des réalisations culturelles. C'est ainsi que l'on dénombre dans le pays plus de 3 800 bibliothèques publiques /ce nombre ne comprend pas les bibliothèques spécialisées, celles des écoles, etc./, qui comptent en tout 2 200 000 abonnés, soit 22% de la population. Les musées reçoivent chaque année 7 millions de visiteurs environ, soit 71% de la population. Le nombre des entrées dans les centres culturels est de 50 millions par an, ce qui montre à quel point les gens ont soif de culture, lorsqu'on sait que la Hongrie compte 10 millions d'habitants. Les chiffres suivants donnent également un aperçu de l'importance des réalisations culturelles: on compte annuellement 80 millions de spectateurs dans les cinémas, 5,5 millions dans les théâtres, et 800 000 dans les salles de concert. Mais il ne s'agit là que d'indices quantitatifs. Il est un point plus important encore: ces possibilités culturelles sont accessibles à toutes les bourses. L'Etat socialiste, contrairement à ce qui se passe aux Etats-Unis, par exemple, où l'industrie des loisirs réalise des profits énormes /4/, ne permet pas de transformer en entreprise lucrative les services culturels présidant aux loisirs des travailleurs. Il n'existe pas d'industrie des loisirs et du divertissement déterminant la structure des activités de loisirs d'in-

dividus manipulés, où seuls ceux qui ont de l'argent peuvent
avoir accès aux véritables valeurs culturelles. Grâce au développement socialiste, cet accès à la culture en Hongrie ne se
heurte plus, pour les masses, à des obstacles d'ordre financier.
Cette tendance générale a encore une autre composante, à savoir
la mise en relief des valeurs et des qualités dans la culture
socialiste: si les chiffres sont élevés, la qualité des possibilités culturelles offertes à la population a une importance
plus grande encore. Les bibliothèques, les théâtres, les cinémas, l'ensemble du réseau des mass media fournissent des possibilités d'un niveau élevé.

C'est l'ensemble des valeurs socialistes /avec les 2,5 millions d'abonnés à la télévision et à la radio, chacun ou presque, peut suivre les programmes radio-télévisés/ qui a créé en
Hongrie les conditions permettant d'utiliser dans un sens positif le temps gagné grâce à la réduction des horaires de travail.
Répétons-le: ce gain de temps ne suffit pas en soi, c'est seulement en le combinant avec un système complexe de conditions que
l'on peut en créer la base d'une utilisation intelligente des
loisirs. Ce n'est qu'ainsi que la réduction des horaires de travail ouvre la voie à des activités de loisirs ayant une valeur
culturelle. C'est l'ensemble des processus sociaux qui doit être
examiné à cet égard, y compris la motorisation en plein essor,
les effets de l'urbanisation et la progression de l'industriali-
sation. Dans le développement propre à la Hongrie, tous ces éléments ont une incidence sur l'évolution des loisirs et le développement de la culture, et modifient la structure des différentes activités.

On s'aperçoit aisément, en analysant les tendances et les
données dont nous faisons état ici, du danger qu'il y aurait à
interpréter d'une manière simplifiée les rapports entre loisirs
et culture. Juger en elles-mêmes les activités de loisirs, et
notamment les activités culturelles mènerait à une impasse, du
fait qu'on les isolerait du système des rapports sociaux qui
influencent la culture. La réduction du temps de travail intervenue en Hongrie, de même que l'élargissement des activités de
loisirs qu'elle a entraînée, prouvent de manière convaincante
que les efforts conscients du système social sont d'une impor-

tance fondamentale pour la mise en valeur du contenu culturel
des loisirs. En l'absence de certaines conditions matérielles
/développement des équipements culturels, des transports en commun, etc./ et d'une politique concertée des loisirs, la réduction de la durée du travail ne conduirait pas à un développement
des habitudes de loisirs, et encore moins automatiquement à un
essor culturel.

Le rapport loisirs-culture est un rapport indirect. Il passe
par une série d'intermédiaires parmi lesquels la conscience des
loisirs, le respect, la valeur du temps libre sont ceux qui
poussent à les bien utiliser. En cela, la couche le plus indis-
cutablement caractéristique est constituée par la culture absor-
bée pendant le temps libre, qui fait d'ailleurs l'objet d'une
grande attention, comme le montrent les sondages pratiqués en
Hongrie.

Une étude de 1974 faisant la synthèse des différents sondages
effectués par l'Institut des Mass media de la Radiodiffusion et
Télévision Hongroises nous apprend /5/ que le type d'activités
liées aux mass media le plus répandu parmi les Hongrois est
l'écoute de la radio et la vue de la télévision /les personnes
interrogées ayant désigné à 92% la première et 88% la seconde
comme activité la plus fréquente/. 48% de la population déclare
lire fréquemment des ouvrages littéraires, et 34% aller souvent
au cinéma. La régularité avec laquelle les personnes interrogées
se consacrent à ces activités est également très importante,
puisqu'elle va de 70 à 80% /6/. Ces chiffres indiquent que certains types d'activités culturelles bien définies sont passés
au premier plan. Les mass media jouent un rôle de plus en plus
notable dans la formation culturelle. Dans le même temps, on
assiste à un développement plus lent, et même à un net recul
de certaines formes traditionnelles de culture /c'est la fré-
quentation des cinémas qui en souffre le plus, comme d'ailleurs
dans le monde entier/.

Lors de la spécification des activités culturelles exercées
dans le cadre des loisirs au-delà des formes traditionnelles de
la culture, il faut également prendre en considération toutes
les formes liées aux mass media. L'interprétation moderne de
la formation culturelle met l'accent sur l'intégration de ces

moyens /la mise au point des émissions télévisées, les débats
sur la production de la télévision dans des clubs, à l'école,
etc., contribuent à en augmenter l'effet et la valeur profes-
sionnelle/.

Partout dans le monde, les téléspectateurs passent un nombre
considérable d'heures devant le petit écran. En Hongrie également, la télévision occupe une fraction importante des loisirs
de la population, et tous les sondages montrent qu'elle est le
passe-temps le plus favorisé. C'est ce qui ressort des analyses
au sujet de l'introduction des samedis libres dans les grandes
entreprises comme c'était déja l'usage au cas des travailleurs
de la métallurgie /7/. Dans une entreprise métallurgique géante
installée dans la banlieue de Budapest, 81% des ouvriers considèrent la télévision comme un passe-temps fréquent, et près
de 55% citent l'audition de la radio comme activité fréquente.
La télévision et la radio mobilisent les gens dans une mesure
très importante, même si les statistiques ne révèlent pas des
proportions aussi effarantes que, par exemple, aux Etats-Unis
où, selon un sondage de la CBS datant de 1973, l'Américain moyen
passe 22 heures par semaine devant son téléviseur. Et il ne s'a-
git encore là que de l'aspect quantitatif du problème. Il serait
intéressant d'enquêter également sur le contenu du temps ainsi
passé et sur la qualité des programmes absorbés par les téléspectateurs.

La télévision est un véritable tyran, qui agit à la façon
d'un aimant sur les individus disposant d'un peu de temps libre,
et c'est bien pour cela qu'il faut attacher une grande importance à la fonction culturelle de la télévision lors de l'élaboration des programmes télévisés. Les programmes artistiques
et littéraires, les films, les feuilletons de la télévision
éveillent l'intérêt des masses pour la culture. C'est ainsi que
l'on peut considérer comme un succès non négligeable pour la
politique culturelle de la télévision hongroise le fait qu'un
nombre extraordinaire de téléspectateurs ont acheté l'Odyssée
d'Homère à la suite d'un feuilleton diffusé sur le petit écran.
Le public aime également beaucoup les émissions musicales de
vulgarisation artistique de Leonard Bernstein. Il n'en demeure
pas moins vrai que la "consommation" inconsidérée d'émissions

télévisées et, en général, l'"art en conserve" font préjudices
à l'assimilation active de l'art et provoquent - ou renforcent
- une attitude passive de réception. Mais une conception culturelle socialiste peut fort bien se baser sur le rôle dominant
de la télévision dans les loisirs pour s'en servir comme d'un
instrument de la diffusion culturelle parmi les masses, en met-
tant au point des programmes bien choisis et en les adaptant
aux formes culturelles traditionnelles.

Compte tenu de l'évolution des cadres du temps libre, il faut
considérer la réduction des heures de travail, qui se traduit
dans l'institution des samedis libres, comme une condition essentielle au développement des activités de loisirs. Les études
effectuées avant le régime des samedis libres montrent que l'on
peut fixer en moyenne à trois heures par jour les loisirs des
travailleurs hongrois. Les travailleurs non actifs jouissent de
3,5 heures libres quotidiennement, les travailleurs intellectuels et assimilés de 3,3 heures, et les travailleurs manuels de
2,7 heures par jour. Mais la situation est autre dès que l'on
procède à des statistiques groupées par sexes. En effet, les
femmes n'ont pratiquement pas de loisirs, puisqu'elles consacrent
la majeure partie de leur temps "libre" au ménage et à l'entre-
tien de la famille, et que leurs activités exigent beaucoup de
temps. Depuis l'introduction des samedis libres, la situation
s'est quelque peu améliorée, mais l'image d'ensemble n'a pas
changé fondamentalement.

Toujours en tenant compte de l'évolution des cadres des loisirs, il est intéressant de se pencher sur la proportion grandissante du temps consacré à la culture. Comment les gens réagis-
sent-ils à ces possibilités accrues? Les enquêtes sociologiques
effectuées au cours des dernières années nous ont mis en garde
contre les déductions hâtives et les attentes exagérées: il serait illusoire de croire que la réduction des heures de travail
suffit à entraîner aussitôt une recrudescence de l'activité culturelle. Mais des tendances très nettes sont perceptibles.

Dans la situation actuelle, selon certaines enquêtes /8/, on
peut évaluer à 30% environ ceux qui se cultivent "activement".
Ce groupe de gens a connu une croissance brusque dans les premiers temps du développement socialiste - exprimant ainsi la soif

de culture des masses -, pour progresser plus lentement depuis
quelques années. On observe bien entendu des écarts importants
dans l'utilisation culturelle des loisirs. De nombreux facteurs
entrent en jeu: âge, formation, conditions financières, situation familiale, etc. Les chiffres montrent aussi que la majeure
partie de ceux qui manifestent la volonté de se cultiver se trouve
parmi les jeunes, et principalement parmi les moins de tente ans
/23%/ /9/. Cette proportion n'est que de 10% chez les paysans,
mais elle est de 30% chez les O.S. issus de familles ouvrières.
Le rôle du niveau scolaire est particulièrement important: l'intention de se cultiver activement est particulièrement vive chez
les ouvriers et les O.S. ayant passé le baccalauréat. Les sondages mettent également en lumière l'importance, outre celle du
facteur temps, des attitudes psychiques, montrant ainsi combien
l'activité culturelle est loin d'être uniquement fonction du
temps libre. Le potentiel créatif existant dans les masses est
particulièrement important et propre à stimuler les besoins culturels. Cette créativité est déjà développée chez les écoliers
par toute la structure de l'enseignement, dès l'école maternelle,
et à tous les échelons de la scolarité. La formation des adultes
contribue également au renforcement de la créativité. Le lieu de
travail et l'entourage peuvent jouer également un rôle capital
dans le progrès de l'activité culturelle.

On est donc en droit de conclure qu'il serait illusoire de
considérer automatiquement la réduction du temps de travail comme
un gain de temps libre "culturel". Il ne fait pas de doute qu'une
place fondamentale revient dans toute typologie des activités de
loisirs aux activités culturelles, mais celles-ci ne les constituent pas exclusivement, et nombreuses sont les activités qui
peuvent être considérées comme des passe-temps. /L'esquisse ty-
pologique de 'The Use of Time' énumère 21 groupes d'activités,
notamment le ménage, les soins aux enfants, leur éducation, les
achats, les besoins personnels - repas, sommeil, repos, prépara-
tion professionnelle, distractions, activités sociales, loisirs
actifs, loisirs passifs, télévision, lecture, voyage... Et encore, les auteurs, Katja Boh et Stane Saksida n'ont-ils pas centré leur énumération sur les activités culturelles./ /10/ Dans
cet ordre d'idées, les rapports qui existent entre le temps libre

164

et la culture s'expriment avant tout, conformément à la pratique de la société hongroise, dans la constatation suivante: le temps libre donne un cadre à la formation culturelle, et l'une des activités de loisirs les plus caractéristiques est constituée précisément par les activités culturelles. L'exploitation des rapports existant entre culture et loisirs constitue dans la société hongroise un élément important de développement du mode de vie moderne, socialiste, et de la mise en lumière des qualités socialistes de la vie.

C'est là une tendance fondamentale. Mais il ne faut pas négliger le fait que l'épanouissement de cette tendance est entravé par de nombreuses tendances contraires qui mettent au premier plan d'autres valeurs dans l'utilisation des loisirs. Parmi ces tendances figurent les conceptions qui donnent la priorité aux rapports matériels, et surtout à la consommation et à l'acquisition des biens matériels comme buts en soi. Ces conceptions peuvent avoir une influence néfaste et déformante sur les qualités et les valeurs socialistes de la vie, en contrariant l'utilisation intelligente et fructueuse des loisirs qui permettent à la personnalité et à l'homme socialiste d'atteindre à un développement multilatéral. C'est précisément pour cette raison que la politique des loisirs doit tenir pour un objectif de première importance la création des conditions objectives permettant d'utiliser intelligemment les loisirs, ainsi que "l'éducation aux loisirs". Il s'agit de mettre les valeurs culturelles à la portée des masses, même si ces dernières n'ont actuellement pas encore suffisamment recours aux possibilités qui leur sont offertes. La politique des loisirs n'a donc pas seulement pour tâche de satisfaire les exigences culturelles existant d'ores et déjà: elle doit en même temps - et c'est peut-être là une tâche encore plus importante - développer ces besoins et éveiller dans les individus des besoins culturels élevés, répondant aux qualités de la vie socialiste. Dans le système culturel socialiste, le développement homogène et concerté de la culture des masses représente le grand avantage de notre développement socialiste. Il n'a pas les mains liées par les limites imposées par le système capitaliste, où la structure unifiée de la formation culturelle fait défaut et la concurrence et les points de vue commerciaux passent avant tout.

Cette différence, cette contradiction fait que, si le progrès socialiste permet de faire une large place aux activités culturelles dans les loisirs, la réduction du temps de travail dans les pays capitalistes entraîne beaucoup moins l'accroissement de la culture des masses car les gens, loin de multiplier leurs activités de loisirs, y semblent au contraire ne pas savoir quoi faire de leur temps. En outre, ils sont fondamentalement conditionnés par l'acquisition des biens et des moyens financiers, et l'on voit souvent que les faits justifient la formule de Harvey Swados: "moins d'heures de travail - moins de temps libre" /11/.

C'est ainsi que l'on constate des différences considérables entre le monde capitaliste et le monde socialiste dans le domaine du livre et des besoins qui s'y manifestent. Il est notoire que dans les pays socialistes les livres jouissent d'un véritable culte. L'édition y produit en grandes quantités des livres de valeur qui sont à la portée de tous et de toutes les bourses, tandis que dans les pays capitalistes, les livres sont chers et presque inaccessibles pour les masses. C'est ce qui explique en partie le fait qu'il n'est pas rare de trouver chez un ouvrier hongrois une bibliothèque de plusieurs centaines de volumes - phénomène pratiquement inconnu dans les pays capitalistes les plus riches même. Les habitudes de lecture se forment dès la première jeunesse, et l'on a constaté, en effectuant des sondages sur les samedis libres, que les ouvriers adultes considéraient la lecture comme une activité régulière, après la télévision, la radio, la lecture des journaux et le jardinage, dans une proportion relativement élevée, soit 47,6% de l'échantillon /12/. Cela aussi montre que la crise prédite par Mac Luhan, la "fin de la galaxie Gutenberg" /13/, c'est-à-dire la disparition du goût pour les livres avec l'extension des "canaux magiques" /les moyens de télécommunication, les mass media/, est enrayée par le penchant pour la culture et par les exigences culturelles de l'homme. Dans la Hongrie d'aujourd'hui, l'ouvrier qui dispose d'une bonne formation générale et se cultive, s'efforce d'élargir ses connaissances en fonction des besoins de la vie et s'intéresse à bon nombre de choses, tels les grands problèmes du monde environnant et l'univers plus restreint de son

entourage, de son lieu de travail, constitue à cet égard un personnage type.

Ainsi, la culture joue dans l'utilisation féconde du temps
libre un rôle irremplacable et fondamental. Bien que nous ayons
repoussé l'identification automatique des loisirs à la culture,
il n'en apparaît pas moins entre loisirs et culture des rapports
directs, et derrière ceux-ci des rapports indirects. Les loisirs,
en tant qu'éléments de l'emploi du temps, font partie intégrante
du système des conditions qui président à la culture. Dans le
même temps, la création et l'utilisation intelligente du temps
libre interviennent également dans le processus culturel. Il ne
faut pas négliger l'importance des influences culturelles exercées sur les habitudes de loisirs. Le développement culturel de
l'individu objectivé dans la culture stimule le désir d'acquérir
un niveau culturel encore plus élevé. La proportion du temps consacré à la culture est plus importante chez ceux qui ont déjà
atteint un niveau culturel assez important, et qui ont reçu une
formation scolaire ou autre plus poussée. Dans ce sens, le niveau de culture acquis a une influence directe sur la transformation du temps libre en loisirs au plein sens du terme, et sur
son utilisation intelligente. Un certain degré de culture assure
de meilleures possibilités à son développement ultérieur, la
"vitesse d'absorbtion" est plus importante chez les individus
déjà cultivés, leurs affinités avec les activités culturelles
sont plus nettes.

Le rôle de la culture de base dans l'utilisation intelligente
du temps libre apparaît à deux niveaux: d'une part comme degré
d'exigence intellectuelle, et d'autre part comme réceptivité.
Pour reprendre un lieu commun, on sait que les gens cultivés
sont plus exigeants en général dans tous les domaines de la vie
et sur le plan culturel en particulier. La présence d'une culture de base a une incidence sur toutes les catégories d'activités de loisirs, et est à l'origine de la recherche de formes
plus élevées de repos, de détente, de distractions. Elle entraîne
généralement des habitudes de loisirs plus raffinées. Il est in-
dubitable que l'exigence intellectuelle ne va pas automatiquement de pair avec un plus haut degré de culture, et que celui-ci
n'entraîne pas toujours des activités culturelles d'un niveau

élevé. Il n'est par exemple pas rare que des intellectuels se détendent précisément en changeant totalement d'occupation, par exemple en pêchant à la ligne, en lisant des romans policiers ou en jouant aux cartes.

En analysant les rapports entre loisirs et culture, nous devons également considérer les relations existant entre la culture et le travail. Contrairement à ce que certains affirment à tort, notamment que la culture serait identifiable aux activités de loisirs et serait donc par son essence exclue du domaine des activités professionnelles, donc qu'il existe un rapport binaire entre les loisirs et le travail, les premiers constituant une compensation au second, ce sont précisément les cadres fournis par le travail qui fournissent une bonne base pour le développement culturel en reliant les phases convergentes de la culture dans les loisirs et de la culture dans le travail. Il arrive fréquemment que l'on nie purement et simplement le rôle culturel du travail pratiquant une approche à courte vue, comme si la culture était pour l'individu une affaire privée, indépendante de son travail et appartenant strictement au domaine des loisirs. Partant de ce principe, certains mettent en doute également le prestige social de la culture et refusent de reconnaître sa valeur sociale et son importance du point de vue des bases de la production et des forces productrices. C'est pourtant justement dans l'élévation du niveau du travail et dans l'activité de l'homme en tant que force de production, qu'apparaît l'importance énorme de la culture, du savoir. Ce phénomène est encore accentué par la révolution scientifique et technique à laquelle nous assistons, par ses conséquences, par les exigences accrues manifestées à l'égard de la culture et du savoir, par le renouvellement et le dépassement constant des sciences, par l'apparition permanente de nouvelles connaissances, et par l'abandon d'une partie des connaissances anciennes au fur et à mesure qu'il en apparaît de nouvelles.

Outre le rôle grandissant des activités culturelles qui se développent dans le cadre des activités de loisirs, on voit croître également, dans la Hongrie d'aujourd'hui, l'importance de la culture liée au travail. C'est par exemple ce qui ressort de la décision du Conseil des Ministres sur la nécessité pour les entreprises de pourvoir à la formation continue des ouvriers. En dehors de son importance de principe, cette décision a également des incidences pratiques: la culture liée au travail, la formation continue, et même tout simplement l'extension de la culture générale, impliquent aussi des réductions du temps de travail dans la mesure où ces activités culturelles sont poursuivies dans les cadres des horaires de travail.

Les rapports culture-travail viennent compléter les rapports loisirs-culture, sans réduire pour autant la valeur culturelle des loisirs, pas plus que ne la réduit le fait que nous considérons l'homme aussi du point de vue de la production, comme étant la "force productrice". Il ne s'agit pourtant là, comme chacun sait, que de l'un des aspects de l'existence humaine, de la totalité humaine. La place, le rôle de l'homme dans la société sont loin de se borner à sa formation comme force de production. Il faut considérer la formation culturelle de l'homme /et cela tout autant dans le travail que dans les loisirs/ comme en premier lieu un élément servant le développement multiforme de la personnalité socialiste; c'est là qu'il faut mettre le point de départ et tenir compte ensuite de la totalité humaine afin de mettre en lumière les besoins culturels des loisirs. Il faut partir de là aussi pour pouvoir apprendre aux gens l'importance et l'usage à avoir des loisirs intelligents. Et il faut rechercher les rapports existant entre les loisirs et la culture - comme on l'a fait lors des conférences "Culture et Loisirs" tenues à Budapest sous l'égide de la Société Hongroise de Vulgarisation Scientifique /TIT/, et de l'UNESCO en 1971, 1974, 1977, 1980 - et s'efforcer de mettre en place toutes les conditions objectives et matérielles nécessaires à une utilisation culturelle du temps libre /14/.

BIBLIOGRAPHIE

Annotated Bibliography on Leisure. Hungary, 1960-1969. Bibliographic Series 1. Prague, 1970. ECLE. 43 p. Compiled by S. Heleszta.

The Use of Time. Daily Activities of Urban and Suburban Populations in Twelve Countries. Edited by A. Szalai. Mouton, The Hague and Paris, 1972, p. 868.

Comptes rendus de la conférence "Culture et Loisirs", tenue a
    Budapest les 15, 16 et 17 avril 1971, p. 25.
Szabad idő és müvelődés /Loisirs et culture/. Budapest, 1972.
    Publié par la TIT, p. 520. - A nap 24 órája /Les 24 heures
    de la journée/, pub. par le KSH /Off. Central des Statis-
    tiques/. Budapest, 1965.
Miklós Szántó: Életmód, müvelődés, szabad idő /Mode de vie, cul-
    ture et loisirs/. Budapest, 1967. Akadémiai, p. 169.
György Fukász: Munka, technika, kultura /Travail, technique, cul-
    ture/. Budapest, 1972, pp. 393-448.
A szabad idő felhasználásának rétegek szerinti vizsgálata, külö-
    nös tekintettel a müvelődésre és a szórakozásra /Sondage sur
    l'utilisation des loisirs selon les couches sociales, portant
    plus spécialement sur la culture et les distractions/, réali-
    sé par Iván Vitányi. Budapest, 1974. MRT TK, p. 121.
Leisure and Education. Budapest, 1974. TIT.
A szabadidő szociológiája /Sociologie du Loisir/. Budapest, 1976.
    Gondolat.
Idő a mérlegen /Le bilan de notre emploi du temps/. Budapest,
    1979. Gondolat.

NOTES

/1/ J. Dumazedier: Criteriology for a policy of cultural leisure
     activities. International Congress: Leisure Activities in
     the Industrial Society. Brussels, 5-7 IV. 1973.
/2/ Cf.Munka és müvelődés /Travail et culture/ Budapest, 1967.
     IIe Conférence internationale sur la formation extra-scolaire
     des Adultes, Budapest, 1966. Cf. la loi V de 1976 sur la cul-
     ture populaire.
/3/ A kultura fejlesztésének távlati koncepciója - 1970-1985
     /Projet à long terme [1970-1985] du développement de la cul-
     ture/, par le groupe de travail de planification culturelle
     de la Commission à la Main-d'oeuvre et au niveau de vie.
     Budapest, juin 1972.
/4/ "L'essor sans précédent du commerce des loisirs". In: US
     News - World Review, No 16, 1972.
/5/ Sondage sur l'utilisation des loisirs selon les couches so-
     ciales, réalisé par Iván Vitányi. Budapest, 1974.
/6/ Ibid., pp. 7 et 13.
/7/ Cf. Munka, technika, kultura /Travail, technique, culture/
     par György Fukász. Budapest, 1972, pp. 418-435. Cf. A szabad-

idő szociológiája /La sociologie du Loisir/. Budapest, 1976. Gondolat. Cf. Leisure and Education, Budapest, 1974.

/8/ Sondage sur l'utilisation des loisirs selon les couches sociales, portant plus spécialement sur la culture et les distractions, réalisé par Iván Vitányi. Budapest, 1974. MRT TK, p. 77.

/9/ Ibid., pp. 79-80.

/10/ The Use of Time. Daily Activities of Urban and Suburban Populations in Twelve Countries. Edited by A. Szalai. The Hague-Paris, 1972. Katja Boh-Stane Saksida: An attempt at a typology of time use, pp. 229-247.

/11/ In: Larrabe-Meyersohn: Mass Leisure, Glencoe, 1958.

/12/ Cf. Gy. Fukász: "A szabad szombatok bevezetésének hatása a munkások hétvégi tevékenységeire" /L'incidence de l'établissement des samedis libres sur l'emploi que font les ouvriers de leur week-end/ in Szociológia, 1973/4.

/13/ Cf. Marshall Mac Luhan: Die magischen Kanäle. Düsseldorf-Wien, Econ Verlag, 1967.

/14/ Comptes rendus de la conférence "Culture et Loisirs", tenue à Budapest les 15, 16 et 17 avril 1971, p. 25.

CULTURE AND MORALITY

ÜBER DAS VAKUUM DER SITTLICHEN KULTUR:
ÜBER DIE GLEICHGÜLTIGKEIT

É. ANCSEL

Nennt man Gleichgültigkeit Vakuum, so bedeutet es nicht, dass
sie ethisch indifferent, jenseits von Gut und Böse wäre. Es geht
eher um ein Zeitsymptom, ein Übel, welches zwar alt ist, allen
Anzeichen nach aber um sich griff und welches in seiner Art das
Jahrhundert erschreckend vervollkommnete und ausserdem auch noch
mit neuen Zügen versah.

Indem der Prozess der Menschenwerdung den Menschen von der
Alleinherrschaft der biologischen Bedürfnisse befreite, zerriss
er die Hülle tierhafter "Gleichgültigkeit" und befähigte ihn,
auch unabhängig von seinen primären Bedürfnissen zu sehen, zu
denken und zu fühlen, mit einem Wort, er machte den Menschen
fähig, universal zu reagieren.

Diejenige praktische Universalität, mit der der Mensch die
ganze Natur in seinen Tätigkeitsbereich zog und sie auf diese
Art zu seinem unorganischen Körper machte, verwandelte ihn selber
in ein auf alles reagierendes Wesen.

Mit der Erwerbung von jedem neuen humanen Bedürfnis wurde der
Mensch für neue, bislang neutrale Wirkungen empfänglich. So wurde
er, wie Marx in den Ökonomisch-philosophischen Manuskripten
schrieb, zum gegenständlichen sinnlichen und infolgedessen leidenden Wesen und weil er seine Leiden empfindet, zum leidenschaftlichen Wesen.

Diese Leidenschaftlichkeit des Menschen ist ein Produkt der
Humanisierung, sie ist gleichzeitig auch Bedingung ihrer Weiterentwicklung. Allein auf dieser Grundlage kann sich die praktische, geistige und emotionelle Universalität in gleichem Masse
entfalten.

Die in ihrer Potenzen universale menschliche Empfindlichkeit schuf die Arbeit, es war jedoch gerade ihre bestimmte historische Form, die warenproduzierende Lohnarbeit, die diese Eigenschaft "zurückzog".

Marx wies nach, dass in der rationalisierten Grossindustrie die bestimmte Art der Arbeit, das, was der Arbeiter produziert, vollkommen zufällig, infolgedessen gleichgültig ist und dies degradiert den Menschen zum passiven Zuschauer seiner eigenen Tätigkeit.

In diesem Prozess wird er zur lebendigen Ingredienz von einem unübersichtlichen Mechanismus, dessen Bewegung in beiden Hauptrichtungen im voraus und ohne ihn schon vorgeschrieben ist und der auf ihn, auf seine menschliche Teilnahme keinen Anspruch erhebt.

Da er gezwungen ist, seine Tätigkeit bei Mobilisierung nur eines einzigen Segmentes seines Wesens zu verrichten, so geraten die tieferen Zonen seiner Persönlichkeit auch in die Macht der Leidenschaftslosigkeit.

Der Mensch ist ein Wesen, der Ziele setzt und Ziele verwirklicht. Falls nicht er das Ziel seiner Tätigkeit setzt und in dem Prozess der Zielsetzung nicht einmal teilnimmt, sich die Mittel der Zielverwirklichung nicht einmal im nachhinein aneignet und nicht er diese Mittel auswählt, vielmehr selber zum Instrument wird - dann wird seine Gleichgültigkeit geboren. Der Einzelne, der mit keinem Strang zur Welt gefestigt ist und dessen Wahrnehmungsfläche zusammenschrumpft, wird zuletzt bloss zum Zuschauer auch dessen, was Geschichte genannt werden kann wie er auch zum Zuschauer seines eigenen Lebens gemacht wird.

Dies bildet die Grundlage auch der Bedrohtheit von den Empfindungen, da Emotionen gerade die subjektive Relation des Menschen zur Welt, seine subjektive Antwort auf deren Angelegenheiten ausdrücken. Stellt die Wirklichkeit an ihn keine Fragen, so hört auch er auf, überhaupt zu antworten. So setzt ein erheblicher Schwund der Reagierungsfähigkeit ein.

Diejenigen Bedürfnisse werden schwach, diejenigen Leidenschaften werden ausgelöscht, die den Menschen für die Phänomene der Welt empfindlich machen oder machen könnten.

Die Empfindlichkeit des Menschen den kleinen, sowie seine
Unempfindlichkeit den grossen Dingen gegenüber - kann laut Pas-
cal als Symptom einer besonderen Verirrung angesehen werden. Woher stammt aber dieses Paradoxon?

Richten sich die Aspirationen des Menschen auf blosse Selbstreproduktion, sei es auch auf luxuriösem Niveau der Fall, bleibt
seine Empfindlichkeit limitiert. Wie für die Menschen, die von
dem ausschliesslichen Bedürfnis des Habens geleitet sind, alles
gleichgültig bleibt, was mit dem Besitzen nichts zu tun hat,
gleichgültig bleibt aber für einen Menschen diesen Schlages auch
der zu erwerbende oder erworbene Gegenstand selbst als Träger
effektiv sinnlicher Eigenschaften oder als ästhetisches Phänomen.

Das Zur-Geltung-Bringen der ihrer Vernunft losgewordenen
Vernünftigkeit bedeutet in der individuellen Lebensführung so
viel, dass der Einzelne "vernünftig" lebt, wenn er mit der geringsten Investierung emotiver Energien existiert und jede
"überflüssige", mit der Selbstreproduktion nichts zu tun habende
Wirkung aus dem Kreis seiner Empfindlichkeit aussperrt, den
Spielraum seines Lebens und die durch seine Emotionen umfasste
Welt so vollkommen wie möglich verengt. Es geht um den Abbau
der "unvernünftigen Fähigkeit des Mitleids", wie dies viele
aus Nietzsche herausinterpretierten - um den Abbau dieser Gegen-
kraft der Gleichgültigkeit.

Unter unseren Verhältnissen des zwanzigsten Jahrhunderts
führt dieser Prozess weiter als je. Dem Menschen als universa-
lem Wesen steht das Teilindividuum als blosser Träger einer
Teilfunktion entgegen, das seinerseits auch mit Anderen als
Teilindividuen in Verbindungen eingeht und dies macht unmöglich,
dass die Beziehungen die Ganzheit seines Wesens in Bewegung
setzen.

Indem man den Wurzeln des Umsichgreifens von der Gleichgültigkeit nachgeht, muss man auch einsehen, dass Leidenschaftslosigkeit nicht nur als spontane Konsequenz erscheint, sondern
auch als scheinbar "vernünftige" Verteidigungsweise vor vermeid-
barem, d.h. fremden Leid und so auch vor "überflüssiger" Belas-
tung des Verantwortungsbewusstseins. Als innerer Panzer, Ska-
fander erscheint sie, die vor Wirkungen schützt, die die fal-

sche Ruhe mit Umsturz bedrohen. Millionen von Menschen nehmen
diese "seelenkonditionierende Vorrichtung in Anspruch" gegen die
die Ruhe des Lebens attackierenden, bedrohlichen Ereignisse, denen gegenüber man sich für wehrlos hielt.

Die Gleichgültigkeit hebt in der Tat die Spannung zwischen
Mensch und Welt auf, und zwar um den Preis einer Auslöschung
von menschlichen Bedürfnissen.

Mangels humaner Leidenschaften setzt man sich in der Tat nicht
so vielen Qualen aus. Man kann dem eigentümlich faustischen Leid
aus dem Wege gehen, indem man die Qual des engen menschlichen
Daseins nicht empfindet.

Von dem Grad der Humanisation abhängig wird überhaupt eng,
was auf einer niedrigeren Stufe noch überhaupt keinen Druck ausübt, und weil Qualen nicht gleichrangig sind, verändert sich
auch ihre Rolle im Leben, weil das Niveau der Humanisierung auch
auf das Leiden des Menschen zurückgreift. Unter gewissen Umständen gilt gerade das für einen Beweis der Entfremdung, wenn man
nicht leidet, wenn Leiden notwendig wäre.

Diejenige unmenschliche und eiskalte Gleichgültigkeit ist es,
auf welche sich der Faschismus stützte und die er bis zum Äussersten vervollkommnete, indem er vorzeigte, dass Leidenschaftslosigkeit nicht einfach Synonym der Passivität ist, sondern in
gewisser gesellschaftlichen Situation geradezu zur Grundlage
aktiver Grausamkeit wird. Für den Faschismus war - unter anderen - gerade die "rationelle Leidenschaftslosigkeit", sogar
sachkundige und kalte Brutalität charakteristisch.

Die Alternative von Gleichgültigkeit und Leiden ist falsch,
auch wenn - scheinbar - allein nur zwischen diesen beiden extre-
men Verhaltensweisen gewählt werden kann. Von der Basis des ein-
samen und auf diese Art ohnmächtigen Einzelnen aus erscheinen
die Möglichkeiten in der Tat in einer Zweiheit von Gleichgültigkeit und unfruchtbarem Leid, von unfruchtbarem Mitleid und bloss
die Innenwelt des Einzelnen umstürzender Unruhe.

Nietzsche hielt Mitleid nicht nur für unfruchtbar, sondern
auch für gefährlich, weil es seiner Auffassung nach im Gegensatz zu denjenigen "tonischen Empfindungen" steht, die die Le-
bensenergie vergrössern - und folglich depressiv auswirkt.

Seine Argumentation lautet so /es sei noch darauf hingewiesen, dass hier keine umfassende Analyse der Nietzscheschen Philosophie beabsichtigt wird/: Der Mensch verliert Kraft, wenn er "mitleidet". Das Mitleid vergrössert, vervielfacht nur diejenigen Kräfteverluste, die schon das Leiden allein verursacht. Dadurch wird Leiden sogar ansteckend und aus diesem Grunde direkt lebensgefährlich, weil es das Gesetz der Entwicklung durchkreuzt, d.h. aufrechterhält, was reif ist, zugrundezugehen. Laut einem so interpretierten Gedanken Nietzsches ist es nur eine nihilistische Philosophie, die aus Mitleid Tugend macht, Mitleid sogar zu "der" Tugend ausruft und es ist eine Philosophie, die die Verneinung des Lebens auf ihre Fahne schreibt. So wird Mitleid bei ihm ein depressiver und ansteckender Trieb, der die lebenserhaltenden Kräfte durchkreuzt. Sie vervielfältigt das Elend, konserviert alles Erbärmliche und wird zum Hauptmittel einer Steigerung der Dekadenz. In ihm wird lebensfeindliche Tendenz zum Ausdruck gebracht.

Das sich in Taten nicht verwirklichende Mitleid, das bloss emotive Zusammenleben mit den Ereignissen der Welt erweist sich wirklich als unfruchtbar, wenn diese Empfindlichkeit dem Gang der Welt gegenüber nichts als die Qualen eines vereinsamten Selbstbewusstseins ergibt.

Die universelle Empfindlichkeit des Menschen, diese notwendige Folge der Humanisierung steigert gleichzeitig in der Tat sein Ausgeliefertsein. Die bislang geschützten Terrains seines Wesens, seine im sozialen Sinn "schlafenden Zellen" sensibilisieren sich und werden so naturgemäss auch verletzbar. Und es erfolgt auf um so mehr Punkten und um so tiefer, je mehr menschliche Bedürfnisse und Leidenschaften sich einer bereits erworben hat. Diese Empfindlichkeit vertieft sich nur, wenn Verbindungsfäden zur Welt und zu Anderen reicher werden. Das damit zusammengehende Leid wird aber nur unter Umständen unfruchtbar, die es nicht erlauben, das es sich in vernünftige Taten verwandelt. Die Gleichgültigkeit als Negation von der elementaren menschlichen Eigenschaft des Mitleides sowie als die von jedem Ausgangspunkt der Humanisation wird typisch, wenn die Wege zur Tat verbarrikadiert sind. In diesen Fällen verliert das Mitleid scheinbar tatsächlich seinen Sinn, wenn es einmal nicht zum Motiv der Kooperation und der gemeinsamen Tat werden kann.

In dem Umsichgreifen von dem Phänomen der Gleichgültigkeit drückt sich also auch das Fiasko von passivem Mitleid aus.

Gleichgültigkeit gilt als Auslöschung von der leidenschaftlichen und leidenden Beschaffenheit des Menschen. So paradox es auch lauten mag, büsst der Mensch, der nicht mehr leiden kann, eine seiner menschlichen Eigenschaften ein. Darauf weist auch Kierkegaard in seiner Schrift <u>Der Unglücklichste</u> hin, indem er den Menschen beschreibt, der nicht einmal mehr leiden kann. Dies ist der Grund, warum sich Kierkegaard beklagt, dass seine Epoche nicht so sehr böse als vielmehr kläglich und elend ist - weil es keine Leidenschaften mehr hat.

Gleichfalls Kierkegaard versucht es, Qual und Leid voneinander zu unterscheiden. Die Qual hängt mit Handeln, und zwar mit tragischen Taten zusammen, weil tragische Qual gleichzeitig stets Taten gleichbedeutend war und umgekehrt. Vom Leid hingegen wird der Mensch heimgesucht, wenn er unschuldig ist. So wird das eine durchsichtig und das andere dunkel.

Kierkegaards Gedanke lässt sich in der Richtung weiterführen, dass es hier eigentlich um die Differenz von souveränem bzw. zufälligem Leid geht.

Während Qual über das Mitleid hinaus Respekt einflösst, weil hinter ihm ein Mensch steht, der für irgendein Ziel als Folge vernünftiger Taten sie auf sich nahm, lässt das Leid - mit den Worten Hegels - nur gemeines Mitleid entstehen.

Der Mensch kann sich zu seinen Leiden nur frei verhalten, wenn sie nicht zufällig sind, sondern aus souwerän gewählten und durchgeführten Taten stammen und insofern vernünftig sind.

Falls die leidende und leidenschaftliche Beschaffenheit des Menschen als Produkt der Humanisation sowie als Bedingung ihrer weiteren Entwicklung angesehen werden kann, so lässt sich die "Geschützheit" der Gleichgültigkeit nur um den Preis von Verengung, Verkümmerung oder von gänzlichem Abbau von menschlichen Bedürfnissen, Fähigkeiten und Verbindungen, d.h. um den Preis einer vollendeten Dehumanisation verwirklichen. Es geht um Selbstzerfleischung und Selbstverblendung, um die Abstumpfung von - praktischen und geistigen - menschlichen Sinnen, um eine Zurücknahme der Humanisation.

So eine Abstumpfung von menschlichen Sinnen kann also um den Preis der Entmenschlichung ein illusorisches Gegenmittel zu dem

individuellen Leid abgeben, sie konserviert aber gleichzeitig
das kollektive Leid.

Zum abgestumpften einmütigen und zuletzt völlig gleichgülti-
gen Zustand führt ein Prozess, der mehrere Phasen durchläuft.

In der Resignation, auch wenn sie in Klammern gesetzt ist
oder von der Ferne der Erinnerung erlebt wird, ist noch das einstige Bedürfnis und die dessen Unbefriedigtsein begleitende Trau-
er vorhanden. Der resignierte Mensch kann noch nicht gleichgültig
genannt werden, er erlebt noch seine eigene Resignation. In dieser Phase sterben noch die menschlichen Sinne nicht ab, sie sind
nur "beiseitegeschoben".

Das ist ein Aufgeben der auf seinen Gegenstand energisch hin-
arbeitenden menschlichen Wesenskraft, und zwar auf dem Wege einer
Aufhebung von dem Widerspruch zwischen Mensch und Welt. Die Aufrechterhaltung dieser falschen Harmonie erfordert aber die stete
Bestätigung der Ohnmacht, sowie eine mythische Vergrösserung von
den Schwierigkeiten oder Irrealität der Veränderung, solange sich
die völlige Gleichgültigkeit noch nicht einstellt.

Die Verneinung des Menschen als leidenden und leidenschaftlichen Wesens vertreten diejenigen Richtungen in ihrer Art fol-
gerichtig, die eine Auslöschung jedes menschlichen Wunsches als
Bedingung von der Aufhebung des Leides, den radikalen Selbstverlust und die radikale Amnesie des Menschen selbst bezeichnen.
Deshalb ist nicht rätselhaft, dass der auf dem Boden uralter
Gesellschaften entstandene Buddhismus, diese eigentümliche "Psychotechnik" des Weltverlustes, des Abbaus von jedem von Gesellschaftlichkeit infizierten menschlichen Restes auch dort sich
einbürgert, wo alles fern von der legitimen Basis seiner Entstehung liegt.

Die eigentümliche Bewusstseinsform von der Unveränderlichkeit
der Welt, bzw. die der menschlichen Ohnmacht findet sich also
neue Wirklichkeitsgrundlage, bzw. deren innere Entzweiung.

Die sich selber legitimieren wollende Ohnmacht "entdeckt"
wieder die Grundlehre des Buddhismus, nach welcher die Ursache
des Leidens der Durst - _trsna_ - ist, die zusammenfassende Bezeichnung für diejenigen Wünsche, die mit der Versuchung der
Unmöglichkeit gleichbedeutend sind. Unmöglichkeit ist aber die
menschliche Selbstverwirklichung selbst. Der radikale Verzicht

auf sie und damit zusammen der Abbau von menschlichen Fähigkeiten und Bedürfnissen führt also zur Beseitigung des Leidens.

Wie Allan W. Watts exakt über den Buddhismus feststellt, ist die Beseitigung des Leidens die des Durstes und zwar durch eine absolute Sehnsuchtslosigkeit, durch ein Aufgeben und einen Verzicht auf jeden Willen sowie durch die Befreiung von ihnen. Dies ist aber nunmehr mit der totalen Gleichgültigkeit identisch, mit dem Verzicht des Menschen auf sich selber sowie mit einer Abschneidung der Fäden, die einen mit der Welt verbinden.

Es geht hier um einen Versuch, die den Menschen vernichtende Welt abzuleugnen und dieser Welt verlustig zu werden, was das Wesentliche aller Mystik ausmacht.

Mit einer Schliessung von den Toren der Sinnesorgane kann auch das Bewusstsein "gereinigt" werden, wobei auch die Brücken in Brand gesetzt werden müssen, die den Einzelnen zur Welt hinführen und das bezieht sich auch auf die Brücken der Kommunikation, auf die Worte. Wie Thomson dies in seiner Arbeit über Ayschylos und Athen formuliert: Diejenigen, die wissen, sprechen nicht. Diejenigen, die sprechen, wissen nicht.

So geht es weiter, bis der Mensch aufhört, sich mit dem Wahren und Falschen auseinanderzusetzen, zu lieben und zu hassen - überhaupt zu wählen - und sich mit dem Unveränderten und Unveränderlichen identifiziert.

GLEICHGÜLTIGKEIT UND EKSTASE

Wie ist es möglich, dass der Gleichgültige zur Ekstase fähig ist und warum ist sie für ihn notwendig? Für das Alltagsbewusstsein bedeutet nämlich dieser Zustand eine Steigerung, einen Paroxysmus, nicht aber einen Mangel an Empfindungen.

Woher kommt diese Ekstasesucht der Unempfindlichen, wie kann es möglich sein, dass Leidenschaftslosigkeit und Ekstase in der gleichen Zeit Konjunktur haben, darüber ganz zu schweigen, dass auch alles gefragt wird, was einem hilft, die Ekstase zu erzeugen, bzw. aufrechtzuerhalten?

In der Tat geht es hier nicht um Gegensätze. Denn die Ekstase ist nichts anderes, als ein extremer und eigentümlicher Grad der Gleichgültigkeit, ein Stadium derselben, welches kaum weiterzutreiben ist. In dem Zustand der Ekstase, in dem von dem Verlust der persönlichen Identität sowie jeder mentalen und sittlichen Kontrolle wird die wirkliche Welt auf weit radikalere Weise als in der "gemeinen" Gleichgültigkeit in Klammern gesetzt. Sie braucht sogar nicht einmal in Klammern gesetzt zu werden, weil das Wesentliche der Ekstase eben in dem Verlust der Welt, in einer völligen Loslösung von derselben besteht, in einer Rückkehr in einen Zustand, in dem die physiologischen Prozesse zum Bewusstseinsverlust führen und dieser selbst noch die Erinnerungen an Gesellschaftlichkeit forttreibt.

Im Stadium alltäglicher Gleichgültigkeit lebt der Mensch noch inmitten der Welt. Er manipuliert mit ihren Gegenständen, er beobachtet ihre Sehenswürdigkeiten, er tut es eben - sofern er es kann - so, dass er bloss reagiert, aber nicht antwortet. Die Ekstase ist jedoch Emigration aus der gesellschaftlich=menschlichen Wirklichkeit. Und in dieser Emigration sind keine menschlichen Empfindungen mehr, sie sind höchstens nur in Fetzen, zerrissen und von ihrer realen Basis abgeschnitten vorhanden. Diese Scheinempfindungen werden nicht von der realen Welt ausgelöst, so haben sie auch keine Konsequenzen.

Die Ekstase ist eine Flucht vor dem Alltag, vor dem Druck effektiver Kräfte. Sie ist eine Selbstaufgabe, Aufgabe von Wille und Freiheit, vor welcher nur solche nicht zurückschrecken, die ihre Herrschaft über sich verloren haben.

Die Suche nach der Ekstase war auch schon in der fernen Vergangenheit eine deutliche Offenbarung von dem Verlust der Hoffnungen.

Die Ekstase ist das Optimum negativer Freiheit. Etwas, wodurch man auf einen Schlag von der Aussenwelt sowie von der inneren Welt der Persönlichkeit befreit wird.

Dies erklärt, warum sie in unserer Zeit als ein Instrument zur "Erkämpfung" der Gleichgültigkeit erscheint, was gleich signalisiert, dass es nicht leicht ist, selbst diese falsche Geborgenheit zu sichern.

Alternativen der Konfrontierung mit der Wirklichkeit sowie der Abkehr von ihr, als mögliche modi von der Beziehung zu der jeweiligen Zeit waren jederzeit existent. In unserem Jahrhundert wird der Zwang und die Notwendigkeit der Konfrontierung gleich

stärker, während gleichzeitig auch der Drang dieser Abkehr auch
in den Vordergrund tritt.

Die Weltsituation wird für die Mehrheit der Menschen erst
jetzt aufnehmbar, sie wird jetzt für sie zu einer Realität, die
die Informationen in unaufhaltbarem Prozess ausstrahlt und, was
noch wichtiger ist, zu einer, die ins Dasein der Menschen brutal
eingreift.

Gesellschaftliche Ereignisse lokalisieren sich in unserem
Zeitalter nicht. Kommt es irgendwo zu einer Bewegung der Erde,
so wird sie in allen Punkten der Welt nicht nur registrierbar,
sie kommt in ihren weiteren Nachwirkungen zu den weitesten Terrains, wobei sie die Aufmerksamkeit eindeutig auf sich lenkt.

Da die Wirklichkeit uns mit allzu vielen äusserst erdrücken-
den und drohenden Tatsachen konfrontiert, meldet sich wieder und
wieder der verzweifelte Versuch: Man müsste die schwache Struktur der Vernunft und des Gewissens vor den Lasten erretten und
den Blick von dem unbarmherzigen Licht abwenden. Dem eilt oft
auch eine Art "dauerhafte und allgemeine Betäubung" zu Hilfe.
Es ist insbesondere der Fall, wenn die Chance von einer Beein-
flussung der Geschichte nicht real oder eben im Vergleich zu jener Wirkung scheinbar unbedeutend wirkt, die die soziale Wirklichkeit auf das menschliche Leben ausüben kann und in der Tat
auch ausübt.

All dies verstärkt das Bewusstsein der Ohnmacht. Scheint es
jedoch so, dass Handeln unmöglich ist, so wird selbst auch eine
blosse Wahrnehmung der Wirklichkeit sinnlos.

Die "klassische" Gleichgültigkeit ging von einer Akzeptierung
der gegebenen Welt aus. Und obzwar sie selbstverständlich auch
heute noch /sogar noch in einem absolut nicht vernachlässigbaren
Masse/ existiert, müssen wir doch die der totalen Ablehnung der
Welt entstammende oder mit derselben zusammengehende Gleichgültigkeit als das typisch neue, das zwanzigste Jahrhundert charak-
terisierende Phänomen ansehen. Während in der Vergangenheit also
die Leidenschaftslosigkeit ein mit Passivität harmonisierendes
Phänomen war, stellt sich heute eigentümlich heraus, dass die
Schwierigkeiten von der Erkämpfung der Gleichgültigkeit von att-
raktiven und mit grosser Lautstärke durchgeführten ekstatischen
Aktionen markiert werden.

184

An der Stelle von dem Menschen, der sich selber verloren hat
und indem er in eine fremde Welt hineingeboren wurde, die Entzweiung seiner Existenz und Situation nicht wahrnahm, erscheint
der Mensch, der sein übrig gebliebenes Selbst, sowie auch noch
die Erinnerungen an seine Gesellschaftlichkeit bewusst verlieren
will.

Un da der Mensch mit der Welt des Menschen identisch ist - hat
diese "Selbstbefreiung" keinen anderen Weg als die Welt in Klammern zu setzen, bzw. zu verlieren, was auch mit der Selbstver-
nichtung des Einzelnen gleichbedeutend ist. So erscheinen in unserem Jahrhundert die paradoxen Bestrebungen nach absichtsvollem,
schon an der Grenze der Bewusstheit liegendem Selbstverlust.

Angefangen von dem Konsum der Rauschmittel bis zu den künstlerischen Richtungen, die auf Ekstase aus sind, zeugt eine ganze
Reihe von Erscheinungen davon, dass der Mensch in dieser sein
gesellschaftlich-Tätiges Wesen niederdrückenden Lebensführung
immer weniger seine Ruhe findet und dieser Zustand immer weniger
"natürlich" für ihn ist.

Der Sinn individueller Existenz lässt sich für ein isoliertes
Individuum immer schwieriger legitimieren. Dann muss man ihn
vergessen, verlieren, und gerade dies erklärt das gesteigerte
Bedürfnis nach Ekstase. Die Ekstase bietet nämlich dadurch eine
"Lösung", dass sie den Selbsverlust und mit ihm zusammen den
Verlust der fremdgewordenen Welt noch radikaler macht: Sie macht
ihn so radikal, dass das Bewusstsein, aber auch die Ahnung des
Verlustes verdrängt wird.

Aus diesem Grunde erscheinen die verzweifelten Versuche, sich
so weit wie möglich von dieser Welt zu entfernen, obwohl allein
diese "schiefgegangene" Welt die Bedingungen ihrer eigenen Überwindung enthält und deren einzige mögliche Grundlage darstellt.
Wohin aber entferne man sich von dieser Welt? Auf diese Frage
wiederholen viele - und zwar nicht nur in Worten, sondern auch
in einer Art illusorischer Praxis - im wesentlichen die Antwort
jeglicher Mystik.

Un das ist nicht mehr die Antwort von einem Menschen, der
sich selbst verloren hat, sondern die von dem, der einen noch
vollständigeren Verlust im Auge hat. So ist die Ekstase ein
Versuch, eine in jeder Einzelheit negative Freiheit zu schaffen,

die Gesellschaftlichkeit, also das menschliche Wesen auszulö-
schen. Es ist eine eigenartige "Psychotechnik", mit deren Hilfe
einer Schritt für Schritt die Amnesie erreicht und alles ver-
gisst, was ihm von der gegenständlich-menschlichen Umgebung gegeben war. Und es geht so weit, bis nichts aus ihm übrig bleibt,
nur was ihn mit irgendwelchem beliebigen Lebewesen, lebendigen
oder unlebendigen Erscheinungen des Universums vereint.

So ein Versuch, die Einheit von Mensch und Natur zu verwirklichen, als nämlich die gesellschaftliche Vermittlung dieser
Verbindung ausgeschaltet und die unpersönliche Auslöschung im
Universum zum Ziel wird, drückt eine Ablehnung von den zur Wirklichkeit hinführenden Beziehungen aus. In einer mystischen Erkenntnis von der unmittelbaren Einheit mit der Natur - möge sie
irgendeine beliebige Form annehmen - schafft der Mensch nicht
seine Harmonie von neuem, sondern "gibt" etwa sich der Natur
"zurück".

Philosophy and Culture
J. Lukács and F. Tőkei eds.

DER BEGRIFF DER ERWAHLTHEIT
BEI THOMAS MANN

I. HERMANN

Zu erfinden, zu erschliessen,
Bleibe, Künstler, oft allein;
Deines Wirkens zu geniessen,
Eile freudig zum Verein!
Dort im Ganzen schau, erfahre
Deinen eignen Lebenslauf,
Und die Taten mancher Jahre
Gehn dir in dem Nachbar auf.
/Goethe: Künstler-Lied/

Der Erwählte ist nicht unvermittelt, nicht plötzlich zu Thomas
Manns erwähltem Problem geworden. Latent zieht sich der Begriff
der Erwähltheit seit dem Tonio Kröger durch Thomas Manns Lebenswerk. Er war eines der Probleme, die Thomas Mann mit seinem Zeitalter konfrontierten. Schriftsteller und Dichter, ja auch die
Massen suchten in der Welt des modernen Imperialismus den Erwählten, die Erwähltheit. In ihren Tiefen barg die Zeit den Auf-
bruch der Menschheit zur Schaffung der Grundlagen von Gesetz und
ethischen Normen, aber der gleiche Mythos, dem sich Thomas Mann
so intensiv zur Zeit des Joseph und schon vordem - zugewandt
hatte, barg auch schon die Lehre von der Erwähltheit, vom auserwählten Volk in sich. Die europäische Kultur, der das Zeitalter
des Imperialismus mit Kriegen und der Vorbereitung von Kriegen,
mit grauenvollen, Wunderwaffen genannten Mitteln der Vernichtung
an tausend Stellen tiefe Wunden geschlagen hatte, war auf dem
zweifachen Prinzip der Gleichheit der Chancen der auserwählten
Völker und damit der auserwählten Menschen sowie der ethischen
Normen aufgebaut.

Die der Kultur der Völker Europas immanenten Widersprüche
wurden noch vertieft durch die Widersprüche innerhalb des Bürgertums. Die auf die Zeit der Aufklärung zurückgreifenden inneren
Widersprüche des Bürgertums liessen die Umrisse eines grossen
und unlösbaren Widerspruchs ahnen. Zuerst tauchte dieses Problem
in aller Schärfe und Entschiedenheit bei Rousseau und in den
Diskussionen um Rousseau auf. In den Augen des Bürgertums waren
Kunst und Moral unvereinbar. Im Zuge der Entwicklung der Produk-

tivkräfte der Gesellschaft, so meinte das Bürgertum, trete zwangsläufig ein innerer Widerspruch ein: Die objektive Seite der Pro-
duktivkräfte, die Entwicklung der Produktionsmittel, würde zum
Hemmnis für die Entfaltung der subjektiven Seite der Produktiv-
kräfte, das heisst der menschlichen Moral werden. Dieser hoff-
nungslose Widerspruch, um den Künstler und Denker in bester Absicht herumzukommen versuchten, blieb im Verlauf der bürgerlichen
Entwicklung bis zu Ende unlösbar. Soweit Denker wie Kirkergaard
oder im 20. Jahrhundert Spengler diesen Widerspruch aufzeigten,
kamen sie nicht über die Phänomenologie hinaus. Das Kirkegaard-
sche Entweder-Oder und die Spenglerschen starren Gegensätze von
Kultur und Zivilisation sind nur die Spiegelung der Tatsachen
und zugleich ihre Mythisierung zum Allgemeinmenschlichen. Im
Ganzen gesehen, sucht Thomas Mann in seinen Werken die Überwindung
des Problems, die Auflösung des Widerspruchs. Ihn interessierte
die Dialektik dieser Frage, und er nahm dazu in entschiedener
Weise Stellung, indem er dem Denker der Renaissance Pico della
Mirandola diese Worte in den Mund legte:
"Versteht mich wohl! Ich lobe diejenigen sehr, die sich der Schönheit anmahnen, solange sie die Sache einigen weniger war und
die Moral dumm und unangefochten auf ihrem Stuhle sass. Aber
seitdem die Schönheit ein Geschrei der öffentlichen Gassen geworden, beginnt die Tugend im Preise zu steigen".
    Diese Frage, die Frage der Scheidung und der dialektischen Ein-
heit von Moral und Ästhetik blieb Jahrzehnte lang eines der Haupt-
probleme Thomas Manns, das ihn nicht wieder losliess. Und es
geht hier nicht nur um die Frage der Moral. Etwa zehn Jahre nach
der _Fiorenza_, wo die zitierten Worte stehen, kommt er wieder und
wieder darauf zurück und sagt:
"Ich liess meinen kleinen Mediceer-Kardinal den Hof-Humanisten
damit ärgern, und dass sie durchaus nicht 'historisch' gemeint
waren, wurde aufgefasst, glaube ich, von dem wachsameren Teil
meiner Leser. _Fiorenza_ war ja nicht nur eine Satire auf die De-
mokratisierung des Künstlerischen, auf den kindlichen Eifer, mit
welchem die Zeit, unsere Zeit und Welt sich der Kunst und Schönheit bemächtigt hatte, dergestalt, dass sie das Geistige nur noch
im Zeichen und Sinn des Ästhetischen begriff; und zu dieser Satire gehörte es, dass ich eine ganz andere Art von Geist, den Geist

188

als Moral, als eine neue und faszinierende, weil in freien Zeit-
läuften nicht mehr für möglich gehaltene Möglichkeit innerhalb
meiner Dichtung hervortreten und über die Gemüter Herr werden
liess".

Bemerkenswert ist hier nicht nur die Dauerhaftigkeit des Gedankens, sondern dass Mann damit gleichsam eine Charakterologie
seiner Kunst gab. Das Wesentliche dieser tief moralischen bürgerlichen Kunst ist die Herausarbeitung der Dialektik von Ästhetik
und Ethik, das Aufzeigen des konkreten Zusammenhangs von Ästhetik
und Ethik. Damit erhält Thomas Manns Lebenswerk gegenüber der
von György Lukács der Verengung der Dimensionen geziehenen Eigenart der modernen Richtungen polemischen Charakter. Manns Erkenntnis, dass das der Kunst im modernen bürgerlichen Zeitalter
gebotene Kettenglied das Erfassen dieser Dialektik sei, sichert
ihm einen besonderen Platz in der bürgerlichen Kunst der Epoche,
einer bürgerlichen Kunst, die zeitweilig, wohl ohne Schlagworte,
aber umso radikaler die Trennung von Ästhetik und Moral vollzog,
wobei das Artistikum zum Ausdruck der unbewussten, das heisst
amoralischen triebbedingten Sphäre wird, mit einem Wort, wo sie
die Kunst das Entweder-Oder nicht nur theoretisch, sondern auch
praktisch auf ihre Fahne schreibt. Daraus ist die Verengung der
Dimensionen, die innere Eigenart der Avantgarde, zu erklären,
und eben daraus auch Thomas Manns Multidimensialität. Eine der
Eigenarten von Thomas Manns erster Epoche war es bekanntlich,
dass er sich ausserordentlich tief von Schopenhauers und dann
Nietzsches Philosophie beeinflussen liess. Der Widerspruch liegt
auf der Hand. Noch nie war es vorgekommen, dass ein Dichter von
so tiefmoralischer Haltung unter den Einfluss sosehr moralfeind-
licher, auf die Umwertung aller Werte bedachter Philosophie geraten wäre. Doch hier geht es um die Frage der Auffassung der
Philosophie. Thomas Manns Verhältnis zu Nietzsche ist ausserordentlich interessant und lehrreich. Lehrreich vor allem von
dem Gesichtspunkt, dass Nietzsche, im Gegensatz zu Thomas Manns
moralischer Haltung, die Philosophie des Übermenschen verkündete.
Thomas Mann aber akzeptierte nicht einen Augenblick lang das
antidemokratische Wesen von Nietzsches Philosophie. Manns Nietz-
scheanismus äusserte sich in scharfer Polemik gegen den Philosophen des vorigen Jahrhunderts. Seine Methode auf diesem Gebiet

entspricht dem allgemeinen Verhältnis des Künstlers zur Philosophie. Das bedeutet aber im Zeichen des von Lukács so häufig
zitierten je prends mon bien où je le trouve, dass Mann Nietzsches
ausserordentlich geistreiche Kritik der bürgerlichen Dekadenz
übernahm, aber das ganze philosophische Gefüge Nietzsches aufs
schärfste ablehnte.
"Wenn aber eben diese Grundstimmung mich nicht zum Verfallspsy-
chologen machte, so war es Nietzsche, auf den ich dabei als
Meister blickte; denn nicht so sehr der Prophet eines unanschau-
lichen 'Übermenschen' war er mir von Anfang an, wie zur Zeit
seiner Modeherrschaft den meisten, als vielmehr der unvergleich-
lich grösste und erfahrenste Psychologe der Dekadenz".
    Und an anderer Stelle heisst es:
"Nietzsches Lehre also war für Deutschland weiniger neu und re-
volutionierend, sie war für die deutsche Entwicklung weniger
wichtig -, wichtig im guten oder schlimmen Sinne, wie man nun
will - als die Art, in der er lehrte. Mindestens, allermindes-
tens ebenso stark, wie durch seinen Militarismus und sein Macht-
Philosophem".
    Manns Verhältnis zu Nietzsche ist also nicht nur keine Wider-
legung unserer Behauptung, sondern stützt sie. Der Begriff der
Erwähltheit entsteht bei Mann auch nicht am Anfang im Zeichen
des Übermensch-Kults, für ihn besteht der ganze Problemkreis
der Erwähltheit im Suchen nach der künstlerischen Aufgabe, im
Forschen nach dem künstlerischen Weg und den gebotenen Möglichkeiten. Wenn wir es paradoxal ausdrücken wollten, so könnten wir
sagen, Mann sei der antinietzscheanischteste Nietzscheaner gewesen, der je eine Feder in die Hand genommen hat. Nietzsche
war in Manns Augen kein philosophisches Vorbild. Nietzsches Probleme bedeuteten für Mann ein künstlerisches Problem, für ihn fand
in Nietzsche und seinen lebensphilosophischen Gedankengängen das
Entweder-Oder der modernen Kunst seinen plastischsten Ausdruck.
Mann hat sich, wie wir gesehen haben, für die Moral entschieden
und ist für ethisches Verhalten eingetreten. Der grosse bürgerliche Rettungsversuch für die moderne Kunst kam im Zeichen der
Moral in Gang und mündete in zwei parallele Werke, den Erwählten
und den Verdammten, in den Gregor-Roman und den Doktor Faustus.

Das philosophische Vorbild war also kein philosophisches Vorbild, sondern das Modell des modernen Künstlerschicksals. Später
schreibt Thomas Mann über sein Verhältnis zu Nietzsche:
"Mit einem Worte: ich sah in Nietzsche vor allem den Selbstüber-
winder; ich nahm nichts wörtlich bei ihm, ich glaubte ihm fast
nichts, und gerade dies gab meiner Liebe zu ihm das Doppelsich-
tig-Passionierte, gab ihr die Tiefe. Sollte ich es etwa 'ernst'
nehmen, wenn er den Hedonismus in der Kunst ausspielte? Was war
sein Machtphilosophem und die Blonde Bestie? Beinahe eine Verlegenheit. Seine Verherrlichung des Lebens auf Kosten des Geistes,
diese Lyrik, die im deutschen Denken so missliche Folgen gehabt
hat - es gab nur eine Möglichkeit, sie mir zu assimilieren: als
Ironie... Diese Verbürgerlichung schien mir und scheint mir noch
heute tiefer und verschlagener als aller heroisch-ästhetische
Rausch, den Nietzsche wohl literarisch entfachte. Mein Nietzsche-
-Erlebnis bildete die Voraussetzung einer Periode konservativen
Denkens, die ich zur Kriegszeit absolvierte. Zuletzt aber hat
es mich widerstandsfähig gemacht gegen alle überromantischen
Reize, die von einer inhumanen Wertung des Verhältnisses von
Leben und Geist ausgehen können und heute so vielfach ausgehen".
Diese 1930 gesprochenen Worte beleuchten die reale Situation.
In Nietzsche fand Thomas Mann viel eher das, was ihn gegen die
inhumanen, geistfeindlichen Tendenzen wappnete, als etwa einen
Ansporn zum modernen Geniekult. Daraus folgt, dass für Manns
Lebenswerk Nietzsches Tragödie, die Tragödie der Dekadenz und
des Irrationalismus das lebendige Veto bedeutete. Das Erleben
des Vetos, das Erleben der Negierung und der Tragik einer Philosophie wandte ihn der Seite zu, die jedweden Antihumanismus
verwarf.
Das Erkennen des Vetos ist nicht blosse Negierung, obwohl
das omnis determination est negatio nicht stimmt, sondern omnis
negatio determinatio est. Dies natürlich unter der Voraussetzung,
dass die Negierung nicht abstrakt, sondern konkret, nicht leer,
sondern gehaltvoll, nicht chastisch, sondern schöpferisch ist.
Thomas Manns tiefste künstlerische Qualität lag eben darin, dass
bei ihm, wie die Gestalten Marios und des römischen Herrn des
Zauberers bezeugen, die Verneinung nie abstrakte, nie passive,
sondern aktive, gehaltvolle Verneinung war. Manns Lebenswerk,

das von einem Gesichtspunkt als die positive Negierung der
Nietzscheschen Philosophie angesehen werden kann, der auch viele
andere dekadente Strömungen, wie etwa auch der Freudismus im
gleichen negierenden Sinn ihren Stempel aufgedrückt haben, baut
eben in diesem Zeichen eine wirklich künstlerisch ökonomische,
zusammenhängende und überschaubare Welt auf. Verneinung bedeutet
nämlich nie starre Ablehnung. Sie bedeutet nicht und kann nicht
bedeuten, dass die Probleme, deren Lösung und letzte theoretische Antworten der Dichter ablehnt, für ihn einfach nicht exis-
tierten. Thomas Manns ganze künstlerische Tätigkeit ist von diesen
ausserordentlich schwerwiegenden Fragestellungen und von dem
Gegensatz von Erwähltheit und Gesetz, von Kunst und Moral durchdrungen, und aus dem Gewirr von Widersprüchen ragt gleich einem
drohenden Veto Nietzsches Gestalt. Die Angst vor der drohenden
menschlichen und künstlerischen Tragödie, hervorgerufen durch
falsche Lösungen der Widersprüche, die Verkündung des Hedonismus
der Kunst, der Erwähltheit und des heroischen Rausches liess
Thomas Mann bestürzt vor allen den künstlerischen Wegen zurückschrecken, die in die Sackgasse führen und in menschliche Tragödie münden. Der Autor des Doktor Faustus betrachtete es also
als die wichtigste Frage, wie sich die besondere widerspruchs-
volle Lage des Künstlers in der modernen bürgerlichen Gesellschaft definieren lasse, welche Wege sich dem Künstler bieten,
was der Künstler durchmache, damit er die Anforderungen des Tages
wirklich fühle.

Kein Zweifel, Thomas Manns ganze Auffassung entwickelte sich
zwangsläufig im Zeichen einer eigenartigen Variante des romanti-
schen Antikapitalismus. Anders als jene, die das Leben und die
Kunst als Gegenpole des bürgerlichen Daseins bezeichneten, erkannte Mann, dass sich in diesem Leben unbedingt das bürgerliche, und zwar das moderne bürgerliche Dasein fortsetze. Das
grosse Problem des wahren Künstlers besteht schon seit dem Tonio Kröger darin, dass er die tausendfachen inneren Widersprüche
des Lebens besser durchschaut als der Durchschnittsmensch, dies
aber nicht ohne Sehnen nach dem Durchschnittlichen tut. Das Er-
lebnis des Widerspruchs zwischen der Problemstellung und der
künstlerischen Methode führte Thomas Mann dahin, dass er ständig
die Auflösung dieses Widerspruchs sucht und in diesem Zeichen

die spezifische Tongebung seiner Werke zustandebringt. Daher
kommt es, dass er in einem ein Schriftsteller von tragischer
und für Komik empfänglicher Anschauungsweise sein konnte. Er
vermochte sich zugleich in die Tragik und die welthistorische
Komik eines Geschehnisses einzuleben. Und das ist kein verein-
zelter Fall. Mit Recht weist Lukács darauf hin, dass bei Mann
Tragödie und Komödie, Ironie und Verzweiflung einander durch-
dringen.

Die Auflösung der Diskrepanzen des Lebens kann an sich sowohl tragisch als auch komisch sein. Thomas Mann bejaht für sich
die sokratische Forderung aus dem Gastmahl, dass derselbe Dichter Tragödien und Komödien verfassen soll. Eine solche Vereini-
gung des Tragischen und des Komischen beinhaltet naturgemäss
ihre Relativierung.

Diese Ineinanderspielen des Komischen und des Tragischen ent-
sprang zwangsläufig der moralischen und ästhetischen Situation
des Künstlers, mit anderen Worten, dem Umstand, dass nur die
Persönlichkeit des Künstlers die Starre des Entweder-Oder auf-
zulösen vermag. Mann selbst erkannte diese Situation klar, und
eben deshalb wollte er, ausgehend von fast jedem tragischen Geschehen, gleich ein Satyrspiel über das Geschehen schreiben.
Lukács leitet das satirische und spielerische Gepräge des Felix
Krull von einem Grundmotiv ab, das Thomas Manns ganzes Lebenswerk durchzieht, und wie recht er hat, erhellt aus der Tatsache,
dass Der Zauberberg ursprünglich als Satyrspiel zu der tragischen
Erzählung Der Tod in Venedig gedacht war.

Die Darstellung des Verhaltens und der gesellschaftlichen
Rolle des erwählten Künstlers ist die Fortführung der romanti-
schen Tradition, die im Künstlertum, in der Genialität etwas
Heroisches, über dem Durchschnittsmenschen Stehendes, im Künstler also einen Erwählten sah. In Wirklichkeit aber war in Thomas Manns Augen die Eigenart des Künstlertums, das Künstlerprob-
lem, nicht Absonderung, nicht eine Abart des Geniekults. Davon
zeugt nicht nur das Ineinanderspielen und Nebeneinander des tragischen und des komischen Moments, sondern auch der Grundzug
von Thomas Manns Lebenswerk, den wir als Sehnen nach dem Durchschnittlichen bezeichnet haben. Neben Gustav von Aschenbach,
der sich vergebens von der Welt der Blonden und Blauäugigen an-

gezogen fühlt, steht Hans Castorp, der selbst zur Welt der Durchschnittsmenschen gehört, neben Josef Felix Krull und neben Adrian
Leverkühn der Papst Gregor. Neben den besonders Erwählten finden
wir die Durchschnittlichen, neben dem zum Bösen Erwählten der
zum Guten Erwählten. Doch die Frage ist: Wie kann man das Letzte
erreichen, wie ist es möglich, zur wahrhaft abgeklärten, zur wahrhaft tiefen Weisheit zu gelangen; mit anderen Worten, wie kann
man das Gesetz, die Gleichheit der ethischen Normen und die Erwähltheit vereinigen. Darin liegt nämlich der Weg zum Leben. Und
Thomas Mann hat sein ganzes Leben lang den Weg zum Leben gesucht.
Von diesem Gesichtspunkt deckt sich Manns Gedanke vollständig
mit dem, was Hans Castorp an einer Stelle zu Madame Chauchat
sagt:
"Zum Leben gibt es zwei Wege: der eine ist der gewöhnliche, direkte und brave. Der andere ist schlimm, er führt über den Tod,
und das ist der geniale Weg".

Und diese Auffassung ist im Zeitalter des Imperialismus die
einzig mögliche für den Künstler. Für ihn kann es den ersten Weg
nicht geben. Er wird ihm vom Zeitalter selbst, der Gesellschaft,
dem von Lukács in Theorie des Romans Zeitalter der vollendeten
Sündhaftigkeit genannten Zeitalter versperrt. Aus diesem Zeitalter findet der Künstler nur einen Ausweg, wenn er den zweiten
Weg wählt, wenn er die Tragödie durchlebt, über das Nietzsche-Er-
lebnis hinauswächst und so zum Leben selbst zurückkehrt.

Die Dialektik des Tragischen und des Komischen, von Moral und
Leben als leitendes Prinzip bildet die Grundvoraussetzung für
Manns Multidimensionalität, seine Vielseitigkeit. Nicht zufällig
hielt Thomas Mann eine Bemerkung Saint Beuves für sehr richtig,
der über einen genialen Reaktionär, Josef de Maistre, schrieb:
dazu, dass er Schriftsteller werde, habe er nur die Begabung be-
sessen. Die Überwindung der ausserordentlich verschärften Widersprüche des Bürgertums konnte nicht von einer Seite allein, weder
von der Seite der Kunst noch von der Seite der Moral geschehen.
Deshalb dachte Thomas Mann, in der wahren Kunst müssten sich
Ästhet, Moralist und der politische und gesellschaftliche Kämpfer
vereinigen. Der Gedanke, es auf bürgerlichem Boden zu versuchen,
offenbarte sich bei Thomas Mann wohl am bewusstesten. Ohne einen
solchen Versuch, ob bewusst wie bei Thomas Mann oder Semprun, ob

weniger bewusst wie bei Martin du Gard oder William Styron, ist
im 20. Jahrhundert Kunst nicht möglich. Grundvoraussetzung für
die Kunst des 20. Jahrhunderts ist, soll sie wirklich grosse
Kunst sein, der von Thomas Mann als der schlimmer bezeichnete
Weg zum Leben über den Tod. Doch auch die über den Tod führenden
Wege scheiden sich. Der eine, Adrian Leverkühns Weg, führt aus
dem Tod über den Tod zum Tod. Der andere, Papst Gregors Weg,
führt über den Tod dazu, dass Glockendröhnen die Ewige Stadt
überströmt. Möglich ist der Tod in Venedig und möglich ist das
Leben auf dem Zauberberg. Es ist also jeder Weg möglich, nur
führt der eine, der Weg des blossen Lebens, der blossen Ästhetik
dazu, dass der Mensch die Beziehung zum Leben kündigt, und der
andere, der moralische, dazu, dass wir über den Tod das Leben
aufs neue finden. Leverkühn wird nie zum verdorrten elenden Wurm,
zieht aber die 9. Symphonie zurück. Papst Gregor schrumpft zu
einem Igel zusammen, aber seine Rückkehr zum Leben lässt die
Glocken erschallen.

Das Leben des Künstlers, also das über den Tod führende Leben
formuliert sich in Thomas Mann geradezu in Attila Józsefschen
Worten: Wer Dudler werden will, fahre zur Hölle, dort muss er
lernen den Dudelsack pfeifen. Sich durch die Hölle hindurchquälen
ist für den Künstler des zwanzigsten Jahrhunderts Voraussetzung
dafür, dass er nicht aus der Perspektive der Bequemlichkeit und
des Luxus auf die menschlichen Probleme herabblicke, sondern in
jedem Nerv das Pulsieren der Wirklichkeit empfinde. So wurde Mann
das Begreifen und Erfüllen der Probleme des Zeitalters des Imperialismus möglich. Von diesem Gesichtspunkt ist ausserordentlich
lehrreich, was Lukács in seinem Werk Wider den missverstandenen
Realismus /Hamburg 1958/ geschrieben hat. Darin stellt er die
Frage: Kafka oder Thomas Mann? Das Wesentliche des Problems besteht darin, dass Kafka und Thomas Mann die Problematik des gleichen Weges aufwerfen. Mit dem Unterschied jedoch, dass für Thomas Mann die Rückkehr zum Leben die zentrale Frage ist, während
Kafkas Helden /hier ist nicht von der meisterhaften Erzählung
Verwandlung die Rede, sondern von seinen Romanen/ den Weg zurück
zum Leben nicht finden und auch nicht finden können. Bei einer
Gelegenheit schrieb Thomas Mann über Kafkas Roman Das Schloss:
"K. - ein Mensch guten Willens. Wünscht die Einsamkeit nicht,

möchte gern ein tätiges Mitglied der menschlichen Gesellschaft
sein... Alles misslingt. Kalte Isolierschicht um ihn. Bevölkerung
des Dorfes schliesst sich von ihm ab. Spezifisch jüdisch, aber
auf den Künstler, den Menschen ausgedehnt. ... Hat es mit der
Berufung zum Landvermesser seine Richtigkeit?"

Diese Kritik Manns drückt, so glaube ich, den Gegensatz zwischen ihm und Kafka am tiefsten aus. In Manns Augen ist das im
Schloss geschilderte Problem nicht das Problem des Durchschnittsmenschen. Der K. - des Romans "Schloss" steht, wenn wir das Problem für sich betrachten, Gustav von Aschenbach näher als Hans
Castorp. Im Hinblick auf seine gesellschaftliche Situation jedoch
ähnelt Kafka in seinem Typus mehr Hans Castorp. Mann hat richtig
gefühlt, dass Hans Castorps Schicksal, das Schicksal des Durchschnittsmenschen, nicht das Schicksal Aschenbachs sein kann und
dass umgekehrt Aschenbachs Schicksal nicht geeignet ist, für
Hans Castorps Schicksal zu stehen. Manns Meinung nach liegt Kafkas künstlerischer Fehler darin, dass er ein spezifisches Künst-
ler- und spezifisch jüdisches Problem zu einem allgemein menschlichen ausweitet und so die von einer engen Schicht erlebten besonderen Probleme über diese Schicht hinweg verallgemeinert. Thomas Manns feine Distinktion zwischen den Problemen des Durchschnittsmenschen und denen des Künstlers ist selbstverständlich
nicht nur eine prinzipielle Frage, sondern auch eine Frage der
Darstellungsweise. Das unterscheidet nämlich Mann in seiner Darstellungsweise von der allgemeinen Methode des Avantgardismus.
Die dem Avantgardismus eigene Ahistorizität findet darin ihren
Ausdruck, dass die Träger der vom Dichter erlebten Probleme sehr
oft nicht Dichter, sondern Durchschnittsmenschen sind. Wenn wir
zum Beispiel das Problem der Fremdheit ins Auge fassen, dem in
der Avantgarde eine so grosse Rolle zugedacht ist, so sehen wir,
dass Camus' Mersault oder auch Virginia Woolfs Orlando, von einem
höheren Gesichtspunkt gesehen, das Problem des Künstlers visio-
när erleben, und eine ausserordentliche Verwandtschaft zwischen
den avantgardistischen und den Künstler-Helden Thomas Mann besteht. Aber dadruch, dass Thomas Mann fähig ist, Platz und Beziehungen der eigenen Probleme zu fixieren, wird bei ihm die Darstellung ausserordentlich konkret, während die Darstellungen der
Avantgarde verwischte Konturen aufweisen. Bei Thomas Mann ist das

Hindurchkommen durch den Tod, die dialektische Verneinung des
Todes der Weg des Dichters, des Künstlers - und daraus ergibt
sich, aus dieser Konkretizität entspringt die Plastizität der
Thomas Mannschen Darstellung.

Manns Helden stehen ebenso wie Kafkas Helden einer kalten und
entfremdeten Welt gegenüber. Nur ist es bei Thomas Mann vollkommen klar, wann der Held Künstler und wann er Durchschnittsmensch
ist. Bei ihm hat auch der Durchschnittsmensch konkreten Inhalt,
konkrete geistige und praktische Zielsetzungen, und darum hat er
im Zuge des epischen Geschehens etwas zu verlieren. Kafka zeichnet die nachgerade gespenstisch werdende Welt genial, doch dieser
gespenstischen Welt stellt er nicht einen konkreten, sondern einen
abstrakten Menschen gegenüber. Den abstrakten Menschen, der kein
entschiedenes geistiges und intellektuelles Profil und - nicht
zufällig - nicht einmal einen Namen hat, das heisst, den Menschen
schlechthin. Der Menschen schlechthin, der keinen konkreten Inhalt zu verlieren hat, sondern nur abstrakt zu leiden vermag.
Der Mensch geht also ganz allgemein im Zuge des epischen Geschehens physisch zugrunde, geistig ist nichts mehr in ihm, was ver-
nichtet werden könnte. So, wie um Hans Castorps, ja auch um Adrian Leverkühns Seele gekämpft wird, wäre es beinahe unmöglich,
dass jemand im geistigen Sinne um K. kämpfen würde. Die im <u>Schloss</u>
an K.'s Seite stehende Frieda will den Kafkaschen Helden natürlich unterstützen, doch ihre Unterstützung beschränkt sich darauf,
ihm in dem Dorf einen Platz zu verschaffen. Doch niemand ist da
und kann auch nicht da sein, der vor K. einen neuen Horizont auf-
schlösse. Während bei Mann das Problem des geistigen Horizonts
immer von neuem aufgeworfen wird, bildet bei Kafka an Stelle des
geistigen Horizonts der Kampf und das nackte Leben das zentrale
Problem. Und Mann hat recht, wenn er die Dinge so sieht, dass
sich zwischen dem Leben und dem Individuum eine ganze Reihe von
vermittelnden Elementen einschaltet, und darunter ist in unserem
Zeitalter die Weltanschauung eines der entscheidenden Elemente,
über die der Weg zum Leben führt. So gelangt zwischen das Individuum und das Leben, das Individuum und die Wirklichkeit als
entscheidendes Kettenglied der "Geist", der Gedanke. Mann hat
nämlich erkannt, dass die Einschaltung des Gedankens, wie jede
Einschaltung, die Beziehung von Menschen und Natur auf eine hö-

here Ebene hebt. Als Hegel in der Phänomenologie des Geistes zu
der genialen Entdeckung gelangte - die Lukács in seiner Schrift
über den jungen Hegel hervorhebt -, dass die Quantität und die
Qualität der zwischen Mensch und Natur vermittelnden Einschaltun-
gen dem Menschen Grösse verleihe, hatte er eine der grundlegenden Besonderheiten des menschlichen Daseins erschlossen. Nur
weist Hegel als idealistischer Denker diesen vermittelnden Elementen ihren Platz zwischen dem Gedanken, dem Geist und der Wirklichkeit an. Der Künstler Thomas Mann geht weiter als Hegel, für
ihn ist der Gedanke selbst vermittelndes Element, eines der Mittel, durch die der gesellschaftliche Mensch über die Wirklichkeit
Herr zu werden vermag. Von diesem Gesichtspunkt ist Kafka unfähig
zu solcher Weiterentwicklung. Bei ihm fehlt infolge des abstrakten Wesens der Visionen und als Ergebnis seiner zugespitzt abstrakten Anschauungsweise das auflösende Moment zwischen den
beiden Polen, dem Menschen und der Wirklichkeit. Und wenn Hegel
gewisse Menschentypen "erhaltende Elemente" nennt, schafft Mann
einerseits Gestalten wie zum Beispiel Hans Castorp und Zeitblom,
und entdeckt andererseits nicht nur die erhaltenden Elemente, sondern auch das Element, das im Zeitalter des modernen Imperialismus die grössten Künstler entdecken müssen - das auflösende Element. Infolge der Erscheinungen neuer Entfremdung im Zeitalter
des Imperialismus offenbart sich die Spaltung und Zerrissenheit
des Menschen darin, dass er sich von der Wirklichkeit gelöst hat,
der Bürger findet nicht mehr die Beziehung zur Wirklichkeit. Das
Bürgertum als Klasse kann diese Beziehung zur objektiven Wirklichkeit auf dem Wege sehr fragwürdiger, neue Formen der Entfremdung gebärenden Manipulation neu schaffen. Der unter den Qualen
der Entfremdung leidende Mensch kann diese Beziehung zur Wirklichkeit - es sei denn, er wolle auf dem Wege des Manipulierens ver-
harren - nur mit Hilfe des Geistes, des Gedankens zustandebrin-
gen.

Für die höhere Kunst bietet sich also in der modernen Welt
nicht der Weg der Ästhetik und auch nicht der abstrakte moralische
Weg für die Darstellung der Beziehungen von Mensch und Wirklichkeit. Der eine Weg ist der Weg Kafkas, der die Situation darstellt,
da der Mensch Opfer des Manipulierens, der Entfremdung wird. Der
andere Weg ist der Weg Thomas Manns, der die Versuche des Durch-

bruchs dieser im Zeitalter des Imperialismus gegebenen Situation darstellt. Mann sieht, dass dieser Durchbruch ausschliesslich nur über den Geist, mit Hilfe des Geistes möglich ist. Dieser Einsicht entsprangen die meisten seiner nicht in der Art eines Satyrspiels verfassten Werke, sein essayistischer Stil, die zentrale Rolle des Essays bzw. der philosophischen Formulierungen in der formalen Lösung seiner Werke. Und wenn dieses Essayhafte auch sehr vielen die Mannsche Form unsympathisch erscheinen lässt, so bot sie Mann doch die einzige Möglichkeit, die Schranken wirklich zu durchbrechen, die sich dem modernen Künstler in den Weg stellen, wenn er das Bild der dialektischen Einheit von Wirklichkeit und Individuum darzubieten versucht.

In diesem Sinne war für Mann das Nietzsche- und später das Freud- und das Kierkegaard-Erlebnis entscheidend. Individuell gibt es nämlich für den Bürger keinen anderen Weg zurück zur Wirklichkeit, von der er sich einmal gelöst hat, als den Weg über die Erlebnisse, den die erwähnten Denker beschrieben haben. In einem anderen Zusammenhang habe ich darauf hingewiesen, dass das bürgerliche Denken in sehr vielen Fällen eine ausgezeichnete Phänomenologie der bürgerlichen Wirklichkeit bietet /s. István Hermann: Sigmund Freud avagy a pszichológia kalandja /Sigmund Freud oder das Abenteuer der Psychologie/, Budapest, 1964./. Das Problem liegt nicht darin, dass das bürgerliche Denken die Erscheinungen verfälscht darstellt, sondern darin, dass es der einen oder anderen solchen Erscheinung nicht konkrete, sondern allgemeine menschliche Geltung zumisst. Mann aber hat in diesen Phänomenologien verständlich gemacht, wie ausserordentlich kompliziert für das einzelne menschliche Individuum seine Beziehung zur Wirklichkeit geworden ist, und welche Hindernisse zu bewältigen sind, damit der Mensch zum Leben zurückfinden kann. In diesem Sinne gilt jedoch, was Hans Castorp zu Madame Chauchat sagt: dass man über den Tod zum Leben gelangen kann. Hier ergibt sich das wahre Problem. Was für Kafka im modernen imperialistischen Zeitalter eindeutig ist, dass nämlich der direkte Weg nicht zum Leben führt, das ist für Thomas Mann, der nach dem mittelbaren, über den Tod zum Leben führenden Weg sucht, schon problematisch und doppeldeutig. Die Doppeldeutigkeit besteht seit dem Tonio Kröger darin, dass Thomas Mann klar sieht, dass es über den Tod einen Weg zurück zum Leben gibt, so wie es auch für Joseph einen Weg zurück über die Grube und den Kerker gibt, wie Gregor einen Weg zurück über das Einschrumpfen hat und dass das Steckenbleiben im Tode möglich ist. Das Steckenbleiben im Tod wird das Los Aschenbachs und Leverkühns und auch Naphtas. Sehr klar kommt das dann zum Ausdruck, wenn Thomas Mann im Zusammenhang mit Adrian Leverkühns Problem sagt, er habe hier den Helden unserer Zeit modellieren wollen, der allen Schmerz unseres Zeitalters in sich trägt, und wenn Thomas Mann auch mit seinem Helden in höchstem Masse sympathisiert, hat er doch seine Kälte, die Armut seiner Seele und seine Verdammtheit zur Unmenschlichkeit empfunden. "Nach einer abendlichen Vorlesung fragte mich Leonhard Frank, ob mir bei Adrian selbst irgend ein Modell vorgeschwebt habe. Ich verneinte, und fügte hinzu, dass die Schwierigkeit gerade darin .bestehe, eine Musiker-Existenz frei zu erfinden, die ihren glaubhaften Platz zwischen den realen Besetzungen des modernen Musiklebens habe. Leverkühn sei sozusagen eine Idealgestalt, ein Held unserer Zeit, ein Mensch, der das Leid der Epoche trägt. Ich ging aber weiter und gestand ihm, dass ich nie eine Imagination, weder Thomas Buddenbrook, noch Hans Castorp, noch Aschenbach, noch Joseph, noch den Goethe in Lotte in Weimar - ausgenommen vielleicht Hanno Buddenbrook - geliebt hätte wie ihn. Ich sprach die Wahrheit. Buchstäblich teilte ich die Empfindungen des guten Serenus für ihn, war sorgenvoll in ihn verliebt von seinen hochmütigen Schülertagen an, vernarrt in seine Kälte, seine Lebensferne, seinen Mangel an Seele, dieser Vermittlungs- und Versöhnungsinstanz zwischen Geist und Trieb, in sein Unmenschentum und verzweifeltes Herz, seine Überzeugung, verdammt zu sein."

Die moderne bürgerliche Philosophie war also in Thomas Manns Augen die Überzeugung, verdammt zu sein, aber der Weg zum Leben führt nur über die Verdammnis, über den Tod. Nietzsches Tragödie ist nicht nur Nietzsches Tragödie, sondern die Tragödie aller Erwähltheit, die Tragödie jeder solchen Erwähltheit, mit der sich auch schon Tonio Kröger gedanklich beschäftigt hat. Und deshalb sind die erwähnten polaren Widersprüche für Mann die Widersprüche der realen Situation, aber überwindbare und mit Hilfe des Geistes auflösbare Widersprüche. So bietet uns Thomas Manns Kunst inhaltlich und in der Form in vollendeter Einheit ein ausser-

ordentlich vertieftes Spiegelbild des modernen Denkens, des bürgerlichen Denkens des Zeitalters des Imperialismus und die Überwindung dieses Denkens. Die beiden Formen der Überwindung sind
die Rückkehr zum Leben oder die Verneinung des Lebens, der gegenüber Mann kritisch ist. Entweder muss die 9. Symphonie zurück-
gezogen werden, oder aber man muss zu ihr zurückkehren. Und im
gegebenen Fall bedeutet die 9. Symphonie das Leben selbst.

Die Trennung des Künstlers vom Leben ist also ein eigentüm-
liches Spiegelbild der Entfremdung des Menschen im heutigen Kapitalismus. Der blosse künstlerische Weg ist, wie wir gesehen
haben, nicht geeignet zur Aufhebung und Beseitigung dieser Trennung. Der wirkliche Weg ist der Weg des Geistes, der Geist im
Thomas Mannschen Sinne, wo das Ästhetische und das Ethische ineinander aufgehen. Thomas Manns Joseph ist Künstler und Nicht-
Künstler zur gleichen Zeit. Künstler, soweit als er den Traum
erlebt. Er reisst sich von seiner Umgebung von seinen Brüdern,
von seiner Verwandtschaft los. Seine Brüder verstossen ihn auch.
Doch derselbe Träumer findet eben mit Hilfe seines Traumgesichts,
da der Traum Wahrsagung und nicht Wahrsagertum war, zu seinen
Brüdern zurück und wird zum verzeihenden Helden. Die Losreissung
von der Wirklichkeit kann zu einer tiefergreifenden Losreissung
führen, zu unmenschlicher Erwähltheit, sie kann aber auch zur
Wirklichkeit, zur ursprünglichen Gemeinschaft zurückführen. In
Manns Kunst dominiert das Problem der Losreissung, und wir wollen
hier dieses eigentümliche Problem, das heisst, das der Erwähltheit kurz beleuchten.

Wenn für Mann das Wesen der Kunst die Losreissung von der
Wirklichkeit und das Zurückfinden zur Wirklichkeit ist, so wirft
er das Problem des Goetheschen Wilhelm Meister auf. Bei Goethe
bedeutet der schöpferische Prozess die Einsamkeit, in seiner Auswirkung führt er aber in die Wirklichkeit, in die Gemeinschaft
zurück. In Manns Augen ist das Problem noch schwieriger. Der moderne Kapitalismus schafft die schwerwiegende Möglichkeit, dass
der Mensch, einmal von der Wirklichkeit gelöst, nicht wieder auf
die Erde zurückfindet und im Zustand der Schwerelosigkeit die
Verbindung mit der irdischen Sphäre verliert. Diese Gefahr haben
die Mann so sehr beeinflussende Kierkegaardsche Philosophie, aber
auch die Psychologie Nietzsches und Freuds ganz klar ausgespro-

chen. Oben haben wir gesehen, wie tief Thomas Mann die Möglichkeit dieser Gefahr erfasst hat, und wie sehr er sich - reisst
doch die Parallelität in seinen Schriften nicht ab - auch die
Perspektive der Aufhebung, der Wiederkehr zur Wirklichkeit vor
Augen gehalten hat. Doch taucht für ihn von Anbeginn seiner Laufbahn immer wieder das Problem auf, dass ein solcher Trennungs-
prozess im Endergebnis entweder schmerzhaft und tragisch wird
oder in einem anderen Fall den Dichter und den Menschen einfach
zum Hanswurst werden lässt. Bisher haben wir, als von Adrian Leverkühn die Rede war, den tragischen Aspekt des Prozesses behan-
delt. Doch der Prozess hat auch seinen tragikomischen Aspekt.
Er taucht schon in Königliche Hoheit auf, als Fräulein Inna sagt:
"Nein, Prinz, das ist in der Tat zuviel verlangt! Haben Sie mir
nicht von Ihrem Leben erzählt? Sie sind zum Schein zur Schule
gegangen, Sie sind zum Schein auf der Universität gewesen, Sie
haben zum Schein als Soldat gedient und tragen noch immer zum
Schein die Uniform; Sie erteilen zum Scheine Audienzen und spielen
zum Schein den Schützen und der Himmel weiss, was noch alles; Sie
sind zum Schein auf die Welt gekommen, und nun soll ich Ihnen
plötzlich glauben, dass es Ihnen mit irgend etwas ernst ist?"

Dann entwickelt sich bei Thomas Mann der tragikomische Charakter des Scheindaseins bis zur Kritik der Trennung von der Wirklichkeit weiter. Adrian Leverkühns Losreissung von der Wirklichkeit ist bereits Künstlertragödie, seine Erwähltheit ist die
gleiche Erwähltheit in moderner Variante, wie es seinerzeit die
Erwähltheit des Prinzen gewesen ist. Bei Adrian verläuft das Motiv der Erwähltheit ins Tragische, denn er durchlebt seine Erwähltheit bis ins letzte, missbraucht sie aber nicht. Darum ist
der Thomas Mannsche Künstlertypus von Aschenbach bis zu Leverkühn noch echter Künstler, der das Artistikum, das ästhetische
Leben in seiner Ästhetik zu Ende lebt, was zu seiner Tragödie
wird. Der andere Typus, der vom Scheindasein ausgeht, ist im
Endergebnis die überspitzte, übertriebene Variante des anderen.
Er wählt die gleiche ästhetische Lebensführung, das Ästhetische,
wie auch Adrian es getan hat, nur führt die Magik des Artistikums
nicht zum persönlichen Untergang, nicht zum persönlichen Zusammenbruch. Er wendet diese Magik - und das ist die andere Seite der
Nietzsche-Tragödie - auf das Leben an. Täte er es ungeschickt,

wäre er ein blosser Hanswurst. Führt er es aber mit gewaltiger
Kraft zu Ende, dann wird er, obzwar er weiter die Züge eines
Clowns trägt, zu einem den Faschismus verkörpernden Magier. Diese
magische Kraft erscheint im Cipolla von <u>Mario und der Zauberer</u>
wieder, das gleiche Motiv finden wir in <u>Willi das Medium</u>, und
momentartig taucht es schliesslich auch in der Gestalt des in-
cubus im <u>Doktor Faustus</u> auf.

Aus all dem ergibt sich für uns als eine der wichtigsten Lehren,
dass Mann die ganze Nietzsche-Tragödie, die Tragödie der Erwähltheit, die Tragödie der Empfindlichkeit der Dekadenz gegenüber auf
zwei Ebenen löst. Soweit das Problem der Dekadenz, der Trennung
von der Wirklichkeit auftaucht und jemand dieses Problem intellek-
tuell erlebt und dieses Erleben zur Tragödie führt, bestehen zwei
Möglichkeiten: die eine im tiefen Erleben der Tragik der Situation und im Hineinrennen in die persönliche Vernichtung, die andere im Vernichten. In dem einen Fall wird der Künstler zum un-
tergehenden Künstler, im anderen Fall wechselt und wandelt sich
die ästhetische Lebensführung vom Künstlerischen zum Gaukleri-
schen. So löst Mann die Problematik der dekadenten Philosophie
zweifach, und sein Lebenswerk zeigt auch auf, wie die Dekadenz
selbstzerstörerisch wird und wehrlos dem Faschismus gegenüber,
und wie andererseits dieselben Motive in Spiegelfechterei und
Magie, in den Faschismus umschlagen können. Aus Nietzsche kann
also die Tragödie der Persönlichkeit und auch die Tragödie der
Menschheit entspriessen. Die Totalität des <u>Doktor Faustus</u> zum
Beispiel entsteht daraus, dass die aus Nietzsche entspriessenden
zweierlei Tragödien voneinander scheinbar unabhängig, aber zugleich tiefer im Zusammenhang miteinander erscheinen und hinter
Adrians Tod als Hintergrund der Tod des Hitlerschen Deutschlands
aufdämmert. Alles, was aus Nietzsche entspringt, geht zugrunde,
auch die aus ihm entspringende Kunst und Gaukelei. Beide, Kunst
und Gaukelei, haben nämlich den gemeinsamen Zug, dass Nietzsche
die Erfordernisse des Tages nicht begriff und auch nicht begriff,
dass die Tugend wieder möglich zu werden beginnt.

Es ist durchaus kein Zufall, dass unter den Thomas Mannschen
Parallelitäten /wir befassen uns nicht mit der spezifischen Rolle
des <u>Felix Krull</u>-Romans, die Lukács herausgearbeitet hat/ beim
Abschluss des Lebenswerkes neben dem <u>Doktor Faustus</u> und <u>Der Er-</u>

wählte steht. Man könnte die Gegenüberstellung Leverkühns und des grossen Papstes als symbolisch ansehen, wir wollen aber es nicht tun. Die Symbolik dieser Gegenüberstellung hätte nämlich den Sinn, dass dieser die Abenddämmerung des westlichen Artistikums bedeute, während jener eben dabei ist, in romanhafter Form den anbrechenden Morgen dieses Artistikums darzustellen. Bekanntlich setzte mit Papst Gregor in der Christenheit eine relativ freiere Bewegungsmöglichkeit der Kunst ein. Obzwar bei Gregor die Kunst bloss didaktischen Zwecken diente, begann dennoch mit ihm die Möglichkeit der künstlerischen Entwicklung, die dann in der christlichen Welt vom ducento an immer mehr zur Herrschaft gelangte. Doch nicht diese Symbolik, an die Thomas Mann kaum gedacht haben mag, ist für uns wichtig. Viel bedeutsamer ist, dass hier der Mythos, und zwar der westliche Mythos, zu neuem Leben erweckt wurde, jener Mythos, der Adrian Leverkühn gegenüber, der die menschlichen Beziehungen desanthropomorphisiert hat, auch das Unmenschliche anthropomorphisiert. Und eine der wichtigsten Lehren dieses Mythos, ja des ganzen Romans, knüpft sich eben an unser Problem an. Zweifellos zeigen sich auch hier die bereits charakterisierten Merkmale der schriftstellerischen Methode Thomas Manns. Auch hier muss sich die Hauptperson, um zum Leben zu gelangen, durch den Tod hindurchkämpfen. Das Hindurchkämpfen durch den Tod geschieht, wie auch im Joseph, in mehreren Phasen. Joseph kann nur nach Grube und Kerker zum Leben gelangen, und so geschieht es hier auch. Gregors Weg ist nicht weniger schwierig und problematisch. In der Sünde geboren sein, das Begehen der Sünde, das freiwillige Büssen sind die Stationen, die der grosse Papst zu durchlaufen hat, damit er zum "Erwählten" werde. Das Erwähltsein ist also eben das Ergebnis des Leidens, der Besiegung des Todes. Dadurch kommt bei Thomas Mann das Gegenstück zu Doktor Faustus zustande. Faust musste sich noch, um sich zu verjüngen und in die neue Welt - in die Welt des Kapitals - zu gelangen, dem Teufel verkaufen. Thomas Manns Faustus wird aber schon in der Welt des Kapitals geboren. Er verkauft sich dem Teufel nicht, um in die neue Welt zu gelangen, sondern um in der von ihm selbst erbauten alten Welt, der Welt des Artistikums, verweilen zu können. Und die Besonderheit dieser Welt ist, wie Thomas Mann nachweist, nicht die gleiche wie die der Welt

Peter Schlemihls. Chamissos Held verkauft dem Teufel nur seinen
Schatten, er selbst bleibt aber erhalten. Manns Held Adrian verkauft sich selbst und es bleibt von ihm nichts wie sein Schatten.
Seine Kunst ist als Kunst Schatten und Scheinkunst, da Adrian
den Weg zurück zum Leben nicht zu finden vermag. Eben darum bleibt
ihm die Erwähltheit versagt. Gregors Verhältnis zu den Fragen
des Lebens ist gerade das Gegenteil. Er sagt zu seiner Frau:
"Ehrwürdigste, wir wollen das Gott anheimgeben und es ihm über-
lassen, ob Er einem Teufelswerk, wie unserer Ehe, Gültigkeit beimessen will oder nicht. Mir stände es wenig an, den Scheidungs-
spruch zu sprechen und unser Verhältnis auf das von Mutter und
Sohn zurückzuführen. Denn auch Euer Sohn wäre ich, alles recht
erwogen, ja besser nicht... Da siehst du, ehrfürchtig Geliebte,
und Gott sei dafür gepriesen, dass Satanas nicht allmächtig ist
und es nicht so ins Extreme zu treiben vermochte, dass ich irr-
tümlich auch noch mit diesen in ein Verhältnis geriet und etwa
gar Kinder von ihnen hatte, wodurch die Verwandtschaft ein völli-
ger Abgrund geworden wäre. Alles hat seine Grenzen. Die Welt ist
endlich."

Wie also der eine Roman der Sieg Satans über den Menschen ist,
so ist der andere Roman als Pendant der Sieg des Menschen über
Satan. Bei Thomas Mann führt das blosse Artistikum, der rein
ästhetische Weg entweder zum Sieg Satans über den Menschen oder
zur Verwandlung des Menschen in einen Teufel. Der andere Weg,
der nicht rein artistische, der die Möglichkeit der Tugend in
Betracht zieht, führt zum Sieg über Satan, zur Erwähltheit.

In Papst Gregors Worten ist die deutliche Polemik mit Freud
kaum zu überhören. Freud hat die Lösung der menschlichen Probleme bekanntlich nur im Wege der Analyse für möglich gehalten. Für
ihn waren alle, auch die noch nicht konkret hervorgetretenen,
sondern nur im Komplexen vorhandenen, unterdrückten seelischen
Vorgänge Objekt der Analyse. Manns Papst Gregor sagt dagegen,
die Hinwendung zur Vergangenheit sei nutzlos, die Analyse sei
wertlos, wertlos sei "die Zurückführung auf das Mutter-Sohn
Verhältnis". Was für Freud Gegenstand der Analyse ist, das ist
für Thomas Mann Lebensvorgang und objektives Geschehen, das man
nicht heraufbeschwören, sondern überwinden solle. Gregor wurde
tatsächlich in Geschwisterliebe empfangen und hat die eigene

Mutter zu seiner Frau gemacht. Er wird gross, weil er sich über die Vergangenheit hinwegzusetzen vermag. Damit sind wir zu dem entscheidenden und zugleich tiefsten Zug der Auffassung Thomas Manns vom Menschen angelangt. Nachdem er im Doktor Faustus die Nietzsche-Tragödie und im Erwählten die mit der Nietzsche-Tragödie zusammenhängende Satire der Freudschen Theorie geschrieben hatte, gelangte er soweit, dass er sich schliesslich über beide bürgerliche Theorien hinwegsetzte.

Dass in Manns Augen Nietzsche und Freud die gleiche Tendenz zum Ausdruck bringen, nur jeder von einem anderen Aspekt, erweist sich aus folgendem Gedankengang im Zusammenhang mit Wagner: "Und wir wollen uns erinnern, dass auch bei Freud, dessen seelische Radikalforschung Tiefenkunde bei Nietzsche in grossem Stil vorweggenommen ist, das Interesse für Mysthische, Menschlich-Urtümliche und Vorkulturelle mit dem psychologischen Interesse aufs engste zusammenhängt". Und dieser Zusammenhang, mag er wissenschaftlich auch nur relativ haltbar sein, der aber Thomas Mann ausserordentlich wichtig schien, ermöglicht die Aufstellung der Parallelität der Nietzsche-Tragödie und der Freud-Parodie. Hier gelangt Mann, der den Erwählten als typisches Spätwerk bezeichnet, zu dem früher erwähnten Menschenbild, und dies jetzt schon endgültig in beinahe abgeschlossener Weise. Die Einheit vom Ästhetischen und Ethischen, der vielseitigen Probleme von Psychologie und Philosophie, der Anschauungen des Politikers und der Protest des Politikers gegen das blosse Literatentum und den Salondemokratismus ist wiederhergestellt. Und diese Einheit ist nichts anderes als die erlebte Überwindung der bürgerlichen Philosophie. Das "erlebt" bezieht sich in gleicher Weise auf Schopenhauer und Nietzsche, Freud und Kirkegaard, aber auf sie alle bezieht sich auch die Überwindung der Philosophie. Welche Bedeutung dies für Thomas Man hatte, geht ganz klar auch aus dem Joseph-Roman hervor, in dem Mann eine eigentümliche Einheit der geträumten und der ethischen Anschauung formuliert hat. Die Überwindung der Philosophie aber konnte nur darum erfolgen, weil Mann die Vergangenheit im ganzen zu überwinden vermochte. Dass Überwindung der Vergangenheit oder Steckenbleiben in der Vergangenheit und Überwindung der bürgerlichen Philosophie oder Steckenbleiben in ihr bewusst einander gegenübergestellt werden, erhellt

schon daraus, dass sich bei Mann, wie wir gesehen haben, die
Beziehung zum Leben über die Weltanschauung, das geistige Profil
als vermittelndes Element abzeichnet. Der Zusammenhang von Vergangenheit und Philosophie ist /im erwähnten Sinne/ offenkundig.
Auf jede bürgerliche Philosophie und insbesondere auf den bürgerlichen Irrationalismus ist Hegels These anwendbar, dass Minervas
Eule nur nach Eintritt der Dunkelheit fliege. Es ist die Eigen-
heit dieser Philosophie und jedweder Philosophie, die sich angesichts neuer Erscheinungen nicht selbst zu erneuern vermag,
dass sie zur Vergangenheit gehört. Im Sinne solcher Philosophie
herrscht die Vergangenheit über die Gegenwart und auch über die
Zukunft... Eben deshalb muss man sich über diese Philosophie erheben.

So wird Thomas Manns Lebenswerk zu einer Reihe von Kunstwer-
ken, in denen die den Künstler auf tragische und parodistische
Irrwege führenden Tendenzen des bürgerlichen Weltbildes schonungs-
los entlarvt werden. Ich möchte im Zusammenhang damit einen beinahe anekdotisch anmutenden Briefwechsel zitieren, der zeigt, wie
sehr ein von Mann ausserordentlich geschätzter Repräsentant des
bürgerlichen Weltbildes Mann missverstand und wie kalt ihn dessen
Versuche liessen, es zu überwinden. Mann schickte Freud ein Exem-
plar des ersten Bandes des Joseph-Romans, und Freud dankte dem
Autor in einem langen Brief für die ihm erwiesene Ehre. Darin
schrieb er, die folgenden Umstände könnten dem Joseph-Problem
Aktualität verleihen. Auch Napoleon dürfte einen Joseph-Komplex
gehabt haben, darum sei er nach Ägypten gegangen, und das ganze
ägyptische Abenteuer erkläre sich aus dem Joseph-Komplex. Aus
der Begründung dieser Ansicht dürften einige kurze Zitate genü-
gen:

"a/ Er /nämlich Napoleon-d. Verl./ war Korse, der zweite Sohn
unter einem Haufen Geschwister. Sein älterer Brüder hiess Josef,
und dieser Umstand wurde, da das Zufällige und das Unausweichli-
che im Leben zusammen auftreten, schicksalhaft für den Jüngeren.
In der korsischen Familie war das Privileg des ältesten Sohnes
von einer speziellen heiligen Arkana umgeben...

b/ Als Napoleon General wurde, empfahl man ihm, eine junge
Witwe zu heiraten, die älter sei als er, sehr anmutig und sehr
einflussreich. Es hätte sich viel gegen die Frau einwenden lassen,

aber zu ihren Gunsten entschied wahrscheinlich die Tatsache, dass sie Josefine hiess. Diesem Namen war es zu verdanken, dass Napoleon die zärtlichen Gefühle, die er für seinen älteren Bruder empfand, auf sie zu übertragen vermochte...

c/ Beim Hören des Namens erwachte grosse Liebe in Napoleon zu Josefine B., aber das war natürlich noch nicht die Identifizierung mit Josef. Deren schönster Ausdruck war Napoleons berühmte Expedition nach Ägypten..." /s. Jones: Sigmund Freud, Life and Work, New York, III. B.S. pp. 462-463./

Diese Stellen haben wir angeführt, um klar zu sehen, wie wenig Verständnis über ihren Ausgangspunkt hinausgewachsene und darüber hinwegschreitende Kunst Thomas Manns bei denen finden konnte, die sich mit seinem Ausgangspunkt identifiziert hatten. /Bei Kirkegaard, Schopenhauer und Nietzsche, die noch im 19. Jahrhundert starben, wäre es wohl das gleiche gewesen, hätten sie erlebt, was Thomas Mann über die Geschichte ihres Einflusses geschrieben hat. Es ist ausgeschlossen, dass welcher konsequente Nietzscheaner auch immer bei Thomas Mann die für Nietzsches Philosophie charakteristische Gedankenwelt fände. Vom Gesichtspunkt seines Verhältnisses zur Philosophie ist das Element der Aufhebung des aufhebenden Bewahrens für Mann vielleicht charakteristischer als für irgend einen anderen/.

Nur auf der Grundlage der Erhebung über Philosophie und Vergangenheit lässt sich Thomas Manns Menschenbild begreifen. Der begabte Mensch gelangte schon seit Hanno Buddenbrook in den Mittelpunkt von Thomas Manns Interesse, und zwar so, dass Mann die Begabung mit Empfindlichkeit und Empfänglichkeit gleichsetzte. Doch Empfindlichkeit, abstrakte Begabung waren für ihn nicht alles. Die wahre Begabung sah er darin, dass der Mensch eine Neigung besitze, die ihn sehnsüchtig oder nicht sehnsüchtig in die Welt der Durchschnittsmenschen zurückführt, zurückführt über den Tod ins Leben. Daher kommt der Unterschied des von Thomas Mann ein fauler Säugling genannten Künstlers Tonio Krögers und Tristan Spinells. In Tonio Kröger lebt noch das Sehnen nach Ingeborg Holmok, Spinell ekelt sich einfach vor Klöterjahn. Joseph reisst sich von seinen Brüdern los, kehrt aber zu ihnen zurück, Adrian Leverkühn bricht endgültig mit der 9. Symphonie, der grosse Papst dagegen kehrt ins Leben zurück. In einer Zeit, da die Pflege des blossen Artistikums zur Tragödie führt, ein solches Artistikum in Gaukelei umschlagen und die subjektive Tragödie zur Welttragödie werden kann, in einer solchen Zeit ist es nötig, den Begriff der Erwähltheit zu klären.

Und wer sind die Erwählten? Die Cipollas, die Medien, die Repräsentanten der Verzauberung der Welt, welche die Vergagenheit, den Zauber, den mythischen Magier in die Gegenwart heben? Nein! Sind Auserwählte diejenigen, die auf der Ebene des Artistikums die vom blossen Artistikum gebotenen Möglichkeiten erschöpfen, die in der Erfüllung der letzten, aber von der Wirklichkeit gelösten Möglichkeit des blossen Artistikums auf Leverkühns Weise das Leben verneinen und die 9. Symphonie zurückziehen? Nein! Jene richten die Welt, diese sich selbst zugrunde. Erwählte können nur diejenigen sein, die sich durch Hölle und Sühne und Weltanschauungen von fürchterlichsten Folgen hindurchkämpfen, die alten und neuen Entfremdungen mit allen ihren Qualen durchgestanden und sie überwunden haben. Das Beispiel des Erwählten Gregor zeigt, dass der Erwählte nichts anderes ist als der Mensch selbst, der sich über seine eigene Vergangenheit zu erheben vermag. Der Erwählte ist eben derjenige, der erkannt hat, das es keinen erwählten Menschen gibt, der weder im Leiden noch im Siege einen Privileg sieht, sondern auch über den Tod hinweg das Leben erobert.

AUSTRIA AND HUNGARY

Philosophy and Culture
J. Lukács and F. Tőkei eds.

THE CULTURAL LEGACY OF THE AUSTRO-HUNGARIAN MONARCHY

L. MÁTRAI

The downfall of the Monarchy is somewhat of a tricky subject,
not only because of the enormous amount of information and facts
at our disposal, but also because it carries a certain "ideological" burden. Therefore it may not be out of place to preface
this article with a few remarks on my approach.

x

Since the subject is the disintegration of a great power with
a major historical role in its time, and the concomitant cultural
effects, the historian is bound to find himself confronted with
the obstacles which arise from different systems of values and
different attitudes. Without indulging in historical relativism,
or even scepticism which contradicts the very meaning of historiography, we are all aware that a man's appreciation of progress
or decadence, of well-merited decline or an end considered deplor-
ably premature greatly depends on his whole system of values. A
brief survey of the studies on the Monarchy is enough to convince
us that the majority of them provide no direct and objective knowledge of historical relations: these can only be acquired indirectly, after an evaluation of the author's ideological position
/not that I claim that this is anything new in considering questions of methodology or historical philosophy/. In these "fundamental" questions, therefore, any concealment of my own ideological position would not serve the interests of scientific truth;
on the contrary, it should be made as clear as possible: the sail-
or who navigates in continually changing waters must, for his own
sake, know his own position exactly.   213

I am discussing this subject primarily from the Hungarian
point of view, but I shall not limit myself to Hungarian problems. In fact, for the purpose of "comparative cultural history",
I shall extend this study to include Austrian and Czech problems
as well. As a result, the general scope of the material will be
rather more limited, and the examples and illustrations mainly
taken from literature and science. The other branches of cultural
history, such as music or fine arts are furnishing only one or
two supplementary examples or parallels.

THE COMMON LANGUAGE

The first question in this comparative study of culture de-
fines itself sharply and clearly. Did the peoples living in the
Monarchy have some common culture, did some sort of "Gesamtkul-
tur" exist built on the economic and political basis of the "Ge-
samtmonarchie"? To give a definite answer to this question is
at least as difficult /in fact even more difficult and compli-
cated/ as to decide whether an independent Austrian or Swiss
literature exists or they are merely the Austrian or Swiss branches of German literature? I think it can be safely assumed as a
simple fact of cultural history that the peoples in the Monarchy
had, in fact, a "more or less common" culture, in the sense that
national characteristics merged into it. It was common to them
all to the extent to which common experiences in one cultural
field made it possible and indeed necessary. But within this
"more or less" common culture an inner paradox remained present:
the people who shared this general culture marked it with their
own particular history, and hence fractured its common character.
Let me start with the most difficult question. The language
of the "Kaiserliche und Königliche Monarchie", translatable as
Imperial and Royal Monarchy, but universally known as "K. u. K.",
increasingly learnt and used by some sectors of the non-Austrian
peoples /the ruling classes and the majority of the intelligen-
tsia/, bore all the marks of the origin of the non-Austrians
using it and was - to say the least - unfit to play the role of
a literary language. At the same time this same German language
played a very positive part after the 1860s, when it opened the

doors of international science to the intelligentsia, because
at that time the main language of science was German in certain
branches of science /i.e.in history of philosophy, medicine and
in many branches of the natural sciences/.

This common language was also useful to other social classes
because it could be used throughout the Monarchy: it was the
language of human contact, commerce and negotiation, and its
use produced a certain kind of joviality and good humour, because it was known that this Viennese dialect was less and less
the classical language of Goethe and Schiller. Historians /and
psychologists/ will easily understand that the common German
language spread among the social classes directly benefiting
from the position of the Monarchy as a larger economic unit,
and the effect this had on the development of capitalism in the
last quarter of the nineteenth century.

THE COMMON WAY OF LIFE

Around 1900 the upper and middle classes of the bourgeoisie,
the groups going up or down in the world, the civil servants
and army officers also enjoyed a common way of life, together
with their use of a common language. In this environment and
way of life the character of K. u. K. Vienna overshadowed the
national character of the non-Austrian groups /it would be difficult to say in what proportion/. This common character was
not only visible for instance in the eclectic style of the
public buildings or the railway statitons built according to
the same pattern from Trieste to Lemberg and from Prague to
Orsova; there was a deeper common denominator appearing in the
customary behaviour and thinking of the population as a whole,
and this was much more important, constituting an effective sociological and historical factor. In Prague, Vienna and Budapest an average flat consisted of three rooms; a dining-room,
a bedroom and a children's room: as it has been described, e.g.,
in the works of Kafka, Joseph Roth and Ferénc Molnár - any difference upwards or downwards indicated with almost mathemetical
accuracy the precise conditions of that bourgeois family; a
member of the upper bourgeoisie also had a drawing room, the

intellectual a study or a consulting room, and the petty bourgeois contented himself with the "dining-room" alone. No dining-
-room was conceivable without the "Kredenz" or "credenza", the
special cupboard in which china and silver were proudly displayed.
This was probably the most widely used German word in the non-
-Germanic territories, second only to the military Habt-Acht
/Attention!/. In the middle of the dining-room would stand a
large table surrounded by leather-covered or plain chairs, always in exact accordance with the economic and social status of
the family, and, if possible, slightly above it... Such a family
had three to five children who all went to school; the clever
boys notched their way upwards by becoming civil servants or
members of the intelligentsia, the others went into their father's
business, eventually taking over the shop, workshop or office.
The household was run by the mistress of the house, but the work
was done by a maid, usually taken from one of the national minorities, because they were more obedient, cheaper, or, in Hungary, from among the landless peasants because they were notori-
ously "unassuming". Apart from the general maid the family also
kept a nurse - the more well-to-do families had a "Fräulein" instead - but they almost never employed male servants /a valet or
lackey because this was understood as the privilege of the aristocracy, and it would therefore have been a form of cheating to
overstep this barrier/. /The Heizer, Kafka's masterpiece, translated the fact into literary form that the furnacemen and domes-
tic servants in the Monarchy were mainly chosen from the Slav
population/.

This way of life continued to develop and expand after 1900,
along with undeniable capitalist development in the Monarchy,
to which it was so closely linked that it provided inspiration
and themes for contemporary literature, and was doomed to perish
with it. Splinters of it survived, however, and not only in literature. How, and to what extent they continue to exist in the various "successor-States" is one of the most interesting questions
in the cultural sociology of the peoples of this region.

This upward trend around 1900 had only been progress for the
bourgeois classes. The nobility, the high-ranking civil servants
and the financial aristocracy found it most undesirable, as they

did every kind of democratization lessening the power of the
existing ruling classes, because it would obviously and cate-
gorically express a decline in their own status and the rise
of the bourgeoisie.

THE DISADVANTAGES OF THE POOR

The living conditions of the exploited and poorer sectors of
the population at the end of the century can be seen in the following story. The German language, which opened larger practical
and intellectual vistas to the bourgeois sectors, was also the
official language of the army, and as such, proved a horrible
straitjacket for all recruits whose mother tongue was not German.
A veteran artillery sergeant of the K. u. K. Army recounted how,
looking through the papers of a private in the artillery, he
found some mysterious notes. He promptly interrogated the suspect, a young peasant, and found that the poor fellow had made
study-notes not to disgrace himself in training. I quote here
only one of his hieroglyphs: _süta-plitagangicse_. Solution: _Schild-
zäpfchen samt Angiessen_ - a more or less important part of a
gun -, knowledge of its German name was indispensable to any
decent gunner of the K. u. K. Army. There is no need to explain
that in such a social-psychological situation the language, the
carrier of thought, consciousness and culture, ceases to spread
culture and friendship between the people; on the contrary, it
becomes a tool of a deaf and blind authority, only increasing
the loneliness and alienation of those who are at its mercy.

If the state is an organ of coercion, its most "coercive"
tool is the army; when the oppressed people rise against the
state, the first obstacle to confront them will be the army.
It is no mere accident that the K. u. K. Army played a major
part not only in unleashing and then losing the First World War,
but also in the disintegration of the Monarchy in a very concrete form, in that the soldiers streaming back from the front
after immeasurable sufferings were important factors in the
destruction of the Monarchic framework of the state. The army
also played a social-psychological role because, already well
before the War, the K. u. K. Army had been the institution cre-

ating the greatest number of enemies for the Monarchy. Robert Musil, for instance, discovered terrible hopelessness of human existence in a military school - though this could have been a consequence of his own personal sensitivity. /Very oddly, despite the fact that he had become a writer, he later adjusted quite well to the absurdities of military life/. But if we consider all the works dealing with this problem in the culture of the peoples of the Austro-Hungarian Monarchy, from Jaroslav Hasek's <u>The Good Soldier Schweik</u> to Alban Berg's <u>Wozzeck</u>, it is clear that there is much more to it than simply the difficulties of a soldier's life, hard on civilian gentleman and peasant alike. The multinational or supranational state, its whole apparatus, or one of its essential institutions, was challenged in these works: and this was an important sign that the centrifugal forces of the Monarchy were gaining the upper hand and threatening the very existence of this "medium-size Great Power". At the same time it seems that the diagnosis according to which an early internationalism appeared in a Monarchy burdened with vestiges of a late feudalism was correct.

COMMON CHARACTERISTICS IN LITERATURE

The evidence furnished on this point by the concrete facts, as reflected in Austrian, Czech or Hungarian literature, must here be evoked if we wish to obtain an authentic picture of what was common to all and what was individual to each in the Monarchy at the end of the century and in the following period of disintegration.

The tripartite kingdom of Austria, Hungary and Bohemia /which could not come into existence constitutionally, primarily because of the energetic opposition of the Foreign Minister of the Austro-Hungarian Monarchy, the Hungarian Count Gyula Andrássy/ was, nonetheless, a more or less accomplished fact spiritually in the intellectual life of these three peoples, and it is these common features I am investigating.

A somewhat limited change occurred at around the turn of the century in the literary history of these three peoples and the individual destinies of their writers. A much more profound

change took place after the First World War and the subsequent
disintegration of the Monarchy. It is, of course, true that "consciousness" follows changes in the situation, but not always in
timed sequence: historical crises may be foreshadowed in poetry
well in advance of the actual happenings, and echo it long after
they have subsided.

Hugo von Hofmannsthal, Rainer Maria Rilke and Franz Kafka are
the greatest representatives of this type of literature, which
came into being in the "golden age" of the Monarchy and ended
after its disintegration, at which time it was incorporated in
the national literatures of the new states. These great writers
are modern in all the good and bad senses of the word. They are
modern from the historical viewpoint, because every line they
wrote is an attempt to discover an answer to the most burning
questions of their own time, and they are also modern in aesthetic terms because they experimented with new /or partially
new/ forms in the description of reality. Enough has been written
about them to fill a library, treating them under various literary
categories: they have been described as expressionists, the representatives of the "Wiener Dekadenz", existentialists, and so on,
and all these classifications provide valuable insights, especially when the analysis of concrete details has revealed some new
philological-historical connection or some fresh psychological
nuance. The historian, however, asks in the first place - and
to this question there is no reply - what is the common feature
belonging to these important works which can be said to bear the
unique stamp of the social and historical background of the Austro-Hungarian Monarchy?

THE RELATIONSHIP TO DEATH

These three great writers are the classics of loneliness,
alienation and the transiency of life. Some would claim that
such characteristics are also found in the works of other writers.
True, but not in this kind of amalgamation. It is, of course, true
that in a certain sense every literature and art concerns itself
with the fleeting nature of life because its human function is
to find "something perdurable" in the ceaseless flow of birth and

death. This perdurable "something" could be called immortality from the emotional angle, the unchanged essence behind changing phenomena from the philosophical angle, or the universal and eternal system of values in terms of humanity in its historical process, from the historical angle - but it is a fact that all art has an inner connection with death. Even if Schopenhauer's extremist and pessimist statement that every art inspired by death is incorrect, there is considerable truth in the words of a Belgian Shakespearean scholar: "Have you never noticed, Sir, that all great art is sad?" Consequently, this connection with death is not, and cannot be, a specific characteristic of writers of the Monarchy, since it characterizes every literature from Aeschylus to Dante, from Shakespeare to Tolstoy.

But a deeper relationship with death also existed, which came into being in the general crisis of European society, around 1900. Its outstanding figures are Proust and Joyce. The melancholy emanating from their works is deeper than the melancholy of earlier bourgeois novelists. Balzac and Flaubert described the transitory character of the external world, but with Proust not only the external world but creation and even the writer's existence became a matter of doubt. Hence the very existence of the realistic great novel became a question in itself, and thus it concentrated its themes on the writer himself as the subject. The writer, who had formerly taken the whole external world as his province, now - as it became increasingly suspect and hostile, withdrew within his own "inner boundaries" and became more and more introverted.

KAFKA

These signs of development, however, were not the result of an arbitrary choice on the part of the writer, but the inevitable impression on art of the substantial changes taking place throughout Europe. Thomas Aquinas rightly said that man could not help his thoughts, neither can a writer freely choose the content of his works. In fact, he does not even choose the attitude he adopts towards them because his opinions about the outer world, whether constructive or not, are determined by the objec-

tive circumstances of his own individual existence. The point
that weighs with the historian is that the great literary documents of the crisis of the Monarchy are not really in the same
category with the works of Proust and Joyce, which are concerned
with the crisis of the novel. Franz Kafka's genius developed and
reached its peak in the period of the Monarchy, but the crisis
he represented is far more profound than that revealed in the
two French and Irish classics, respectively. It is worth noting,
however, that Joyce himself was temporarily within the Monarchy
/see Stephen Bloom's relations in Szombathely, and Joyce himself
in Trieste/. Kafka's work is the extreme example of alienation,
loneliness and transience, for Proust's world was alienated from
the present, Joyce's from society as well, but Kafka, in addition,
was also alienated from himself.

                              x

It is no secret that this fatal "extra" was due to the fact
that Kafka lived in the period of the Monarchy, so the specific
K. u. K. character preciously described must be sought in his
work. He was, by the way, the last representative of the trend
that began with Hofmannsthal and Rilke. Kafka's importance in
the universal history of civilization lies precisely in the fact
that in his person and work the general decline of European bourgeoisie merged with the main literary trend expressing the decline of the Monarchy.

HOFMANNSTHAL

In many respects Hofmannsthal's work occupies a key position
between old and new in literature: he wrote his first poems and
plays at the end of the century, when capitalism in the Monarchy
still possessed its last reserves of vigour: the world was still
open to the poet and he was free to experiment with different
literary methods and attitudes. His first period, therefore, was
influenced by the prevalent aestheticism and the cult of classical Greece /as if he were an archetype of Stefan George/ and
a further unfortunate feature of this period of his was his epi-

gonism /1/, well known to literary historians. A decisive change
in his life and art occurred around 1898 /almost exactly at the
turn of the century/ when he - himself did not quite understand
why - found he had to choose a new direction in his life and
work, for he was unable to continue in the old ways. The "Letter
of Lord Chandos" was a poignant manifestation of this poetic
crisis. In the somewhat stilted, archaic style of the era a
youth confessed to Lord Bacon of Verulam, his spiritual father,
that he was abandoning writing because he realized the hopeless
impractibility of poetry, the impossibility of faithfully convey-
ing reality. This work, in my opinion, lies on the borderline
between impressionism and expressionism; driven by the desire
to express outward reality fully and absolutely. He found himself faced with the choice of either substituting the subjective
for the objective as the matter of literature, or of renouncing
art completely. Can poetry seize and hold from passing reality
something like "the smell of freshly washed stone blocks in a
lonely corridor" - this wording of the crisis is akin to Proust.
Hofmannsthal overcame the crisis with a "positive" solution /he
chose the world, external reality/, while Rilke, his fellow poet,
chose the "negative", the introvert way, and became Kafka's
predecessor. As a consequence, Hofmannsthal was able to remain,
or rather develop to be the poet of Austria, while Rilke became
the poet of the Monarchy... An impatient historian might ask
why I find it necessary to go into all these hyper-aesthetic
details; why not leave them to elegant essayists? The answer is
clear: writers put into words the consciousness a society possesses of itself; without their evidence we can learn a great
deal of the history of an epoch, but not what happened to the
subject of the whole story, man himself.

RILKE

The Aufzeichnungen des Malte Laurids Brigge /The Notebooks
of Malte Laurids Brigge/ is a shockingly "Proustian" short story
which clearly demonstrates that Rilke chose "the other way": he
withdrew into the privacy of his soul. His chief character lives
in a pathologically extreme condition of complete separation

from the world; he lives half in a trance, but at the same time
suffers from this divorce from reality and from his fearful loneliness. This is indeed the position proclaimed by existentialism,
in which death is a permanent companion but by no means a solution. Rilke himself could live his life in the special world of
art which was independent of place and time - for a period he
was Rodin's secretary - it was his hero, Malte Laurids Brigge,
who had to suffer the inhuman, schizophrenic tortures of his
Sein zum Tode /Being for death/.

It is as if Rilke had sketched a design for living for Kafka,
for his life and work. Kafka's writing bore the stamp of this
dual suffering, in which the general crisis of the European bourgeoisie and the special crisis of the Austro-Hungarian Monarchy
were merged. It is for future researchers to investigate more
fully this double uncertainty of existence as demonstrated by
Hofmannsthal, Rilke and Kafka. Here and now I must limit myself
to the assertion that these three great authors, belonging to
the same historical trend, experienced and described in their
work three different degrees of the incertitudes of existence.
Hofmannsthal: beware, the world has become uncertain; Rilke:
withdraw into your inner self; Kafka: there is no help, we must
all die a miserable death.

These crises were determined by history: at the turn of the
century they forecast the social crisis and the approaching world
war; apprehended unconsciously in the writers' sensitive minds,
even if, like Rilke, they aristocratically turned their heads
away from "daily politics". "He who has not built himself a house
so far will not build one any more": this might be no more than
an over-sensitive poet speaking, but it is in fact a "concrete"
historical prediction of the long years of homelessness, loneliness and suffering which awaited the people of this region.
In an unstable country and a perishable world all three tried
to discover the "indestructible in us" /das Unzerstörbare in
uns/ - as Kafka put it. Hofmannsthal found it in an Austrian
sense of vocation /2/, Rilke in an interior fiction of a religious character and Kafka found it nowhere at all.

THE CHOICE BEFORE THE WRITER

A writer in 1900 had two alternatives: to cling to the past - but then he could not be an artist - or to find his way to the masses -, but then he could not remain a bourgeois. Those who could not "commit" themselves forwards or backwards chose the way upward, or inward, which amounted to the same thing. Like St. Augustine: noli fores ire... in interiore hominis habitat veritas /3/; they chose religion, Utopia, the existentialist nihil or some other "third way". Rilke's words /given a new colour recently by György Lukács in his theory of catharsis/ warned us: "You must change your life!" We seem to hear Erasmus of Rotterdam, who said: "Nothing will be good and perfect until men are good and perfect!" The only trouble is - and this is at the bottom of the vicious circle of every bourgeois humanism and every "reformism" - that man is not a Baron Münchhausen to lift himself out of the morass: he must rid himself of the morass around him if he really wants to get out. Marx, referring to the French materialists and Bentham in an early work of his, the Holy Family, wrote that if man was shaped by circumstances - and this was a fact - we had to make these circumstances more human in order to make men human. In short, the design for the "new world" so keenly awaited by Rilke amounted to change the world and your life will also change.

x

The crisis and downfall of the Monarchy in the context of cultural history can only be fully described through an exhaustive study of the voluminous material and extensive information about its interconnections which is available. So it is understandable that up to the present I have had to treat it qualitatively, rather more in the manner of an essay. So, similarly, I can only add a few facts to show the main lines of the common, centripetal features of the three territories of the Austrian Monarchy at the turn of the century, and its diverging, centrifugal characteristics after the collapse.

THE "LOSS OF REALITY"

The human and artistic attitudes represented by Franz Kafka
/apart from personal talent/ were, in fact, the expression of
the complete hopelessness of a man chained to the Monarchy: as
can again be seen in the problems which his "spiritual cousin"
Robert Musil, chose to deal with. Musil, although he did not
suffer from as many problems as Kafka, could never make up his
mind between the devil and the deep blue sea, between the "österreicher" /Austrian/ and the "Preusse" /Prussian/, /Ulrich and
Arnheim/, and I myself believe that this "definite inability to
choose" was the reason why Der Mann ohne Eigenschaften /The Man
without Qualities/ remained finally a truncated torso, like Kafka's great works: it also explains why he wanted to abandon art
for science, and then he longed to return to art again: i.e. for
him the borderline between the subjective and the objective was
blurred, and he himself described his position as "Essayismus".
/A similar break with traditional forms appears in the works of
the third "spiritual cousin", Hermann Broch/.

The same "loss of reality", increasingly observable in literature also appeared, mutatis mutandis, in Viennese science. Ernst
Mach was a world famous physicist, but he built a philosophy on
his physics which dissolved the objective outer world in the
"inner" world of subjective perception, and he destroyed even
this remnant of certainty when he declared: das Ich ist unrett-
bar /the Ego cannot be saved/ - as if he were speaking for Kafka /4/. The Böhm-Bawerk theory of marginal profit was a highly
intellectual economic concept but, marred by the same error,
it transferred the objective value-producing force of labour
to the relativist realm of subjective appreciation. Or again
Ludwig Wittgenstein, who lived and worked in the more stormy
atmosphere of the steadily approaching collapse of the régime,
and with whom the scientific claims of positivism went side by
side with an extreme intellectual mysticism which negated every
objective science /or dissolves in it/. All these are signs of
a deteriorating relation to reality, or its loss.

Further comparative information shows that the common cause
of all these similar phenomena was the gradual contraction of

the future of the Monarchy, the ensuing loss of perspective and, in its extreme form, the loss of a sense of reality. Those, such as the Hungarians and Czechs, for whom the downfall of the Monarchy did not mean the extinction of a great power with which they identified, but the birth of their own national independence, had something to cling to during the cataclysm: the existence of their own people and country. The future had not contracted for them; on the contrary, it opened newer vistas, and they had every reason, and did not lack the means, to seek a realist solution in concrete reality instead of turning to religion, Utopia or the innermost reaches of the soul. The amalgamation of the "Monarchic" elements of the past and of the national and popular elements of the future produced such brilliant works as Jaroslav Hasek's The Good Soldier Schweik which, it is true, may lack the poetic melancholy of temps perdu but certainly also lacks its morbidity. Where Karl Kraus, in his apocalyptic "danse macabre" /Die letzten Tage der Menschheit/ could only despair, where Franz Kafka could only reveal the hopelessness of all human existence, this brave Czech who used humour equally well as a defensive and offensive weapon, found the way to the future.

THE HUNGARIAN REACTION

A similar but original combination appeared in Hungary around 1900 and later during the "collapse", in which the common elements of the Monarchy and specific Hungarian elements of culture merged. The struggles and traditions of the independence of the past centuries determined a priori that Hungarian writers and artists took over only the best from Vienna. This "best" was obviously the still progressive cultural inspiration provided by a capitalism which still had some reserves of vigour at the time. Here I am referring in the main to the ideas of bourgeois radicalism, which probably exerted more influence on development in Hungary than in Austria, and which had started many progressive thinkers and politicians on their way to democracy, such as the poet Endre Ady, the sociologist Ervin Szabó, the political scientist Oszkár Jászi and the politician Mihály Károlyi.

226

It was only natural that other trends also exerted an influence, trends which became outdated along with the Monarchy, even though around 1900 they had seemed to promise - owing to the peculiar optical delusion of the bourgeoisie - sensational prospects of a "new culture". The partisans of the early expressionist movement, the "Wiener Dekadenz", aroused enormous interest in Budapest. Béla Balázs, who later became internationally known as a film expert and critic, wrote in 1909 the "Aesthetics of Death" which contained all the irrationalist, aestheticizing, mystical and pessimistic elements which belonged to the arsenal of the "Wiener Dekadenz", and which also attempted to answer the question of the Unzerstörbare, in a relation to death. It was around that time that the young Lukács wrote his Die Seele und die Formen /The Soul and the Forms/ which also proclaimed experimentation with death, the priority of art over reality, and crossed the borderline between literature and science, subordinating Tolstoy to Dostoevsky, just as Béla Balázs downgraded Mozart to "nothing but a fairy tale" in comparison with the "transcendent" Schubert.

Both Lukács and Balázs were representatives of the prewar era of the Monarchy, but their development took them further from it, and later they found solid ground amidst their own people and in the Marxist ideology of the proletariat. The same process of "growing away" is admirably shown in music, for example, in the works of Béla Bartók who, in a modern form of music which did not deny but expressed crisis, found his way to the people. This is where he differs from Schönberg, of whom a /non-Hungarian!/ critic wrote that "he became a revolutionary only to enable him to remain a conservative...".

The Monarchy has left a further literary "legacy" in Hungary, which is still operative in our day but hardly known to the public abroad. In the following generation of writers, now around sixty years of age, are two characteristic novelists who have both followed the example of Proust in their masterly pursuit of "temps perdu". Their childhood was affected by the after--effects of the historical storm which had swept away the Monarchy, and they became, as it were, specialists on decay. But the Hungarian society in which they grew up was no longer attached to that failing world; at most it only carried traces of the former ties. These traces were, however, only memories: they did not decide the writer's future in any way, nor constrict his prospects: they were no more than a theme, a subject for him which, for all its melancholy, opened up future vistas. Two such works exist: <u>Confession and Farewell</u> by Pál Granasztói, the other <u>School on the Frontier</u> /Harcourt, Brace and World/ by Géza Ottlik, which is the real counterpart of Robert Musil's <u>Törless</u>, although Ottlik had never read Musil's book.

GYULA KRUDY

Both these novels are unimaginable without the work of Gyula Krudy /1878-1933/, the Hungarian writer best acquainted with the last period of the Monarchy. If a comparative literary history of the Monarchy ever cam to be written, an analysis of the works of Musil of Vienna, Kafka of Prague and Krudy of Budapest would be most rewarding in scholarly and philosophical terms. Krudy also specialized in decay and the fleeting impermanences of life; he was a <u>narrator temporis acti</u>: his works are full of the lost figures of the dead and gone Monarchy; one of his characters openly declared that "everybody who still wants to live here after Franz Joseph's death is a fool". Nonetheless, there is a cathartic effect in everything he writes because it is attached to a realist tradition in Hungarian literature which saves Krudy from extreme irrealism, from the lack of any future perspectives for the poetic and the tragic. His works are practically untranslatable, which is why he is considered one of the most "Hungarian" of our writers. They are also characterized by a subtle interpretation of real and dream worlds, but there is nothing Kafkaesque in them because he never oversteps the boundary between poetry and morbid fear. His chief work, <u>In my past days as a young gentleman</u>, relates the story of an afternoon: the scene is set in a small inn in a petty bourgeois district of Budapest. It is called "To the City of Vienna" and is famous far and wide as the only place throughout the country where they keep "Schwechat Lager Beer". The characters are the ordinary people of the neighbourhood to whom the most peculiar things are happening

228

with the approach of dusk. We never learn whether all these happenings are only the illusion of their quiet drinking; at the
peak of the illusion a mysterious foreigner appears who is a
real Austrian archduke. All these things happen in 1906, on the
last afternoon of the "To the City of Vienna". This last afternoon is not tragic in the sense that no further afternoons are
to follow: it is only the last because the old couple who keep
the inn are retiring and giving way to the young, with whom certainly quite different things will happen. Life is a dream, but
life continues - this can, perhaps, sum up the attitude of Gyula
Krudy, the best Hungarian writer on the atmosphere of the dis-
integrated Monarchy.

x

A short definition of the last two periods in the cultural
life of the Monarchy based on the foregoing is now worth attempt-
ing. Due to the collapse and final end of the Austro-Hungarian
Monarchy as an economic and political base, its cultural superstructure first found itself in a state of crisis and was later
overcome by a condition of extreme irreality, the typical condition of a superstructure which has lost its base. This explains
the often peculiar phenomena which made their appearance, as is
inevitable in every similar historical situation, when a great
power has ceased to be a great power, but the habitual forms
of thinking still persist among the people for some time to
come.

NOTES

/1/ See Requardt, Paul; H.v. Hofmannsthal /in Friedmann-Mann,
    Deutsche Literatur im 20. Jahrhundert, Heidelberg, 1961.
    II. Bd. p. 60./.

/2/ Literally he speaks of unzerstörbar Österreichisches /in-
    destructibly Austrian/ in his moving essay on Grillparzer.
    Ganzheim to his credit also pointed out that poetry and
    politics were healthily related in his work.

/3/ "Don't crave for the outside World... the truth is within
    man".

/4/ Mach, E.: Die Analyse der Empfindungen. Jena, G. Fischer,
    1900. p. 17.

Philosophy and Culture
J. Lukács and F. Tőkei eds.

ÖSTERREICH UND UNGARN.
EINE PHILOSOPHISCH-SOZIALPSYCHOLOGISCHE SKIZZE

J.K. NYÍRI

Die viele Jahrhunderte umfassende gemeinsame Geschichte von Österreich und Ungarn, insbesondere aber die Jahrzehnte des Dualismus, haben beide Länder mit tausendfachen engen Fäden auf
wirtschaftlichem, politischem und geistigem Gebiet miteinander
verbunden. Die wechselseitige Verflechtung des ungarischen und
österreichischen geistigen Lebens war Ende des neunzehnten und
Anfang des zwanzigsten Jahrhunderts für die Zeitgenossen derart
selbstverständlich, dass sie deren besondere Erwähnung gewiss
erstaunlich gefunden hätten. Sie betonten, im Gegenteil, die
unterscheidenden Züge, so dass in unserer geschichtlichen Erinnerung heute eben das Bewusstsein der auf diese Weise in den Vordergrund gerückten Unterschiede vorherrschend ist, und wir hinter den einstigen kulturellen Kämpfen, aufeinanderprallenden
Leidenschaften und geistigen Abneigungen mit Überraschung die
beträchtliche Gemeinsamkeit der Lebensformen, die Verwandtschaft
in Geschmack und Denken und jene zahllosen persönlichen Verbindungen entdecken, die zwischen den Repräsentanten der ungarischen
und der österreichischen Kultur bestanden. Wir empfinden es als
eine Entdeckung, wenn wir auf die Tatsache stossen, dass etwa
der liberale Politiker Ernst von Plener die staatstheoretischen
Schriften von József Eötvös hocheinschätzte und später eine Toch-
ter von Eötvös heiratete; dass der bekannte ungarische Philosoph
der Jahrhundertwende, Bernát Alexander, ursprünglich in Wien,
bei Zimmermann Philosophie studierte; dass der Politiker und
Rechtsgelehrte Ágost Pulszky in Wien geboren ist, Theodor Herzl
aber in Budapest, wie ja auch Arthur Schnitzlers Vater in Ungarn
aufgewachsen ist, György Lukács' Mutter indes in Wien erzogen

wurde; oder dass der Psychiater Hugó Lukács, bei welchem der ungarische Dichter Endre Ady in Behandlung war, später in Wien auch Robert Musil zu seinen Patienten zählte. Dabei waren diese Verbindungen durchaus keine Ausnahmen, die Fälle der persönlichen und geistigen Begegnungen waren nicht selten. Die ungarische und die österreichische Gedankenwelt hatten in der hier betrachteten Periode zweifellos bedeutende gemeinsame Bereiche, und es ist keineswegs überflüssig, dies von vornherein festzustellen, denn eine Untersuchung der Unterschiede dieser beiden Gedankenwelten wird nur vor dem Hintergrund einer geistigen Gemeinsamkeit überhaupt sinnwoll. Nur wenn wir davon ausgehen, dass die ungarische Kultur und Bildung während der Jahrzehnte des Dualismus in wichtigen Aspekten sehr nahe zueinander standen, gewinnt die Erscheinung Interesse und bedarf der Erklärung, dass in philosophiegeschichtlicher Hinsicht das ungarische und das österreichische Denken zu dieser Zeit voneinander radikal verschieden waren. Das österreichische Denken zeigte in der betreffenden Periode im allgemeinen eine starke philosophische Neigung; das ungarische Denken hingegen war grundlegend nichtphilosophischer Natur.

Diese Verschiedenheit lässt sich letzten Endes durch zwei Faktoren erklären. Der erste: Die bürgerliche Entwicklung in Ungarn ging im Vergleich zur österreichischen verspätet vor sich, das ungarische Bürgertum war sowohl zahlenmässig als auch in wirtschaftlicher Hinsicht schwach. Die klassische Rolle des Bürgertums - auch seine ideologische Rolle - musste in Ungarn dementsprechend vom Adel, der natio Hungarica der Adeligen übernommen werden. Der zweite Faktor ist der multinationale Charakter des im weiteren Sinne verstandenen /also ausser Deutsch-Österreich auch Böhmen, Mähren, Galizien usw. miteinschliessenden/ Österreichs, demzufolge innerhalb dieses Gebietes zentrifugale nationale Bestrebungen auftraten, und das österreichische Nationalbewusstsein /waren doch die Deutsch-Österreicher eigentlich auch Deutsche/ von einer inneren Unsicherheit gekennzeichnet war. Die bedeutenden Leistungen der deutsch-österreichischen Philosophie und Kultur im allgemeinen entstanden gerade im Ringen mit dem deutschen Bewusstsein, im Konflikt der nationalen und dynastischen, nationalen und supranationalen Verpflichtun-

gen: An diese Leistungen denken wir, wenn wir über österreichische Kultur sprechen. Die österreichische Kultur war von vornherein eine Krisenkultur, von vornherein /spätestens aber seit
1806, als der österreichische Kaiser Franz II. auf die deutsche
Kaiserkrone verzichten musste/ Ausdruck einer gewissen Entzweit-
heit, obwohl dieses Gefühl des Zwiespalts erst nach 1866, nach
dem preussisch-österreichischen Krieg und dem Ausschluss Österreichs aus dem Deutschen Bund traumatisch wurde, und auch danach
nicht mit gleichem Gewicht auf den verschiedenen gesellschaftlichen Schichten lastete. Für österreichisch - d.h. nicht-national - konnte sich ohne Vorbehalt die Bürokratie und das berufs-
mässige Offizierskorps halten - zwei Schichten, die durch den
Zerfall des Habsburger Reiches in ihrer Existenz bedroht gewesen
wären; und das Judentum, das von vornherein nicht-national, d.h.
recht eigentlich österreichisch war, auch wenn es sich in den
österreichischen und böhmischen Gebieten der deutschen Kultur
anzupassen versuchte. Ein tatsächliches Assimilationsbestreben
setzte um die achtziger Jahre eigentlich nur unter der Intelligenz ein; zu dieser Zeit jedoch nahm der deutsche Nationalismus
bereits eine antisemitische Färbung an, so dass die Juden Österreichs in ihren Bindungen sowohl deutsch als auch von den Deutschen abgestossen wurden. Allerdings war auch die Situation
der Deutschen nicht eindeutig. In der Monarchie konnten sie sich
als die herrschende Nation fühlen. Die Loslösung der slawischen
und ungarischen Gebiete und Österreichs Anschluss an Deutschland
hätte die österreichischen Deutschen eine zumindest relative Ver-
schlechterung ihrer gesellschaftlichen und wirtschaftlichen Lage.
bedeutet. 1866 hat dann die Österreicher vor der europäischen
Öffentlichkeit zu minderwertigen Deutschen degradiert, und bei
vielen das bis dahin bloss schlummernde nationale Gefühl aufge-
wühlt - wobei dasselbe auch in Österreich Niederlagen erleiden
musste. 1867 erhielten die Ungarn die Selbständigkeit, die achtziger Jahre brachten bereits einen erheblichen tschechischen
Einfluss: Die Deutschen Österreichs haben sich in dem Reich, das
sie als ihre Heimat betrachteten, immer weniger zu Hause gefühlt.
Um die Jahrhundertwende haben sich die Nationalitätenkämpfe der-
massen verschärft, dass die parlamentarische Regierungsform gänz-
lich gelähmt war. Wenn sich jetzt der Kaiser entschloss, seine

233

Deutschen gegen die Slawen und seine Juden gegen die Deutschen zu verteidigen, konnte er das nur auf absolutistische Weise tun - und was da das deutsche und deutsch-jüdische Bürgertum feierte, war die endgültige Niederlage seiner eigensten liberalen Grundsätze.

Nicht dass der ungarische Liberalismus und das ungarische Nationalbewusstsein frei von inneren Widersprüchen gewesen wären. Die zu den Ereignissen von 1848 führende Bewegung war im Grunde eine Bewegung des liberalen Klein- und Mitteladels, doch die Revolution, der Freiheitskrieg und sein Ausgang - die plebejischen Initiativen, der Aufstand der Nationalitäten gegen Ungarn, schliesslich die russische Intervention - übten eine abschreckende und desillusionierende Wirkung auf den ungarischen Adel aus. Seine Erlebnisse und Erkenntnisse - welche in erster Linie von Zsigmond Kemény, József Eötvös und Imre Madách in einer mehr oder minder abstrakt-begrifflichen, doch eher philosophiefeindlichen als philosophischen Form dargestellt wurden - führten diesen Adel notwendigerweise zum Ausgleich von 1867, und nicht nur die Deák-Partei und ihre politischen Nachfolger sahen sich in Bezug auf die Forderung der ungarischen Selbständigkeit und auf die liberale Nationalitätenpolitik zu ständigen Kompromissen gezwungen, nämlich zu Kompromissen auch mit sich selbst, sondern auch die Gegner des Ausgleichs meinten es mit der Unabhängigkeit nicht wirklich ernst, wie dies später die Entwicklungen von 1905/06 - der Opportunismus der Parteien der sog. nationalen Koalition - sehr klar bewiesen.

Die Wendepunkte der österreichischen und ungarischen Philosophiegeschichte in der zweiten Hälfte des neunzehnten und Anfang des zwanzigsten Jahrhunderts - bei den Ungarn wäre es allerdings treffender, von Wendepunkten in der Geschichte der Philosophiefeindlichkeit zu sprechen - hingen einerseits mit den Krisen der bürgerlichen Entwicklung bzw. des Bürgertums in Österreich und in Ungarn, andererseits mit den Krisen des österreichischen und ungarischen Nationalbewusstseins zusammen. Die deutsche bürgerlich-liberale Politik war in Österreich eigentlich schon seit 1861 die führende. Allerdings hatte das deutsch--österreichische Bürgertum diese Wende nicht seiner eigenen politischen Kraft, sondern den militärischen Misserfolgen und dem finanziellen Bankrott des kaiserlichen Absolutismus zu verdanken. Das mit Preussen rivalisierende Österreich erhoffte nur dadurch die Sympathie der kleineren deutschen Staaten zu gewinnen, wenn es den österreichischen Deutschen, also eigentlich der Bourgeoisie, eine angemessene Stellung gewährleistete; und auch in den Augen der internationalen Finanzwelt konnte nur ein liberales, konstitutionell eingerichtetes Österreich als kreditfähig gelten. Das sog. Februarpatent sicherte dem deutschösterreichischen Bürgertum eine wirksame Vertretung, ja ein Übergewicht im Reichsrat; noch mehr befriedigt wurden die liberalen Wünsche durch die im Dezember 1867, gleichzeitig mit der Inartikulierung des Ausgleiches verabschiedete Konstitution. Diese proklamierte die Immunität von Person und Eigentum des österreichischen Staatsbürgers, die Freiheit der Meinungsäusserung und der Presse, die Gleichheit vor dem Gesetz, und erklärte, dass die bürgerlichen und politischen Rechte, unabhängig von konfessioneller Zugehörigkeit, jedem zustehen – d.h. sie hob die Diskrimination der Juden auf. Ungelöst blieb jedoch die Nationalitätenfrage. Die zentralistischen Deutschen stimmten der ungarischen Selbständigkeit nur ziemlich missmutig, nur unter dem kaiserlichen Druck, zu; die Tschechen hingegen verlangten eine der ungarischen ähnliche Rechtsstellung, und boykottierten den Reichsrat. Die eine Hälfte Österreich-Ungarns hiess Königreich Ungarn; die andere Hälfte – dasjenige Gebiet, das von den deutschen Liberalen regiert wurde – hatte keinen Namen. Der Bezeichnung "Österreich" hätten die Tschechen oder die galizischen Polen niemals zugestimmt: Der offizielle Wortgebrauch sprach von den "im Reichsrate vertretenen Königreiche und Länder", inoffiziell wurde allgemein der Name "Zisleithanien" benutzt, während die Deutschen natürlich "Österreich" sagten. Die sozialpsychologische Lage der Österreicher war unter solchen Umständen in der Tat nicht einfach. Diese Lage wurde von keinem besser beschrieben, als von Robert Musil in seinem Roman Der Mann ohne Eigenschaften. "Man tut heute so", schreibt Musil, "als ob der Nationalismus lediglich eine Erfindung der Armeelieferanten wäre, aber man sollte es auch einmal mit einer erweiterten Erklärung versuchen, und zu einer solchen lieferte /Österreich-Ungarn/ einen wichtigten Beitrag. Die Bewohner dieser kaiserlich und königlichen kaiser-

235

lich königlichen Doppelmonarchie fanden sich vor eine schwere
Aufgabe gestellt; sie hatten sich als kaiserlich und königlich
österreichisch-ungarische Patrioten zu fühlen, zugleich aber auch
als königlich ungarische oder kaiserlich königlich österreichische. Ihr begreiflicher Wahlspruch angesichts solcher Schwierigkeiten war 'Mit vereinten Kräften!' ... Die Österreicher brauch-
ten aber dazu weit grössere Kräfte als die Ungarn. Denn die Ungarn waren zuerst und zuletzt nur Ungarn, und bloss nebenbei
galten sie bei anderen Leuten, die ihre Sprache nicht verstan-
den, auch für Österreich-Ungarn; die Österreicher dagegen waren
zuerst und ursprünglich nichts und sollten sich nach Ansicht ihrer Oberen gleich als Österreich-Ungarn oder Österreicher-Ungarn
fühlen, - es gab nicht einmal ein richtiges Wort dafür". Das
Krankheitsbild im Mann ohne Eigenschaften wurde freilich nachträglich gezeichnet. Doch bereits vor dem Krieg konnte Musil als
Zeitgenosse ähnliche Beobachtungen machen. "Es muss irgendwo in
diesem Staat ein Geheimnis stecken, eine Idee", schrieb er 1912.
"Aber sie ist nicht festzustellen. Es ist nicht die Idee des
Staates, nicht die dynastische Idee, nicht die einer kulturellen
Symbiose verschiedener Völker /Österreich könnte ein Weltexperi-
ment sein/, - wahrscheinlich ist das Ganze wirklich nur Bewegung
zufolge Mangels einer treibenden Idee, wie das Torkeln eines Rad-
fahrers, der nicht vorwärtstritt".

Ein Blick aus philosophiegeschichtlicher Sicht auf Österreich
zwischen 1848 und 1867 beweist, dass die Enttäuschung über die
Misserfolge der Revolution - und über die Misserfolge der deutsch-
österreichischen bürgerlichen Politik überhaupt - anfangs zweifellos ein gewisses Bedürfnis nach einer philosophischen Aufar-
beitung der entsprechenden geschichtlich-gesellschaftlichen Erfahrungen weckte. Seit der zweiten Hälfte der 1850er Jahre gewann
jedoch das österreichische Bürgertum seine Tatkraft allmählich
wieder zurück, der österreichische Liberalismus erwachte zum
neuen Leben. Der österreichische Bürger suchte nunmehr nicht in
abstrakt-begrifflichen Paradoxien seine Erfahrungen und Wünsche
in Einklang zu bringen, sondern betrat das Feld der wirtschaftlichen und politischen Handlungen. Man kann mit Bestimmtheit
von einem Verblassen des philosophischen Gefühls in Österreich
zu jener Zeit sprechen. Robert Zimmermann etwa hat in der ersten

Ausgabe /1852/ seines Lehrbuches Philosophische Propädeutik noch
die harmonieverkündenden und wertgläubigen Kategorien seines
böhmisch-deutschen Philosophenmeisters Bolzano verwendet, die
jedoch eine gewisse Spannung zwischen der harmonischen Welt der
Werte und der empirischen Welt andeuteten. In der zweiten Ausgabe von 1860 traten bereits Herbartsche Kategorien an die Stelle
der Bolzanoschen, und diese wiesen schon eher auf eine tatsäch-
liche und verwirklichte Harmonie hin. Zimmermann behauptete zwar,
dass die Änderungen nur terminologischer, nicht inhaltlicher Natur seien; man muss sich auch vergegenwärtigen, dass der 1841
verstorbene deutsche Philosophieprofessor Herbart um diese Zeit
sozusagen zum offiziellen Philosophen Österreichs deklariert
wurde, die Änderungen in Zimmermanns Buch also eher äusserliche
als immanent philosophische Gründe haben - doch das Vorherrschen
von äusserlichen Überlegungen in den zeitgenössischen Werken
weist eben auf eine Abkehr vom philosophischen Denken. Nach 1854
- als die scharfsinnige Schrift Vom Musikalisch-Schönen des offensichtlich unter Bolzanoschem Einfluss stehenden Musikästhe-
tikers Eduard Hanslick zum erstenmal herausgegeben wurde -, fand
in Österreich während etwa anderthalb Jahrzehnten kein nennens-
wertes philosophisches Ereignis statt.

Auch in Ungarn war nach den bereits erwähnten philosophischen
Versuchungen der 1850er Jahre eine extreme Abnahme jeder Neigung
für abstraktes Philosophieren zu beobachten. In den sechziger
Jahren trat zwar etwa Ferenc Mentovich auf, seine Schriften sind
aber viel eher eine optimistische Popularisierung des naturwissenschaftlichen Weltbildes als eine solche Erscheinung, welche
darauf hindeuten würde, dass das zeitgenössische Denken vor
praktisch unlösbaren Fragen in begriffliche Spekulationen hätte
flüchten wollen. "Das nutzlose Werk einer Definition des Stoffes
der Philosophie überlassend", schreibt Mentovich in seinem Buch
Az uj világnézlet /Die neue Weltanschauung/, "sind wir, was uns
betrifft, vollkommen befriedigt durch die Einsicht, dass es im
mächtigen Lager jener, die sich mit der Entdeckung von den Wahr-
heiten der Natur befassen, von dem die enormen Himmelskörper
messenden Astronomen bis zum das Leben der Aufgusstierchen unter-
suchenden Zoologen keinen gibt, der in Verlegenheit kommen würde
in Bezug auf die Frage, welchen Begriff er mit der Bezeichnung

Stoff verbinden solle". Weder die politische Aktivisierung in
den sechziger Jahren noch die mit dem Ausgleich beginnende Periode, welche freilich einerseits von einem unbestreitbaren Aufbau
des Landes, andererseits aber von fruchtlosen staatsrechtlichen
Kämpfen und damit im Zusammenhang von einem leer - aber um so
lauter - werdenden Nationalismus charakterisiert wurde, hatten
ein Bedürfnis nach einer philosophischen Darstellung von geschichtlich-gesellschaftlichen Dilemmen. Der ungarische Nationalismus im Zeitalter des Dualismus, bekanntlich eine Minorität
im Königreich Ungarn repräsentierend, musste zwar um so konsequenter an der Abhängigkeit Ungarns von Österreich festhalten,
je extremer sein Programm der Magyarisierung wurde. Dieser Nationalismus war aber immerhin an der Macht, sein Dilemma war politischer, nicht begrifflicher Natur: Dieses wurde politisch gelöst, verursachte eine moralische Desillusionierung und schaffte
eine Lyrik der Einsamkeit und des Abwendens vom Leben, brauchte
aber nicht in philosophische Formeln gefasst zu werden. In diese
Periode fällt zwar das Auftreten von Károly Böhm, und es wäre
nicht richtig, ihn einfach als einen Schulphilosophen abzutun.
Nicht durch akademische Ambitionen, sondern durch persönliche,
erschütternde Erlebnisse wurde er zu seinen philosophischen Stu-
dien angeregt. In seiner ersten publizierten Schrift, 1867, äus-
sert er sich dahingehend, dass "die eigentliche Philosophie die
Anthropologie ist"; sein vielbändiges Hauptwerk, dessen ersten
Teil er 1883 als Professor des Budapester Evangelischen Ober-
gymnasiums veröffentlichte, trägt den zusammenfassenden Titel
Ember és Világa /Der Mensch und seine Welt/. Károly Böhm übte
aber keine derartige Wirkung aus und war kein so bedeutender
Denker, dass man in Hinblick auf ihn von einem wirklichen Aufschwung des philosophischen Denkens sprechen könnte. Im Ungarn
der Ausgleichsperiode kam der Wunsch, den Menschen und seine
Welt zu verstehen eher in der Dichtung als in der Philosophie
zum Ausdruck. Der später besonders in Deutschland bekannt ge-
wordene ungarische Denker, Menyhért Palágyi schrieb 1885, dass
"bei uns der philosophische Geist weit hinter der dichterischen
Schaffenskraft zurückgeblieben ist"; wobei man allerdings hinzufügen muss, dass seit den 1870er Jahren das dichterische Schaffen geradezu philosophisch veranlagte Werke in Ungarn hervor-

brachte. Der von Palágyi sehr geschätzte Dichter János Vajda
etwa - der, wie darauf Aladár Komlós mit Recht hingewiesen hat,
in den siebziger Jahren keine ungarische Partei fand, welcher
er sich mit voller Überzeugung anschliessen und die Teilnahme
in deren Kämpfen seinem Leben Sinn verleihen könnte - entdeckte
nach 1872 seinen wahren Stil.

   Das wirtschaftliche Leben in Österreich nach dem Ausgleich
wurde von einer liberalen laissez faire-Politik geleitet. Die
Unternehmungslust erlebte unter der Wirkung der günstigen politischen und finanziellen Umstände einen ungeheueren Aufschwung.
Die Jahre nach 1866 waren zweifellos eine wirtschaftliche Blüte-
zeit in Österreich. Wirtschaftlicher Natur war auch das erste
bedeutende quasi-philosophische Werk in Österreich nach dem Ausgleich. 1871 erschien Mengers aufsehenerregendes Buch, die Grundsätze der Volkswirtschaftslehre. Diese Arbeit scheint derart ein
Ausdruck der Weltanschauung des österreichischen Liberalismus
zwischen 1867 und 1873 zu sein, dass deren ausführlichere Darstellung hier am Platz ist. Carl Menger, Gründer der österreichischen Schule der Nationalökonomie, wurde 1840 als Sohn eines
katholischen Grundbesitzers in Galizien geboren. Er studierte
Jura in Prag und Wien und trat anschliessend in den Staatsdienst.
Die Grundsätze verhalfen ihm 1873 zu einer Professorenstellung,
1876 wurde er dann für zwei Jahre Hauslehrer des Erzherzogs Rudolf und impfte dem unglückseligen Thronfolger liberale Ideen
ein. Menger vertrat einen eigenartigen Liberalismus. Er war davon überzeugt, dass die Wirtschaft der freien Konkurrenz, d.h.,
die wirtschaftliche Macht der bürgerlichen Mittelklasse, das
wirklich Segensreiche für den grösseren Teil der Bevölkerung
ist; er betrachtet indes diese Wirtschaft nicht vom Standpunkt
des Produzenten, sondern vom Standpunkt gleichsam des Konsumenten - genauer vom Standpunkt des für den Konsumenten sorgenden
Staatsbeamten. Der Produzent rechnet auch mit den Produktions-
kosten, der Bürokrat jedoch fast nur mit dem Bedarf - mit dem
Bedarf der einzelnen Haushalte und des Staatshaushalts. Das

Wesen der Mengerschen Ökonomie liegt in einer bedarf-zentrischen, psychologischen Werttheorie, welche eher von der englischen Erkenntnisphilosophie als von der englischen politischen Ökonomie inspiriert ist. Die Arbeitswertlehre akzeptierte Menger nicht, er bestimmte den Wertcharakter und die Wertgrösse der Güter durch ihr Verhältnis zur inneren Welt des wirtschaftlichen Subjektes - ähnlich, wie der britische Empirismus die Realität der Aussenwelt durch ihr Verhältnis zu seelischen Vorgängen bestimmte. "Wie eine tiefer gehende Untersuchung der seelischen Vorgänge uns die Erkenntnis der Aussendinge lediglich als die zu unserem Bewusstsein gelangte Einwirkung der Dinge auf uns selbst, das ist in letzter Reihe als die Erkenntnis eines Zustandes unserer eigenen Person erscheinen lässt, so ist auch alle Bedeutung, welche wir den Dingen der Aussenwelt beimessen, in letzter Reihe nur ein Ausfluss jener Bedeutung, welche die Aufrechterhaltung unserer Natur in ihrem Wesen und ihrer Entwicklung, das ist unser Leben und unsere Wohlfahrt für uns haben. Der Werth ist demnach nichts den Gütern Anhaftendes, keine Eigenschaft derselben, sondern vielmehr lediglich jene Bedeutung, welche wir zunächst der Befriedigung unserer Bedürfnisse, beziehungsweise unserem Leben und unserer Wohlfahrt beilegen und in weiterer Folge auf die ökonomischen Güter, als die ausschliessenden Ursachen derselben, übertragen". Es ist ein klassisches Phänomen des bürgerlichen Denkens, die innere seelische Welt des in seiner Isoliertheit betrachteten Einzelnen philosophisch in den Mittelpunkt zu stellen. In Österreich freilich trat dieses Phänomen zweihundert Jahre später als in Westeuropa auf: Doch die Entwicklung der Bourgeoisie selbst hat sich ja verzögert. Und wie die Entwicklung des österreichischen Bürgertums individuelle Züge aufweist, so hat auch die österreichische bürgerliche Ideologie besondere Elemente - ein solches ist der Bedarf-Zentrismus der Mengerschen Werttheorie. Es könnte fast scheinen, dass Menger konsequenter ist als die Engländer, die den Wert, trotz ihrer subjektivistischen Anschauungsweise, doch von etwas Objektivem, von der Arbeit herleiteten - obwohl auch Adam Smith eine psychologische Erklärung gab, als er die Gleichheit der Werte durch die Gleichheit der Arbeitsmengen definierte, die Gleichheit des Opfers, welches die Arbeiter bringen. Der Unterschied liegt eher darin,

dass Menger bloss die Psychologie des Anschaffens untersucht,
nicht aber die Psychologie der Produktion; und erst recht nicht
die Psychologie des Arbeiters. Die Arbeitstätigkeit kann zwar,
meint Menger, Elemente haben, die beim Arbeiter "unangenehme
Empfindungen" erwecken, doch die überwiegende Mehrzahl der Menschen hat Freude an ihrer Arbeit, und die "Unthätigkeit" hat
keineswegs einen so grossen Wert für den Arbeiter, wie das allgemein angenommen wird. Die wirtschaftlichen Ungleichheiten lassen sich, letzten Endes, auf die Naturtatsache zurückführen, dass
im Vergleich zum Bedarf der Menschen die Menge der verfügbaren
Güter gering ist. Die Institution des Eigentums ist also eine
Notwendigkeit. "Wohl mag es für den Menschenfreund", schreibt
Menger, "betrübend erscheinen, dass die Verfügung über ein Grund-
stück oder ein Capital innerhalb eines bestimmten Zeitraumes
dem Besitzer nicht selten ein höheres Einkommen gewährt, als die
angestrengteste Thätigkeit dem Arbeiter innerhalb desselben Zeitraumes. Der Grund hievon ist indess kein umoralischer, sondern
liegt darin, dass in den obigen Fällen eben von der Nutzung jenes Grundstückes, beziehungsweise jenes Capitals, die Befriedigung wichtigerer menschlicher Bedürfnisse abhängig sind, als
von den in Rede stehenden Arbeitsleistungen". In der Arbeitswertlehre sieht Menger nichts als Propaganda - und fühlt keine
Veranlassung, diese Propaganda weiter zu verbreiten.

Menger nennt den Kreis der Naturdinge Güter, die zur Befriedigung menschlicher Bedürfnisse geeignet und dem Menschen in der
Tat zugänglich, und deren Eigenschaften dem Menschen bekannt
sind. Güter, die nicht in unbegrenzter Quantität zur Verfügung
stehen, werden von Menger wirtschaftliche Güter genannt. Der
wirtschaftliche Charakter der Güter ist kein objektives Moment:
Erst durch die Erkenntnis ihrer Knappheit wird dieser Charakter
konstituiert. Jede einzelne konkrete Teilquantität der wirtschaftlichen Güter hat einen Wert für den Menschen. Der Wert ist eigentlich ein Urteil, indem er bloss im subjektiven bedeutungverlei-
henden seelischen Akt existiert; seine Grösse wiederum hängt davon ab, wie gross die Bedeutung ist, welche das Subjekt dem zu
beurteilenden Gut bzw. der zu beurteilenden Güterquantität für
sein eigenes Leben und seine eigene Wohlfahrt beimisst. - Indem

die Wertbeurteilung eine genaue Kenntnis der wirtschaftlichen
Umwelt voraussetzt, wendet Mengers Theorie eigentlich die Anschauung der präkapitalistischen Verhältnisse auf die kapitalistische Wirtschaft an, jedoch auf solche Weise, dass sie auch
gewisse Elemente der gerade zu jener Zeit lebendig werdenden Anschauung der ebenfalls durchsichtige Angebote und Nachfragen
schaffenden monopolkapitalistischen Wirtschaft aufnimmt. Die ver-
spätete österreichische ökonomische Entwicklung war von einer
in einem präkapitalistischen Rahmen sich vollziehenden intensiven Monopolkapitalisierung gekennzeichnet. Die Mengersche Theorie ist ein ineinander projiziertes Bild dieser widerspruchs-
vollen politischen Lage der österreichischen Liberalen.

Obzwar ihr politischer Einfluss auch weiterhin erheblich blieb,
wurden die österreichischen Liberalen 1879/80 in die Opposition
gedrängt. Bereits nach dem spekulären Bankrott der liberalen
Wirtschaftspolitik im Jahre 1873 und noch mehr seit den achtziger Jahren, mit der wirtschaftlichen Unsicherheit der vom
Grosskapital bedrohten Schichten, mit dem zunehmenden Antisemi-
tismus und dem Aufflammen des tschechenfeindlichen deutschen
Nationalgefühls verlor die liberale Partei allmählich ihre Mas-
senbasis, da sich ihre Anhänger den sich vom Liberalismus los-
lösenden radikalen Fraktionen anschlossen. Die antisemitischen
alldeutschen und christlichsozialen Bewegungen wurden Ende der
achtziger Jahre organisiert bzw. neuorganisiert und die Sozialdemokratie wurde um diese Zeit zu einer beträchtlichen Kraft.
In den Wahlen von 1897, welche auf Grund des erweiterten Wahl-
rechts abgehalten wurden, erlitten die Liberalen eine katastro-
phale Niederlage. Die enorme Belebung des Interesses an der Literatur hatte 1899 Karl Kraus, dessen Laufbahn um diese Zeit
begann und der im österreichischen geistigen Leben am Anfang
des Jahrhunderts eine ganz besondere Bedeutung erlangte, mit
politischen Gründen erklärt, namentlich mit der notgedrungenen
Emigration des österreichischen Liberalismus in das Reich der
Kunst; und diese Erkenntnis wird auch heute von den hervorragend-
sten Kulturhistorikern vollkommen akzeptiert und verallgemeinert.
Die Grundlagen des Elfenbeinturms, der in den neunziger Jahren
aufgebaut wurde, waren allerdings schon früher gelegt. Die Künste
bedeuteten für das Wiener Bürgertum von vornherein einen Möglich-

keitsraum des gesellschaftlichen Aufstiegs: Die Bourgeois konnten
neben der Geburtsaristokratie als der Neuadel des Geistes auftreten. Die Kunst war ein natürliches Lebenselement für die Generation, welche in den sechziger und siebziger Jahren geboren
wurde. Eine hohe künstlerische und psychologische Sensibilität
charakterisierte besonders die jüdischen Intellektuellen. Geistig
hervorzuragen, war geradezu eine Lebensbedingung, eine conditio
sine qua non des Akzeptiertwerdens für sie. Und die Juden waren
ja, ausserdem, von den antiliberalen Massenbewegungen, als antisemitischen Bewegungen, besonders stark bedroht; die Juden mussten
das Gefühl des Nirgendswohingehörens besonders stark empfinden.
Eine berühmte Formulierung dieses Gefühls gab Gustav Mahler. "Ich
bin dreifach heimatlos", schrieb er. - "Als Böhme unter den Ös-
terreichern, als Österreicher unter den Deutschen und als Jude
in der ganzen Welt".

Da sie ihre Niederlage nicht so sehr der Übermacht ihrer Gegner
als vielmehr der Verwirklichung ihres eigenen Programms - der Ka-
pitalisierung und dem erstarkenden Parlamentarismus - verdankten,
waren die österreichischen Liberalen in einer psychologisch schweren Lage. Je wirkungsvoller sie gegen das konservative Etablisse-
ment kämpften, um so gefährdeter wurden sie von den - unter den
liberalen Verhältnissen sich verstärkenden - sozialistischen, na-
tionalistischen und antisemitischen Bewegungen. Je erfolgreicher
andererseits die deutsch-österreichischen Nationalisten das Nationalbewusstsein der Deutschen Österreichs weckten, desto schwä-
cher wurden die Grundlagen des multinationalen Staatsgefüges, in
dem sie immerhin beträchtliche Vorteile genossen. Und je erfolgreicher die tschechischen Nationalisten die Verbindungen zwischen
Böhmen und Deutsch-Österreich lockerten, desto wehrloser wurden
sie gegenüber den grossdeutschen und panslawistischen Eroberungs-
tendenzen.

Es ist kaum überraschend, dass in der hier dargestellten Atmo-
sphäre von geschichtlich-gesellschaftlichen Dilemmen, politischen
Paradoxien und nationalen Identitätskrisen das philosophische
Denken geradezu aufblühte. 1872 wurde der Leseverein der Deutschen
Studenten Wiens gegründet, welcher den deutschnationalen Gefühlen
der Universitätsstudenten gedanklichen Ausdruck verlieh und ein
Zentrum des Wiener Wagner- und Nietzsche-Kultes wurde; 1874 wurde

243

der Süddeutsche Franz Brentano, Autor eines inzwischen klassisch
gewordenen präphänomenologischen Werkes, später Lehrer von Masaryk, Husserl und Meinong, an die Wiener Universität zum Professor
berufen; 1875 konnte sich der Krakauer Ludwig Gumplowicz auf
Grund seiner geschichtsphilosophischen Dissertation Rasse und
Staat in Graz habilitieren; Masaryk hat 1878 die erste Fassung
seiner philosophisch-anthropologischen Arbeit Der Selbstmord als
sociale Massenerscheinung der modernen Civilisation beendet. In
den achtziger Jahren liess der Aufschwung des philosophischen
Denkens in Österreich, mit Ausnahme Böhmens, wieder nach, in Prag
begann jedoch 1884 der Physiker Ernst Mach, der sich zwischen
den tschechischen und deutschen nationalen Gegensätzen aufrei-
bende Universitätsrektor, sein philosophisches Werk Analyse der
Empfindungen zu schreiben. In diesem Werk wird sozusagen die
Physik zur Metaphysik: Die unmittelbare theoretische Vorgeschichte
von Machs Philosophie ist zum grossen Teil von jenen wissen-
schaftsmethodologischen Ansichten konstituiert, welche er sich
im Laufe seiner Arbeit in der Mathematik und Physik gebildet hatte.
Darauf, dass die Anfänge dieser eigentümlichen Philosophie des
Ich-Verlustes bereits in seiner früheren wissenschaftstheoreti-
schen Auffassung vorhanden waren, weist u.a. die Tatsache hin,
dass Fritz Mauthner, der als Universitätsstudent Anfang der siebziger Jahre Mach in Prag kennenlernte, und 1901/02 in Deutschland sein die Wirklichkeit des Ichs ebenfalls bezweifelndes
sprachphilosophisches Hauptwerk herausgab, als eine Quelle seiner
Ansichten eben Machs Vorlesungen bezeichnete.

Die grundlegende Quelle von Mauthners Sprachphilosophie war
allerdings, wie er betonte, nicht diese oder jene Ansicht, sondern seine böhmische Existenz. Obwohl Mauthner, während er seine
Theorien ausarbeitete, nicht in Österreich lebte, wurde seine
Anschauungsweise - wie er in seinen Erinnerungen berichtet -
grundlegend von den Jahren in Prag geprägt. Mauthner war einer
der ersten, die unter die Macht des Sprachzentrischen im spätbürgerlichen Denken gerieten. Die linguistische Wende des zwanzigsten Jahrhunderts hängt, allgemein gesprochen, mit den ökonomischen und gesellschaftlichen Veränderungen zusammen, durch
welche das Ideal der Individualität dahinschwindet, und einer
realen Erkenntnis von der überragenden Rolle des Gemeinschaft-

lichen den Platz räumt; die Bürger der multinationalen Monarchie aber, für die das Sprachproblem, als ein wichtiges politisches Problem, in der zweiten Hälfte des neunzehnten Jahrhunderts eine hervorragende Bedeutung gewann, waren für einen Ansatz linguistischer Art von vornherein empfänglich. Mauthner selbst lernte als Kind drei Sprachen kennen - die deutsche, die hebräische und die tschechische; man musste aber weder Jude noch Deutschböhme sein, um in Österreich auf die das Denken gestaltende und das Denken verzerrende - nicht bloss das Gedachte mitteilende - Rolle der Sprache aufmerksam zu werden. In seinem faszinierenden Essay über Grillparzer und Österreich bezeichnet J. P. Stern Wien als "ein wahrhaftes Babel an Sprachen und die Alma mater der Sprachphilosophie" und hebt die eigentümliche Lage hervor, in der sich die Schriftsteller und Dichter dieser Stadt befanden, die als ihre Muttersprache den Wiener Dialekt sprachen, ihre Werke jedoch in Hochdeutsch formulieren mussten. Grillparzers Situation charakterisierend, führt Stern einen von 1938 datierten Brief Josef Weinhebers an. Als Weinheber, schreibt Stern, "darüber klagte, dass er 'in zwei Sprachen zu denken habe', - 'Wienerisch und Hochdeutsch', dass das Wienerische keinerlei Anspruch auf eine sprachliche /und daher auf eine wahre/ Harmonie erheben kann, schilderte er die Zwangslage, in der sich auch Grillparzer ohne Ausweg befunden hatte". Seinen Anspruch auf diese Harmonie hat das Wienerische "'schon seit etwa 1800 verloren, als die deutsche Klassiker den Sieg des Hochdeutschen entschieden. Die Verzichtgeste Kaiser Franzens auf die Römische Kaiserwürde ist nichts anderes als der sichtbare, wenn auch unbewusste Ausdruck dessen, dass der kaiserliche Dialekt darangeht, sich als eine Stammesmundart zu bescheiden...' Der Streit geht natürlich" schreibt Stern, "nicht nur um die Sprache. Der Mangel einer ausgeprägten Sprachform, über den Weinheber klagt, die Ungewissheit der sprachlichen /'und daher realen'/ Lage, sie spiegeln jenes unglückliche 'österreichische Problem' wider, mit dem wir aus der jüngsten Geschichte vertraut sind". Ein ähnliches Problem wie Weinheber hatte auch der Trieser Ettore Schmitz, der den Namen "Italo Svevo", "der italienische Schwabe", angenommen und das Italienische als die Sprache seines literarischen Wirkens gewählt hat, obzwar er sich nicht ohne Schwierigkeiten in dieser

Sprache ausdrücken konnte: War es doch für ihn nicht möglich, in jenem von deutschen und slawischen Einflüssen gefärbten italienischen Dialekt zu schreiben, den er als seine Muttersprache sprach.

Dass Mauthners Name heute ziemlich bekannt ist, lässt sich darauf zurückführen, dass ihn an einer Stelle Wittgenstein selbst, zweifellos der hervorragendste österreichische Philosoph, erwähnt; ausser Mauthner waren indes auch andere Sprachphilosophen um die Jahrhundertwende in Österreich tätig. Die - etwa Adolf Stöhr oder Richard Wahle - sind fast unbekannt gewesen und geblieben; dennoch darf man behaupten, dass die sprachphilosophischen Werke Wittgensteins - sowohl seine 1918 abgeschlossene Logisch-Philosophische Abhandlung als auch die in den dreissiger und vierziger Jahren geschriebenen, von der Erlebniswelt des alten Österreichs jedoch keineswegs unabhängigen Philosophischen Untersuchungen lediglich ein Gipfelpunkt jenes Prozesses sind, in dem die Sprachphilosophie im Österreich der Jahrhundertwende aus einem unterirdischen Bach der klassischen deutschen Philosophie zu einer Hauptströmung vom bürgerlichen Denken des zwanzigsten Jahrhunderts wurde.

Machs oben erwähntes Buch wurde 1886 veröffentlicht - übte aber in Österreich zunächst keine nennenswerte Wirkung aus. Das philosophische Interesse der Österreicher scheint in den achtziger Jahren merklich nachgelassen zu haben. 1893 jedoch, mit Hugo von Hofmannsthals Drama Der Tor und der Tod - welches, wie auch Leopold Andrians 1895 erschienenes dichterisches Werk Der Garten der Erkenntnis, vom hoffnungslosen Sich-selbst-Suchen des Menschen und vom Tod als vom Abschluss dieses Suchens handelt - begann eine grosse Zeit des österreichischen Geistes und insbesondere des österreischen philosophischen Denkens. 1894 erschien das Buch des Brentano-Schülers Kasimierz Twardowski, in dem Brentano von einem Bolzanoschen Gesichtspunkt aus umgedeutet wird. 1899 veröffentlichte der damals schon seit einem Jahrzehnt in Wien lebende Engländer H. St. Chamberlain sein Buch Die Grundlagen des neunzehnten Jahrhunderts, welches "das Vorwalten des Provisorischen, des Übergangsstadiums, de/n/ fast gänzliche/n/ Mangel an Definitivem, Vollendetem, Ausgeglichenem" als das Charakteristische der Zeit bezeichnete. Im selben Jahr erschien Freuds grundlegendes Werk Die Traumdeutung. 1902 stellte der Brentano-Schüler Alexius Meinong, Professor in Graz, in seinem Buch Über Annahmen die Welt der Begriffe entschieden der wirklichen Welt gegenüber; zur selben Zeit erschien Hofmannsthals sog. Chandos-Brief, welcher von der Unanwendbarkeit der Begriffe auf die Welt, letzten Endes von der Unmöglichkeit jeder Kommunikation, handelt. Auch Mach wurde populär. Die Analyse der Empfindungen erlebte um die Jahrhundertwende plötzlich drei Neuauflagen. 1903 erregte Otto Weiningers Buch Geschlecht und Charakter grosses Aufsehen - der Verfasser verübte im selben Jahr, im Alter von dreiundzwanzig Jahren, Selbstmord. Sein ethischer Rigorismus wird später mit mathematisch-logischer Strenge in Wittgensteins Abhandlung zu neuem Leben erweckt.

Demgegenüber kann man in Bezug auf Ungarn zur Zeit des fin de siecle und der Jahrhundertwende keinesfalls von einem intensiven philosophischen Leben oder vom Entstehen einer grossen Philosophie sprechen. Die ungarische Philosophie war zu jener Zeit eine epigonhafte Kathederphilosophie. Es fragt sich indessen, ob dieser Mangel an philosophischer Schaffenskraft - oder philosophischem Spekulationszwang - als Zeichen einer tatsächlichen gesellschaftlich-menschlichen Harmonie aufgefasst werden darf oder vielmehr als eine ideologische Erscheinung, als Manifestation eines überentwickelten Nationalbewusstseins bezeichnet werden muss. Bestanden doch zu jener Zeit bereits zweifellos manche Elemente eines kosmischen Unsicherheitsgefühls in der ungarischen Gesellschaft, auch wenn dieses Gefühl keine philosophische Fassung erhielt. Ich habe bereits den dichterischen Ausdruck dieses Gefühls erwähnt, und man kann auch auf seinen existentiellen Ausdruck hinweisen - vor allem auf die sich häufenden Selbstmorde. Etwa seit 1896 übertraf, laut den Statistiken, die Selbstmordhäufigkeit in Ungarn bereits jene in Österreich. Es ist jedenfalls eine Tatasache, dass seit 1906 die Anwesenheit des philosophischen Denkens in der ungarischen Kultur nicht mehr zu übersehen war, und dass das österreichische und das ungarische Denken gerade in Bezug auf ihren philosophischen Inhalt sich immer näher kamen. Der Bolzano- und Meinong-Einfluss wurde in den zwanziger und dreissiger Jahren zu einer bestimmenden Quelle der un-

garischen Katnederphilosophie, der österreichische Platonismus
übt jedoch bereits auf den jungen Georg Lukács und auf Béla Zalai seine Wirkung aus. Die Unterschiede zwischen der Geschichte
der Philosophie in Österreich und in Ungarn im Zeitalter des Dualismus dürften vielleicht bloss als Phasenverschiebung, nicht
aber als Wesenmerkmale gedeutet werden. Es ist jedoch schwer,
hier eine eindeutige Formel aufzustellen, besonders wenn man
im Spiegel der Philosophie die Wirklichkeit der ungarischen Gesellschaft erblicken möchte.

Denn wenn wir vom Mangel an Philosophie in Ungarn sprechen,
so tun wir das fast unvermeidlich mit einem negativen oder positiven Wertakzent, und es fragt sich, ob unsere Wertung nicht
auf Fiktionen beruht. Die Grundlage der negativen Wertung ist
doch sehr oft jene - vielleicht als messianistisch zu bezeich-
nende - Fiktion, derzufolge die politische Handlungsfähigkeit
oder gar die künstlerische Schaffenskraft einer Gesellschaft
gering sein muss, wenn diese nicht von irgendeiner grossen Philosophie durchdrungen ist. Diese Ansicht vertrat z.B. der junge
Georg Lukács, als er die Abwesenheit von "wirklichen" ungarischen
Dramen mit dem Mangel an "lebendiger philosophischer Kultur" erklärte, wobei er eine solche Kultur übrigens der blossen "philosophischen Bildung" oder "gedanklichen Tiefe" gegenüberstellte,
aber ähnlich äusserte sich bereits Károly Böhm, als er sich 1883
im Vorwort zu Ember és Világa darüber beklagte, dass "unsere Literatur, insbesondere in ihrem wissenschaftlichen Teil, keine
höhere Idee, einheitliche Verbindung, keinen beseelenden Gedanken enthält", und darauf aufmerksam machte, dass "der Sinn der
Teile ... nur in der umfassenden Idee zu finden ist". - Die Grundlage der positiven Wertung in Bezug auf die Abwesenheit der Philosophie war andererseits, in der hier betrachteten Periode, sehr
oft jene allgemeine - etwa als borniert-konservativ zu bezeich-
nende - Einstellung, welche in der zeitgenössischen ungarischen
Gesellschaft etwas überaus Organisches, in nationaler Einheit
Verschmolzenes sah und daher jegliches kritisch-weiterblickende
Denken als von vornherein fremdartig empfand, und indem sie gegen die sogenannte Spekulation auftrat, die Sozialwissenschaft
an sich verwarf. Diese Einstellung äusserte sich manchmal in
jener - vielleicht als philosophisches Kurutzentum zu bezeich-

248

nenden - Ansicht, laut welcher es - wenn auch nicht in der Wirklichkeit, so immerhin als etwas Mögliches - eine spezifisch
ungarische, von der deutsch-österreichischen unabhängige Philosophie gibt, und die Aufgabe eben darin besteht, diese zu be-
treiben bzw. auszuarbeiten. Diese Ansicht, deren prominenter
Vertreter z.B. Bernát Alexander war, liess offensichtlich den
allgemeinen Umstand ausser acht, dass - wie dies zu jener Zeit
vom hervorragenden Publizisten Ignotus, u.a. gerade Alexander
kritisierend, betont wurde - das "spezifisch Ungarische" meistens
nichts anderes sei als etwas früher Übernommenes und anderswo
bereits Veraltetes. Diese Ansicht liess auch den konkreten Umstand ausser acht, dass die damalige angeblich selbständige ungarische Philosophie in einem solchen Kulturboden wurzelte, der
- und damit komme ich zum Leitmotiv meiner Ausführungen zurück -
von einer intensiven Wechselwirkung, ja Symbiose, des österreichischen und des ungarischen Alltagslebens gekennzeichnet war.

Spricht man andererseits etwa von der seit 1906 stärker werdenden Anwesenheit der Philosophie in Ungarn, so ist es wiederum
nicht ganz gewiss, ob diese Anwesenheit nicht bloss fiktiv, bloss
scheinbar war. - Um 1906 erfolgten auf fast allen Gebieten des
ungarischen geistigen Lebens grundlegende Wandlungen. 1906 erschienen Endre Adys Uj versek /Neue Gedichte/, sowie die von
Bartók und Kodály bearbeitete und eingeführte Volksliedsammlung
Magyar népdalok énekhangra, zongorakisérettel /Ungarische Volks-
lieder für Gesang mit Klavierbegleitung/. Das Jahr brachte einen
Zusammenstoss der radikalen und der konservativen Kräfte in der
Sozialwissenschaftlichen Gesellschaft /Társadalomtudományi Tár-
saság/; 1906 wurde der Kreis Ungarischer Impressionisten und Na-
turalisten gebildet, aus dem 1907 die Gruppe der "Acht" /Nyolcak/
ausschied. "Literatur, Musik und Malerei", schreibt Zoltán Horváth, "erklären fast zur gleichen Zeit den Krieg, und entscheiden
sich für einen Kampf auf Leben und Tod..." In dieser Periode trat
Georg Lukács auf, der zwischen 1906 und 1909 sein erstes grosses
Werk A modern dráma fejlődésének története /Die Entwicklungsge-
schichte des modernen Dramas/ schrieb, und ab 1907 die später im
Band Die Seele und die Formen gesammelten Essays verfasste. Um
1905 entstanden die ersten Aufsätze /u.a. der deutsch verfasste
Aufsatz Metaphysik als symbolische Summation perseverierender

Bedürfnisse/ des jung verstorbenen Philosophen Béla Zalai, der besonders auf Arnold Hauser und Károly /Karl/ Mannheim eine bedeutende Wirkung ausübte. Die gesellschaftlich-geschichtliche Verwurzeltheit von Zalais Schriften ist freilich viel weniger offensichtlich als etwa jene von Lukács's antiimpressionistischen Essays oder seinen Analysen zu Ady; und auch die Bestrebungen der "Acht" stehen in einem weit weniger direkten Zusammenhang mit den politischen Ereignissen der fraglichen Jahre als etwa die Diskussionen der Sozialwissenschaftlichen Gesellschaft oder gar Adys Gedichte über das "ungarische Brachland". Diese Erscheinungen der geistigen Gärung und Krisen hängen jedoch gewiss miteinander zusammen, und geht man von den eindeutig interpretierbaren Aspekten aus, so lässt sich mit Bestimmtheit behaupten, dass die politische Krise von 1905/06 - der Wahlsieg des radikalen Nationalismus, der Konflikt zwischen der nationalen Idee und dem bürgerlichen Fortschrittsgedanken, das Gefühl, dass der Nationalismus inhaltslos, die bestimmenden Prinzipien und Normen des ungarischen Nationalbewusstseins sinnlos und wertlos geworden sind - ihren Hintergrund bildete. Diese Periode hat in Ungarn zweifellos ein Bedürfnis für Philosophie, und zugleich eine abstrakte Möglichkeit für ihre Entstehung, geschaffen. Eine Analyse der Schriften des jungen Lukács sowie von deren Wirkung zeigt jedoch ziemlich eindeutig, dass die Essays im Band Die Seele und die Formen, diese zweifelsohne philosophischen Werke, eher ein Teil der österreichischen als der ungarischen Geistesgeschichte bilden; während das Dramenbuch, das an die Anfänge der ungarischen Soziologie, an kultur- und wissenssoziologische Anfänge anknüpft, im Grunde genommen eine sozialwissenschaftliche und keine philosophische Arbeit ist. In der Tat: Wenn es zutrifft, dass die philosophische Einstellung ein charakteristischer Zug des bürgerlichen Bewusstseins ist, und dass um die Jahrhundertwende, mit der Herausbildung der spätbürgerlichen Verhältnisse in Westeuropa und in Amerika, das Zeitalter der Philosophie, allgemein gesprochen, zu Ende ging, so konnte das in Ungarn zu dieser Zeit selbständig werdende bürgerliche Denken kaum noch in philosophischem Gewand auftreten. Dies lässt sich eindeutig an Hand den Schriften von Béla Zalai veranschaulichen. Als Georg Lukács im hohen Alter auf die Zeit des

Jahrhundertbeginns zurückblickte, erklärte er, dass damals Zalai
der einzige originell denkende ungarische Philosoph war. Einige
Zeitgenossen Zalais - der Kreis seiner Freunde und Verehrer -
waren ähnlicher Meinung. Unter diesen Umständen ist es recht
auffallend, dass weder damals noch seitdem praktisch niemand beschrieben hat, worin eigentlich das Wesentliche von Zalais Ansichten bestand. Im Briefwechsel zwischen den Dichtern Babits,
Juhász und Kosztolányi taucht der Name Zalai immer wieder auf,
es wird auf seine persönlichen und intellektuellen Vorzüge hingewiesen, aber kein einziges Mal wird erwähnt, womit er sich
eigentlich beschäftigte, was er eigentlich erstrebte. Was Kosztolányi in einem Brief an Juhász über Zalai schrieb: "dieser
Mensch ist für mich heute noch ein Rätsel. Wer ist er?" - scheint
das Problem der zeitgenössischen Philosophen /und der sich mit
Zalai befassenden philosophiegeschichtlichen Versuche/ ziemlich
genau wiederzugeben. Die Schwierigkeit liegt wahrscheinlich darin,
dass Zalais philosophisches Thema die Philosophie selbst war;
dass sich Zalai eigentlich nicht mit philosophischen Fragen be-
fasste, sondern mit dem Problem, aus welchen Bedürfnissen die
Philosophie entsteht, wie und ob Philosophie überhaupt möglich
ist. Obzwar es seine Zeitgenossen kaum ahnten, und vielleicht
auch er selbst nicht ganz klar sah, behandelte Zalai die Philosophie völlig von aussen; er betrieb nicht Philosophie, sondern
Metaphilosophie. Der junge Béla Fogarasi war einer der wenigen,
die das Wesentliche an Zalais Bestrebungen erfasst haben. Hätte
wohl Zalai seine Metaphysik schreiben können - fragt Fogarasi
1916 in seinem In Memoriam - "und nur die Zeit, das Leben fehlte
dazu? Falls dies so sein sollte, würde die tiefe Tragik von Zalais Werk vielfach alle jene tragischen Verluste der Philosophie
übertreffen, von denen wir in der jüngeren Vergangenheit wissen.
Es würde bedeuten, dass sein ganzes Schaffen eine blosse Vorbereitung darauf war, was er nicht mehr niederschreiben konnte,
und was nun keiner an Stelle von ihm niederschreiben kann. - Ich
glaube aber nicht, dass wir seine Philosophie auf diese Weise
beurteilen müssten. In seiner postumen Arbeit, welche in der
endgültigen Vertiefung des philosophischen Formproblems und der
Problematik des Systematisierens ausserordentlich viel Neues
und Wichtiges bietet, kann ich keine Spur dieser sich gestal-

tenden neuen Metaphysik finden. ... Das ausserordentliche Ver-
dienst Zalais besteht darin, dass er die Gesetze, Rechte und
Grenzen des philosophischen Denkens, der 'par excellence' philosophischen Methode festgestellt hat. ... Während die Vision
der Metaphysiker das Wesen des Kosmos, der Seele, der Gottheit
ist, war Zalais Vision das Wesen der Metaphysik selbst". Und es
scheint dann, dass Zalais Auftreten nicht mit irgendwelchem Anfang der ungarischen Philosophie zum Jahrhundertbeginn, sondern
mit der weltweiten Krise der Philosophie überhaupt zusammenhängt;
oder mit anderen Worten, eine abstrakt-begriffliche Antwort auf
eine antinomische geschichtliche Lage bedeutet in einem solchen
Zeitalter, wo sich diese Antwort nicht mehr der klassischen Mittel der Philosophie bedienen kann.

Philosophy and Culture
J. Lukács and F. Tőkei eds.

L'INFLUENCE DE LA PSYCHANALYSE CLASSIQUE SUR LA PSYCHOLOGIE ET LA CULTURE HONGROISES DES ANNÉES VINGT ET TRENTE

T. BALOGH

L'influence de la psychanalyse classique /celle de Freud en premier lieu/ sur la psychologie et la culture hongroises des années vingt et trente a été <u>caractéristique</u>, <u>multiple</u>, <u>intense et durable</u>. Notre intention est de présenter cette diffusion extrêmement dynamique des travaux de Freud en Hongrie. Nous donnerons à cette fin un aperçu des activités les plus représentatives des intellectuels hongrois qui ont contribué à cette intégration particulière du freudisme.

Nous nous excusons de cet exposé restrictif: le cadre chronologique pourrait être élargi dans les deux sens, et la liste de ceux qui mériteraient d'y figurer pourrait se prolonger sensiblement.

Nous nous proposons d'examiner deux questions seulement:
1/ <u>la réflexion de la psychanalyse sur elle-même</u>, ou plus concrètement: les observations d'ordre théorique des psychanalystes de la période considérée sur les idées et la théorie de Freud, et sur les conceptions des disciples du freudisme.
2/ D'autre part, nous voudrions traiter de <u>l'interprétation freudiste de la culture</u>, et en particulier des arts.

x

1/ La première question est d'ordre philosophique: elle concerne le système, les éléments rigoureusement théoriques, la manière d'envisager l'homme et son rapport à son monde. Ici, il faut mentionner <u>Géza Csáth</u> écrivain, esthète, neurologue et psychiâtre, d'orientation multiple et d'une carrière très par-

ticulière. Né en 1887, à l'époque relativement consolidée, mais
pleine de tensions de la Monarchie Austro-Hongroise, il acheva
sa vie tragiquement brève en 1919. Son oeuvre est considérable,
aussi bien en quantité qu'en qualité. En 1912, au moment même où
les premiers disciples /Bleuer, Jung, Abraham, Sachs, Stekel,
Rank, Adler/ s'organisent autour de Freud, il publie un volume
intitulé Le mécanisme psychique des maladies mentales. Il a une
grande estime pour Freud: pour lui, Copernic, Darwin et Freud sont
les garants de la valeur définitive de nos connaissances sur le
monde. En ce qui concerne la découverte décisive de Freud, Géza
Csáth met l'accent sur l'importance de la connaissance de soi
de l'homme en quête du savoir. Cette connaissance garantie la
santé de l'âme et elle est capable de surmonter les grands obstacles épistémologiques.

D'après Csáth, l'évolution sociale a eu pour résultat la dif-
férentiation continuelle des sociétés civilisées et l'accéléra-
tion de l'évolution spirituelle des individus. Il existe une
corrélation entre l'évolution de l'individu et celle de la col-
lectivité, où l'une présuppose et provoque l'autre.

Cette interdépendance nous incite à une connaissance active
de l'homme, comme le font aussi les besoins économiques et l'é-
volution de la vie intellectuelle. Selon Csáth, pour l'homme moderne la connaissance de soi n'est plus spéculative, il n'édi-
fie plus de grandes théories systématisées; sa connaissance est
pratique, son but est de découvrir des relations causales. C'est
la connaissance adéquate de nous-mêmes qui fait nous intéresser
aux autres, et qui nous invite à les mieux connaître. D'après
Csáth, Freud est le guide le plus sûr dans la voie d'une meil-
leure connaissance de l'homme, et le trait le plus caractéristique de la psychologie freudienne est qu'après avoir définitivement rompu avec la philosophie, elle a acquis le statut d'une
science naturelle.

Chez Csáth, l'influence de Freud est plutôt sentimentalement
motivée, elle est basée sur une expérience personnelle et a une
fonction d'initiation. C'est pour cette raison que nous l'avons
mentionné, bien qu'il soit mort avant l'époque que nous nous
sommes proposés d'examiner.

254

Le rapport de Sándor Ferenczi avec le maître viennois est
beaucoup plus complexe. Surtout au début, le rôle de Freud est
dominant dans l'évolution de Ferenczi, mais plus tard, il s'é-
tablit une influence mutuelle. Ferenczi est devenu l'un des re-
présentants les plus connus de la psychanalyse classique. Ses
capacités ont été reconnues par Freud aussi; le fait qu'à la
fin des années vingt, pendant son séjour en Amérique, les vues
de Ferenczi se sont radicalisées et leurs liens se sont relâchés
- amenant Freud à critiquer Ferenczi - est dû, à notre avis, à
des questions de méthode. Ces conflits n'ont pas d'implications
philosophiques directes, ainsi leur importance ne sera pas trai-
tée ici.

Dans le mouvement psychanalytique, du moins jusqu'en 1926,
Ferenczi était le représentant le plus orthodoxe du freudisme.
Il fut responsable, au moins partiellement, de la rupture entre
Freud et Jung. Néanmoins, l'influence de Freud n'a pas empêché
Ferenczi d'élaborer sa propre théorie. En voici un seul exemple:
dans la formation de la perception, Ferenczi distingue quatre
étapes, dont deux sont empruntées à Freud, mais l'ensemble de
la théorie est la réalisation autonome de Ferenczi, c'est sa
théorie qui sera reprise par Rapaport et White, et qui réappa-
raîtra aussi chez Piaget et Canon.

Csáth s'était attaché à la psychanalyse parce qu'il pensait
que l'insistance de celle-ci sur les déterminations, sur la recherche rigoureuse des relations causales lui assurait une pré-
cision comparable à celle des sciences naturelles. L'attitude
de Ferenczi est radicalement différente. Son objectif principal
est de séparer la psychanalyse des sciences naturelles. A son
avis, ce qui, dans les phénomènes mentaux, est mesurable, sché-
matisable et accessible à l'expérience ne constitue qu'une partie élémentaire et infime.

Il écrit en 1912: "La psychologie expérimentale est exacte,
mais elle ne nous apprend rien; la psychanalyse n'est pas une
science exacte, elle découvre des corrélations insoupçonnées
et met en lumière les couches jusque là inaccessibles de l'âme".
Il attend beaucoup, lui aussi, de la psychanalyse: la disparition des dogmes, des opinions préconçues, fondées sur l'autori-
té, la formation et la diffusion de l'autocritique. Et surtout:

l'apparition d'une génération qui ne refoulera plus ses instincts et ses aspirations, ses désirs naturels souvent en conflits avec la culture, mais apprendra à les supporter d'une façon consciente. Il concevait la psychanalyse comme une science théorique, tout en affirmant que les explications psychanalytiques des circonstances et des modalités de la détermination des processus psychiques avaient une valeur directement pratique.

Tout en reconnaissant l'apport de Jung, il pense que son activité - tout comme celle d'Adler - n'avance pas la psychanalyse scientifique, qu'elle constitue plutôt un recul vers d'anciennes tendances erronnées, philosophiques ou théologiques. Il est intéressant de lire ses réflexions à propos des autres analystes et ses réactions aux hypothèses des penseurs qu'il croit proches de la psychanalyse. Il émet des réserves critiques à propos de Kultur und Mechanik de Mach, paru en 1915. Il pense que cet auteur, poussé par ses ambitions et ses expériences relatives à la "ressouvenance réitérée", sera amené à utiliser les acquis de la psychanalyse. Pour traiter de la préhistoire de la mécanique, Mach procède à l'examen systématique de la genèse du psychisme individuel, étant donné qu'on peut, semble-t-il, retrouver chez l'enfant des souvenances appartenant à l'histoire de l'espèce. Une analogie est donc à découvrir entre le développement de la culture humaine et l'évolution psychique individuelle. Mais il est indispensable - nous avertit Ferenczi - de mettre en lumière les besoins comme motifs de l'évolution; les deux composantes de l'analogie ne peuvent être discernées qu'en décrivant les besoins, les associations d'idées, et - en recourant aux méthodes analytiques - l'arrière-fond du subconscient. Tout cela manque chez Mach, ce qui rend son ouvrage sans nuances et partiel, d'autant qu'il ne s'intéresse qu'à l'évolution des facultés mécaniques de l'homme.

L'orthodoxie freudiste de Ferenczi se manifeste dans toutes ses critiques: le critère du jugement reste toujours la profondeur de l'influence freudienne. Il loue par exemple Jones, parce qu'il s'arrête au regroupement des faits et y ajoute de la théorie dans la mesure où elle en surgit d'une manière évidente et directe, tout comme Freud, qui - remarque Ferenczi - ne procède jamais à une systématisation hâtive. A propos de l'école psychiàtrique de Bordeaux, Ferenczi souligne que la psychanalyse est une science en formation, elle doit s'abstenir des définitions rigides et se contenter du recensement des faits et de leur classification. Pour revenir à l'appréciation donnée par Ferenczi sur Jung et Adler, nous savons que le groupe de Jung s'est détaché de Freud en 1914, et que le nouveau courant se nommera psychologie analytique, puis psychologie complexe. Il est à remarquer que dès 1913 Ferenczi désapprouvait les écrits de Jung. Il jugeait inacceptable l'opposition trop poussée des concepts d'extraversion et d'introversion. Il refusait surtout de considérer Freud comme le représentant de l'extraversion, et de voir le trait significatif d'Adler dans l'introversion. Dans la typologie de Jung, Freud apparaît comme un penseur matérialisant, empirique, sensualiste, axé sur la causalité, incapable de systématiser; quant à Adler, il serait idéalisant, croyant, radicalisant, penchant vers la systématisation - et finaliste.

Le plus grand défaut de l'effort adlérien - selon Ferenczi - est sa tendance à établir une philosophie. Ferenczi apprécie les remarques pertinentes d'Adler, ses pensées biologiques et caractérielles très spirituelles, et certains éléments de sa description des instincts d'agression. Mais il pense que l'abandon de la conception du déterminisme psychique est une erreur. En ce qui concerne le penchant philosophique d'Adler, Ferenczi déclare: "les systèmes philosophiques ... ne sont que l'expression de l'impatience due à ce que l'on n'est pas capable de supporter les incertitudes réellement existantes; la construction des systèmes est le résultat de la contrainte de surmonter les doutes; comme par un coup de baguette, elle redonne la bonne conscience au philosophe et le dispense de procéder à des expériences craintives et tâtonnantes. Nous n'envions pas aux philosophes l'harmonie intérieure ainsi acquise mais, tout en y renonçant pour le moment, nous nous contentons des valeurs réelles offertes par la psychanalyse".

Nous pouvons dire que Ferenczi, chef de l'équipe de chercheurs de l'École de Budapest et dirigeant de la Société Psychanalytique de Hongrie, croyait avoir pour tâche de diffuser et de défendre la psychanalyse authentique freudienne.

Ces brèves réflexions ne nous permettent pas de présenter l'influence de Ferenczi sur Freud, notre objectif étant de montrer l'influence de Freud sur le psychanalyste hongrois. C'est de ce point de vue qu'il nous semble important de souligner que Ferenczi /de même que Freud/ met tout son effort à écarter la philosophie de la psychanalyse, à souligner la différence entre celle-ci et les sciences naturelles, à attirer l'attention sur l'importance du concept de déterminisme, et enfin à mettre en relief le rôle de la causalité.

Ferenczi n'est pas seul: ses vues sont partagées par un de ses disciples, également de réputation mondiale, <u>Imre Hermann</u>, dont l'oeuvre la plus importante, <u>Les instincts primitifs de l'homme</u>, parue en 1943, est accessible en français et en italien. En apportant des rénovations à la psychanalyse classique, il y reste pourtant fidèle, suivant en cela aussi son maître.

<u>Lipót Szondi</u>, dans ses recherches analytiques sur le destin, entreprises en 1937, choisit une hypothèse similaire: pour lui, le sort humain <u>n'est pas le fait du hasard</u>. En s'éloignant de Freud, il pense que l'homme naît et mène sa vie suivant un "<u>projet</u>" individuel. Ses actes, ses choix /le choix de ses amis, des compagnons de sa vie et de sa carrière/, ses maladies et même sa mort sont prédéterminés. Selon Szondi, la vie humaine réalise un "plan" dont les éléments font partie d'un ensemble "planifié" - comme une épopée ou un roman. Chez lui, l'analyse du destin, la diagnose des instincts ont pour but de trouver dans chaque destin individuel le plan qui forme sa vie, depuis la naissance jusqu'à la mort, en tant qu'ensemble. La conception du déterminisme et la recherche de la causalité sont les facteurs décisifs de l'oeuvre de Szondi.

Mais pour en revenir à Ferenczi, force est de constater que sa volonté de débarrasser la psychanalyse des tendances philosophiques ne se réalisera pas. Pour s'en persuader, il suffit de lire <u>Totem und Tabu</u> /1913/ et <u>Neue Folge der Vorlesungen zur Einführung in die Psychoanalyse</u> /1932/ de Freud, et <u>Entwicklungsstufen des Wirklichkeitssinnes</u> /1913/ de Ferenczi.

<u>Ces ouvrages montrent clairement que les efforts pour écarter l'intrusion de la philosophie dans la psychanalyse ont fait faillite, du moins provisoirement, aussi bien chez Freud que chez</u>

Ferenczi ou Hermann. L'échec ou l'ajournement de ces tentatives est inéluctable, à notre avis, puisque toute méthode analytique, toute pratique théorique réagissant directement à la pratique analytique suppose plus ou moins ouvertement une théorie philosophique. Et ces éléments philosophiques, nous les retrouvons effectivement dans l'oeuvre de chaque théoricien de la psychanalyse.

2/ Après avoir traité sommairement de la réflexion de la psychanalyse sur elle-même, nous aborderons un autre domaine, celui de l'interprétation psychanalytique de la culture.

La présence de la psychanalyse classique dans l'oeuvre poétique, critique et théorique d'Attila József /1905-1937/, un des plus grands poètes hongrois du XXe siècle, est bien connue en Hongrie.

Ferenczi - dans une de ses études sur Putnam - proteste contre l'idée de subordonner la psychanalyse à une vision du monde. Il accepte par contre - en se référant à Freud - l'explication de certains problèmes de métaphysique par la psychologie, en élaborant ainsi une sorte de métapsychologie; il voudrait que la psychanalyse devienne une critique de la philosophie, tout en restant indépendante des systèmes philosophiques. Pour lui, la psychanalyse est une science, tandis que la philosophie travaille avec des intuitions et des notions, comme la religion ou les arts.

Attila József a cherché à concilier la psychanalyse et la philosophie marxiste, pour arriver à harmoniser les problèmes interférants de la société et de l'individu. A son idée, les questions existentielles de l'homme soulignent l'importance de la psychanalyse aussi bien du point de vue ontologique que du point de vue épistémologique et axiologique.

Dans son texte intitulé Personnalité et réalité /1932/, la logique d'Attila József est le suivant: l'individu, la personnalité font partie du processus social. L'individu est à la fois produit et production, objet et sujet de la production, objet et sujet social. L'individu - ou plutôt la personnalité - dès avant sa naissance est l'objet de l'activité d'autres personnes; c'est déjà socialisé qu'il devient l'objet des sujets sociaux. Mais en même temps, l'individu - ou la personnalité - comme su-

259

jet, a un rapport actif avec les autres. Dans cette étude, Attila
József relie la névrose à l'opposition du sujet à l'objet social.
Le névrosé est névrotisé par sa socialisation particulière, qui
le réduit soit en objet social, soit en sujet social. Il en résulte le paradoxe de la personnalité névrosée: elle souhaite so-
cialiser individuellement l'objet social individualisé, ce qui
est un non-sens, étant donné que l'individu est lui-même le produit et la production d'un processus social. L'activité du névrosé est inconsciente, son objet n'est pas la réalité matérielle,
mais le domaine de la morale qui en est détachée. Attila József
accepte la suggestion de Totem und Tabu de Freud, selon laquelle
les "peuples primitifs" ne sont pas névrosés, justement parce
que leur vie mentale comprend des connaissances adéquates à leurs
institutions socio-historiques.

D'après le poète hongrois, le marxisme est la science de la
libération du prolétariat opprimé, et la psychanalyse est celle
de la guérison de l'âme chargée de refoulements. Il souligne
l'idée importante, démontrée par le marxisme: la formation de
la conscience se réalise toujours dans des conditions historiques
concrètes; la philosophie marxiste est la philosophie de l'évolution de la conscience humaine. L'idée marxienne de l'"homo
oeconomicus" n'est pas véritablement étrangère à Freud, puisqu'il retrouve dans les névroses le principe économique - dit
Attila József.

C'est en s'opposant aux théoriciens vulgarisateurs du marxisme
qu'il opère les tentatives les plus marquées pour "allier" Marx
et Freud. Citons la conclusion caractéristique de son étude intitulée Hegel, Marx et Freud, datée probablement de 1935:
"... Marx envisage donc l'homme en tant que réalité visible,
sensible, et c'est de ses conditions de vie et de son 'moi réel'
qu'il déduit son avenir. Il peut le faire, puisqu'il estime que
l'existence de l'individu est objectivement donnée pour sa propre conscience. 'La conscience /Bewusstsein/ ne peut jamais être
autre que l'être conscient /bewusstes Sein/, et l'être des hommes
est leur véritable processus vital'. 'Ce n'est pas la conscience
qui détermine l'existence, mais c'est la vie qui détermine la
conscience'. C'est à cela que se rattache sa conception selon
laquelle l'homme se développe en transformant ses conditions de

vie, et ces conditions de vie, à leur tour, le transforment. Par conséquent, nous ne pouvons pas former directement notre existence au moyen de notre conscience.

"Cependant, une nouvelle science naturelle, la psychanalyse est devenue capable de guérir en découvrant que la conscience peut bel et bien façonner directement l'existence, en rejetant, en refoulant les idées suggérées justement par cette existence réelle, naturelle; et que, parallèlement à ce refoulement, elle transforme l'existence à tel point qu'elle entraîne la maladie du sujet; et, dans l'être pensant, raisonnable, on voit se développer cet 'esprit religieux', cet état d'âme réel, dont Engels a trouvé la notion si ridicule chez Feuerbach. Un homme de ce genre - et dans le passé de l'humanité on ne peut trouver que des hommes de ce genre - est sans aucun doute un être réel, mais sa conscience ne correspond pas à son existence instinctive /générique, sexuelle/, elle produit l'image d'une existence qu'elle avait déjà déformée. Ce n'est pas l'image de l'existence que cette conscience déforme, mais l'existence elle-même en tant que nature, et elle conserve plus ou moins fidèlement cette image déformée. 'Tout ce qui met en mouvement les hommes - écrit Engels - doit nécessairement passer par leur tête, tout, même le manger et le boire, qui aboutissent à la satiété, ressentie également par la conscience'. -- Depuis, la psychologie a découvert, dans le développement de l'individu, de l'être social, tout une série de phénomènes que le philosophe du XIXe siècle devait nécessairement ignorer. Il ne pouvait qu'effleurer certaines questions qu'il pourrait reformuler aujourd'hui et les utiliser afin de vérifier son propre système de pensées. Ainsi, depuis, nous avons appris qu'entre la faim et la conscience, le désir sexuel et la conscience, le contact peut se rompre; et que la conscience ne se rend pas toujours compte de la satiété et du plaisir sexuel, bien que tout se soit normalement passé, conformément aux lois de l'existence physiologique. En général, elle ne s'en rend pas compte du tout s'il y manque /pour utiliser une formule populaire/ 'la bénédiction de Dieu'".

Freud, dans son ouvrage de 1930, Das Unbehagen in der Kultur, affirme que la culture freine trop les désirs érotiques de l'homme, et par conséquent il devient nerveux; elle freine encore

plus radicalement son désir d'agression, ce qui développe en lui
le sentiment de la culpabilité, en le rendant mécontent, irri-
table et désagréablement tendu. La culture déclare la guerre à
l'agressivité, mais il n'en résulte rien de bon. L'homme - grâce,
en grande partie, à la pression exercée par la culture - retient,
n'extériorise pas, ne manifeste pas son agressivité, mais il
s'attaque à soi-même, ou périodiquement, il réduit les tensions
accumulées par des manifestations brutales de l'agression.

Aux yeux de Freud, la tâche véritable et immanente de la culture est la lutte pour la vie; elle est incapable d'autre chose,
p. ex. d'établir ou de faire établir des liens d'amitié. Freud
déduit la propriété privée du désir d'agression, en affirmant
que ce désir déterminera le sort de l'humanité: tout dépend de
sa capacité à surmonter l'agression et le désir de se supprimer.
Il semble bien, qu'après avoir rejeté la religion comme illusion
/Die Zukunft einer Illusion, 1927/, Freud envisage de se déba-
rasser de la culture, étant elle aussi une illusion.

Toute différente est la position d'Attila József. Il affirme
que le produit artistique /marchandise comme n'importe quel autre
produit/ sert à satisfaire aux besoins sociaux. Selon lui, l'o-
rigine de l'activité artistique remonte à l'instinct de l'homme
d'accomplir des activités sensorielles. Cet instinct s'accompagne
d'une force qui le détache, sinon de l'objet sensoriel, du moins
de son objectif sensoriel, en le dirigeant vers des ambitions
spirituelles. Attila József pense que l'oeuvre d'art est un
aspect ultime de la perception qui donne à son destinataire la
perceptibilité d'une totalité; à chaque époque, toute objectivation ayant une vraie valeur artistique, est une totalité perceptible qui représente une vision globale du monde. L'aspiration sensorielle à la totalité, le désir de la perception de
la totalité constituent la justification de l'oeuvre d'art - en
tant que besoin fondamental, argument final - aussi bien du côté du créateur que de celui du destinataire.

En dehors des différences purement individuelles dans l'assimilation de l'oeuvre d'art - écrit Attila József -, les mem-
bres des différentes classes sociales sont souvent différemment
prédisposés, au niveau sentimental et conscient, à l'assimilation de l'oeuvre, mais aussi de ses éléments constituants /par

exemple, dans la littérature, "le sens même des mots varie selon les classes sociales"/. Cet effet est partiellement amoindri
par l'intervention d'un autre phénomène: les divergences d'interprétation dues aux différences sociales sont atténuées par
un sentiment irrésistible, présent dans la culture, lié aux
sphères motrices de l'organisme humain et qui ignore les différences sociales: le sentiment, l'expérience de l'appartenance
à la même espèce /humaine/. La nature humaine commune peut se
manifester dans le comportement psychique et intellectuel des
différents groupes. Le reflet dans l'art /dans la création, dans
l'oeuvre, dans l'assimilation de l'oeuvre/ de la structure sociale définie par l'existence des classes /comme aspect spéci-
fique/ s'accompagne d'un aspect /général/ qui peut être perçu
dans le caractère fondamental-originel, donné par nature, mais
développé dans la société et dans la culture, de l'être humain.

Ferenczi attribue à la psychanalyse la capacité de former
une nouvelle génération plus parfaite; Freud parle de la pression gênante de la culture. En ce qui concerne Attila József,
il pense que le mouvement social est le facteur qui assure à
l'individu /à la personnalité/ la possibilité de se construire,
de se perfectionner; l'art est nécessaire, et les rapports de
l'activité artistique à l'instinct sont, d'après lui, tout particuliers. La psychanalyse peut aider le mouvement social, parce qu'elle est capable de dissoudre ou de corriger les troubles
de la socialisation, mais elle ne peut pas remplacer le mouvement social.

L'influence de Freud est sensible aussi dans la poésie d'Attila József, mais nous n'avons pas l'intention d'en parler ici.
Par contre, nous ne pouvons pas nous dispenser de faire un tour
d'horizon pour montrer l'influence de Freud sur la culture et,
plus particulièrement, sur la littérature hongroises des années
vingt et trente, car cette influence était aussi profonde et générale que dans le domaine de la psychologie et de la psychiatrie.
L'époque de l'épanouissement du freudisme dans la littérature
hongroise correspond à celle de l'apogée de la revue Nyugat /Oc-
cident/. Outre les auteurs déjà mentionnés, nous énumérerons
quelques écrivains chez qui cette influence a été significative.

Mihály Babits, dans son roman La cigogne calife /1916/ donne la peinture des instincts refoulés et des rêves, en suivant l'enseignement de la psychanalyse. Le héros de Babits a une vie double: en présentant un cas de schizophrénie, l'auteur transforme l'analyse psychologique en une oeuvre fantastique.

L'influence de la psychologie freudienne sur Frigyes Karinthy est également manifeste. C'est l'étude de la psychologie - et celle de Freud surtout - qui l'a incité à représenter l'aliénation mentale, les rêves, les visions extrêmes, et à employer un ton grotesque dans la description du délire. Il n'est pas moins significatif que Gyula Krúdy écrit son Livre des rêves sur l'encouragement de Ferenczi. Il serait facile de multiplier les exemples, mais nous croyons que cet échantillon témoigne assez fidèlement de l'extension et de la profondeur de l'influence de Freud en Hongrie à l'époque considérée.

Pour terminer ce tour d'horizon, nous voudrions citer quelques phrases de l'étude intitulée Freud et la psychanalyse de László Németh, écrivain, essayiste et jeune médecin alors, en 1929: "Et faut-il parler des écrivains pour qui la psychanalyse est une stimulation, un encouragement? Les uns connaissent Proust, les autres ont lu Alouette ou Absolve Domine de Kosztolányi. La mélodie des temps chante aussi bien dans les théories scientifiques que dans les vers des poètes. Darwin est beaucoup plus proche des poètes qu'on ne le croie, et c'est la conception artistique de l'âme, surgie depuis le milieu du siècle dernier, qui entre dans la science avec Freud".

x

Nous nous sommes limités jusque-là au recensement des faits. Il nous a été plus facile de parler de la nature de l'influence du freudisme que d'en chercher les causes, qui sont - bien sûr - beaucoup plus complexes. Les auteurs des volumes de l'Histoire de la littérature hongroise affirment que Freud a essayé de transposer, de traduire à l'aide de la science les phénomènes que seuls les arts avaient abordés jusque-là. Après Dostoïevsky, Freud n'avait d'autre tâche que d'arriver à prendre conscience de ces phénomènes.

264

Si nous admettons cette position, force nous est de poser la question suivante: Qu'y a-t-il au fond des phénomènes dont il a fallu prendre conscience?

Pour trouver une réponse, nous nous adresserons à György Lukács. Sa Théorie du roman avait paru en 1920, et dans la préface d'une édition ultérieure, datée de 1962, il affirmait que l'essentiel de son entreprise avait été de remonter aux sources des idéologies des années vingt et trente. La nouveauté ou le véritable but de son ouvrage aurait été une analyse complète de l'oeuvre de Dostoïevsky. Il est bien regrettable que Lukács n'ait jamais mené cette tentative à sa fin, et que son analyse s'arrêtât à Tolstoï.

Selon Lukács, la totalité humaine et celle des événements ne peuvent se réaliser que dans et par la culture, et cela indépendamment de notre attitude envers elle. Mais si la culture ne satisfait pas l'homme substantiel /ne touche pas à la substance de l'homme/ parce qu'elle lui est étrangère, l'homme commence à chercher la réalité plus substantielle de la nature, et cette recherche peut se lier avec une sorte de vécu sentimental, romantique. L'amour et la mort reçoivent, chez Tolstoï, une place particulière, entre la nature et la culture: ils sont enracinés dans les deux et leur sont en même temps étrangers. Chez Tolstoï, dans l'amour, c'est la nature primitive qui devrait l'emporter sur le faux raffinement de la culture; mais, en fait, l'amour devient "l'engloutissement peu consolant de toute supériorité et de toute grandeur humaines par la nature vivant dans l'homme; mais cette nature, pour vivre sa vie - dans notre monde civilisé - ne peut arriver à son but qu'en s'accomodant des conventions les plus basses et les plus dénuées d'esprit". L'homme de Tolstoï n'est capable de connaître et de vivre la substance de la nature que dans des moments exceptionnels: tels les moments de la mort. Toute la vie antérieure "se perd dans le néant devant cette aventure: les conflits de la vie, les souffrances, les tourments, les égarements paraissent mesquins et sans importance".

Lukács affirme que dans les romans de Tolstoï, c'est dans la sphère de "l'âme pure" que "l'homme apparaît en être humain et non en être social, mais ce n'est plus une intériorité isolée, incomparable, pure et par conséquent abstraite; c'est dans cette

sphère, une fois là en tant qu'un _allant-de-soi_ naïvement vécu
comme la seule réalité véritable, qu'il peut se construire la
nouvelle plénitude de toutes les substances et relations poten-
tiellement contenues en elle, plénitude qui laisse derrière elle
notre réalité déchirée et ne l'utilise que pour arrière-plan;
de même que notre monde de dualité sociale intériorisé a laissé
derrière lui le monde de la nature. Mais on ne peut jamais réaliser cette transformation par la voie de l'art..."

Nous avons cité Lukács, parce que _nous avons la conviction_
que la cause profonde de l'influence de Freud réside dans son
penchant romantique qui l'a poussé à décrire, d'une manière par-
ticulière, le caractère illusoire de la religion et de la cul-
ture. Il fait appel à la nature de l'homme en la débarassant
de tout ce qui lui est extérieur, de toutes conventions étran-
gères à sa substance /cf. la religion et la culture/.

La manière de traiter des notions de l'amour et de la mort,
chez Tolstoï, en les confrontant à la nature et à la culture,
nous semble analogue à l'utilisation des symboles d'_Eros_ et de
Thanatos, par Freud. Le besoin de construire ces deux pulsions
amène Freud à faire des réflexions métapsychologiques abstraites
dont les composantes de base sont la nature /nature primitive
- perçue comme biologique - de l'homme/ et la culture. Chez
Freud, l'homme se privatise, et si, de ce point de vue, dans
une certaine mesure, Ferenczi diffère de lui, il reste dans
le sillage du romantisme propre à Freud quand il espère que la
psychanalyse formera une génération capable d'assumer ses conflits avec la culture.

En tout cas, il est à noter que, dans la période qui nous
intéresse, les analystes disciples de Freud restent plus fi-
dèles à lui que les écrivains, poètes et esthètes. Dans les productions de ces derniers, l'influence de la mentalité freudienne n'est jamais exclusive, et dans certains cas, elle n'apparaît que provisoirement. Dans la majorité des cas, elle ne
constitue qu'une des composantes des oeuvres. Nous pensons à
la tentative de synthèse d'Attila József, ou à Frigyes Karinthy
qui, tout en puisant beaucoup dans le freudisme, s'attaque vi-
olemment aux écoles psychologiques - freudisme y compris - dès
1923, dans son roman intitulé _Voltige_.

Dans ce bref tableau, nous avons présenté l'influence de la psychanalyse classique à travers l'analyse succinte des vues d'un analyste "orthodoxe" /Ferenczi/ et de celles d'un poète-esthète /Attila József/ qui a tenté de procéder à une synthèse de Marx et de Freud.

Nous n'ignorons pas que l'influence de Freud sur la psychologie et sur la culture hongroise des années vingt et trente a été plus complexe que l'image que nous en avons présentée. Nous avons donné plutôt des indices qu'une analyse systématique du caractère fondamental de l'influence freudienne et de ses traits particuliers, tels qu'ils apparaissent dans des oeuvres souverainement originales.

LUKÁCS AND HUNGARIAN CULTURE

LUKÁCS AND HUNGARIAN CULTURE

F. TŐKEI

György Lukács and Hungarian culture is a subject so vast that
all I can really do on this occasion is to throw some light on
certain of its aspects which, in my opinion, have not been given
the attention they deserve by Lukács scholars, neither in Hungary
nor elsewhere.

My starting point is simply to ask: Was György Lukács a Hungarian thinker, or a German philosopher who happened to live in
Hungary? This question may seem absurd, since everyone is aware
that important facts and periods of Lukács's life were undoubtedly closely linked to Hungary /at least also to Hungary/. Indeed,
it may seem even superfluous given that Lukács's lifework, in
the eyes of Marxists and non-Marxists alike, is of international significance. However, the question is not absurd when we
consider how closely Lukács was tied to the German philosophical
tradition, that he wrote his principal works in German and, furthermore, he spent a great deal more time and effort on German
than Hungarian literature. His life's work can therefore also
be regarded as part of German culture. Nor must it be forgotten
that Lukács, the scion of a Budapest Jewish haute-bourgeois family, already in early youth, at the turn of the century, turned
sharply against the Hungary of that time, and against the gentry
and gentry-imitating - pseudo-gentry, gentroid-Hungarian mentality. All his life he emphasized his solitude as a thinker in Hungary /though, true enough, also in Germany/. Following a stay
in Florence and Heidelberg in his early years, he lived in exile
between 1920 and 1945, first in Vienna, then Moscow, Berlin and
again Moscow. While in Berlin, he played an important role as a

leader of the Association of German Proletarian Writers. There
is, therefore, every reason to wonder how deep and how strong
were the threads linking Lukács to Hungary and Hungarian culture,
that is, in what sense one should look on him as a Hungarian
writer and on his work as something Hungarian culture can be
proud of. This way of putting the question makes it perhaps already clear that it is certainly not besides the point to examine
what being Hungarian meant for Lukács. And if there were strong
ties between Lukács's work and Hungarian culture, then the facts
of Hungarian history and the characteristic features of Hungarian
culture must be borne in mind if we are to understand Lukács's
work, even on a most elementary level. It seems to me one of the
more serious weaknesses of the large and expanding literature
dealing with Lukács that scholars are not able to understand the
actual relationship between him and the culture of his native
country. Even in Hungary there is, frankly, still a great deal
of uncertainty in this respect, few of the prejudices involved
have been overcome yet and research into the problem can be said
to be only in its initial stages.

Let us see, first of all, the answer provided by Lukács himself. In 1970, he published a voluminous selection of his essays
written in Hungarian and on Hungarian topics /1/. In a preface,
specially written for that volume in 1969, he described how he
saw his relationship to Hungarian culture, and the way in which
this relationship developed. I should like to quote from this
most interesting autobiographical piece at length, particularly
from those sections which refer to his origins and early oppo-
sitional attitude. "It is well-known that I was born into a capitalist family living in the Lipótváros district of Budapest. I
would like to indicate that since early childhood I was thorough-
ly dissatisfied with the Lipótváros way of life of those days.
And since the business activities of my father brought us into
daily contact with the city's patricians and gentry bureaucracy,
this rejection was automatically extended to them also. Consequently, from an early age I harbored oppositionist sentiments
toward the whole of official Hungary. It was a reflection of my
immaturity that this opposition extended to all domains of life,
from politics to literature, and was obviously expressed in some

272

kind of callow socialism. /.../ It does not matter how childish-
ly naive I now consider this uncritical and generalized hostility,
extended to all phases of Hungarian life, history and literature
alike /with the sole exception of Petőfi/; it is certain that
those views had dominated my way of thinking. The real counter-
force, the firm soil which alone existed for me, where I could
dig in my heals, was the European literature of those days, with
which I became acquainted around the age of fourteen or fifteen.
I was influenced primarily by Scandinavian literature /mainly
Ibsen/, the Germans /From Hebbel and Keller to Gerhart Hauptmann/,
the French /Flaubert, Baudelaire, Verlaine/ and English poetry
/first of all Swinburne, then Shelley and Keats/; later Russian
literature became important to me. It was out of these that I
put together that complex of forces which was meant to destroy
spiritually the Lipótváros Jewish and gentry /gentroid/ attitude
surrounding me. /.../ This not entirely accidental conjunction
of circumstances led to my attempts at liberation from spiritual
servitude to official Hungary, taking on the accents of a glori-
fication of the international modern movement as opposed to what
I regarded as narrow-minded Hungarian conservatism, which under
those circumstances I identified to a great extent with the entire official world of the time" /2/.

Yet Lukács then goes on to speak of two Hungarian contemporaries whose uncompromising moral attitude had a positive influence on him. He continues by describing his role in Budapest's
theatrical life of the time, pointing out that "It was at that
stage that I realized ..., as an important negative circumstance,
that I could participate in literature only as a theoretician
and not as a creative writer. The practical consequences of this
realization led me away from the stage; I began to prepare for
theoretical and historical research into the essence of literary
forms and turned towards scholarly and philosophical work. This
again made me more acutely aware of the importance of the contradiction between influences from abroad, mainly German, and
Hungarian life. It is hardly surprising that under those circumstances my starting point could only be Kant. Nor can it be
surprising that when I looked for perspectives, foundations -
and the methods of application - of philosophical generaliza-

tions, I found a theoretical guide in the German philosopher Simmel, not least because this approach brought me closer to Marx in certain respects though in a distorted way. Moreover, interest in the history of literature carried me back from the prominent names of the present to those mid-19th century scholars in whose writings I found methods of a higher order in the understanding of society and history. I deeply despised Hungarian literary theory and literary history from Beöthy to Alexander. But important counterweights acting against this theoretical one-sidedness were soon to appear in my life. Ady's volume, Uj versek /New poems/, was published in 1906; in 1908, I read the poems of Béla Balázs in Holnap and within a short time Balázs and I were linked by both personal friendship and a close literary alliance" /3/.

This takes us to a decisive moment in Lukács's life, decisive also when it comes to understanding Lukács's work. The friendship between Lukács and Béla Balázs was important in itself, the more so in virtue of the close cooperation between Balázs and Bartók. More important still, however, was Lukács's encounter with the poetry of Endre Ady, one of the outstanding oeuvres of 20th century Hungarian literature, but unfortunately almost inaccessible to those who do not read Hungarian. This encounter proved decisive for further developments in Lukács's philosophical orientation. It would be difficult to formulate the philosophical importance of this encounter in a clearer and more precise way than Lukács himself did: "My encounter with Ady's poems was a shock, as one would call it today. It was a shock the effect of which I began to understand and to digest seriously only years after. My first efforts to come to terms with the intellectual significance of this experience occurred in 1910; but it was only much later, at a more mature age, that I was really able to grasp the decisive importance of my encounter with Ady's poems for the evolution of my view of the world. Although I may be upsetting the chronological order, I believe that this is the place to describe that influence. To sum up briefly: although the German philosophers, not only Kant and his modern followers, but Hegel too -- whose influence I came under only years later -- appeared to possess a subversive Weltanschauung, they remained

274

conservatives in regard to the great questions pertaining to the development of society and history; reconciliation with reality /Versöhnung mit der Wirklichkeit/ was a basic tenet of Hegel's philosophy. Ady's decisive impact came to a head precisely because he never, not for a single moment, became reconciled to Hungarian reality and, through it, to reality as a whole as it then was. I had felt a longing for such a view of the world since adolescence though I had not been able to generalize these feelings conceptually. For a long time I did not truly understand the clear expression of this attitude in Marx, even after several readings, and so I was unable to utilize him to oppose Kantian and Hegelian philosophy in a thoroughgoing way. But what I missed there, hit home in Ady's poetry. Ever since I became familiar with Ady's work this irreconcilability had been present in all my thoughts as an inevitable accompaniment, although for a long time I was conscious of it to the extent its importance required. To clarify these thoughts let me quote a few lines of Ady which he wrote much later. In Hunn, új legenda /New Hun Legend/, he described this attitude to life, history, yesterday, today and tomorrow as follows: 'Vagyok... protestáló hit és küldetéses vétó: Eb ura fakó, Ugocsa non coronat' /I am ... a protesting faith and a veto with a mission... I am my own master, Ugocsa /one of the smallest counties in Hungary/ non coronat/. It is peculiar how that feeling about the world, which at the level then reached by me, could hardly have been called a world view or even an idea, had a broad and deep transforming influence on the whole world of my ideas. It caused me to fit into my picture of the world the great Russian writers, above all Dostoyevsky and Tolstoy, as decisive revolutionary factors which shifted me slowly but safely in a direction where the internal transformation of man stood expressly in the focus of social transformation, where ethics methodically overwhelm the philosophy of history. Such became the ideological foundation of this feeling about the world, and in the last resort it grew out of my experience with Ady. This did not, of course, mean the total elimination of an objective socio-historical foundation. On the contrary, it was exactly at this stage of my development that French syndicalism began to influence me in a decisive way. I was never able to see

eye-to-eye with the social democratic theory of those days, especially with Kautsky. My knowledge of Sorel, mediated by Ervin
Szabó, helped me to developed the combined Hegel-Ady-Dostoyevsky
influence into a sort of Weltanschauung which I felt to be rev-
olutinary, and which made me oppose the journal Nyugat, isolated
me even from the circle of the periodical Huszadik Század, and
placed me in the position of an 'outsider' also among my later
German friends" /4/.

As can be seen from this quote, the meeting with Ady's poetry
had a decisive influence on Lukács's development as a thinker.
However, it was not enough in itself to ensure that he should
regard himself as a Hungarian thinker. In a 1966 interview Lukács said:

"Ady's Uj versek really changed me. Roughly speaking, that
.was the first Hungarian literary work which allowed me to find
my way home, the first that I could identify with. What I now
think of the Hungarian literature of the past is another question,
and the result of a long experience. At that time, I must admit,
I felt no inner relationship with classical Hungarian literature,
having been only influenced by world literature, primarily by
German, Scandinavian and Russian literature, and also by German
philosophy. German philosophy influenced me throughout my life,
but the moving experience which Ady afforded me did not essentially change this, did not put an end to it, did not take me
back to Hungary. One could say that, at the time, Ady's poems
meant Hungary to me" /5/.

                                x

In the close ties with Hungary, Lukács almost became German.
He describes this in his 1969 Preface: "The experience of meeting Bloch /1910/ convinced me that philosophy in the classical
sense was nevertheless possible. I spent the winter of 1911-12
in Florence under the influence of this experience, wishing to
be undisturbed while working out my aesthetic theory as the first
part of my philosophy. In the spring of 1912, Bloch came to Florence and persuaded me to go to Heidelberg with him where the
environment was favourable for our work. What I have said so

far must have made it clear that there was no motive keeping me from moving to Heidelberg for a longer period, even permanently. Although I always preferred Italy to Germany, the hope of finding understanding was stronger. I thus went to Heidelberg without knowing for how long I intended to live there" /6/.

Lukács spent 1915 and 1916 in Budapest as a member of the Auxiliary Services. At that time a circle of friends gathered around him that led to an interesting experiment, the "Free School of Humanities" /Geisteswissenschaften/. To a certain extent, however, Lukács already felt isolated, even amongst his friends, owing to his revolutionary left-wing attitude. Looking back, Lukács writes: "Towards the end of the war a group gathered in Budapest around Béla Balázs and myself, which soon grew into the 'Free School of Humanities'. My earlier work no doubt played a certain role in its formation. The group became important later thanks to the role played abroad by some of its members /Karl Mannheim, Arnold Hauser, Antal Frigyes, Charles de Tolnay/; its influence in Hungary is often overestimated today for the same reason. It did not really mean anything important to me since it was essentially linked to a way of thinking and behaviour that I had already surpassed" /7/.

Then certain events occurred which proved to be the decisive experiences of Lukács's life -- the 1917 Russian, and the 1918-19 Hungarian revolutions. "By chance," Lukács was caught by them in Budapest.

"The Russian revolution and its reverberating echo at home gave the first inkling of the contours of the answer. This road first opened up before me at home, but it was not an ideologically conscious homecoming, not a necessary consequence of my evolution. Seen objectively and intellectually it was mere chance. /That from the aspect of my purely personal evolution, it was not mere chance, that it was a help in this sense, a fate pointing towards the true path, is one of the facts of my life and beyond the scope of this analysis./ But even if my staying at home before and during the revolutions was purely chance-like as far as the immediate causes were concerned, it created entirely new contacts for my life which, having become conscious in the course of internal struggles lasting many years, produced an entirely new attitude in me" /8/.

277

19

Lukács immediately understood that in 20th-century Europe
a plebeian revolution could only be a socialist revolution. Not
long after the foundation of the Communist Party in Hungary in
1918, Lukács joined it as one of its leaders. This meant giving
up his past ways of thinking in favour of a thorough study of
Marxism. He became a People's Commissar in the Hungarian Republic
of Councils, in charge of cultural policy. He realized that Hungary was not destined to be the country of "revolutionaries without a revolution", that in Hungary, too, outstanding individuals
could be united together with the masses in revolution. "The cultural policy of the Hungarian proletarian dictatorship was," in
Lukács's words, "the first attempt to unite on the part of all
those forces in Hungarian society that truly wished for progress
and sought a genuine rebirth" /9/.

We are, I believe, entitled to say that by becoming a communist,
Lukács became decisively tied to Hungary also; that his becoming
an internationalist at the same time meant a strengthening of
his ties to a particular nation. And this is certainly not a contingent connection, but follows necessarily from the concepts
involved.

The Hungarian Republic of Councils was suppressed and, in
1920, Lukács was forced into exile. In Vienna, he began an intensive study of Lenin, initiating that decade-long period in
his intellectual development which can justly be called his "road
to Marx". Lukács himself said that in the 20s he had still tried
to reconcile a "right-wing epistemology" with a "left-wing ethics",
producing a "messianic sectarianism". It is rather interesting
that this "messianic sectarianism" was manifested primarily in
his philosophical and international political views, while, re-
garding the problems of the Hungarian working-class movement, he
supported the Landler faction against Béla Kun and therefore also
against his own general theoretical views. Landler's more realistic ways of thought served as a basis for his overcoming of
that "ultraleftism" which Lenin also criticized.

x

Following Landler's death, Lukács formulated the so-called "Blum-theses" which saw the future of the Hungarian working-class movement in a democratic dictatorship of the working class and the peasantry. Lukács's theses were rejected by the party leadership of the time, and he was expelled from the central committee of the party. Nevertheless, this setback did not alienate him as a philosopher from Hungary. On the contrary, it made the links still closer. Lukács said of the importance of the Blum-theses for his own development that it was there that "in my case a general theory allowing for further generalization grew directly out of a proper observation of reality, that is where I first became an ideologist who took his cue from reality itself, what is more, from Hungarian realities" /10/.

Lukács was therefore ready consciously and finally to accept his role as a part of Hungarian culture precisely at a time when, following his removal from political office, he shifted his concentration to German as well as English, French and Russian literary problems. Let me quote again Lukács himself at some length.

"The 'Blum-theses' put an end to my political career and took me away from the Hungarian party for many years. At the same time, as a direct consequence of this crisis, my theoretical and critical work as an aesthetician received a new impetus. I was able to take an active part in the struggle against literary sectarianism on the German and Russian fronts, I was able to lay down the theoretical foundations of socialist realism, in uninterrupted but quiet opposition to the Stalin-Zhdanov views which were then prevalent. This took me to the 7th Congress of the Comintern, which came out with the first public statement summing up the popular front policy and, at the same time, reopened the door to the Hungarian party for me. When, after this Congress, the paper of the Hungarian popular front, Uj Hang, appeared, I became an active contributor from the very start, and was once again working with József Révai after a long time. It was there that, for the first time since I became a Marxist, I discussed Ady and the Babits of The Book of Jonah. It was there that I attempted to criticise the false antithesis between urbánus /urban/ and népi /populist/ writers from the point of view of a true Hungarian democratic popular front. These articles I wrote as a Marxist communist, but they never centered on the opposition of Marxism and bourgeois ideology but on a united Hungarian popular resistance to the Horthy regime. This meant a break with the critical practice of Hungarian communists, in which ideological standpoints expressed in Hungary were judged by nothing but Marxist standards. Thus when arguing against the urbánus outlook, I pointed out the distortions caused in the Hungarian development of revolutionary democracy by liberal prejudices such as the criticism of radical land reform in the interest of the undisturbed capitalist development of large estates. Though these were contradictions between liberalism and democracy, and not between socialism and democracy, and both Révai and I always recognized and supported the spontaneous plebeian democratic faith of the népi writers, we only reproached them for often expressing those ideas inconsistently /making concessions to reaction at the expense of the people/. But in an important debate I, for instance, pointed out that, even when judging their ideology by Tolstoyan and not by Marxist standards, their inconsistencies meant a danger to democratic evolution in Hungary. In this way I joined the mainstream of the best traditions of Hungarian literature. Csokonai and Petőfi, Ady and Attila József all took as their starting point action that grew out of the people's attempts to determine their own fate. And if Hungarian literary history and criticism – apart from exceptions such as János Erdélyi, later Ady, and then György Bálint in the Horthy era – scarcely proceeded along this path, this does not call into question the correctness of the way the question is put, nor does it lessen its rootedness in the life of the Hungarian people. Due to this radical change in my intellectual evolution, my return to Hungary in 1945 in no way resembled the coincidence to which I owed my presence in Hungary during the 1918 revolution. On the contrary, it was a conscious decision made in the face of concrete offers from German-speaking circles" /11/.

Lukács's self-analysis must be accepted as decisive in regard to his relationship to Hungary: he has unambiguously declared himself to be Hungarian. Following his return he passionately threw himself into the literary and cultural struggles and wrote a number of important papers dealing with basic problems of Hungarian culture. Summing up this period of his life which lasted more than twenty years, he said: "If I wished to characterize this whole period ideologically, I must point out that in addition to Ady the influence upon me of the plebeian democratic nature of Bartók's art /Cantata Profana/ became stronger and stronger. It would give a false picture of the totality of my activities, including the part concentrating on Hungarian problems, if I made it appear as if Hungarian literary and cultural topics had then dominated my entire activity. This was by no means the case. At the time of the Uj Hang period, I wrote a book about the young Hegel, after the Liberation I produced The Destruction of Reason, Particularity, and later Die Eigenart des Aesthetischen, and I am now about to formulate my views on the philosophical nature of social being. The core of my ideological activities has all the time been to deal with general philosophical problems. These must necessarily point beyond Hungarian reality. Not even a member of the greatest people of world history would be able to think out a valid philosophy /including of course an aesthetics/ merely on the basis of his own national experience" /12/.

Every page of the volume of selected studies on Hungarian literature and culture bears out what Lukács says in the Preface. One soon discovers, looking through the volume, that Lukács's critical and theoretical work is in accord with the description he gives of his own development. All I should like to do now is to draw attention to certain particularly interesting aspects. In 1908, the young Lukács wrote that Ady "had no need of tradition, did not accept any Hungarian values or join any existing trend" and that it was precisely to this that he owed his greatness as a Hungarian poet /13/. In another article Lukács said that for Ady Hungarian existence always carried tragic connotations /14/. In 1909, in a book on the history of the modern drama, he opposed the vulgar interpretation of "international modernism" and pointed to Mihály Vörösmarty's fairytale play Csongor és Tünde as the "most alive, and perhaps only genuinely organic Hungarian play" in classical Hungarian literature. He argues that "it was not chance, not a meeting of fortunate outer and inner circumstances that proved successful in this instance, but the conscious and artistic welding of elements of Hungarian folktales and folk-humour with the mood and techniques of Shakespearean comedy. The main reason why Hungarian fairy-comedy ceased later to be organic was that it lost the relationship with Hungarian life which is there still present" /15/. In an article on Ady published in the same year he wrote that the peculiar character both of Ady and of Hungarian radicalism was to be found in the fact that "there is no Hungarian culture which one could join, and since the old European one does not mean anything from this point of view, only the distant future can produce for us the communion of which we dream". Looking ten years ahead, he predicted the events of 1919 by saying that Ady was "a fighting song, a trumpet and standard around which all can gather if there should ever be a struggle" /16/. That same year, writing about a volume of short stories by Zsigmond Móricz, Lukács said: "One can only speak of this vol-ume with genuine joy. It contains true Hungarian short stories, Hungarian ones in the simplest, most common and most customary sense of the term" /17/. Reading such formulations one might well wonder whether Lukács did not exaggerate somewhat in his Preface quoted above when he said that he had no "inner" relationship to the Hungarian literature at that time.

In 1918, when Mihály Babits accused Béla Balázs and Lukács of being "German", Lukács proved that Babits wanted to protect Hun-garian literature against philosophical "depth". Lukács showed how retrogade the Hungarian "stiff upper-lip" and "nil admirari" spirit was. Lukács asks "whether one is permitted to say that there will not and must not be /any philosophical/ depth in Hun-garian literature in the future, just because there was none in the past?" "Has the Hungarian soul reason to be afraid of depth?" /18/ It is clear that at that time Lukács was already fighting the same fight as Ady and Bartók, the leading spirits of Hun-garian cultural life.

A picture of Lukács without his relationship to Hungarian culture would be pretty anaemic even discussing the 1920s. In 1925, for instance, only two years after his History of Class Consciousness appeared, right in the middle of his "Messianic sectarianism", Lukács published a short article on Mór Jókai, who dominated post-1867 Hungarian literature. Lukács argued that

Jókai "wanted no more in '48 than was realized in '67". "Jókai's
narrative style," Lukács goes on, "is still fully interwoven with
the old Hungarian manner of telling a tale, which is humourous
and imaginative and anecdotal, a style that only loosely links
events. As against his contemporaries, /Zsigmond/ Kemény and József Eötvös who insist upon forcing the style of the foreign novels of the time onto nascent Hungarian prose, Jókai's style
grows organically out of the Hungarian life of his own period.
In this respect Jókai's prose can justifiably be compared to
Petőfi's prosody. Though it is true that this manner of writing
is full of loose and undisciplined elements... it was nevertheless the only road along which Hungarian narrative prose could
progress right up to Zsigmond Móricz, while the artificial prose
of his contemporaries remained an episode in the development of
Hungarian literature" /19/.

x

All his life, Lukács remained true to the simple principle
that "the true greatness of poets rests in their being welded
to the life of their nation" /20/. What is more, in his own work
he put this principle into practice in an increasingly consistent manner. That is why his internationalism has nothing to do
with cosmopolitanism, and that is why his criticism of the népi
and urbánus movements of the Thirties is still valid today. He
explains the real achievements of both as the effect of the 1919
Hungarian revolution, and that, it seems to me, is interesting
even from the point of view of world literature. By and large,
he considered the népi movement to be the more important of the
two, precisely because of the close links with the peasant masses
and the life of the people. When in 1947 he read an article by
Béla Zsolt in which népi writers were viciously slandered, while
writers of Jewish origin were praised to the skies in an unprin-
cipled way, Lukács first of all demonstrated how the author applied double standards, and then went on to say that this whole
method and attitude have their own social background... To put
it briefly, what is involved is the literary and cultural role
of the Lipótváros district. Béla Zsolt describes its style with

great affection, applying positive standards only, allowing at
the most for certain tragic features. But that social and national rootlessness which the Lipótváros culture meant for Hungarian
writers of Jewish origin at the time /i.e., at the turn of the
century/ only rarely grew into a genuine tragedy. ... The break
with genuine Hungarian folk culture bred the false extremes of
snobbery and literary prostitution, though there were, of course,
writers with a happier temperament who, protected by a sort of
narrow specialization, preserved their human and literary integ-
rity. But one cannot, without applying double standards, argue
that tragedies like those of /János/ Vajda or /Lajos/ Tolnai
took place, not to mention Kálmán Mikszáth. It is Ady's great
historical merit, and that of the Nyugat-revolution as a whole,
with all its limits and contradictions, that they started to
demolish these barriers. The real work of demolition was, however, done by the class struggles of the counter-revolutionary
period, and by the népi literature which arose as a part of them.
Until then there had only been an occasional writer who rose a-
bove the dilemma of snobbery and literary prostitution; the counter-revolutionary period produced a new type of writer, liberated
from "Lipótváros", perhaps not many, but respectable numbers
nevertheless, and of a quality that commanded respect. ... and
... that ideal and artistic, meaningful and formal engagement
in the great social and national problems of the Hungarian people
which destroys, in the eyes of all unprejudiced men and women,
every difference of origin, became part of the flesh and blood
of more than one outstanding writer alive today - helping there-
by to root out the ideological bases of antisemitism in the field
of literature. /.../ At the time of the first revolutionary up-
rising of the Hungarian nation the Jews had only reached a stage
of development where they could provide thousands of brave soldiers for the liberation army. The social backwardness of Hungary made it impossible for this fight for freedom to become
manifest among the Jews in an ideological form. In Germany, a
more developed country /at the middle of the 19th century/ Heine
... was the true representative poet. The like of that could
not have happened in the sultry atmosphere of the 1867 Ausgleich
and of the Lipótváros gentroid ghetto. The breeze of the revolu-

tion was needed to bring it about. That is what started with
Nyugat, and was continued, at a higher level of social development, in the period between the two world wars. As Marx rightly
says: 'The soil of counterrevolution is also revolutionary' /21/.

There are not too many people in Hungary who could criticize
'Lipótváros culture' with greater justification and therefore
with greater persuasive force than Lukács who was born and bred
in the Lipótváros district, but who became a revolutionary and
who established qualitatively different ties with his country.

Writing of Ady's importance and influence in 1969 Lukács said:
"It can be said that those who were not satisfied with the Ausgleich did not consider the situation from a specifically Hungarian point of view" /22/. The passages I have quoted in the
foregoing, will indicate how this sentence is to be interpreted.
Lukács continues: "I have not lost touch with Ady, not even for
a day, since reading Uj versek more than sixty years ago. But
this is only a biographical detail, and, without wishing to exaggerate my importance, I cannot really consider my development
typically Hungarian" /23/. It is my suspicion that Lukács, in
this case, did not use the term "typical" in the sense of his
own aesthetics but in the everyday sense of the word; his language would have been more exact if he had said "average". I am
convinced that, taking the term as used in aesthetics, Lukács
was a most typical manifestation of Hungarian culture, though
he was of course no more average than Endre Ady, Béla Bartók or
Attila József.

It is certainly worth investigating how Hungarian culture
managed to accomplish a whole series of achievements of international significance in the 20th century. This seems to me necessary even for a proper understanding of these achievements
themselves. All that I have here said can of course serve as
no more than one of the premises necessary for asking the right
questions - in this instance, the right questions for a proper
understanding of Lukács's work.

/1972/

POSTSCRIPT 1982

Although the above was written ten years ago, its basic ten-
ets have by no means become obsolete. I would, however, like to
add a few remarks and references. The growing literature on the
subject of "Lukács and Hungarian culture" points in many directions. There are some who discuss Lukács's views on this or that
achievement of Hungarian culture, examining the depth of his
understanding of this or that work and analysing his judgments.
There are others who examine the impact on Lukács's thought of
the fact that his career, naturally, began in Hungary and remained - through his connection with the Hungarian Republic of Councils, through his activities in exile, and with his return in
1945 - in close connection with that country. The latter interpretation of the subject is in some measure the more serious one.
It points to many problems of detail which are worth examining.
These researches cannot, however, do anything more than produce
new data, cannot facilitate the exploration of Lukács's accomplishment as a thinker, unless by telling us of how central problems
in his work originated in Hungarian history and in the peculiar-
ities of Hungarian culture and society in the 20th century.

In 1969, in the above-discussed preface to Magyar irodalom
- magyar kultura /Hungarian literature - Hungarian culture/, Lukács outlined the story of how he became a communist and traced
his ideological development. He described as decisive his struggle
to understand Hungarian social reality, which is directly docu-
mented in the so-called "Blum-theses". That is what he wrote on
the subject: "I seriously doubt the objective value of the 'Blum-
-theses' as a theoretical document of the labour movement. This
is chiefly because, compelled by tactical considerations, I made
quite a few concessions to the political prejudices of that time
... in order to be better able to assert my essential ideas concerning the cardinal issue. Yet it is a historical fact that,
on the one hand, the course of development followed by Hungary
has borne out the general perspective of the 'Blum-theses' and
that, on the other, I was after all the only one who foresaw that
development". Lukács then went on to emphasize /see the quote
earlier in my paper/ that for his own development those "Theses"

286

had been crucially important. He saw his becoming a Marxist and
his conscious attachment to Hungarian culture as processes occurring side by side in such a way as to form a unity, despite
all contradictions, processes that bore fruit in his works of
the émigré years in Moscow. Evidently, Lukács's oeuvre /like
other major achievements in Hungarian culture/ could not rely
solely on Hungarian sources. But his becoming a Marxist and growing attachment to Hungarian culture were undoubtedly related
developments, and an analysis of their relation must necessarily
be of significance for an understanding of his work. When this
topic is treated on its merits, it will be clear that Lukács's
oeuvre is among the highest achievements of Hungarian culture
in the 20th century and, what is more, is of a paradigmatic importance from the viewpoint of the relation of modern Hungarian
history and communism, of modern Hungarian culture and Marxism,
that is, problems vital to Hungary and to Hungarian culture.

Seen in this light the subject "Lukács and Hungarian culture"
will rid itself first of all of that distortion of an ostentatiously Hungarian provincialism that rejects Lukács and his consistent radicalism because he belongs to all the world. But it
will rid itself also of that equally ostentatiously non-Hungarian
provincialism which, under the sway of "New Left" utopias, rejects the popular and national problems that are so important
in Lukács. Both sets of views in fact underestimate Hungarian
culture; the first is, after all, afraid of measuring our culture against the standard of world history, world literature,
etc. They represent extremes which, with their shared element,
the underestimation of Hungarian history and culture, were alien
to György Lukács.

In 1948, Lukács published his A Magyar Kommunista Párt és
a magyar kultura /The Hungarian Communist Party and Hungarian
culture/. It was the opening essay in the volume Uj magyar kul-
turáért /Toward a new Hungarian culture/. In it he pointed to
a central problem of Hungarian culture, namely "... the absence
of Hungarian philosophy of any kind. A great Hungarian literature
does exist which, chiefly on account of its poetry, is on par
with the literature of great European peoples. Our modern music
is highly esteemed throughout the world. For a long time our

fine arts have been of a European standard. We have had achievements of international stature in the natural sciences, mathematics and certain areas of historiography. We have not, however, had any thinker who so far would deserve to be ranked even a modest second-rate internationally".

It is clear from this passage that Lukács compares Hungarian culture with the greatest and most original European cultures. He continues to point out that "What I speak of is not the history of philosophy in the professional sense. What I have in mind is the productive impact of philosophy on culture, the interplay of national culture and philosophy. ... What Descartes or Diderot did for French culture, Kant or Hegel for German culture, Belinsky or Chernyshevsky for Russian culture had been unknown to us, and one cannot find even a remote analogy. In fact, we have not had a demand for it either". Lukács is at this point raising problems of national history. "Philosophy at its best is the most abstract summation of man's relation to the world, that is, to nature, society, his own self and thought. From this standpoint the connection between a nation's social character and philosophical culture is important and serious".

Further on Lukács gives the following characterization of two of Europe's greatest philosophical cultures -- "French development in an earlier period, and the upturn in Russian thinking that started in the early 19th century. In both cases philosophy was the prime theoretical weapon in ... the elimination of mediaeval vestiges, in the revolution that eradicated feudalism. In what lay the strength of the two trends of philosophy in France and Russia? What was the secret of their profound impact on the two national cultures? They explored reality with great perseverence, conceptualized the findings shrewdly and without fear of the consequences, and went on to discover the laws inherent in them. They did so with the conviction that the generalized knowledge which they were amassing would be translated into reality and become the guideline by which the people might transform society, that, by enlightening the people, philosophical enlightenment would become the guideline for a superior, meaningful and happy way of life for society, nation and mankind".

The great era of French philosophy paved the way for the bourgeois revolution, and the upturn in Russian philosophy prepared the ground for the socialist revolution. "The golden age of German philosophy also coincided with the intellectual preparations for the bourgeois democratic revolution. /Yet this latter development may be characterized briefly as follows: that its highly refined intellectual generalizations and syntheses lacked the lively and real social basis which lent exceptional courage and insight to the French and Russian philosophies. German philosophy was, consequently, basically idealistic. Though in philosophy's most general and abstract sphere it has managed to make a transition to dialectical thought and, on an idealistic basis, to create the most sophisticated form of dialectic /Hegel/, concerning reality it has necessarily been more obscure and backward and less courageous than the other two philosophies. Its statements of principle are of a very high standard, yet in applying the principles to practice, it has been hesitant, abstract and vague. Hence it follows that the resultant philosophy and culture have exerted a profound influence on high accomplishments in ideology /Goethe, Schiller, Heine/, without having shown themselves capable of influencing the innovative tendencies of the people at large. It is no accident that this intellectual preparation for the German democratic revolution was the preparation for a revolution that failed. It is no accident that the impact of the most refined new German philosophy, materialist dialectic, has had the least influence upon the culture of its homeland. Neither is it an accident that after the downfall of the revolution of 1848, all the negative aspects of philosophical development multiplied in Germany, and that German thought became the guideline for reactionary thinking around the world".

We can see from this passage that Lukács did not idealize even German philosophical culture. The less so the English one. As he put it: "Concerning its type, the first period of modern English philosophy /Bacon, Hobbes/ resembled the French development. Yet after the 'Glorious Revolution', the class compromise between the nobility and bourgeoisie, which facilitated the prosperity of capitalism in Britain, the social function and entire character of philosophy underwent a radical change. Since then philosophy has sought to clear the way for the development of capitalist production and capitalist ideology in such a way so as to use 'epistemological' considerations for eliminating from the thinking of the people all problems that could disturb the class compromise. The resultant hypocrisy, which manifests itself philosophically in agnosticism and skepticism, has since determined the official mainstream of English thought".

While English philosophy became the ideology of the compromise between the nobility and bourgeoisie after a victorious revolution, in Hungary the pre-1848 philosophical endeavours were arrested just because the revolution had been put down and the compromise of 1867 shut the door before radical thought for a long time.

"Hungarian development has been marked by a cant that strongly differs from the English one, a particular hypocrisy that thrives on Hungarian soil: it is a general agreement among 'responsible' persons that to speak of the vital and decisive problems of the Hungarian nation is forbidden, not polite, unbecoming of gentlemen".

The vital problems are oppression, exploitation, the relationship between Hungarians, the ethnic minorities and neighbours, and Hungarian national independence. The set of Hungarian compromises was abrogated first and most forcefully by Endre Ady, whose radicalism, Lukács holds, makes him the greatest poet in the world literature of the beginning of the century. The compromise, again, was cancelled by Béla Bartók, whose art has ascended to becoming one of the greatest achievements of music in the 20th century. And finally, in part under the influence of Ady and Bartók, György Lukács strove to annul the compromise in the sphere of philosophy. Since that sphere was all but a terra incognita for Hungarian culture, his was the most difficult task. Within a period of twenty to thirty years, his endeavours had begun to produce internationally recognized works, the first products of Hungarian thought which were of a world standard. The secret of these internationally recognized achievements lies in this: that only communism has been able to solve the fundamental problems of the Hungarian people in the 20th century. It is convincingly proved by Lukács's work that a new Hungarian culture is inconceivable without identification with the Marxist method and with the application of its theory.

Lukács's philosophical accomplishment provides only the opportunity for thought to play a serious role in Hungarian culture. It is absolutely necessary to oppose that trend of the literature on Lukács which alleges that with the advance of science the epochal ideas in his work have become obsolete, or which claims that his works are sketchy, doctrinaire or abstract, or - most importantly - which attempts arrogantly to discredit his analyses of Hungarian culture. Only if literature of this kind is rigorously criticized can that Marxist philosophy of which Hungarian praxis was the basic source, be capable of exerting its full influence on Hungarian culture.

NOTES

/1/ Magyar irodalom, magyar kultura /"Hungarian literature, Hungarian culture"/. Budapest, 1970. Gondolat

/2/ Lukács, op. cit. pp. 5-7, Preface.

/3/ Op. cit., pp. 7-8.

/4/ Op. cit., pp. 8-9.

/5/ Conversation with György Lukács, in: Irodalmi Muzeum, Emlékezések I, Budapest, 1967. p. 21.

/6/ Lukács, Magyar irodalom..., p. 12.

/7/ Op. cit., p. 14 /see also Emlékezések, pp. 31-34/.

/8/ Ibid.

/9/ Op. cit., p. 15.

/10/ Op. cit., p. 18.

/11/ Op. cit., pp. 18-19.

/12/ Op. cit., p. 20.

/13/ Op. cit., p. 26. "Kosztolányi Dezső" /1907/.

/14/ Op. cit., pp. 34-36. "A Holnap költői" /"The Poets of Holnap"/, 1908.

/15/ Op. cit., p. 38, "A magyar drámáról" /"On Hungarian drama"/, 1909.

/16/ Op. cit., p. 45 and 51, "Ady Endre", 1909.

/17/ Op. cit., p. 60, "Móricz Zsigmond novellás könyve" /"Zsigmond Móricz's volume of short stories"/, 1909.

/18/ Op. cit., pp. 133-145, "Kinek nem kell és miért Balázs Béla költészete" /"Who rejects Béla Balázs's poetry and why"/, 1918.

/19/ Op. cit., pp. 150 and 151, "Jókai", 1925.

/20/ Op. cit., p. 158, "Ady, a magyar tragédia nagy énekese" /"Ady, the great bard of the Hungarian tragedy"/, 1939.

/21/ Op. cit., pp. 443-444, "Egy rossz regény margójára" /"Margin notes on a bad novel"/, 1947.

/22/ Op. cit., p. 606, "Ady jelentősége és hatása" /"Ady's significance and influence"/, 1969.

/23/ Op. cit., p. 609.

Philosophy and Culture
J. Lukács and F. Tőkei eds.

CULTURE ET CIVILISATION CHEZ LE JEUNE LUKÁCS

F. L. LENDVAI

La carrière de Lukács a commencé à la fin du XIXe et dans les premières années du XXe siècle. Le jeune Lukács -- et cela est valable aussi pour les périodes ultérieures -- s'intéressait surtout à l'histoire et à la théorie de la culture de l'humanité, et plus spécialement de l'art. C'est ainsi que sa pensée se trouve centrée sur la philosophie de l'art, sur l'esthétique et ses problèmes. Dès le début, cependant, il se refuse à traiter ces questions de manière subjectiviste /ou, pour reprendre ses termes: dans l'esprit de l' "impressionnisme"/, considérant aussi comme absolument nécessaire de jeter des fondements plus profonds relevant de l'épistémologie et de la philosophie de l'histoire.

Ainsi, par ses objectifs, la pensée du jeune Lukács se rattache sur le plan artistique et philosophique, aux grandes tentatives de synthèse du tournant du siècle. Ses premiers idéaux furent le "distingué" Oscar Wilde, et Richard Wagner, le père de l'idée du Gesamtkunst /art global/, et surtout le grand critique de la vie bourgeoise moderne que fut Henrik Ibsen. "Ibsen, Nietzsche et Tolstoï seront les classiques de l'âge moderne", écrit-il dans l'un de ses tout premiers articles /1/. Au plan philosophique, outre Nietzsche, Lukács fut bientôt influencé aussi par Kierkegaard, qu'on découvrit à cette époque, et par Georg Simmel, dont il fit aussi la connaissance personnelle. Se ralliant à la critique culturelle allemande du tournant du siècle -- et en accord, d'ailleurs, avec la terminologie allemande et hongroise --, Lukács comprenait à l'origine par "civilisation" la culture de caractère technique, et par "culture" celle de l'esprit.

Quant à la notion de l' "impressionnisme" qu'il condamna à plusieurs reprises, le jeune Lukács l'utilisait dans un sens assez large, et en pratique comme synonyme de la décadence bourgeoise; en l'occurrence, il fut certainement influencé par le célèbre livre de Richard Hamann paru en 1907, Impressionismus im Leben und Kunst. Et lorsque, adoptant la position de Rudolf Kassner, il s'efforça d'être "critique", il comprenait par là avant tout une critique de l'art et de la vie bourgeoise modernes. Toute sa vision du monde était typiquement conservatrice, et même aristocratique. Dans l'un de ses écrits se rattachant encore directement à Ibsen, il a recours à la catégorie du "romantisme attardé" pour décrire le mode de penser auquel il veut se rallier: il caractérise l'univers d'Ibsen en se servant des notions de romantisme et de désillusion, et le met en parallèle avec la philosophie de Fichte, Schopenhauer et Kierkegaard, mais aussi avec la poésie de Grillparzer, Baudelaire et Flaubert. "Tout romantisme était déjà brisé et périmé lorsqu'ils vécurent", écrit--il à leur sujet, "à une époque ou leur ennemi juré, le rationalisme, régnait déjà dans tous les domaines... Ils étaient déja passés par la désillusion" /2/.

Les temps anciens, souligne à plusieurs reprises le jeune Lukács, étaient plus propices que les temps modernes à l'épanouissement du grand art. C'est ainsi qu'on peut lire dans l'un de ses essais que "ce sont précisément les peintres les plus modernes, ceux qui stylisent le plus systématiquement, qui sentent avec le plus de force quel avantage indicible représentait pour Giotto son "primitivisme" /qui nous parle/ de beautés tout à fait spéciales et inaccessibles de nos jours, issues justement de cette démarcation" et qui n'existent plus ni chez Bellini, ni chez Giorgione /3/. En effet, les plus grands peintres des temps modernes, Van Gogh, Cézanne et Gauguin, se trouvent dans une situation tragique. "Après les victoires décisives" écrit à leur sujet le jeune Lukács, "lorsque tous les moyens nécessaires à une grande peinture se trouvèrent réunis, /.../ ils durent réaliser à leur profonde douleur, qu'il ne pouvait être question aujourd' hui de grande peinture. L'impressionnisme ne peut être qu'un matériau dans un grand édifice, mais où est cet édifice?" /4/ En effet, l'homme des temps modernes ne vit plus dans les cadres

294

d'une culture close "dans laquelle un même instinct détermine quels doivent être la demeure de l'homme, ses vêtements, ses meubles et ses tableaux; l'anarchie est totale" /5/.

Aussi l'intérêt de Lukács se tourne-t-il de plus en plus vers la possibilité de l'existence ou plutôt du renouveau d'une culture close. Il traite de ce problème dans nombre de ses écrits, parmi lesquels l'un des plus beaux et des plus profonds est la grande étude qu'il consacra à Theodor Storm, et qu'il devait inclure dans son célèbre recueil d'essais <u>A lélek és a formák</u> /L'âme et les formes /1910/, paru en allemand en 1911 sous le titre de <u>Die Seele und die Formen</u>/, ouvrage qui exerça une influence considérable a l'époque, et qui est centré sur les questions de la "forme", autrement dit de la nature "formable" de la vie humaine. L'idée de la "mise en forme" s'y mêle à l'idée de l'appartenance à une communauté existant réellement. Une telle communauté existait par exemple au Moyen Age, à propos duquel Lukács notait: "/.../ que l'art fût achevé en lui-même et n'obéit qu'à ses propres lois, cela n'était pas la conséquence d'un violent détachement de la vie; au contraire, il existait pour l'amour de lui-même, de la même manière que tout travail accompli avec probité existe pour l'amour de lui-même. Cela parce que l'intérêt de l'ensemble, pour l'amour duquel tout naît, recommande que le travail soit accompli comme s'il n'avait d'autre but que lui-même et n'existait que pour l'amour de la perfection achevée en elle-même" /6/. Si Storm fut capable de créer une poésie reflétant un univers spirituel qui était pratiquement celui de la bourgeoisie des corporations médiévales - souligne Lukács, dont la force fut toujours l'analyse des racines sociologiques des oeuvres d'art - c'est parce qu' "en Allemagne, de nombreuses transformations, en particulier dans le domaine économique, ont eu lieu beaucoup plus tard qu'autre part, tandis que de nombreuses formes de société, et encore bien plus d'anciennes formes de vie, se sont conservées plus longtemps ici qu'autre part. Au milieu du siècle dernier, il y avait encore en Allemagne, particulièrement à la périphérie, des villes dans lesquelles l'ancienne bourgeoisie était restée forte et vivante, cette bourgeoisie qui constituait la plus forte anthithèse de celle d'aujourd'hui" /7/.

Pour cette raison, Lukács rejette catégoriquement le "progrès" purement technique de l'âge moderne. En effet, le développement de la civilisation technique n'est pas allé de pair avec le progrès de la culture spirituelle, et il est même en contradiction expresse avec ce dernier. "Certains", écrit-il, "parlent d'aéroplanes lorsqu'il est question de culture, et de chemin de fer, de la rapidité des télégrammes et de la sûreté des opérations; ils parlent du fait que tant de gens pourraient lire /si leur vie était telle que leur âme souhaitait la lecture/ et -- du nombre de ceux que le "démocratisme" de l'époque actuelle prive cependant de tous leurs droits/.../ Mais n'oublions jamais une chose, à savoir que ce ne sont là -- tout au plus -- que des voies d'accès à la culture, des possibilités, des facilités; moyens par lesquels la culture exerce son pouvoir. /.../ Et on se demande si un voyage vaut davantage pour nous parce qu'il ne dure qu'une journée, au lieu d'un mois. Si nos lettres sont plus profondes et plus émouvantes du fait que la poste les fait arriver plus vite à destination. Les réactions manifestées devant la vie sont-elles à présent plus fortes et plus homogènes du fait qu'un plus grand nombre peut avoir accès aux choses et à un plus grand nombre de choses?" /8/ Et, face au démocratisme formel de l'époque moderne et à son "nivellement" - pour utiliser un terme de Kierkegaard -, Lukács exige une sorte d'idée communautaire, en se retournant contre l'individualisme, dans un texte qui est pratiquement un programme de par son caractère et son titre, et qui a été écrit presque au même moment que le précédent. Le nouvel art, écrit-il dans son article Az utak el-váltak /Les chemins se sont séparés/ qui rejette désormais définitivement et globalement l' "impressionnisme", doit avoir pour devise ceci: "la guerre à tout impressionnisme, à toute sensation et à toute atmosphère, à tout désordre et à toute négation des valeurs, à toute vision du monde et à tout art écrivant "je" pour premier et dernier mot" /9/.

Après l'analyse de grande envergure des possibilités de la culture close et "mise en forme", Lukács écrit l'une de ses oeuvres capitales, la Théorie du Roman /10/. Formellement, l'ouvrage relève simplement de la théorie et de l'histoire des genres, mais en réalité, comme l'indique son sous-titre, il s'agit d'un

"essai de philosophie de l'histoire". Le premier chapitre de la
première partie, qui a pour titre "Cultures closes", est le développement d'une gigantesque confrontation dans le cadre de la
philosophie de l'histoire, des temps anciens et des temps modernes
-- confrontation qui est présente dans les oeuvres du jeune Lukács dès le départ -- et prend en l'occurrence trois formes concrètes et parallèles: monde grec - monde moderne, âge de l'épopée - âge du roman, et enfin, enfance - âge d'homme. La première
période est caractérisée par l'unité du monde et du moi; l'homme
y parcourt le monde avec un naturel naif. La première définition
concrète que Lukács applique à cette période est qu'elle est
l'âge de l'épopée; puis, tout de suite après, il la définit aussi
comme l'enfance de l'humanité; et étant donné qu'il ne considère
-- en dernière analyse -- comme épopées que les oeuvres d'Homère,
il s'agit en même temps de l'âge de l'hellénité. Ici, la notion
d' "hellénité" doit être prise dans un sens très général; elle
désigne en effet une hellénité homérique abstraite-idéalisée.
Et, bien que l'influence de Hegel soit évidente dans l'ouvrage,
cette notion d'hellénité rappellerait plutôt l'image de l'hellénité que Marx propose dans l'introduction de l'ébauche du Capital. /Le jeune Lukács connaissait certainement ce texte, qui
avait été publié par Karl Kautsky dès 1902-1903/. En dernière
analyse, la totalité naive de cette hellénité relevant de la
philosophie de l'histoire repose sur l'unité de l'individu et
de la communauté, et prend ses racines dans la "culture close".
Cependant, comme le montre Lukács dans les analyses suivantes,
cette hellénité change aussi au cours de son développement ultérieur, et le monde grec original, clos et mis en forme, se
désagrege. Il est vrai qu'une fois encore, la totalité naive
opere un retour, durant la période prospere du moyen-age, et
que l'Eglise devient une sorte de nouvelle polis -- l'auteur
y voit une survivance de l'hellénité --, mais ce sera la der-
niere fois. Le monde moderne est déjà le monde des individus
solitaires. Alors que l'épopée était la grande forme épique de
l'enfance de l'humanité, le roman est la grande forme épique
de "l'âge d'homme mûr" de l'humanité. En conséquence de quoi,
tandis que la totalité de l'épopée était donnée, la totalité
du roman reste à faire. Les anciens dieux ont quitté le monde,

et l'avènement des nouveaux dieux ne s'est pas encore produit:
notre monde est donc celui de la démonité, car "les dieux dé-
chus et ceux qui n'ont pas encore d'empire reconnu deviennent
des démons" /11/.

Mais l'avènement de nouvelles divinités peut-il encore se
faire dans ce monde abandonné de dieu, ou bien ce monde reste-
ra-t-il à jamais abandonné de dieu? Dans un texte également paru en 1916 /12/ Lukács attend explicitement l'avènement d'une
nouvelle divinité: "Et s'il y avait vraiment un Dieu? Si un dieu
seulement était mort, et qu'un autre, issu d'une génération plus
jeune, d'une autre essence et ayant avec nous d'autres rapports,
allait venir maintenant? ...Dans ce cas, sa clarté qui ne nous
apparaît que faiblement n'est-elle pas plus importante que la
trompeuse splendeur du héros, et la maisonnée de celui qui vient
n'est-elle pas davantage et plus proche de l'essentiel que le
héros et son éthique génératrice de solitude?" /13/ Et Lukács
nous dit aussi clairement où et par qui il voit annoncer ce dieu
nouveau: par Dostoïevski, en Russie. "C'est de cette dualité",
écrit-il, "que sont issus les héros de Dostoïevski: le prince
Mychkine aux côtés de Nicolaï Stavroguine, et aux côtés d'Ivan
Karamazov son frère Aliocha" /14/. Dans un autre texte de 1916,
il est encore plus net: "C'est là le mysticisme de ceux qui sont
véritablement croyants aujourd'hui, celui des athées modernes.
Les chemins /y/ deviennent évidents, ils conduisent à la patrie
de la religiosité d'aujourd'hui, à la Russie de Dostoïevski"/15/.
Par sa première femme, l'anarchiste-révolutionnaire russe Léna
Grabenko, Lukács chercha un contact direct avec ce monde; et,
comme on sait, la Théorie du roman parut avec la dédicace: "Jel-
jena Andrejewna Grabenko zu eigen" /A Jeliena Andreievna Graben-
ko/.

On sait également que l'ouvrage se termine sur le nom de Dostoïevski. Comment Lukács est-il donc arrivé jusqu'à Dostoïevski?
Dans les premiers temps, il ne s'intéresse qu'à la "véritable"
éthique des héros de Dostoïevski, allant au-delà de l'éthique
formelle, mais la recherche de la "communauté" commence à l'attirer de plus en plus vers le monde décrit par Dostoïevski. A
l'origine, la Théorie du roman devait être le premier chapitre
d'une monographie de grande envergure sur Dostoïevski, et l'on

298

trouve dans l'ébauche de l'ouvrage des points tels que "Mystique russe -- communauté. La Russie et l'Europe" /16/. Selon Lukács, en effet, il n'est plus qu'un vain effort de protester de l'intérieur contre la civilisation occidentale, aliénée et sclérosée. Le premier exemple qu'il cite est celui de Rousseau: "Même chez Rousseau, dont la vision romantique du monde a pour contenu le rejet de toute structure sociale liée à la culture, la contestation prend une forme purement polémique, c'est-à-dire rhétorique, lyrique, réflexive; la culture de l'Europe occidentale plonge de si fortes racines dans les structures sociales sur lesquelles elle se fonde que, lorsqu'elle prend position contre elles pour leur échapper, ce ne peut être que sur le mode polémique" /17/. Et à ce stade, Lukács franchit un pas qui sera d'une importance déterminante pour son développement ultérieur: il déclare sa rupture avec la civilisation occidentale et s'engage en faveur de la nouvelle culture orientale -- bien qu'il fasse tout cela sur un plan entièrement abstrait et purement spirituel. Mais le milieu historico-philosophique et sociologique réel est aussi présent dès le départ: "Pour que pareille contestation devînt créatrice, il a fallu qu'avec l'avènement de la littérature russe du XIXe siècle, elle se trouvât plus proche des états organiques naturels donnés à cette littérature comme substrats de ces dispositions intérieures et de ces actes structurateurs" /18/. Cependant, dans la conclusion de l'ouvrage, Lukács pose la question suivante, sceptiquement malgré tous ses espoirs: "/peut-être/ sommes-nous effectivement sur le point d'abandonner l'état /fichtéen/ de parfaite culpabilité ou /peut-être/ de simples espérances annoncent-elles seulement le début d'une ère nouvelle, -- signes d'un avenir si faible que la force stérile de ce qui se borne à exister peut toujours l'anéantir comme en se jouant" /19/.

Quittons à présent les sommets éthérés des analyses théoriques pour descendre parmi les réalités crues de l'histoire de l'Europe orientale. Les pays de cette région du continent faisaient partie au Moyen Age, à peu près depuis leur formation intervenue aux Xe et XIe siècles, de la "Respublica Christiana" européenne, surtout les pays catholiques dits centre-européens. A partir du début des Temps Modernes, cependant, une rupture très marquée se

produisit entre les moitiés Ouest et Est de l'Europe: alors que
la société bourgeoise moderne prenait forme à l'Ouest, les conditions partriarco-féodales traditionnelles se stabilisèrent à
l'Est. Il devint alors évident que le régime des ordres qui ca-
ractérisait les Etats occidentaux n'existait pas réellement au
Moyen Age en Europe orientale. La proportion faible de la bourgeoisie, la masse imposante de la noblesse et son poids social,
tout cela rendait impossible la constitution à l'Est de monar-
chies absolues qui jetterent les fondements des Etats-nations
de l'époque moderne et qui servirent aussi de cadre au développement de la civilisation moderne. L'Etat nobiliaire hongrois dé-
fendit avec succès son autonomie contre les souverains de la
maison des Habsbourg, au prix, cependant, de la conservation des
conditions arriérées. La Hongrie ne fit ses premiers pas hési-
tants sur la voie de la civilisation moderne qu'à l'époque de
l'absolutisme éclairé de Marie-Thérèse d'Autriche et de Joseph II.
Pendant la révolution et la guerre d'indépendance de 1848, de
grands projets virent le jour en vue d'édifier une société et
un Etat hongrois modernes, mais la plupart d'entre eux ne purent
être réalisés qu'après le "Compromis" austro-hongrois de 1867.
La Hongrie fut alors le théâtre d'un développement bourgeois réellement rapide et de vaste envergure, mais assez inégal. Il se
produisit surtout dans les villes, et avant tout à Budapest, qui
se transformait en métropole, tandis que les conditions qui ré-
gnaient dans les villages étaient pratiquement -- selon les critères occidentaux -- semi-barbares. Les tensions sociales s'ag-
gravèrent de façon insoutenable dans le pays, qui comprenait
alors de grandes régions habitées par diverses éthnies. La Hongrie se trouva au seuil d'une nouvelle révolution.

Si le jeune Lukács était opposé au conservatisme régnant de
l'aristocratie et de la grande bourgeoisie, il ne se rallia pas
non plus aux tendances libérales et modernes de l'opposition dé-
mocratique bourgeoise. Ennemi des conditions politiques et sociales réactionnaires-bureaucratiques /qu'il qualifia plus tard,
avec une certaine exagération, de "prussianisme"/, il considérait
avec non moins d'inquiétude les conditions aliénées du capitalisme
moderne, qu'il condamnait sous l'influence de Neitzsche, Kierkegaard, Weininger et d'autres penseurs /20/. Il se refusa donc à

se joindre aux groupes d'opposition hongrois parce qu'il trouvait que ceux-ci -- les radicaux et les sociaux-démocrates --
ne se dressaient pas avec assez de virulence contre les conditions en place et souhaitaient aboutir en Hongrie aux conditions
du capitalisme occidental et de la démocratie bourgeoise /qu'il
méprisait profondément/. Dans l'avant-propos à la nouvelle édition de la Théorie du Roman /Luchterhand, 1962/, Lukács caractérise en ces termes ses positions de l'époque de la première guerre
mondiale: "les puissances centrales battront vraisemblablement
la Russie; le résultat en sera peut-être la chute du tzarisme
-- d'accord. Il existe une certaine probabilité pour que les
puissances occidentales l'emportent sur l'Allemagne; si leur
victoire aboutit au renversement des Hohenzollern et des Habsbourg, là aussi je suis d'accord" /21/. "Mais la question est
de savoir qui nous sauvera de la civilisation occidentale". /+/

/+/ Cette phrase a dû être retraduite, car elle figure sous une
    forme erronée dans la version française, qui dit "Mais la
    question est de savoir qui sauvera la civilisation occiden-
    tale là où l'original allemand /et de même le texte hongrois/
    dit "Aber dann entsteht die Frage: wer rettet uns vor der
    westlichen Zivilisation?" /22/ N.d.t.

C'est ainsi que l'intérêt de Lukács se tourne vers le "monde
nouveau" dépeint par Dostoievski, mais pas seulement vers la
"révolution de l'âme". Comme il l'écrivit en avril 1915 à Paul
Ernst à propos du livre du célèbre anarchiste Boris Savinkov-
-Ropchetchine, "un nouveau type d'homme est né /dans le mouvement révolutionnaire russe/, que nous devons apprendre à connaître".

C'est à partir de cette base spirituelle profondément contradictoire que Lukács se trouve confronté aux questions posées
par la révolution hongroise de 1918/19. Dès le début, il ne souhaite pas une simple réforme politique des conditions existant
alors en Hongrie, mais des changements sociaux fondamentaux.
"Nous voulons une renaissance intérieure de la Hongrie, tant
économique que sociale; ...nous devons voir clairement que les
véritables ennemis du progrès sont les latifundia, le grand ca-

pital et la bureaucratie irresponsable" /23/. De tels objectifs
ne furent bien entendu formulés, fixés pour la révolution que
par les communistes hongrois -- qui suivaient en cela l'exemple
des bolchéviks russes. Néanmoins, dans son premier article consacré au bolchévisme, qui vit également le jour en novembre 1918
et portait le titre de Le bolchévisme en tant que probleme moral
/A bolsevizmus mint erkölcsi probléma/, Lukács rejette encore
"les méthodes du bolchévisme". L'article est écrit dans l'optique
d'un socialiste qui doit politiquement faire son choix entre la
social-démocratie et le bolchévisme; mais ce choix était en l'occurrence motivé surtout par des considérations relevant d'une
éthique formelle. Lorsqu'il prend -- à contre-coeur -- la défense
de la position des sociaux-démocrates, c'est en fait Dostoievski
qui s'exprime à travers ses paroles: le censeur de la violence,
celui qui appelle les moines à se lever et à precher sur l'heure.
Et effectivement, ici c'est à Dostoievski que Lukács emprunte
son principal argument contre le bolchévisme: "Le bolchévisme
est basé sur la supposition métaphysique que le bien peut sortir
du mal et qu'il est possible, comme le dit Razoumikhine dans
"Crime et Châtiment", de mentir jusqu'à parvenir à la vérité"/24/.
Mais lorsque l'article en question fut publié, en décembre 1918,
son auteur n'était plus d'accord avec son contenu, à tel point
qu'il demanda alors son admission au sein du Parti des Communistes
de Hongrie. /Il devait bientôt devenir l'un des chefs du parti et,
comme on sait, son engagement envers l'idée de communisme et le
mouvement communiste dura jusqu'à son dernier souffle/. Que s'é-
tait-il donc passé entre-temps, comment Lukács était-il "devenu
Paul, de Saül qu'il était", selon l'expression de l'époque? Outre
des motifs personnels tels que le rapport que lui fit personnelle-
ment un ami de longue date sur les conditions de la guerre civile
en Russie et sur la lutte de la terreur rouge et de la terreur
blanche, on peut trouver, sans trop de difficulté, une explication à cela aussi sur le plan théorique. En Hongrie, tout comme
en Russie, dans des conditions semi-barbares, la lutte pour la
civilisation et le progrès /au sens le plus général du terme/
était encore largement à l'ordre du jour. Mais nous avons aussi
mentionné l'antipathie profonde de Lukács à l'égard de la civilisation aliénée. /Il vaut peut-être la peine de noter en passant

que, lorsqu'on objecta à Dostoïevski qu'il ne s'agissait pas
d'adopter cette civilisation-là, l'écrivain répondit: mais si,
puisqu'il n'y en a pas d'autre/. Dans son étude déjà citée,
Esztétikai kultura /Culture esthétique/, Lukács reprend les propos de Bernard Shaw selon qui "le meilleur programme serait de
faire sauter toutes les églises du monde avec leurs orgues,
peintures et tout, malgré tous les gémissements des critiques
d'art et des amateurs de culture" /25/. Bien entendu, cela ne
veut nullement dire que Lukács ait voulu détruire la culture en
général; simplement, il souhaitait, à la place d'une culture
décadente, l'avènement d'une nouvelle culture "mise en forme"
et close, comme celle que la chrétienté avait édifié à la place
du monde antique qui avait sombré dans la décadence et s'était
désagrégé.

Or, il est extrêmement intéressant de voir que Lukács établit
très tôt un parallèle historico-philosophique entre le marxisme
et le christianisme. Dans son premier ouvrage important, A modern
dráma fejlődésének története /Histoire du développement du drame
moderne/, il écrit: "comme système et vision du monde du socialisme, le marxisme est une synthèse. Peut-être la plus impi-
toyable et la plus stricte des synthèses depuis le catholicisme
médiéval. Pour s'exprimer, lorsque viendra pour lui le temps
d'avoir une expression artistique, seule sera adéquate une forme
d'une rigueur comparable à l'art véritable de celui-ci /je pense
surtout à Giotto et à Dante/ /.../ De nos jours, la plupart des
véritables socialistes ne le sont encore que dans leur pensée,
dans leurs convictions politiques et sociales, etc.; leur vision
du monde n'a encore nullement pénétré celles de leurs formes de
vie qui n'y sont pas liées. C'est ainsi que seul un petit nombre
d'entre eux sentent pour le moment que leur conception de l'art
ne peut être que dogmatique/.../ Que leur art ne peut être autre
que l'art du grand ordre, celui de la monumentalité" /26/. Pour
l'essentiel, il reprend le même point de vue dans Esztétikai
kultura /Culture esthétique/: "C'est dans le prolétariat, dans
le socialisme que nous pouvons placer notre unique espoir. L'espoir que viendront des barbares qui mettront en pièces avec
leurs mains grossières tout raffinement outré. /.../Mais ce que
nous avons vu jusqu'ici ne promet pas grand'chose de bon. Le

socialisme, en apparence, n'a pas la force religieuse emplissant l'âme tout entière que l'on trouvait dans le christianisme primitif. Il a fallu la persécution de l'art des premiers chrétiens pour que puisse naître l'art de Giotto et de Dante, de Maître Eckhart et de Wolfram von Eschenbach: le christianisme primitif nous a donné la Bible, et l'art de plusieurs siècles s'est nourri de ses fruits. Et parce qu'il s'agissait d'une religion véritable, douée d'une force qui a donné la Bible, elle n'avait pas besoin de l'art; elle ne le souhaitait pas et ne le tolérait pas auprès d'elle, elle voulait régner seule sur l'âme de l'homme car elle en était capable. C'est cette force qui manque au socialisme, et c'est pour cette raison qu'il n'est pas autant qu'il le voudrait et qu'il le faudrait l'ennemi véritable de l'esthétisme né de la bourgeoisie" /27/.

Seulement, par "socialisme" et "socialistes" il faut comprendre chaque fois la social-démocratie telle que Lukács l'a connue en Hongrie et en Allemagne autour des années 1900. C'est pour cela que la découverte du bolchévisme fut pour lui un tel choc, et que celui-ci représenta à ses yeux un "problème moral"! Lukács hésita un moment: pouvait-il assumer avec toutes ses conséquences cette révolution qui n'était pas la "révolution de l'âme"? Et il se trouva alors placé devant un choix dans lequel Dostoïevski, précisément, auquel -- nous l'avons vu -- il se référait, ne pouvait lui être d'aucun secours. En effet, la sympathie de Dostoïevski pour la révolution -- qu'il condamnait pour la forme -- est par trop évidente /que l'on pense, par exemple, au célèbre chapitre de "La Révolte" dans Les frères Karamazov !/: de toute la littérature russe c'est probablement ce qui lui fit choisir Dostoïevski à cette époque, étant donné que celui-ci ne déclarait pas a priori avec Tolstoi, avec passivité et résignation: "Ne résiste pas au mal par la violence !". A la fin de 1918, la situation sociale et politique due à la révolution révéla clairement que la "révolution de l'âme", et ses pareilles n'étaient que des utopies. Or si Lukács, donc, ne voulait pas opérer un retour à la démocratie bourgeoise à caractère formel, il lui fallait nécessairement, dans la situation donnée, choisir entre le fascisme naissant et le communisme ! Un choix de ce type se fût imposé a Dostoievski lui-même si l'écrivain n'était pas mort

avant même que la "sainte Troupe" et les "Cent Noirs" ne tentent
de réaliser ses idées tout en recourant à des méthodes qu'il
avait condamnées. Ce n'était certainement pas une pure coïnci-
dance si certains éléments de la démagogie nazie /par exemple
les tristement célèbres "Actes des Sages de Sion"/ ont été em-
pruntés à la panoplie de la réaction russe préfasciste...

Au plan éthique, Lukács motivait son choix du bolchévisme en
tenant le raisonnement suivant: soit je choisis le bolchévisme,
et je suis responsable, il est vrai, des vies humaines détruites
dans le combat mené en son nom, mais je me sacrifie aussi moi-même
pour une grande idée et pour un objectif historique d'envergure
mondiale; soit je tolère la terreur blanche, et je dois assumer
la responsabilité de davantage encore de vies humaines détruites
/pas seulement dans le présent, mais aussi au cours des guerres
nouvelles qui se produiront sûrement, etc./, mais sans sacrifice
personnel qui justifierait ma décision. Cependant, en réalité,
le motif fondamental de son choix n'était en l'occurrence pas
d'ordre éthique. Lukács ne pouvait opter pour le préfascisme
sans contredire toute la critique de la culture qu'il avait professée jusque-là et son rejet de la décadence. En effet, le préfascisme ne promettait aucun changement fondamental dans les
conditions économiques et sociales de fond qu'il condamnait profondément. En effet, il n'était pas difficile de découvrir dans
le fascisme une décadence générale, son incapacité d'édifier
une grande culture, et sa médiocrité au plan de l'histoire universelle. C'est pour cela que, par exemple, un homme comme Os-
wald Spengler qui avait des idées proches de celles du jeune
Lukács sous bien des aspects, mais qui influença pourtant sur
bien des points l'idéologie du fascisme, s'éleva contre celui-ci
lorsqu'il prit le pouvoir; cela explique aussi le fait que le
bourgeois conservateur allemand Thomas Mann ait écrit dans son
grand roman "Le Docteur Faustus": "En ma qualité de bourgeois
allemand, je considère le règne de la classe inférieure comme
un état idéal, comparé au règne de la lie". Lukács, qui, comme
nous l'avons vu, sympathisait en théorie depuis longtemps avec
l'idée socialiste, put enfin découvrir dans le mouvement ouvrier
révolutionnaire russe, qui avait grandi dans des conditions pa-
triarcales et semi-barbares et différait radicalement de la so-

cial-démocratie occidentale, le grand mouvement messianique prometteur d'un monde nouveau et d'une nouvelle culture qu'il cherchait et attendait depuis si longtemps.

L'on pourrait citer nombre de ses textes de l'époque pour prouver que Lukács concevait alors, à l'époque de la République hongroise des Conseils, le développement de la société humaine d'une façon profondément messianique, dans le cadre d'un schéma typiquement eschatologique. Prenons parmi ces écrits celui qui est peut-être le plus caractéristique; il représente une sorte de transition entre sa critique culturelle romantique antérieure et son révolutionnarisme messianique d'alors, et a pour titre L'ancienne culture et la nouvelle culture /28/. Lukács y oppose on ne peut plus clairement culture et civilisation. "Le concept de culture", écrit-il /par opposition à celui de civilisation/ "renferme tous les produits et toutes les activités de valeur qui sont indispensables à la subsistance directe" /29/. Il est à remarquer qu'ici Lukács n'identifie pas la culture au savoir humain, pas plus qu'il ne comprend par civilisation la science technique et professionnelle. L'essentiel est l'aspect de l'utilité dans l'ordre de la production marchande, dans le monde de l' "homo oeconomicus". "La libération du joug du capitalisme signifie la libération du joug que représente le règne de la vie économique" /30/. Il s'agit donc de conditions sociales dans lesquelles -- tout comme dans les cultures closes des époques antérieures au capitalisme -- l'homme redevient un but en soi: "Car la culture représente le règne intérieur de l'homme sur son environnement au même titre que la civilisation représente sa domination extérieure sur son environnement /.../ L'autonomie de l'homme est la condition sociologique préalable de la culture" /31/.

Lukács se rallie là à une tradition philosophique ayant des racines profondes et qu'il est coutume de désigner brièvement par le terme de "négation de la négation". Aux termes de celle-ci, les phénomènes de l'histoire humaine peuvent être répartis en trois grandes phases: l'état naïvement naturel de la période préhistorique primitive, les conditions aliénées-civilisées de la période dite historique, et enfin, la période /résultant de la précédente/ de la "véritable histoire", basée sur la période

"historique" et représentant un retour à l'état naturel, mais
à un niveau élevé. Lukács écrit dans "Histoire et conscience
de classe", en se référant avant tout à Marx: "C'est ainsi que
commence vraiment l'histoire de l'humanité. De même que l'histoire au sens ancien du terme commence avec la civilisation et
qu'elle range les luttes de l'homme contre la nature dans la période de la "préhistoire", l'historiographie des époques futures
fera dater la véritable histoire de l'humanité du communisme
développé" /32/. Marx, bien entendu, a emprunté directement,
comme nous le savons, le schéma de la négation de la négation à
Hegel, mais celui-ci existait déjà en fait chez Kant et chez
Fichte. Et c'est précisément sur le nom de ceux-ci que Lukács
conclut son étude: "De même que le capitalisme crée lui-même les
conditions économiques préalables de sa destruction,/.../ il a
créé/.../ dans la philosophie de Kant et Fichte l'idée de la
société nouvelle qui est appelée à réaliser nécessairement son
anéantissement" /33/. Une investigation plus poussée nous conduirait de toute évidence au dogme chrétien de la rédemption,
mais ce serait pousser trop loin notre analyse. De même, l'analyse de la mesure dans laquelle l'évolution réelle a justifié
ou non les conceptions de Lukács nous mènerait également trop
loin.

NOTES

/1/ Az új Hauptmann /Le nouvel Hauptmann/: "Jövendő" du 23 août
 1903, in: Ifjúkori művek /Oeuvres de jeunesse/, Magvető,
 Budapest, 1977. p. 89.

/2/ Gondolatok Ibsen Henrikről /Pensées sur H. Ibsen/: "Huszadik
 század", 1906/II, p. 127 et suiv., in: "Ifjúkori művek"
 /Oeuvres de jeunesse/, pp. 90 et 92.

/3/ Shakespeare és a modern dráma /Shakespeare et le drame mo-
 derne/, "Magyar Shakespeare Tár", 1. IV, 1911, pp. 129-130.
 Ibid., p. 486.

/4/ Gauguin: "Huszadik század", 1907/I, p. 559 et suiv. Ibid.,
 p. 113.

/5/ Ibid., p. 112.

/6/ Theodor Storm, in: "L'âme et les formes", Gallimard, 1974,
 p. 97.

/7/ Ibid., p. 106.

/8/ Esztétikai kultúra /Culture esthétique/, "Renaissance",
1910/I, p. 123 et suiv., in: "Ifjukori müvek" /Oeuvres de
jeunesse/, p. 422.

/9/ "Nyugat" 1910/I, p. 190 et suiv. Ibid., p. 286.

/10/ Paru en 1916 dans le "Zeitschrift sür Aesthetik und allgemeine Kunstwissenschaft" Bd. 2, p. 225 et suiv., p. 390
et suiv., sous le titre de Die Theorie des Romans; sous
forme de livre chez Cassirer en 1920.

/11/ Théorie du roman, Gonthier, Bibliothèque Médiations, 1963.
p. 82.

/12/ Ariadne auf Naxos, in: "Paul Ernst. Zu seinem 50. Geburts-
tag", München, bei Georg Müller, 1916, p. 11 et suiv.

/13/ Ibid., pp. 17, 18.

/14/ Ibid.

/15/ Tristan hajóján /A bord de la nef de Tristan/. Remarques
sur les nouveaux poèmes de Béla Balázs: "Nyugat", 1916/II,
p. 751 et suiv., in: "Ifjúkori müvek" /Oeuvres de jeunesse/,
p. 651.

/16/ L'ébauche autographe figure dans les collections des Archives
Lukács de Budapest, IV/3.

/17/ Théorie du roman, Gonthier, pp. 146-147.

/18/ Ibid., p. 147.

/19/ Ibid., p. 155.

/20/ Il cite par exemple Maine de Biran comme un "grand philosophe" dans un passage de son Journal de 1910/11. /Akadé-
miai, Budapest, 1981, p. 39./

/21/ Théorie du roman, Gonthier, pp. 5 et 6.

/22/ Luchterhand, 1962, p. 5.

/23/ A köztársasági propaganda /La propagande républicaine/:
"Világ" du 10 novembre 1918.

/24/ In: "Történelem és osztálytudat", /Histoire et conscience
de classe/, Magvető, Budapest, 1971, p. 17.

/25/ Cf. "Ifjukori müvek" /Oeuvres de jeunesse/, p. 429.

/26/ Cf. A modern dráma fejlődésének története /Histoire du développement du drame moderne/, Franklin, Budapest, 1911,
pp. 156-157.

/27/ In: "Ifjúkori müvek" /Oeuvres de jeunesse/, p. 428.

/28/ Régi kultúra és új kultúra. Ce texte parut d'abord dans le
numéro du 15 juin 1919 de l'"Internationale" /publié à Buda-
pest/ et figure dans l'édition hongroise de 1971 de "Histoire
et conscience de classe", p. 29 et suiv.

/29/ In: "Történelem és osztálytudat", /Histoire et conscience
de classe/, p. 30.

/30/ Ibid., p. 31.

/31/ Ibid., p. 43.
/32/ Ibid., p. 31.
/33/ Ibid., p. 47.
/+/ Traduit par Mireille T. Tóth

GEORG LUKÁCS, KRITIKER DER FASCHISTISCHEN PHILOSOPHIE UND KULTUR

L. SZIKLAI

> Wahrscheinlich kann man vom Nichtwollen seelich nicht leben; eine Sache nicht tun wollen, das ist auf die Dauer kein Lebensinhalt; etwas nicht wollen und überhaupt nicht mehr wollen, also das Geforderte dennoch tun, das liegt vielleicht zu benachbart, als dass nicht die Freiheitsidee dazwischen ins Gedränge geraten müsste /1/.

Der Herr aus Rom will nicht tanzen. Er spannt seine Kraft an, widersteht der Hypnose des Cipolla lange, und tut schliesslich doch wie befohlen: Er tanzt im Takt des Peitschenknalls. Er tanzt, noch dazu gerne, wenngleich wider Willen. Er unterliegt, weil er sich bloss aufs Nichtwollen beschränkt hat.

Sooft Georg Lukács in den 30er Jahren Thomas Mann erwähnte, versäumte er vielleicht nie an dieses grauenhafte Bild zu erinnern. Als beinhalte die negative Tat des "römischen Herrn" den letzten Sinn des Werkes, als wäre seine fatale Niederlage der eigentliche Schluss der Novelle. Nie gedenkt er des Mario, als hätte Mario dem Cipolla kein Ende bereitet. In Wirklichkeit sind bei Thomas Mann die zwei Schüsse, die Mario abfeuert, das wirkliche Ende. "Ein Ende mit Schrecken, ein höchst fatales Ende. Und ein befreiendes Ende dennoch -" /2/. Symbolischen Wert misst Lukács aber nur der Tat des "römischen Herrn" bei, und dies kaum von ungefähr. Er erblickt darin die künstlerische Darstellung eines Verhaltens, in welchem sich das Verhältnis der bürgerlichen /insonderheit der fortschrittlich-linksorientiert bürgerlichen/ Intelligenz zum Faschismus symbolisch, in erschütternder Tiefe und Wahrheit offenbart. Sein Interesse gilt aber, ganz besonders zu Beginn der 30er Jahre, vor allem diesem Verhalten, diesem aus blossem Nichtwollen notgedrungen hervorgehenden fatalen Tanz: nicht dem befreienden Schuss des Mario, nein, sondern der schändliche Niederlage davor. Nicht das sowieso sichere Ende des Cipolla, sondern der Zusammenhang zwischen ihrer Macht und dem Nichtwollen als machtfördernden Dienst: der "Zauber" selbst. Tatsächlich liegt das theoretisch-philosophische Problem

eben im "Zauber": nicht an sich in der hypnotischen Macht, natürlich, vielmehr darin, wieso sich die Hypnose durchsetzen kann.
Tragisch ist ja nicht einfach, dass es sie gibt, sondern dass
sie zustande kommen konnte. Wichtig erscheint Lukács das Entstehen des "Zaubers", nicht sosehr von der Seite des Zauberers
als vielmehr des "römischen Herrn". Das Umschlagen des einen
Prozesses - des Nichtwollens - in den anderen: in das Dochtuen.
Was ihn interessiert, ist die Frage, wie die Freiheitsidee ins
Gedränge geraten ist: die Frage der Verantwortung.

DIE VERANTWORTUNG DER INTELLIGENZ

Lukács erblickt in der Rolle der bürgerlichen Intelligenz und
der bürgerlichen Philosophie beim Zustandekommen der faschistischen Ideologie nicht nur /und nicht erstrangig/ ein Problem,
das sich von moralischer Seite beurteilen liesse. Eine Antwort
auf die Frage suchend, wie die faschistische "Weltanschauung"
zur Macht gelangen konnte im Land eines Hegel, eines Goethe,
eines Beethoven, wie der Faschismus überhaupt aufkommen konnte,
stellt er die vielleicht relevanteste geschichtsphilosophische
Frage der Epoche. Die in den 30er und 40er Jahren mehrfach neu-
formulierte, nie aber aufgegebene Fragestellung weist gleichzeitig weit über den Fragenkomplex - eine Problematik von damals
äusserster Aktualität - hinaus: über die Genese der Ideologie
des 20. Jahrhunderts. Sie weist darüber hinaus nicht nur im zeit-
lichen Verständnis, d. h. in dem konkreten Sinn, dass der Faschismus, das Entstehen des Faschismus, wie durch Erfahrungen von
wachsender Fürchterlichkeit belegt, weder 1933 noch 1945, ebensowenig in den 70er Jahren endgültig abgeschlossen war. Sie ist
weiterweisend auch in einem mehr umfassenden, theoretischen Be-
lang. Die Frage von Lukács lautet nämlich, welche Funktion der
Ideologie als falschem Bewusstsein in der Geschichte und der Gesellschaft zukommt; wie reaktionäre, retrograde Ideen selbst wider die persönliche Absicht der Urheber zu einer materiellen
Kraft werden, wie sie sich mit der "schlechten Seite" der Geschichte, mit der blutigen Praxis der Unterdrückerklassen kop-
peln können. Lukács gab in den 30er und 40er Jahren unterschied-
liche, auch nicht in allen Einzelheiten richtige Antworten. Doch

verliert die Warnung dessen ungeachtet nichts an Wert und Aktualität: Was der Philosoph und der Ideologe, der Denker und der
Schriftgelehrte tut, ist untrennbar von der gesellschaftlichen
Verantwortung. Die Verantwortung der Intelligenz ist gesellschaftlicher und geschichtlicher, nicht aber subjektiver oder aus
schliesslich moralischer Natur.

Das Schaffen jenes Lukács, der sich mit den geschichtsphilosophischen und ideologischen Schicksalsfragen des an die Macht
gelangten Faschismus konfrontierte, ist hinlänglich bekannt; dennoch weiss man wenig darüber. Hinlänglich bekannt sind seine Konzeptionen über Realismus und sozialistischen Realismus, ist der
Forscher der "grossen Realisten" des 19. Jahrhunderts, der Auf-
decker und Verteidiger aller Werts der klassischen Literatur,
der unerbittliche Kritiker jeglicher dekadent-bürgerlicher Literatur, der Verfasser von "Beiträgen" zur Geschichte der Ästhetik,
des <u>Historischen Romans</u> und des <u>Jungen Hegel</u>. Weniger bewusst,
eigentlich kaum wirklich zum Bewusstsein gelangt ist aber die
Tatsache, dass die Themenwahl, der Gedankengang, das Suchen eines
ideologischen Weges seit Anfang der 30er Jahre nicht durch persönliche Neigung, die eigenartige Bildung, subjektives Interesse
oder Gesichtspunkte der Disziplin voraus bestimmt war, sondern
immer und überall durch die Alternativen des antifaschistischen
Kampfes als entscheidendes Motiv. Auf Grund seiner marxistischen
Weltanschauung und seines kommunistischen Engagements nahm er
diesen Kampf als Gebot der Zeit auf, und trug ihn, als Denker,
bis zuletzt aus, machte ihm auch subjektiv zu seinem innersten
Imperativ.

Das ist der Grund, weshalb der Kampf gegen den Faschismus für
Lukács nicht Frage der gelegentlich gebotenen Wahl eines Thomas
oder disziplinärer Rahmen ist. Direkt oder indirekterweise setzt
sich der Gesichtspunkt des Antifaschismus in allen Werken durch,
in den ästhetischen wie in den philosophischen auch. Es lässt
sich nicht einfach aus der Welt schaffen, dass Lukács, über Goethe
schreibend /3/, gegen die Faschisierung von Goethe protestiert,
das Andenken Büchners ehrend /4/ den wirklichen Büchner gegen
den faschisierten Büchner verteidigt, dass er Hegel analysierend
/5/ sich gegen die faschistische Verunglimpfung des Philosophen
einsetzt. Ohne dies ins Auge zu fassen wird man nie richtig be-

greifen, warum Lukács nicht einfach die Theorie des Romans "fort-
gesetzt" hat /natürlich mit der Absicht, eine marxistische Theorie
der Gattungen zu entwickeln/, sondern einen Aufriss eben des historischen Romans gab, dessen wirkliche Protagonisten jene Volks-
massen sind, die die Geschichte "machen" /6/. Auf Grund eines
"höheren" Kriteriensystems der Literaturgeschichte kann man Lukács natürlich mit Recht vorhalten /und nur sehr wenige versäumen
ihm den Vorwurf zu machen/, er habe sich mit gewissen bedeutenden
modernen Autoren kaum oder überhaupt nicht, mit anderen widerum
"über Gebühr" beschäftigt. Auffallend viel Publizistisches aus
den 30er Jahren ist etwa Hans Fallada gewidmet. Fallada habe, so
Lukács, in den Frühwerken die erschütternde Wirkung, die die Krise nach dem verlorenen Krieg auf das deutsche Kleinbürgertum in
Stadt und Land ausübte, mit besonderer Empfindlichkeit beschrieben. Als begabter, doch ideologisch ratloser Repräsentant eben
dieser Schicht habe er jedoch nach der Machtergreifung durch Hitler vor dem Faschismus kapituliert. - Nun, eben diesem Typus der
Intelligenz galt das besondere Interesse von Lukács.

Die antifaschistische Plattform ist also nicht eines von vielen
Motiven, das nebenbei auch in den ästhetischen Schriften von Lukács präsent ist: Antifaschismus ist vielmehr eines der entscheidenden konzeptuellen und konstitutiven Prinzipien auch der ästhetischen Werke, das sich direkt oder indirekterweise, doch immer
durchsetzt. Möglicherweise werden Leute, die allzu gerne von der
grundlegend antifaschistischen Orientierung der Lukács-Ästhetik
in den 30er und 40er Jahren Abstand nehmen /zweifellos wirkte
sich diese Position von Lukács u.a. in der Form einer selektiven
Anschauung aus, die nur auf die wesentlichsten Grundsatzzusammen-
hänge konzentriert und Einzelheiten betreffende Momente verdrängt/,
die in diesen Jahren formulierten Ansichten und Bewertungen, Analysen und Urteile einseitig, zuwenig raffiniert, der totalen Wahrheit entfernt, mehr als einmal zu starr finden.

Lukács stürzte sich "a corps perdu" in den Kampf und kümmerte
sich "den Teufel um sein Renommee, um seine 'Unfehlbarkeit', seinen 'Nachruhm'" /7/. Bewusst bekannte er sich zu dieser Einseitigkeit: Es gelte, dass "Richtungen, die für die Weiterentwicklung
gefährlich sind, bekämpft werden müssen, andererseits..., dass
in der Leidenschaft des Kampfes Irrtümer nicht ausgeschlossen

sind. Lenin sagte einmal sehr weise zu Gorki, der sich über die
Härten des Kriegskommunismus beklagte, dass man bei einem Hand-
gemenge unmöglich genau abwägen kann, welcher Hieb noch unbedingt
notwendig und welcher schon überflüssig ist" /8/.

Es kommt freilich nicht nur von der Betrachtungsweise her,
dass man über den Kampf von Lukács gegen die Ideologie des Faschismus eigentlich recht wenig weiss, dass dieser entscheidende denkerische Aspekt seiner Tätigkeit 1930-1945 noch nicht seiner Bedeutung, seinem Umfang gemäss erkannt ist. Bedauerlicher-
weise ist eben der Teil des Lukács-Erbes in Vergessenheit geraten,
bis auf den heutigen Tag unbekannt oder unveröffentlicht geblieben, der eine kritische Auseinandersetzung mit der deutschen Ideologie, mit der Geschichte der bürgerlichen Philosophie im 20.
Jahrhundert darstellt. Dieser Teil des Oeuvres ist auch dem Umfang nach nicht unbedeutend. Ihn so bald wie möglich kennenzu-
lernen könnte nicht nur die Legende zertrümmern, Lukács hätte
sich in den 30er Jahren, vorwiegend aus politischen und taktischen
Gründen, von der Philosophie ab- und - den Jungen Hegel ausgenommen - sich ausschliesslich der Ästhetik zugewandt, sondern auch
eine gewisse Proportionsverschiebung im Lukács-Image aus diesen
Jahren herbeiführen.

Der Bedeutung nach ragen von den unveröffentlichten Werken zwei
Manuskripte von der Stärke je eines Bandes heraus. Das erste,
Wie ist die Faschistische Philosophie in Deutschland entstanden?
wurde 1933 in Moskau zu Papier gebracht /9/, das andere, Wie ist
Deutschland zum Zentrum der reaktionären Ideologie geworden? /10/
entstand fast ein Jahrzehnt später, als Lukács nach Taschkent
evakuiert war /1941/42/; es ist nich sosehr eine Variante, als
eher eine eigenartige Fortsetzung des ersten. Bei der Sichtung
des vergessenen Nachlasses sei ferner eine in Taschkent veröffentlichte Broschüre von Lukács erwähnt: Der Kampf zwischen Humanismus und Barbarei /11/ ebenfalls als selbständiger, einheitlicher
und originaler Band zu betrachten, obgleich gewisse Kapitel /oder
deren Varianten/ bereits früher in verschiedenen Zeitschriften
erschienen waren.

Sehr aufschlussreich sind die zwei, die Genese der faschistischen Ideologie behandelnden Manuskripte auch für das Verständnis der Laufbahn, geistigen Entwicklung von Lukács. Nicht **zuletzt**

weil die Entstehungsgeschichte der Zerstörung der Vernunft erst
im Spiegel all dieser Manuskripte tatsächlich ausgeleuchtet wird:
Erst durch sie kann man sämtliche Frühphasen der Vorgeschichte
dieses mächtigen und - selten genug im Lukács-Oeuvre - abgeschlossenen Monographie konkret einsehen /12/. /Die Forschung im Quel-
lengebiet von Lukács' Kritik an der irrationalistischen Philosophie wird hoffentlich dazu beitragen, dass dieses von so vielen
Seiten und vielen Personen verbittert angefochtene, nur von sehr
wenigen verteidigte Werk, das Michael Lifschitz einmal im Genie-
blitz eine "Kritik der unreinen Vernunft" nannte, schliesslich
die ihm gebührende Einschätzung erhält/.

Von der "versunkenen" Lukács-Literatur muss man nicht sosehr
den Fakten als vielmehr dem Wesen zuliebe sprechen. Zum einen
machte sich Lukács während der 30er und 40er Jahre zweimal daran,
die Genese der deutschen Ideologie ins Auge zu fassen: im Augenblick der Machtergreifung und am Vorabend des Sturzes des Faschismus. Sieg und Sturz der barbarischen Naziherrschaft sind also
die zwei äussersten Punkte, an die die zwei umfangreichen theoretischen Versuche einer Antwort auf die Frage "Wie ist... entstanden /bzw. geworden/" anknüpfen. Doch liegt zwischen den beiden
keine Pause, kein Vakuum: Keinen Augenblick unterbrach Lukács
den Kampf. Selbstverständlich trug er ihn anders aus, als 1930-
1933 oder 1941-1943. Mit "anders" ist aber nicht der eher auf
die Ästhetik /oder eher auf die Philosophie/ verlegte Schwerpunkt
gemeint, sondern die andersgewordene geschichtliche Situation.

Es ist gleichzeitig vollends klar, dass der Antifaschismus
andere Perspektiven hatte bei den Anfängen des Hitlerregimes bzw.
zu dem Zeitpunkt, wo die die Sowjetunion überfallende deutsche
Armee noch vor Moskau, jedoch bereits mit dem Rücken zu Moskau
stand. Darüber hinaus kam es zwischen 1933 und 1943 zu wesentlichen Veränderungen in der Politik der Komintern, es genügt
vielleicht an die Volksfrontpolitik zu erinnern, die 1935, auf
dem VII. Kongress verkündet wurde /13/. Die veränderten Alternativen des antifaschistischen Kampfes hatten entscheidenden Teil
daran, für welche theoretischen Alternativen sich Lukács bei der
Kritik der reaktionären deutschen Ideologie entschied. Bestimmend war nämlich für seine theoretische Tätigkeit, die Kritik
der neueren deutschen Philosophie, Anfang der 30er Jahre ebenso

wie Anfang der 40er Jahre die Tatsache, dass er sich ohne den geringsten kritischen Vorbehalt an den strategischen wie takti- schen Grundsätzen der Kommunistischen Internationale orientierte.

Diese durchaus allgemeinen Zusammenhänge müssen, so einfach sie auch erscheinen mögen, berücksichtigt werden, wenn es gilt, die Zeiträume 1930-1935 bzw. 1941-1945 flüchtig zu betrachten, d.h. die Jahre, in denen sich Lukács unmittelbar mit der Entste- hung der faschistischen Ideologie beschäftigte. Hier soll nur kurz, in den Umrissen gezeigt werden, dass bei Lukács, trotz einer gewissen Kontinuität zwischen den zwei Endpunkten, die ge- danklichen Konturen einer Verfallsgeschichte der deutschen Ideolo- gie im 20. Jahrhundert nicht unverändert bleiben; es verschiebt sich die Beurteilung von Rolle und Verantwortung der Intelligenz für das Zustandekommen der faschistischen Philosophie, für die Tatsache, dass Deutschland zu einem ideologischen Zentrum der reaktionären Ideologie wurde.

Eigentlich erkennt die Menschheit die früheren Entwicklungs- phasen der Geschichte, das Wesen der vorangegangenen gesellschaft- lichen Verhältnisse erst nachträglich, und auch dann nicht immer richtig heisst es bei Marx. Das nachträgliche Bewusstsein ist kritisch, selbst auch Teilnehmer an der Grablegung überholter gesellschaftlicher Formationen. Wie es scheint, hat das nach- trägliche Bewusstsein nicht nur im Fall revolutionärer Verände- rungen, sondern auch nach tragischen Wendungen in der Geschichte, im Leben der Völker eine notwendige Funktion. Für die interpre- tierende Kritik der eingetroffenen Katastrophe ist ein theore- tisches Überdenken der Alternativen kennzeichnend, das nur retro- spektiv und dennoch im Entstehungsprozess wahrnimmt /und wahr- nehmen kann/, inwieweit das Entstandene notwendig war bzw. wie es vermeidbar gewesen wäre. Dieser kritische Bewusstwerdungspro- zess in bezug auf Notwendigkeit und Vermeidbarkeit setzte 1933 ein, zuallererst und am schnellsten bei Leuten, die von Anbeginn gegen die nationalsozialistische Herrschaft kämpften.

Das 1933 entstandene Buch von Lukács über die Entstehung der faschistischen Philosophie kam also im Zeichen eines kritischen, nachträglichen Bewusstseins zustande: "Dieses Buch ist eine Kampf- schrift. Eine Kampfschrift gegen die Ideologie des Faschismus" /14/. Der Verfasser geht von der Überzeugung aus, dass der Na-

tionalsozialismus in Deutschland eine notwendige Entwicklungs-
folge der deutschen Bourgeoisie ist. Scharf wendet sich Lukács
gegen alle, die durch Anerkennung dieser Notwendigkeit die Verantwortung der Handlanger Hitlers /beispielsweise Hindenburgs/
herunterspielen, die sich, vom weiteren, effektiven Kampf Abstand
nehmend, damit begnügen wollten, die Greueltaten der Lumpen in
der Gesellschaft, die Niedertracht der Lumpenbourgeoisie und des
Lumpenproletariats zu entlarven, die gegebenenfalls gemeinsame
Sache machen. Hitlers Faschismus, meint Lukács, sei eigentlich
Form: <u>Die zur Zeit herrschende Form des imperialistischen Mono-
polkapitalismus</u>, die man nicht vom soziohistorischen Unterbau
ihres Entstehens loslösen darf. Um ihn zu überwinden, reicht es
nicht aus, den Kampf des revolutionär vereinigten Proletariats
bloss auf die Form zu reduzieren. Die Form allein lasse sich
kaum aufheben ohne den Inhalt - die kapitalistische Ausbeutung -
zu liquidieren /es sei hinzugefügt: in Lukács' Verständnis, ohne
sie <u>unverzüglich</u> aufzuheben/. Diese abstrakte, recht starre Kop-
pelung von Inhalt und Form, diese unmittelbare Gleichsetzung von
Antifaschismus und Antikapitalismus ist der theoretische Wesens-
kern, der Schlüssel zu Lukács' gesamter Denkweise in jenen Jahren.
Nicht geringen Anteil hatte daran wahrscheinlich auch, dass Lukács angesichts der Attacken gegen die Blum-Thesen stillschwei-
gend seine in den 20er Jahren vertretene Auffassung zurücknahm,
wonach die demokratische Diktatur der Arbeiterklasse und der
Bauern der Übergang zwischen fortschreitend faschisierter bürgerlicher Gesellschaft und Sozialismus sei. Aus der aktuellen
Lukácsschen Alternative /Faschismus oder alles hinwegfegende proletarische Revolution/ folgt aber geradlinig, dass <u>allein das
Proletariat</u>, genauer: <u>das Proletariat allein</u> den tatsächlichen
Kampf gegen den Faschismus, <u>das heisst</u> gegen den Kapitalismus
aufnimmt. Jede Opposition, die auf einer bürgerlichen Plattform
steht, sei teils im vornherein zum Scheitern verurteiltes "Nichtwollen", teils Scheinopposition, die - innerhalb der bürgerlichen
Rahmen verharrend - den Faschismus fördert, ob sie es will oder
nicht. "Wir haben gesehen, dass alle Strömungen der bürgerlichen
Politik in Deutschland - die Sozialdemokratie immer mit inbegrif-
fen - im breiten Strom der faschistischen Bewegung gemündet sind;
dass alle bürgerlichen "Gegner" des Nationalsozialismus in der

letzten, entscheidenden Frage, in der Frage des Verhältnisses
von Bourgeoisie und Proletariat in der Krisenzeit des Kapitalistischen Systems auf dem gleichen Boden mit ihm, auf dem Boden
des Faschismus stehen, dass sie nur durch Fraktionsdifferenzen,
durch taktische Meinungsverschiedenheiten von ihm getrennt sind"
/15/.

Aus Lukács' Charakterisierung der soziopolitischen Grundstruktur fehlt die Alternative eines demokratischen bürgerlichen Antifaschismus /sofern sie erscheint, so bestenfalls in sektiererisch
in Frage gestellter Form/. Die in der kommunistischen Bewegung
damals vorherrschende Auffassung macht - der Theorie über den
Sozialfaschismus entsprechend - die Sozialdemokratie verantwortlich für den ausgebliebenen Bürgerkrieg gegen den Faschismus.
Die Sozialdemokratie, zwischen Bourgeoisie und Proletariat ste-
hend, die für Deutschland den Faschismus für das "kleinere Übel"
hielt, habe die Massen der sozialdemokratischen Partei von den
revolutionären Bewegungen abgeschnürt, den Streik unterbunden,
und halte die Massen auch nach 1933 vom Klassenkampf zurück. Genau wie alle anderen bürgerlichen Scheinoppositionen, die früher
Wegbereiter des Faschismus zur Machtsübernahme waren, sei die
Sozialdemokratie auch jetzt, eben als Opposition, organischer
Bestandteil des faschistischen Systems.

Es schien notwendig diese Grundstruktur ins Auge zu fassen,
denn analog zu dieser Struktur wird, gleichsam parallel, die Verantwortung der Intelligenz und die Genese der faschistischen Philosophie interpretiert.

Lukács zeigt die Parallelität zwischen der Scheinopposition
der Sozialdemokratie und dem Verhalten der Intelligenz als Ideo-
logieproduzenten auf /16/. Zwar unterscheidet er zwischen den
herausragendsten Vertretern der Intelligenz und der breiteren
Schicht, der parasitären Intelligenz, zwischen den aufrichtigen
Kritikern der kapitalistischen Kultur und den korrupten Führern
des Sozialfaschismus, diesen Gaunern, doch ist die "nichtmecha-
nische Parallele" eben auch eine Parallele /17/.

Die radikal oppositionelle Intelligenz stehe auf halbem Weg
zwischen der unterdrückenden und der revolutionären Klasse. Sie
erkenne zwar die endgültige Unauflösbarkeit aller Widersprüche
in der bürgerlichen Gesellschaft, doch erwarte sie im Zustand

der höchsten Verzweiflung die nahende letzte Stunde der Menschheit, oder sie kritisiere die bestehenden Zustände. Allerdings
gehe diese Kritik nicht über eine rein ideologische Kritik der
Gegenwart hinaus. Sie sei zwar unwillig, sich den Befehlen des
Faschismus zu unterwerfen, könne sich aber ebensowenig zum Salto
vitale entschliessen, durch den sie ins Lager des Proletariats
gelangen würde. Die Elite der Intelligenz sei hypnotisiert durch
die feiner gesponnene Abhängigkeit schaffenden Mechanismen des
Kapitalismus, eben weil die Illusion von Unabhängigkeit und Freiheit gestattet ist. Der bürgerliche Intellektuelle sei Teilnehmer
am Totentanz der Weltanschauungen und zugleich ironischer Geniesser
des Anblicks. Die Verachtung dieser Intelligenz für die verfallen-
de bürgerliche Welt und ihre zerfallende Kultur mag noch so auf-
richtig und radikal sein, ideologisch fördere sie dennoch ihr
Fortbestehen. Sie sei verantwortlich: Wegen der Unfähigkeit,
ideologisch wirksam gegen den Faschismus zu kämpfen, wegen der
Zurückhaltung der eigenen Schicht und der Kleinbürger von einer
Annäherung zur revolutionären Arbeiterklasse. "Jede Ideologie
aber, die das Erwachen der Massen zu diesem einzigen Standpunkt,
der ihren wahren Interessen entspricht, verhindert, eilt - ob
gewollt oder ungewollt - der sozialen Demagogie zu Hilfe" /18/,
leistet also dem Faschismus Vorschub.

Die Hauptfrage der Gegenwart sei, so Lukács, die Leninsche
Frage: Wer besiegt wen? Analog zur soziopolitischen Alternative
sei auch in der Ideologie nur eine einzige Möglichkeit gegeben:
"Faschismus oder Bolschewismus ist die Wahl, vor die die heute
Lebenden gestellt sind. Und da sie diese Wahl in ihrer materiellen Praxis zu treffen haben, ist sie für sie auch weltanschaulich nicht zu umgehen. Und weltanschaulich bedeutet heute jeder
Idealismus, jeder Irrationalismus, jeder Glaube an einen Mythos
die Wahl des faschistischen Weges, und allein der dialektische
Materialismus, die Weltanschauung des Proletariats weist auch
weltanschaulich ins Land der Befreiung von Ausbeutung und Knecht-
schaft!" /19/

Das Lukácssche Verständnis der weltanschaulichen Wahl gibt
eine Antwort auf die Grundfrage über die Entstehung der faschistischen Ideologie: So, wie alle Typen der Politik der Bourgeoisie einheitlich den Faschismus zur Macht gefördert haben, sei

die faschistische Philosophie, geradlinig und unmittelbar, aus
der bürgerlichen hervorgegangen. In diesem Geist gibt Lukács
den näheren Gegenstand seiner Untersuchungen an: das Aufzeigen
dessen, "dass jene Weltanschauung, die sich in der nationalsozialistischen Agitation und Propaganda vom dicken Wälzer Rosenberg bis zu den Tagesreden und Zeitungsartikeln offenbart, die
organisch gewachsene, notwendig entstandene Frucht der <u>ideolo-
gischen Entwicklung der deutschen Bourgeoisie im imperialistischen Zeitalter</u> ist" /20/.

Doch noch einmal zurück zum Dilemma der Verantwortung der
Intelligenz. Sieht also Lukács keinerlei prinzipielle Möglichkeit, dass sich die <u>Besten</u> der bürgerlichen Intelligenz dem Faschismus wirksam widersetzen? Doch, es gebe eine, meint Lukács,
vor allem den <u>Salto vitale</u>. Die radikale Forderung nach dem
"Lebenssprung" schwächt Lukács allerding einigermassen, indem
er bei <u>aufrichtigen</u> Intellektuellen, die einer <u>selbstkritischen</u>
Auseinandersetzung mit dem eigenen Gewissen fähig sind, die Möglichkeit auch eines langsamen, schmerzlichen Übergangs annimmt,
in welchem sie die Innervationen ihres bürgerlichen Denkens stu-
fenweise überwinden. /Solche Intellektuellen gehören natürlich
zur antifaschistischen Front, stehen sogar dem Marxismus-Leninismus <u>de facto</u> näher als die "gebildeten Marxisten", die die
Taktik des Sozialfaschismus durch Marx- und Lenin-Zitate unter-
mauern wollen/.

Das ist der Punkt, wo sich Lukács Kritik an dem Weg der bürgerlichen Intelligenz, der hart an den Rand des Abgrunds führt,
und die Konfrontation mit dem <u>eigenen</u> Weg schneiden: die bitter-
-ironische Charakterisierung der von der Illusion der geistigen
Freiheit und Unabhängigkeit zährenden Elite, die sich im Grand
Hotel Abgrund bequem einrichtet, und das Verantwortungsgefühl
des Mannes, der, sich um die in die Klemme geratene Freiheitsidee ängstigend, auf die <u>eigene</u> Vergangenheit zurückblickt; die
Negation des bürgerlichen Scheinradikalismus und die Negation
des <u>eigenen</u> früheren Radikalismus; die unnachsichtige Kritik am
blossen Nichtwollen als Selbstkritik. Lukács will allem, was er
im Buch über die Entstehung der faschistischen Philosophie sagt,
<u>auch subjektive Authentizität</u> verleihen. Die Notwendigkeit prä-
sentiert sich als <u>persönliches Schicksal</u>. "Dieses Buch ist, bald

nach der Machtergreifung Hitlers, nach meiner notgedrungenen Emigration in wenigen Wochen niedergeschrieben worden. Ich kann aber zugleich - ohne grosse Übertreibung - sagen: Dieses Buch entsteht seit über fünfundzwanzig Jahren. Als Schüler Simmels und Diltheys, als Freund Max Webers und Emil Lasks, als begeisterter Leser Stefan Georges und Rilkes habe ich die ganze hier geschilderte Entwicklung selbst miterlebt. Allerdings - vor, bezüglich nach 1918 - auf verschiedenen Seiten der Barrikade. Den Lesern also, die vor den Konsequenzen dieses Buches, vor der Anerkennung der Einheitlichkeit der Entwicklung des bürgerlichen Denkens der imperialistischen Periode bis zum Faschismus zurückschrecken, muss ich hier betonen, dass die Feststellung des Zusammenhanges keine rasche Konstruktion aus polemischen Rücksichten gewesen ist, sondern die Zusammenfassung und Verallgemeinerung eines miterlebten Lebensalters. Manchen Freund meiner Jugend, ehrliche und überzeugte Antikapitalisten habe ich vom Sturm des Faschismus verschlungen sehen müssen. Grosse Hoffnungen der Philosophie und der Poesie habe ich unfruchtbar zwischen den Lagern enden gesehen, weil sie sich nur in den Schlussfolgerungen, nicht aber in den Voraussetzungen ihres Denkens vom Parasitismus der Periode lossagen konnten, weil sie nur äusserlich und nicht bis zu den Wurzeln ihres Seins und Denkens mit der imperialistischen Bourgeoisie gebrochen haben" /21/.

Man hat keinen Grund, die Aufrichtigkeit Lukács' in Frage zu stellen, wie es auch verfehlt wäre anzunehmen, bei der Zurücknahme von Geschichte und Klassenbewusstsein wären einfach taktische Erwägungen im Spiel gewesen. "Seit ungefähr fünf Jahren ist 'Geschichte und Klassenbewusstsein' vergriffen; eine Neuauflage habe ich ... aus der Einsicht in das wesentlich Unrichtige des Buches nicht gestattet. Wenn ich aber heute mit einem neuen Buch philosophischen Inhalts vor den Leser trete, so halte ich mich verpflichtet, auch die Gründe, warum ich mich schon längst nicht mehr mit 'Geschichte und Klassenbewusstsein' solidarisiere, wenigstens kurz aufzuzählen. Dies um so mehr, als es nicht wenige gibt, die dieses Buch noch immer für ein marxistisches Kampfmittel gegen falsche Ideologien halten. Der Kernpunkt der Frage ist die Frage des Materialismus, die Frage, deren weltanschauliche **wie** praktische Bedeutung von jenen, die aus der bürgerlichen In-

telligenz zum Marxizmus kommen, am schwersten begriffen wird.
So auch damals von mir. Wenn ich damals in falscher Polemik gegen Friedrich Engels die Möglichkeit einer dialektischen Erkenntnis der Natur bestritt und die dialektische Methode auf Erkenntnis der Gesellschaft beschränkte; wenn ich die Abbildtheorie mit
dem 'Argument' bekämpfte, dass Prozesse nicht abgebildet werden
können, so liegt diesen und ähnlichen Anschauungen das Nichtlos-
kommen vom bürgerlichen Idealismus zugrunde. Wenn dies in dem
subjektiven Glauben, ganz besonders radikal, radikaler als die
wirklichen, materialistischen Kommunisten zu sein, geschah ...
so ändert dies nichts an der objektiven Tatsache, dass gerade
in entscheidenden Fragen die schwerwiegendsten Konzession an die
bürgerlich-idealistische Weltanschauung gemacht wurden. Die ultra-
radikale Illusion bei Abbiegen der wesentlichen Gehalte ins Bürgerlich-Idealistische ist aber sehr geeignet, die aktuell-poli-
tische Bedeutung solcher Fehler zu unterstreichen... Man glaubt
ehrlich zu kämpfen, liefert aber gleichzeitig - ungewollt - dem
Gegner geistige Waffen" /22/.

Von der Kritik, die er über die bürgerliche Intelligenz gab,
nahm er auch sich selbst nicht heraus, er wandte sie auch auf
das eigene Schaffen an. Im Gestus des subjektiven Zeugnisses,
der Warnung und der Selbstkritik war - nur wenige Tage nach dem
Reichtagsbrand, zu Beginn seiner Exilzeit in der Sowjetunion -
das nachträgliche Verantwortungsgefühl des marxistischen Ideologen und kommunistischen Intelligenzlers stärker mit im Spiel
als alles andere.

DER FASCHISMUS, EINE ENZYKLOPÄDIE DER BARBAREI

"Aber als bestimmtes Gebiet der Arbeitsteilung hat die Philosophie jeder Epoche ein bestimmtes Gedankenmaterial zur Voraussetzung, das ihr von ihren Vorgängern überliefert worden und wovon sie ausgeht", schreibt Engels und fügt hinzu, "aber die Art
der Abänderung und Fortbildung des vorgefundenen Gedankstoffs"
sei durch die ökonomischen Verhältnisse "meist indirekt" bestimmt,
da unmittelbar auf die Philosophie eher die politischen, recht-
lichen und sittlichen Widerspiegelungen einwirken /23/. Der Gedanke von Engels zeigt klar, warum man ein gegebenes philosophi-

sches System nicht einfach aus seinen Quellen heraus verstehen
kann, und warum man es ohne die Ursprünge ebensowenig begreifen
wird. Die Anfang der 30er Jahre entstandene Konzeption von Lukács
über die Genese der faschistischen Philosophie lässt sich nur
bei weitgehendster Berücksichtigung der methodologischen Probleme
in bezug auf die Bedeutung der kontinuierlichen Entwicklung, der
Quellen und der Vorläufer einschätzen.

Wie gesehen, setzt sich, nach Auffassung von Lukács, in der
Geschichte der deutschen Ideologie im 20. Jahrhundert notwendigerweise eine geradlinige, gleichmässige Bewegung, eine Kontinuität durch: der Verfallsprozess der bürgerlichen Philosophie
läuft parallel mit dem Weg der Bourgeoisie, der zum Faschismus
führt. Diese Bewegung der nichtklassischen Philosophie betrachtet
Lukács erkenntnistheoretisch für widersprüchlich: im bürgerlichen
Bewusstsein zeichnet sich die Wirklichkeit falsch ab, erschienen
die realen Klassenverhältnisse verdreht. Die verzerrte Spiegelung, die irrationalistische Mystifikation der Wirklichkeit mag
noch so viele kritische Momente enthalten, mag die bestehenden
Verhältnisse noch so scharf oder geistreich kritisieren /etwa
die Dekadenz der Periode/, sie wird nicht nur das Bestehende
festigen, sondern die Faschisierung fördern, indem sie der Dekadenz gegenüber die Parole einer "Revolution von rechts" prokla-
miert.

Darin, dass sich die deutsche Bourgeoisie nach Lukács' Auffassung einheitlich zum Faschismus hin entwickelt hat, kommt
unseres Erachtens nicht eine Paralelle zwischen Klassenbewegung
und Ideologieentwicklung im vulgärsoziologischen Verständnis zum
Ausdruck, sondern ein Herangehen an die Quellen /an die Philosophieentwicklung der imperialistischen Periode/ vom Endergebnis,
vom Faschismus her.

Die Arbeiten der Faschismus-Ideologen untersuchend weist Lukács ausführlich nach, was sie von den fertig vorgefundenen philosophischen Theorien einfach übernahmen. So etwa, was Alfred
Rosenberg von den Ansichten H. St. Chamberlains und Spenglers,
Riegls und Worringers übernimmt /24/. Nicht weniger Aufmerksamkeit schenkt Lukács der faschistischen Metamorphose der nichtklassischen deutschen Philosophie, der Untersuchung von politischen Mechanismen, die an der Umfunktionierung von Schopenhauer

und Nietzsche, Dilthey und Simmel, Max Weber und Spengler teil-
hatten. Die Absicht ist dabei vor allem vielseitig zu zeigen,
wie Hitler, Rosenberg, Goebbels, Bäumler u.a. aus den wahrgenom-
menen Quellen schöpften, wie sie das übernommene Gedankengut
selektierten und verfälschten, für das Kleinbürgertum simplifi-
zierten und zurechtschneiderten, wie aus diesem Stoff eine eklek-
tische, nichts Originelles beinhaltende, demagogische "Weltanschauung" zusammengetragen und zu einem enzyklopädischen Inbegriff aller reaktionären Theorien der Zeit zusammengebaut wurde.

Lassen sich aber gleichzeitig die Quellen, die Vorläufer selbst
bewerten aufgrund der "weiterentwickelten" Form der von den Vorläufer geerbten philosophischen Ansichten? Lässt sich etwa der
Irrationalismus der Lebensphilosophie als Vorläufer von dem Gesichtspunkt aus bewerten, dass der Irrationalismus im Mythusbe-
griff Rosenbergs seine radikalste Form erhalten hat? Kann man
vielleicht die Idee des charismatischen Führers von Max Weber
und Stefan George für eine frühe Variante der faschistischen
Führerkonzeption betrachten, für eine "bedeutende Vorarbeit" zur
Führerideologie des Faschismus?

Am knappsten formuliert Lukács die Betrachtungsweise von Quellen und Entstehung, in der der Gesichtspunkt "woher – wohin" und
"wohin – von woher" gleichzeitig und zugleich zum Ausdruck kommt,
an Hand von Nietzsche: "Mit allen diesen Grundtendenzen seiner
Philosophie leitet Nietzsche jenen Entwicklungsprozess der bürgerlichen Ideologie ein, der im Nachkriegsimperialismus in die
faschistische Ideologie mündet. Es gibt kein einziges Motiv der
faschistischen Philosophie und Ästhetik, deren Quelle nicht in
erster Reihe bei Nietzsche zu finden wäre" /25/. Es ist selbst-
redend nicht Lukács, der damit die _Quellen_ als faschistisch ab-
stempelt.

Aus dem Bisherigen könnte man leicht zu dem banalen Schluss
kommen, dass die Urteile von Lukács, sofern seine Einschätzung
der deutschen bürgerlichen Philosophie des 20. Jahrhunderts in
den 30er Jahren methodologisch falsch war oder zumindest auf
einer widersprüchlichen Grundlegung beruht, samt und sonders
in Frage zu stellen seien. Die Lage ist aber etwas komplizierter. Zunächst, weil es falsch wäre theoretische und methodologi-
sche Irrtümer überhaupt ungeschichtlich zu betrachten /was frei-

lich nicht heissen soll, dass die geschichtlichen Umstände als
mildernder Umstand gelten/. Zweitens, weil die Irrtümer heraus-
ragender Denker nie auf einer Elementarstufe stehen und nicht
als Offenbarungen gewisser persönlicher Beschränktheit abgetan
werden dürfen. Und drittens, weil - auch wenn es als Widerspruch
in der Sache erscheinen mag, besonders im Auge gestrenger Lukács-
-Kritiker - eine dialektische Beziehung zwischen Fehlern und Tu-
genden besteht, wie durch die Geschichte des philosophischen
Denkens tausendfach belegt.

Die geschichtliche "Einseitigkeit" von Lukács' Antifaschismus
wurde bereits erwähnt. Dies sei höchstens dadurch ergänzt, dass
diese Reduktion in der Regel eine bewusste ist; die Kampfschrift
gegen den Faschismus etwa beruft sich eingestandenermassen nur
auf Tendenzen und Werke, die, nach Meinung des Verfassers, die
wichtigsten Entwicklungsetappen der bürgerlichen Ideologie bis
hin zum Faschismus am prägnantesten widerspiegeln. Sie soll also
nicht einen Überblick der ganzen deutschen Philosophie geben.

Es sei bemerkt, dass die marxistische Literatur kaum andere,
die kritische Analyse des bürgerlichen Denkens im 20. Jahrhundert ähnlich wie Lukács anvisierende Werke kennt, deren Einstellung so weitgehend durch aktuelle politische Erwägung, durch
Agitationsabsicht geprägt wäre. Will man sich davon überzeugen,
was für ein Niveau die theoretischen Feststellungen von Lukács
repräsentieren, soll man die Durchschnittliteratur der Periode
über dasselbe Thema mit seinen Büchern und Aufsätzen vergleichen,
beispielshalber seine Kritik der sozialdemokratischen Ideologie
mit der von Rudas, die fast zur gleichen Zeit zustande gekommen
war /26/.

Indem Lukács an die deutsche Ideologie vom Faschismus, von
dem Endergebnis her herangeht, beschränkt er sich natürlich nicht
auf das Aufzeigen der Verwandtschaft, der übereinstimmenden Motive,
auch nicht auf die Ahnentafel, sondern er ist bemüht, die Totalität der gegebenen Tendenz, das gesamte Auffassungssystem des e-
ben betrachteten Denkers - auch den Widersprüchen Rechnung tra-
gend - zu beschreiben. Innerhalb dieser Beschreibung ist /mehr
als einmal latent/, gleichsam als ordnender und interpretierender
Mittelpunkt, das genetische Herangehen wirksam: Aus diesem philosophischen Stoff konnte, ungeachtet der ursprünglichen Absicht

326

des Originals, die Ideologie der Barbarei entstehen. Doch ist es gerade die Einseitigkeit von Lukács' Methode, die rigide Einseitigkeit der Linearität, durch die es ihm möglich wird, innerhalb der philosophischen Systeme die ursprünglich und objektiv vorhandenen reaktionären Momente und Tendenzen zu erkennen und konzentriert zu kritisieren. Eben die fruchtbar-einseitig zustande gebrachte unmittelbare, genetische Beziehung zwischen den Ideen der Vorläufer und ihren faschistisch ins Extrem getriebenen Fortentwicklungen verhilft Lukács dazu, eine im wesentlichen heute noch gültige Analyse der Zerstörung der Vernunft, d.h. des Irrationalismus zu geben, neue Züge der bürgerlichen Philosophie des 20. Jahrhunderts mit dauerhafter und aktueller Gültigkeit zu beschreiben etwa die Mythenschaffung, den religiösen Atheismus, den Übergang des Agnostizismus in Mystik, die indirekte Apologetik. Es sind vor allem diese Denkerrungenschaften, die eine Kontinuität zwischen den Anfang der 30er bzw. 40er Jahre entstandenen antifaschistischen Lukács-Schriften herstellen.

Neben der Kontinuität müssen aber vor allem die entscheidenden Veränderungen betont und kurz expliziert werden, denn die von früher her aufgehobenen Elemente in Lukács' Taschkenter Manuskript und den 1940/1945 entstandenen Papieren sind ebenfalls nur im Licht der Veränderungen interpretierbar.

Der wichtigste geschichtliche Umstand, der den Geist des 1941/42 geschriebenen zweiten Buches über den Faschismus prägt, ist der Ausbruch des Zweiten Weltkriegs und der Überfall der Sowjetunion. Anfang der 30er Jahre gilt das Hauptinteresse Lukács', wie gesehen, der Kritik der faschistischen Ideologie; obgleich in dieser Kritik auch die Praxis des Nazionalsozialismus entsprechenden Raum erhält, ist ihre Analyse theoretisch nur zweitrangiger Bedeutung. Das durch den Weltkrieg ausgeweitete Genozid, in das sämtliche fortschrittlichen Personen, die Völker und die Kultur einbegriffen wurden, kurz: die in Erfahrung gebrachte Praxis des Faschismus - modellierte den Gedankengang Lukács' in mehr als einer Hinsicht um. Zum einen erhält innerhalb der philosophie- und ideologiegeschichtlichen Untersuchung der Frage, wie der Faschismus zustande gekommen ist, mit gleichem Nachdruck auch die Frage Platz, wie und wieso die faschistische Theorie zur Praxis werden konnte, auf welche **Weise**

Nazideutschland die durch seine Ideologen entwickelten Ideen
mit den Waffen verwirklicht. In diesen späteren Schriften ist
also bereits das theoretische und das praktische System der Barbarei Gegenstand der Betrachtungen. In der Lukácsschen Untersuchung der deutschen Ideologie ist die Rassentheorie freilich
von Anbeginn präsent, betrachtet wird aber vor allem, was etwa
Goebbels und Rosenberg von Gobineau und Chamberlain übernommen
haben. Nun aber verschiebt sich der Nachdruck, indem die Rassentheorie als Quintessenz der nationalsozialistischen "Weltanschauung", als ideologisches Fundament all der Schändlichkeit erscheint,
die die Faschisten verübten und verüben, in Deutschland und ausser-
halb des Reichs, im Krieg wie im Frieden /27/. Auf diese Weise
rücken also Nietzsche und die Gestapo in bedenkliche Nähe zueinander bei Lukács.

Der durchaus aktuelle Gesichtspunkt, wonach Faschismus das
praktische System der Barbarei ist, lässt, zum anderen, ein für
Lukács unerhört schwerwiegendes Dilemma in den Vordergrund rücken:
die Frage nach der Beziehung zwischen Faschismus und deutschem
Volk. Im Augenblick von Hitlers Machtergreifung lautete Lukács'
Frage, wieso Menschenmillionen in Deutschland an die lächerlich
verworrene Ideologie des Faschismus glauben können. Damals schrieb
Lukács die hypnotische Wirkung dem Mystizismus, der Demagogie zu,
sein Ausgangspunkt war also die Beschaffenheit der Ideologie selbst.
Anfang der 40er Jahre lautete die Frage anders: "wie ist das deutsche Volk, einst führend in der europäischen Humanität, bis hier-
her gesunken? Ist es noch dasselbe Volk? Oder ist es durch das
Gift des faschistischen Regimes, der faschistischen Ideologie,
ein durch und durch barbarisches Volk geworden?" Auf das Dilemma,
ob das deutsche Volk schuldig oder unschuldig sei, antwortet er
vor allem mit dem bekannten Gedanken von Marx: "einer Frau und
einer Nation wird die unbedachte Stunde nicht verziehen, worin
der erste beste Abenteurer ihnen Gewalt antun konnte" /28/. Es
gelte zu erklären, wieso der moralische und geistige Fall der
deutschen Nation eintreffen konnte. Dazu aber, so Lukács, müsse
man auch ihre einstige Grösse aufzeigen. Die Antwort ist also
vorwiegend historischer Natur und sie stellt nicht einfach die
ideologiegeschichtlichen Zusammenhänge voran.

Das aber betrifft nur die Genese, nur die Vergangenheit des Dilemmas. Sehr kräftig erscheint in Lukács' Gedankenwelt in der Zeitspanne zwischen den Schlachten bei Moskau und Stalingrad die Zukunft des deutschen Volkes nach dem Zusammenbruch des Hitlerregimes; das Unterpfand des Aufstiegs sei das Ausmerzen der faschistischen Ideologie, der Ausbau und die Festigung der deutschen demokratischen Bewegung. Das Verhältnis zwischen deutschen Volk und Faschismus betrachtet Lukács nunmehr nichtmehr von der Ideologie her, sondern vielmehr vom Gesichtspunkt der Wirkungsmechanismen /Propaganda, Werbung usw./; auch beruft er sich auf Massenstimmungen /Antikapitalismus, Enttäuschung an der Weimarer Republik, Antidemokratismus, nationalistische Gefühle usw./, die die Verbreitung des faschistischen Gifts förderten, die hypnotische Macht des Faschismus stärkten. Da Lukács in diesen Jahren den gesellschaftlichen Funktionen grössere Aufmerksamkeit schenkt, über Mittel nachdenkt, mit deren Hilfe die reaktionären Ideen "auf die Strasse" gelangt sind, erscheinen in seinem Gedankengang neben erkenntnistheoretischen Belängen der Ideologie auch Beschreibungen gewisser ihrer ontologischen Eigenschaften.

Zahlreiche Faktoren waren mitverantwortlich dafür, dass sich die Art und Weise, wie Lukács an die deutsche Ideologie Anfang der 40er Jahre geschichtlich heranging, veränderte: Innerhalb der in den Vordergrund gerückten Erörterung der deutschen Geschichte erscheint die im Faschismus mündende Ideologiegeschichte der bürgerlichen Philosophie im 20. Jahrhundert als Ursprungsgebiet nurmehr aufgehoben, im Doppelsinn des Wortes. Auch früher gab es den geschichtlichen Ansatzpunkt, er war jedoch überwiegend als politische Geschichte präsent; nun aber wird die Analyse der reaktionären Ideologie innerhalb der allgemeinen Geschichte betrachtet /29/. Besonders ausführlich erörtert Lukács die Geschichte Preussens und die Bedeutung der Preussen innerhalb der deutschen Entwicklung /30/.

Einer der Gründe, weshalb der geschichtliche Gesichtspunkt auftaucht, wurde schon erwähnt: zu Beginn der Niederschlagung des Faschismus musste man sich notwendigerweise Gedanken machen über die Zukunft Deutschlands und des deutschen Volkes, auch die Kräfte sichten, die den Kampf gegen die Überreste des Faschismus aufnehmen können im Zeuge der gesellschaftlichen, geis-

tigen und kulturellen Erhebung. Kräfte aber, die als Garanten
der Demokratie von morgen gelten könnten, seien gering und schwach,
meint Lukács; eine Erklärung dafür sei ausschliesslich in Deutschlands Geschichte zu finden. Ein Grund mehr, um sich der Vergangenheit zu konfrontieren.

Ein zweiter Grund, weshalb Lukács auf andere Weise an die Geschichte der deutschen Ideologie herangeht, kommt daher, dass
er sich auch über die ideologischen Aussichten des antifaschistischen Kampfes Gedanken machen musste. Was für Kräfte stehen
überhaupt zur Verfügung, um den ideologischen Zukunftskampf aus-
zutragen, die Reaktion zu überwinden? 1933 betrachtete Lukács
die Geschichte der bürgerlichen Philosophie vom Endergebnis, vom
Faschismus her, schwieg sich aber über den geschichtlichen Gegen-
pol der reaktionären Entwicklung aus. Die Vergangenheit wurde
nicht ins Auge gefasst, als noch keine Zukunft in Sicht war.
1941/42 jedoch erhielt die Grösse des deutschen Volkes, der Humanismus der deutschen Klassik ausserordentliche Bedeutung; angesichts dieses neuen Moments wird die reaktionäre Ideologie
nunmehr als Produkt der Verwüstung dieses Humanismus durch die
nichtklassische deutsche Philosophie dargestellt. /Das ist übrigens die allgemeine Erklärung für den Aufbau des Taschkenter
Manuskripts/. Die Aufgabe - wie auch die Hoffnung - den Humanismus wiederzubeleben, kommen eben daher. Die bekannte Lukácssche
Konzeption über die Philosophieentwicklung nach 1848, über die
Scheidung der Wege - wo die Linien Schelling-Schopenhauer-Nietz-
sche bzw. Kant-Fichte-Hegel-Goethe später streng divergieren -
erhält in diesen Jahren die endgültig ausgearbeitete Form. /Dar-
aus folgt nebenbei auch, dass Lukács nicht bloss aufgrund seiner
Vorliebe für den Klassizismus genau 1940 die Faust-Studien in
Angriff nahm, dass ein sehr tiefer Zusammenhang zwischen seiner
antifaschistischen Gesinnung und der Forschung der klassischen
deutschen Philosophie, der klassischen Kunst besteht/.

Ob aber Lukács in der Gegenwart antifaschistische Kräfte fand,
die die klassisch-humanistischen Traditionen aufbewahrten und
sie zu erneuern vermochten? In den 40er Jahren schon viel eher
als 1933. Eine solche Kraft erblickte er etwa in der humanisti-
schen Intelligenz in Emigration, darunter Künstler wie Thomas
und Heinrich Mann, Lion Feuchtwanger, Arnold Zweig. /Dahin sind

nun die Vorbehalte, die Lukács noch 1936 zu einem gewissen Grade
hegte beispielshalber gegenüber Thomas Mann, wegen dessen Neigung zum Mythos/ /31/.

"Aus Deutschland sind vorwiegend liberale Intellektuelle,
teils mit gewissen demokratischen Neigungen, ausgewandert, sie
haben sich aber unter dem Einfluss der ungeheuren Ereignisse der
vergangenen vier Jahre in der Richtung der revolutionären Demokratie energisch weiterentwickelt... In dieser Hinsicht beleuch-
tet die Wendung in der politischen Weltanschauung der deutschen
Emigration eine Schicksalswende, die sich in der Geschichte des
deutschen Volkes vorbereitet" /32/. Es ist vielleicht überflüssig
eigens zu betonen, wie sehr sich Liberalismus oder revolutionäre
Demokratie, worin Lukács nun die Alternative für die Intelligenz
erblickt, vom Entscheidungszwang zwischen Salto mortale oder Salto vitale unterscheidet. Es gilt auch für Lukács, dass in seiner
"politischen Weltanschauung" ab 1935 eine Wende eintrat. Indem
er sich zur Volksfrontpolitik bekannte, erhielt bei ihm die Alternative "Faschismus oder Demokratie" wachsenden Nachdruck gegenüber "Faschismus oder Bolschewismus".

Verleihen der Humanismus, die revolutionäre /und sozialisti-
sche/ Demokratie Kraft genug gegen den "Zauber", zur Restauration der Vernunft? Wird Cipolla je auferstehen? - Fragen, die
nicht von Lukács gestellt worden sind. Sie sind Fragen unserer
Zeit.

NOTEN

/1/ Thomas Mann: Mario und der Zauberer. In: Gesammelte Werke
    9 /Erzählungen/. Berlin, 1955. p. 756.

/2/ Ebd. p. 764.

/3/ Der faschisierte Goethe. Die Linkskurve, Goethe-Sonderheft,
    Juni 1932. pp. 32-40.

/4/ Der faschisierte und der wirkliche Georg Büchner. Zu seinem
    hundertsten Todestag 19. Februar 1937. Das Wort 2/1937/
    pp. 7-26.

/5/ Der deutsche Faschismus und Hegel. Internationale Literatur
    8/1943/ pp. 60-68. - Von den Gesichtspunkten, die ihn zum
    Schreiben des Jungen Hegel bewogen haben, erwähnt Lukács,
    dass "da der faschisierende Neuhegelianismus diese Periode
    dazu benützt hat, um aus Hegel einen den Faschisten genehmen
    Irrationalisten zu machen, ist es eine nicht unwesentliche

Aufgabe, diese Geschichtsfälschungen mit den historischen Tatsachen zu konfrontieren". Der Junge Hegel. Über die Beziehungen von Dialektik und Oekonomie. Zürich/Wien, 1948. p. 14.

/6/ Diesen Zusammenhang ist nicht nur durch Der historische Roman überhaupt und insonderheit das Schlusskapitel "Der historische Roman des demokratischen Humanismus" belegt, sondern auch durch zahlreiche Aufsätze, wie Der Kampf zwischen Liberalismus und Demokratie im Spiegel des historischen Romans der deutschen Antifaschisten. Internationale Literatur 5/1938/ pp. 63-83.

/7/ Brief an Anna Seghers. In: Essays über Realismus. Georg Lukács Werke 4. Neuwied u. Berlin, 1971. p. 362.

/8/ Ebd. p. 363.

/9/ Das Tiposkript ist im Georg-Lukács-Archiv aufbewahrt. Nr. LAK 3d I/18, 2185.

/10/ Ebd. Nr. LAK 3d I/15, 1885.

/11/ Государственное Издательство СССР. Taschkent, 1943. p.85. Aus dem Deutschen übertragen von R. Rasumowoj.

/12/ Wie ist die faschistische Philosophie in Deutschland entstanden nimmt in gwissen Kapiteln bereits die Struktur der Zerstörung der Vernunft vorweg; zugleich lässt sich der ansehnliche geschichtliche Unterschied zwischen den zwei Werken erkennen. Die Hauptteile des Werkes sind: Vorwort; I. Gibt es überhaupt eine faschistische Weltanschauung? II. Die Kritik der Gegenwart als neue Form der Apologetik; III. Die "Lebensphilosophie" und die Erneuerung der Romantik; IV. Der Anteil des Sozialfaschismus an der Entstehung der faschistischen Philosophie; V. Der Kampf gegen die Wissenschaftlichkeit; VI. Der Mythos. - Das erste Kapitel von dem Werk Wie ist Deutschland zum Zentrum der reaktionären Philosophie geworden? /Der historische Weg Deutschlands, pp. 14-42/, überdeckt sich mit dem ersten Kapitel der Zerstörung der Vernunft. Die Einteilung des Werkes ist folgende: Vorwort; Einleitung: Von Goethe und Hegel zu Schopenhauer und Nietzsche; I. Der historische Weg Deutschlands; II. Der Humanismus der deutschen Klassik; III. Die Destruktion des Humanismus in der deutschen Ideologie; IV. Der Faschismus als theoretisches und praktisches System der Barbarei. -- Die Zerstörung der Vernunft ist die "aufhebende" Synthese der Frühvarienten: Sie reicht mitsamt den /und trotz der/ teilweisen Überdeckungen weiter /den Irrationalismus nach 1945 mit einbegriffen/, und geht auch gedanklich weiter.

/13/ Über gewisse Zusammenhänge zwischen den ästhetischen Ansichten von Lukács und der Komintern-Politik s. L. Sziklai: Die Ästhetik der ungleichmässigen Entwicklung. Annales Sectio Philosophica et Sociologica. Tom. III. Budapest, 1976. pp. 123-137.

/14/ Vorwort, p. 1.

/15/ Ebd. p. 14.

/16/ Dieselbe grundlegende Struktur wendet Lukács auch für den
Expressionismus an /"Grösse und Verfall" des Expressionismus. Internationale Literatur 1/1934/ pp. 153-173./ und
stellt fest, es bestehe eine ideologische "innere Verwandtschaft" zwischen der Kriegsfeindlichkeit der USP und der
Expressionisten. Darüber hinaus beschreibt er ebendort auch
die Ideologie der deutschen Intelligenz im Zeitalter des
Imperialismus. Dort heisst es unter anderem: "Die Unterord-
nung der bürgerlichen Intelligenz unter den sich ausbreitenden und entfaltenden Imperialismus vollzieht sich nicht direkt, nicht widerspruchslos; es entstehen auch oppositionelle
und vor allen scheinoppositionelle Bewegungen, die aber...
mögen sie sich noch so radikal gebärden, mögen sie subjektiv
noch so tief von ihrem 'Radikalismus' überzeugt sein, nur
einen 'internen', einen 'fraktionellen' Kampf zu führen
fähig sind".

/17/ "Hitler oder Dolfuss mögen die sozialdemokratischen Organi-
sationen auflösen, ihre Funktionäre in Konzentrationslager
sperren - die Socialdemokratie bleibt trotzdem die soziale
Hauptstütze der Bourgeoisie in Deutschland oder Österreich,
gerade dadurch, dass sie durch ihr scheinoppositionelles Verhalten die Arbeitermassen von dem wirklich revolutionären
Klassenkampf gegen das faschistische System zurückhält...
Die Literatur, die wir hier charakterisieren, soll damit
nicht in eine mechanische Parallele zur Sozialdemokratie
gebracht werden... Es darf aber nicht vergessen werden, dass
in der imperialistischen Epoche die Grenzen zwischen ehrli-
cher Opposition auf bürgerlicher Grundlage auf ideologischem
Gebiete und zwischen direkter und indirekter Bestochenheit
durch den Kapitalismus zuweilen recht fliessend sind..."
Grand Hotel "Abgrund". Manuskript im Besitz des Georg-Lu-
kács-Archivs. Nr. LAK 230, p. 7.

/18/ Ebd. p. 18.

/19/ Wie ist die faschistische Philosophie in Deutschland entstanden? Vorwort, pp. 30-31. - Alldem zum Trotz glaubte
Lukács freilich nicht, dass alle, die den Faschismus be-
kämpfen wollen, unbedingt zu Marxisten werden müssten. Obgleich einzig der dialektische Materialismus Bewusstheit in
den antifaschistischen Kampf hineinträgt, führe der Kampf
- auch wenn dies nicht bewusst wird - objektiv und unvermeidlich eine Annäherung an den Marxismus-Leninismus her-
bei. /Vgl. ebd. p. 33./

/20/ Ebd. p. 22.

/21/ Ebd. pp. 36-37.

/22/ Ebd. pp. 34-35.

/23/ Fr. Engels an K. Schmidt /27.10.1890/. MEW 37, p. 493.

/24/ Alfred Rosenberg, Ästhet des Nationalsozialismus. In russi-
scher Sprache. Literaturnaja Gaseta, 21.Juli 1934.

/25/ Nietzsche als Vorläufer der faschistischen Ästhetik. Internationale Literatur 8/1935/ p. 90.

/26/ L. Rudas: <u>Der dialektische Materialismus und die Sozialde-</u>
<u>mokratie.</u> Verlagsgenossenschaft ausländischer Arbeiter in
der UdSSR. Moskau-Leningrad, 1934.

/27/ <u>Der Rassenwahn als Feind der Menschheit.</u> Internationale Literatur 1/1943/ pp. 40-51.

/28/ <u>Wie ist Deutschland zum Zentrum der reaktionären Ideologie</u>
<u>geworden</u>? Einleitung: Von Goethe und Hegel zu Schopenhauer
und Nietzsche. A.a.O. p. 2.

/29/ Ebd. Kap.I: Der historische Weg Deutschlands. pp. 14-41.

/30/ <u>Über Preussentum.</u> Internationale Literatur 5/1943/ pp. 36-
47; ursprünglich Teil des in Anm. 11 erwähnten Werkes.

/31/ <u>Der historische Roman.</u> Probleme des Realismus III. /Georg
Lukács Werke 6/. Neuwied u. Berlin, 1965. p. 324.

/Übersetzt von Ágnes V. Meller/

LUKÁCS'S ONTOLOGY AND THE PROBLEM OF SOCIAL FORMATIONS

I. BALOGH

1. WHY ONTOLOGY?

George Lukács, familiar with what his closest disciples thought of the first two volumes of his Ontology, started the third by reiterating his basic ideas as follows: "Presumably no one, least of all the author of this work will be surprised that an attempt which posits being as the philosophic concept of the world, meets with resistance from several directions. Recent centuries of philosophic thought were dominated by epistemology, logic and methodology, and this dominance is far from being over." /1/ Some of these several directions, where resistance was experienced, are obviously within philosophy, but others lead far beyond philosophy, towards social practice. The forms of resistance also vary; some of them are conscious and pondered over, while others are rooted in tradition, and are related to difficulties attendant upon the changing modes of thought and attitude necessary to understand ontology. If we wish to turn our attention to the development and concrete theoretical forms of the tradition within philosophy, we have to focus on the first volume of the Ontology, on the historical chapters: there Lukács critically presents a current of thought – beginning with Cardinal Bellarmin, consummated in Kant, and crystallized into a general mode of thinking, an ideology, in modern neo-positivism – which considers our knowledge about reality and not reality itself as the true object of philosophic inquiry. And even though the thrust of this current is curbed and thwarted by some systems of thought, like that of Hegel, and particularly that of

Nicolai Hartmann or the existentialists, their incoherence, idealism, and other limitations render them incapable of preventing or disputing the victory of epistemological philosophies. The opportunity of halting this triumphal progress arose only with the emergence, and further development of Marxism.

But anyhow, why is it important and necessary to subject the epistemological approach to critique and revision? Lukács's answer to this question is: it is an entirely different matter to base theoretical inquiry on complex social reality, qua being - which includes the transformed natural environment, and the various forms and institutions of thought - and, on the contrary, to set out from a mere segment of reality, the problems of cognition. However much our knowledge reflects reality, we still should not formulate our angle on reality solely with the exploration of knowledge. For if we do so, the basis of philosophical scrutiny will be restricted to a single sphere of the whole of reality, i.e. knowledge. This basis, by dint of its nature - since it is the field of abstraction on the one hand, and, on the other, an activity of cognition developing specific rules and thus becoming relatively autonomous, with a specific position in the division of labour - is particularly capable of captivating philosophical thinking. Then the mind so "enchanted" tends to perceive the world outside the realm of knowledge either not at all, or only in parenthesis, and is willing to consider reality beyond cognizance only as some area of manipulation for the cognitive activity. The various forms of this outlook are analyzed in detail by Lukács. Thus, for instance, he argues in connection with the Neo-Kantians that "... they evade the fundamental problem of the existential particularity of social being, and approach the conceptual difficulties of parts of the whole purely epistemologically, or purely methodologically, from the aspect of scientific theory ... On this point the Neo-Kantianism of the turn of the century is closely concurrent with the then current positivism of Mach, Avenarius etc. But the fine methodological differences, much debated then, are insignificant and irrelevant for the issue they pose, since they are all in agreement about the fundamental question that scientific philosophy knows no ontological questions whatever."/2/

Neopositivism, on the other hand, which is based on modern physics and mathematics "... has succeeded in realizing Bellarmin's programme to a never before experienced degree: the "language" of mathematics is not only the most important medium of the physical interpretation of physical reality, but also the ultimate, purely conceptual, 'semantic' expression of a phenomenon important for people, with the assistance of which the phenomenon can be manipulated with practically unlimited freedom. Any proposition which points farther, toward immanent reality, has no scientific importance according to this theory." /3/ Now it is clear that this narrowing down of philosophy is self-restriction in the first place. This becomes particularly dangerous /almost threatening the very basis of science/ in the social sciences. The consequence of such philosophical self-limitation is that the sciences, and particularly the social sciences - even the various disciplines - disintegrate into parts indifferent, or even opposed, to one another. Thus, for one, an empiricism without theory come to develop and, for another, 'pure' theory gradually losing touch with reality. The theoretical problems of empiricism become narrowed down to the methodological problems of sociological inquiries and the theoretical pretension beyond this produces only meaningless commonplaces. Thus, empiricism degrades itself to become an instrument of all sorts of manipulation, while pure theory, in its disdain of empiricism, does nothing but spell out its alienation from life in secret codes, "rising" into a manipulator. Then the two one-sided attitudes take each other to court; they mistake their rightful censure of their opponent for laying down their own foundations, while what they really prove and confirm is no more than the disintegration of the common basis, of the uniform scientific outlook itself. Lukács's aversion for sociology as a self-sufficient discipline, as well as for pure theory, originates in his understanding of the dangerousness of this situation /4/.

The problem of the opposition of theoretical and empirical research leads far beyond the social sciences to the contradictions of social practice, and - precisely for this reason - distinct social interests are tied up with the maintenance of this opposition. The attempt, therefore, to base a philosophy

337

on being, which, in contrast with the disintegration of scientific foundations, endeavours to philosophically work out their unity, also encounters the resistance of certain modes of social practice. /Whether this resistance is manifest spontaneously, or in a consciously developed form is, naturally, a separate question./ Ontological thought, for Lukács, certainly does not mean a reconciliation of philosophy or social theory with currently prevailing social practice, in order to provide a theoretical quasi-rationale for the latter. On the contrary: he regards this latter form of being clasped to practice just as much a possibility or consequence of manipulation, and, nay, it even lacks the possibility of those partial and limited achievements which full-fledged empirical research and pure theory might offer. Lukács argues that an uncritical attitude to practice, and the direct, unconditional justification of prevailing practice can establish the harshest forms of manipulation, or indeed, it is part of this manipulation. Just as a philosophy getting rid of epistemological conventions must not become a direct and unconditional justification of practice, it must not be dissolved in this practice either. Overcoming conventional philosophy based on epistemology in no way means the elimination of every kind of philosophy. For taking possession of social and natural reality is a total social process which - even though it forms a coherent whole - has relatively independent spheres within this unity carrying out its various functions. Thus, theory and praxis, cognition and practice, the movement of particular social processes and that of the totality of society, can never completely coalesce. Their overlapping indicates also the regeneration, at a higher level, of their differences and of their critical stance toward each other./5/ Thus the social "mission" of a philosophy tied to social practice yet not dissolved in it, is nothing else but the far-reaching analysis of the social practice unifying in various ways, thus falling into relatively separate spheres. Its task is to study the natural and historical conditions of this practice and explore the development of the changing practical relation to these conditions.

"The thinking of every philosopher who lives up to his trade more than in the narrow, academic sense of the terms, is direct-

ed to have a decisive say in the vital conflicts of his age, to
work out the principles of the struggle, thus giving a more distinct direction to the struggle itself. And if that which philosophy states is also only a potentiality, then - if the philosophy is a true one - its import is that it expresses the potentialities of some concrete developmental stage of mankind concretely and dynamically /pointing to the future/ ... The central
object of philosophy is the human species, that is the ontological picture of the universe and of society from the aspect of
what it was in reality, what it has become, and what it is like,
in order to establish the eternally valid type of the genus as
a necessary and possible type; it thus synthetically unites the
two poles, the world and man in the image of a concrete generity."
/6/

Lukács' Ontology is an unfinished attempt worked out with
colossal intellectual effort and imagination to lay the foundation of this philosophical scheme. It should not, then, be looked
on as a product of the failing intellectual and physical powers
of the philosopher, but rather the opposite: as the outline of
a new synthesis of many decades of activity, political and scholarly as well as practical and intellectual, the result of which
must be measured against the size of the task undertaken. It
follows, therefore, that the argument that one ought to go back
from the Ontology to the History and Class Consciousness, sharply
contradicts Lukács's philosophical development, and it is justified from a certain aspect that Die Eigenart des Asthetischen
is thrown into relief against the Ontology.

2. THE RAMIFICATIONS OF A METHODOLOGICAL PROBLEM

Lukács's conception in the Ontology - which claims that philosophy should analyse concrete reality with a view to the perspective of the future - raises the problem of historicity in a
most direct manner. That kind of historicity which consciously
focuses on studying the present, necessarily leaves its mark on
the content of philosophical thinking, on the various categories,
and on the interrelation of these categories alike. Lukács writes
about this in these terms: "...philosophic universality in phi-

losophy proper /that is not in the conventional, but in the above-mentioned sense of philosophy - I. B./ is never autotelic, it is never a merely encyclopedic or educational synthesis of the confirmed results, but a systematization, which is a means for understanding the Wherefore? and Whither? of the human race in the most adequate manner possible./ This implies not only that every philosophy is, in one way or another, rooted in the relations of its time, however universal, independent of time and place, the form may be in which it is expounded. From the point of view of a philosophy oriented toward Marxist ontology, there is much more at stake: a theory that consciously responds to its own age must necessarily abandon its claim to setting up some sort of timeless and unchanging system, and must ensure that the system and the build-up of its categories conform to the actual system of relations of the age.

In order to establish this relationship of reasoning and reality, Lukács turns to the basic methodological principles of Marx, since Marx in the introduction to the Grundrisse thorough-ly examined the relationship between the categories of the various social formations and the most general, most abstract categories, as well as the methodological problems involved in the analysis of this relationship./8/ Even though Marx concentrates princi-pally on the categories of political economy, he usually dis-cusses general philosophical and ideological problems as well.

a/ General Ontology and Social Ontology

To recall the methodological concepts of Marx is important not only because Lukács uses them and builds upon them, but mainly because they lead to the intrinsic and fundamental contra-dictions of the Lukács's Ontology. These contradictions equally affect the inner structure and the outer build-up of the Onto-logy.

Concerning the inner structure, mention must be made primarily of the relationship between general ontology and social ontology. Discussing general ontology, Lukács says: "The ontology of social existence... presupposes a general ontology... General ontology, or more concretely, the ontology of inorganic nature as the basis

340

of each and every being, is general because there is no possibility for any being not to be rooted in some sense in inorganic
nature. New categories emerge in life, but these can be efficient
beings only on the basis of, and in interaction with the general
categories." /9/ Lukács, however, by marking out the realm of
inorganic nature for a general ontology, precludes the possibility
of understanding the higher spheres of existence, organic life
and society on the basis of a general ontology, since the categories of the inorganic sphere of existence "are incapable of
determining the specific feature /of the higher level of being/,
and this preserves its originality and cannot be deduced from
the lower ones." /10/ It is clear now that a general ontology
limited to inorganic nature cannot be the definition of the
general starting point at all, since it serves only as basis
for organic life and society, but does not in the least touch
their specific nature, or even explicitly excludes that. This
ontology is "general" only inasmuch as the higher modes of being,
subject as they are to their specific qualities, include inorganic nature as well, or rather, they could be regarded as general
only if organic life and society were reduced to the laws of
the inorganic world, and were directly deduced from these. Even
though Lukács himself plainly rejected any such reduction, indeed
he sharply criticized the methods of reduction in the Ontology,
this does not change the fact that he himself gives rise to the
possibility of reduction again and again in his concept of general ontology.

The situation is, however, completely different concerning
the problem of the 'general' ontology that we propounded first,
i.e. that the more developed forms of being comprise the lower
ones as well. Here Lukács systematically moves along the path
where, from among the higher-than-inorganic modes of being, it
is organic life that appears first - as the extraneous relationship of inorganic and organic -, and secondly society, the social sphere is defined in a manner that it is none other than
the coexistence and relation of the inorganic, organic and social forms of being. The root of the problem lies in the fact
that Lukács conceives of general ontology not as one the categories of which combine the collective determination of the in-

organic world, organic life, and society - the three spheres of
existence which have their own specific qualities qualitatively
divergent from one another. Thus, with any logical operation
whatever, he is unable to overcome the detachment of these spheres
of being or reconstruct their genuine relationship. The Ontology,
then, has a constant, deep-rooted tendency to have inorganic life,
organic life, and society fall apart into spheres indifferent to
one another. We can therefore say that although Lukács's concept
of a general ontology calls for criticism, this critique does
not necessarily point towards the negation of the dialectics of
nature, and towards the ideas of the <u>History and Class Conscious-
ness</u>. Even if I agree with the authors of the "Notes" in that
- at least on several essential points - "the basic methodological principles had not been fully considered..." /11/, this certainly does not mean that the outcome of this consideration had
to be that "nature as a philosophical theme could arise only as
a ... social problem..." /12/

While in the ontology of inorganic nature appearing as general
ontology, and social ontology detached from this, threaten to
burst apart the whole of ontology, social ontology itself is
threatened by the contradiction of a different kind of duality:
the individual as a complex entity may be confronted with, and
separated from, society as totality, and this may involve that
these two poles are treated in isolation. "We must scrutinize
... the ultimately decisive polar nature of the total complex...
The two poles, which limit its movements of reproduction, and
determine these in a positive sense, as they destroy old restric-
tions, and in a negative sense, as they put up new ones, make
up, on the one hand, the reproduction process in its extensive
and intensive totality, and on the other the individual people,
the reproduction of whom, as individuals, forms the existential
foundation of total reproduction." /13/ And later, confirming
the starting point: "... we must clarify, at least in general,
the kind of structural and dynamic conditions under which this
bi-polar movement takes place. We have just become familiar with
one of the poles, man, as a moving and developing complex. It
is just as clear that the other pole is, by necessity, society
as totality." /14/ In the bi-polar concept of the reproduction

of society and the individual, Lukács relies directly on a definition formulated also by Marx: "We set out, as a matter of course, from the individuals productive in society, hence the socially determined production of the individuals." Why is it then that this starting point never makes Marx perceive society as bi-polar, while in Lukács's conception the individual and society appear as poles, so that he cannot but make repeated efforts to prevent social ontology from disintegration. The answer to be formulated in terms of methodology leads us back to the earlier mentioned problem of general ontology and the ontology of nature, and throws light on these from a new angle.

By treating the conditions of the activity of the productive individuals as social ones, Marx is afforded the opportunity of discussing the actual relationship of individual activity, the social whole, and nature. Indeed, the social conditions of productive activity mediate the relationship between individual activity, and nature as basis. Thus the individual, as producer, always enters into a relationship with nature as a socially producing individual. Therefore, when we examine the activity of the individual, we are to do that only through its relation to the social conditions, and when we examine the relation to nature, we must examine the relation of the social whole, as a totality, to its natural foundations and conditions. Therefore, an examination which disregards the correlation of individual-society-nature and employs categories directly expressing the relation of the individual and nature, is really beyond the scope of social theory. In other words, however much production, a 'response' of necessity given to the natural conditions, is the activity of the individual producer, it is always an activity mediated by a definite community, that is, a social response. So the means of production are not an objective mediation - separable from the social response between individual and nature, but the mediating operation of a definite mode of activity: the mediation of that mode of activity which has been evolved in a definite community. It is also the mediation of that activity with which the instrument was made and taken possession of. Consequently, although production for Marx is the production of individuals, the producing individuals never become independent of society, that is separate poles, but on the contrary, their production is also social production, the reproduction process of their social relations. As opposed to this, with Lukács, due to the methodological problems of general and social ontology, individuals also have to reproduce themselves as biological beings – that is, the inorganic and organic bases of their lives, and the non-social components of their individuality – as a continuously present non-social aspect, somehow isolated from society. Thus, at least in this respect, their metabolic relationship with nature is unmediated by society, and whatever mediation does come about between man and nature in this sphere, it is at most a technical mediation through the instrument of labour.

Lukács makes huge efforts to shun the dangerous ramifications. He repeatedly underlines the importance of the social determination of the individual, devoting a separate chapter to the problems of ontological priority, and concludes that for organic nature as well as for the social being "...reproduction in the ontogenetic as well as in the phylogenetic sense is that decisive, overwhelming motive of the – constantly surviving – interactions with inorganic nature which determines the content and form of every organic being." /15/ But on the other hand, the fundamental methodological problems – indicated also by the treatment of the problem as exemplified in the passage quoted – push through in those concrete concepts with which Lukács characterizes, for instance, social development, and describes it as the increasing socialization of society, or as a process where social development becomes increasingly socialized. For social development may be regarded as the process of becoming increasingly socialized only if society has previously been divided into two sides extraneously independent of one another: a social, and a natural sphere.

b/ The Historicity of the Structure of the Category of Labour

It is well known that the inner structure of Lukács's category of labour differs from that of Marx. Still Lukács does refer – and with good reason – to Marx's definition of labour when laying the foundations of this different category of labour. Marx

344

himself writes that if we postulate labour in a form which is
the exclusive property of man, then purposeful activity, that is
work itself, the object of work, and the instrument of work a-
rise as simple aspects of the process of labour./16/ But Marx
handles this determinated quality of labour as a precondition
which he does not explore in detail, and he uses instead another
pair of opposites, and posits labour partly as a general /phy-
sical and intellectual/ human effort, partly as a concrete purposeful activity /work/. For Marx - as his methodological basic
principles prove it - it was clear that the categories determining the fundamental relations of capitalist production are based,
on the one hand, on such general determinations of labour - developed concurrently with the emergence of man- which could be
found in every social formation, but, on the other, are also
the most developed forms of this general determination of labour.
This characteristic of the basic categories expressing capitalist production is, as Marx puts it, that even the most abstract
categories are products of definite historical relations and have
full validity only in respect to, and within, these relations.
It is not, then, that the duality of the abstract and concrete
aspects constitutes the only determination of labour for Marx
- or that this duality could provide the fundamental definition
of any social formation. And naturally, it is not as if Marx
would deny the duality of teleology and causality, intellectual
and manual work, aim and implementation, and the historical
changes of form of this relation. But while the duality of human
work in general, and the concrete, purposeful human exertion of
effort produces the differences of abstract and concrete labour
at a definite phase of development, and in connection with this
it shapes the separate socio-economic objectivations of one side:
value /exchange value, capital/, the other side, teleology and
causality, aim and implementation do not exhibit such features.
It is true, though, that the difference between causality and
teleology - at least after the differentiation of intellectual
and manual work - can be found in historically different forms
in all social formations. It is also clear that the independent
existence of either side, growing out of the other and establishing a separate system of relations, is an historical fact detect-

able in a multitude of socio-economic formations. Still, the duality of causality and teleology has to date never provided any social formation with the constitutive element from which the determining objectivations of the socio-economic basis, and the categories corresponding to these, develop. And in a philo-sophical analysis whose goal it is to elucidate the course to be followed by the social totality, the most fundamental categories - i.e. causality and teleology in the case of the Ontology -, can be justified only if the categories also express the essence of those specific categories which constitute the specific de-termination of the totality in question. It is not enough there-fore that causality and teleology are found in every social form-ation, this is but an abstract and extensive generality. For Lu-kács an ontological theory to be worked out requires also that causality and teleology should lay the foundation of the deter-mining essence of a specific historical formation. Only in this way can they become intensive-general categories.

Thus when Lukács makes the duality of work in relation to teleology and causality and not concrete and abstract work as the theoretical and structural starting point of the Ontology, he seemingly does no more than step back from the Marxian category of work towards a more general, more primaeval, original category of work. But, by paying no heed to the methodological consequen-ces of this seemingly simple act, he promptly finds himself at a starting point which offers no opportunity for the examination of the concrete course of social history, of the various concrete social formations, and only a pseudo-genetic conceptual analysis can be carried out /17/. Therefore, when Lukács does attempt to draw the various concrete social formations into the sphere of his enquiry, it turns out that his ontological position establish-ed according to the foregoing is not suitable even for a more or less coherent summing up of the already available most important results. The theoretical solution to the problem that "...we are discussing an historical process which, as a whole, never and not in any respect bears a teleological character..." /18/, in no way wards off the difficulties towering here.

346

3. THE "MESSAGE" OF THE ONTOLOGY

Since the fundamental structure of category of the <u>Ontology</u>
has not so far been confirmed by any concrete social formation,
the essence of Lukács's position leads us to assume that the
basic categories of the <u>Ontology</u>, and the relationship of these,
express the basic determination of a social formation to be.
This means that Lukács's philosophic scheme is future bound, it
aspires to the realm of freedom, and envisages the vista of modern communism. Lukács derives the possibility, and also the necessity, of this great undertaking from the fact that, on the
one hand "... the conscious methodological basing of a consistent
social ontology or philosophic generalization onto the real economic process is an historical indication that, in terms of universal history, decision-making has gradually come to the fore
in those conflicts which lead to the end of the "prehistory of
mankind" /19/, and also that with the emergence of socialism,
"for all the problems, a new society is in the offing, with new
human types." /20/. And, Lukács in his <u>Ontology</u> sets about spell-
ing out the philosophical outlines of the basic relations of this
new society which has yet to take shape.

Naturally, Lukács is fully aware that there is a completely
new historical phase here, different from all previous ones,
which can no longer be described using the concrete categories
that applied to earlier phases of development. Following Marx,
Lukács reaches the conclusion that communism is the social formation where teleology appears as an end in itself /the purpose
of man is the improvement to the utmost of his own intellectual
and physical capacities/, and causality, like the economy, turns
into the basis of this end in itself. Lukács describes this relationship as follows: "...Every economic event consists of casual chains moved by teleologic rules..., as I have demonstrated
in the chapter on Marx, the essential laws of economic development - that is the reduction of the social working time necessary
for reproduction, the regression of the bounds of nature parallel
with the increased socialization of society, and simultaneously
with the integration of originally small societies leading towards the establishment of a world economy - also spring from

teleological rules in their essence, but the casual chains activated by these factors assert themselves independently of the content, intent, etc. of the rules that produce these. In this sense, the realm of the economy belongs to the realm of necessity."/21/ Now by this we have come to the fundamental categories of Lukács's concept of work, to the very birth-place of the basic categories of the Ontology. For in Lukács's view communism is the social formation which is based on the world of necessity, of causal connections, that is on the economy, but whose true nature is expressed by the world of freedom. This world of freedom is the sphere in which the true human character of teleology develops and asserts itself: this is where man can become the centre of teleologic rules with his totality, with his omni-sided talent.

In his Ontology Lukács undertakes to present, right from the beginnings, the historical Odyssey of teleological positing and of man realizing this positing. At the consummation of the great undertaking the encounter of teleological positing and of man who posits, becomes possible and complete by man becoming his own goal.

Lukács is firmly convinced that it is now possible to grasp the basic relations of communism at the philosophical level. And when, taking his cue from Marx's tenet concerning the realm of freedom and necessity, he expounds the theoretical-historical relationship of teleological postulation and causal connection, he has to accept a series of theoretical and methodological inconsistencies. All this, however, does not refute Marx's conclusions - about the realm of freedom -, but it implies that while Marx described the definite aspects and features of communism, still we cannot say that these aspects are also the basic categories of the determination of formation of the new society. In other words, they express some aspects of the totality, and not the determined historical totality of the activity. Although Marx's words are employed here to express only certain aspects of society, and this phrase is by no means unscientific, it certainly does not describe communism as such. Contrary to his original intention, Lukács outlines not the timeliness of communism, but rather the fact that the conditions of expounding a scientific theory of communism as such - that is in its social formation-

Conditions are absent
for a sc. theory?
Communism

-determination - do not exist either in reality, or in theory.
Nor are the conditions suitable for working out the basic relations of communism, even at the level of philosophic generality. Science and philosophy /philosophy in Lukács's sense/ for
the time being can undertake only the expounding of various aspects.

This conclusion - which may seem to be formally negative, yet
which is in reality almost limitlessly positive - is what raises
the Ontology high above the majority of its critics. For: in the
Ontology Lukács undertakes to answer a question which certainly
cannot be avoided - in practice - in the course of the development of our society.

The most important specific feature of the Ontology, according to its aim, is that it attempts to look on the long term
programmes of communism as an actual theoretical and philosophical task. What it actually proves - contrary to the intention
of the author - is that at the present stage only an approach
from certain given sides is possible. It must be said that philosophy in Lukács's sense, if it has any hope of solution, may
at this stage undertake a closer theoretical-philosophical task
only. The fundamental - and no longer methodological - contradiction of the Ontology is that Lukács proclaims the undoubtedly
correct philosophical aspiration of the complex analysis of totality in respect of a social formation, of which only some aspects can be partially grasped or approached./22/ The fact that
the methodological and theoretical problems of Lukács's explanation bear on the analysis of socialism most heavily derives
from this.

Ultimately, the innermost, decisive contradiction of the
Ontology is that it postulates the elimination of alienation
with respect to the future, while the basic categories of this
postulation are themselves also expressions of a definite alienation. This contradiction makes it impossible for Lukács to
explain the relationship between the present and the future of
socialism and the concrete historical formation determination
of socialism. The fact that he confines the problem of alienation to the political sphere, the relations of leadership and
implementation, he creates a barrier between theory and practice.

349

23*

But since Lukács aims precisely at theoretically establishing
an organic relationship between the practice of the present and
future perspectives - the interruption of which he himself considers as a development that involves very serious consequences-,
he is forced to make commitment to the cause of communism the
guiding thread of practical action. Considering that Lukács is
ultimately unable to provide any basis for practical action beyond this, István Mészáros /23/ has rightly pointed out that Lukács finds himself in the position of Ethical Utopianism where
commitment and devotion to the cause becomes a medium which has
to dissolve the contradictions developed in the argument of the
Ontology as well as in reality between present and future, particularity and generic nature, tactics and strategy. "If we examine the devotion of people to some cause regarded simultaneously as their own as well as that of the whole of mankind, then
socialism occupies a peculiar position in this problem-complex...
while the motives of the basic attitude related to the cause remain alive, there arise formations of thought and modes of attitude which - however much they may diverge from the correct
image of Marxian socialism - remain socially and humanly superior
to bourgeois irrationalism as well as to bourgeois manipulation..."
/24/ But Lukács also knew that the superiority of socialism was
a /practical/ question and task first of all. Thus, philosophy
in Lukács's sense may contribute to the realization of this practical task first of all by the clarification of the basic relations of socialism, which contain contradictions. The inner division, contradiction, and unity of these basic relations also
shine through the categories of Lukács's Ontology, which for
this very reason take us nearer to a higher level of social self-
-knowledge.

NOTES

/1/ Lukács György A társadalmi lét ontológiájáról /.On the On-
     tology of Social Reality/ Budapest, 1976. Vol. III. p. 7.
/2/ Lukács György Ontológia /Ontology/ Vol. I. p. 18.
/3/ Ibid. pp. 43-44.

350

/4/ "Comte and Taine differentiated between economic and sociology in the 19th century. Thus they came to confront not
only Marx, but also Petty and Smith, and all the older economists, who were both sociologists and economists without
exception. In my view this separation is an altogether un-
sound development. Sociology not rooted in economics is but
empty chatter. No independent science of sociology exists
- sociology is but one aspect of the true, comprehensive
economic inquiry into reality... On the other hand, I should
like to emphasize that while I do not accept an independent
sociology, I am all in favour of sociological research. The
two propositions are not opposed in any sense." /Lukács
György A futurológiáról /On Futurology/ Valóság, 1981.No.11./
The harmony of the two seemingly contradictory statements
is explained by Lukács's aversion to empiricism rising to
theoretical rank on the one hand, and on the other to theory
breaking away from reality.

/5/ Consequently one cannot agree that Lukács did not succeed
in clearly distinguishing between science and philosophy
/See G. H. R. Parkinson, George Lukács, London-Boston, 1977.
pp. 145-146./. According to Lukács ontologically oriented
philosophy encompasses objective reality and science as well,
therefore, albeit it is related to the sciences and scientific theory, it can in no way be identified with these.

/6/ Lukács György Ontológia /Ontology/ Vol. II. pp. 526-529.

/7/ Lukács György Ontológia /Ontology/ Vol. II. p. 526.

/8/ Marx, K., Grundrisse. Foundations of the Critique of Political Economy, "Introduction". Harmondsworth, Middlesex: 1973.
pp. 81-111.

/9/ Lukács György Ontológia, Vol. I. p. 19.

/10/ Ibid. p. 157. Lukács here expounds the views of Nicolai
Hartmann. Clearly expressing his agreement with Hartmann,
he supplements him only on one point: "This profoundly correct recognition concerning the ontological structure of
the world does, however, imperatively demand Genesis, as
a link between these grades of existence..." /p. 157./

/11/ Fehér, F. - Heller, Á. - Márkus, Gy. - Vajda, M. Feljegyzé-
sek Lukács elvtársnak az Ontológiáról 1968-1969. /Notes on
Lukács's Ontology Telos 1976 No.29./ Magyar Filozófia Szem-
le, Vol.XII., 1978. No. 1.

/12/ Ibid.

/13/ Lukács György Ontológia , Vol. II. p. 258.

/14/ Ibid., pp. 185-286.

/15/ Ibid., p. 233. This coexistence leading to unexplained connection appears perhaps even more lucidly elsewhere in connection with work "...work, by its nature, is interaction
between man /society/ and nature, in organic /tools, raw
materials, object worked etc./ as well as organic nature;
and this interaction... leaves its stamps mainly on the
transition, which takes place in working man himself from
the mere biological to social existence." Ibid. p. 14.

/16/ Marx, K., <u>Das Kapital</u>. Vol. I. Berlin: Dietz, 1969. pp. 192 f. Lukács quotes Marx's passage several times in the <u>Ontology</u>, usually in full length. Cf. e.g. <u>Ontológia</u>, Vol. I. pp. 285-286., Vol. II. pp. 17-18., Vol. III. p. 22.

/17/ At this point Lukács does in fact draw the conclusions from his position. Where Hartmann - opposing Aristotle - points out the concrete historic forms of the possibility in contrast with the abstract approach, he adds that in case of unemployment "...the invalid character of this possibility is manifest...", then he goes on to accuse Hartmann of passing over the problem inattentively. "It is unquestionable that many workers really have no opportunity to work during extensive social /he ought to have said economic - B. I./ crises; but it is equally true beyond doubt - and this is the reason why such a profound truth lies in the Aristotelian notion of dynamism -, that they can again resume their work during a boom. How would it be possible to explain this peculiarity from the aspect of the ontology of social existence by anything, but that even the unemployed remain workers - according to his dynamics - as a result of his upbringing, experience etc.?" /Lukács György <u>Ontológia</u>, Vol. II. pp. 38-39./ It is evident that Lukács is not so susceptible to problems as Hartmann.

/18/ Lukács György <u>Ontológia</u>, Vol. II. p. 331.

/19/ <u>Ibid</u>. p. 558.

/20/ <u>Ibid</u>. p. 777.

/21/ <u>Ibid</u>. pp. 515-516.

/22/ Favourable presentation or critique of the dual ontology is really completely needless and meaningless without discussing fundamental contradictions. Cf. Fehér, F. - Heller, Á.- Márkus, Gy. - Vajda, M., <u>Feljegyzések Lukács elvtársnak az Ontológiáról</u> /Notes on Lukács's Ontology. <u>Telos</u> No. 29. 1976./ <u>Magyar Filozófiai Szemle</u>, 1978. No. 1. The critiques of the dual ontology, that is, disregard precisely the fundamental aim of Lukács, and drag back the <u>Ontology</u> to the philosophic level Lukács wanted to rise above. Therefore, from his view-point this critique could not have any other conclusion than that this group of his disciples were right in the usual philosophic sense, but their truth hardly related to the essence of the matter, which had to be explained again in order to make it understood.

/23/ Mészáros, I. <u>Lukács's Concept of Dialectic</u>, London, 1972. pp. 81-91. However, Mészáros interprets Lukács's ethical Utopianism as a problem of the entire view of history of his Ontology.

/24/ Lukács György <u>Ontológia</u>, Vol. II. pp. 776-777.

CATHARSIS ET MIMÉSIS *

D. ZOLTAI

Spätwerk, ouvrage tardif: cette expression connaît de nouveau
un grand prestige dans les publications récentes de la littérature spécialisée. La déterminante chronologique du tardif commence depuis peu à se transformer en notion - clef de dimension
métaphysique. On prétend que ce qui confère son aura au Spätwerk
est le fait qu'il est irrémédiablement en retard, et donc privé
d'avenir. C'est ainsi qu'en 1937, Adorno parlant du Spätstil de
Beethoven, croyait déchiffrer dans les ruines du style de vieillesse des grandes figures de la période bourgeoise une préscience
de catastrophes.

Dissipons tout de suite d'éventuels malentendus, et précisons
que c'est en vain que nous chercherions dans l'oeuvre de Lukács
les traces d'un Spätstil dans cette acception du mot. Il est bien
sur des marques de style, dont il n'est pas difficile de déduire
l'âge avancé d'un auteur. C'est un savant âgé qui écrivit La particularité de l'esthétique /1962/ et qui réunissait les thèmes
de l'Ontologie de l'Etre social. On perçoit dans le style la hâte
et la recherche de la formule qui convainc, le manque de poli,
et le désir élémentaire, faisant fi des répétitions éventuelles,
de dire, d'exprimer, de graver quelque chose d'important dans
la conscience du lecteur. On peut lire dans la préface, datée
de 1969, des Etudes philosophiques choisies publiées en Hongrie
en 1971 sous le titre de Mon chemin vers Marx:

> Quelque paradoxal que cela puisse paraître, aujourd'hui,
> alors que je suis âgé de plus de quatre-vingts ans, je
> suis à la veille d'écrire les plus décisifs de mes
> ouvrages.

* Cet article a paru dans l'Europe, avril 1979, Paris

De même, Lukács déclarait dans une interview parue dans La Quinzaine Littéraire du 15 décembre 1966 que c'était à l'âge de soixante-dix ans qu'il avait commencé à écrire son oeuvre véritable. Voilà donc quelques explications à propos des marques de style en question: mais le paradoxe de ces déclarations n'a pas grand-chose à voir avec l'auto-stylisation psychologisante de la personnalité particulière. Une cause, une vie ayant un sens, l'avenir, la réflexion marxiste rénovable et à rénover, la situation mondiale, constamment dans la fièvre des changements, avec ses alternatives exigeant des décisions toujours nouvelles: c'est sur cela que se concentre en l'occurrence l'attention du penseur. C'est également cette attitude que l'on retrouve dans sa synthèse esthétique tardive. Le calme du Il n'est pas trop tard et l'inquiétude du Que faire? La solidité des principes et la passion de l'interrogation.

C'est seulement dans ce contexte que prend un sens la question de savoir s'il peut encore y avoir de nos jours une esthétique philosophique qui - pour reprendre une remarque de circonstance de Nicolaï Hartmann - "ne cause pas de déception". Philosophique: cet adjectif se rapporte, au sens le plus large, à l'une des formes idéologiques caractérisées par Marx qui, tout comme son objet élu, l'art, est destinée à ce que "les hommes prennent conscience de /leur/ conflit et le mènent jusqu'au bout". /Cf. la préface de Contribution à la critique de l'économie politique/. Esthétique philosophique: conscience théorique et systématisée de l'autoconscience, telle que cette dernière est apparue dans l'art et dans l'univers des objets esthétiques. Si l'on considère la méthode, une telle philosophie de l'art doit, pour ne pas "causer de déception", éviter deux grandes zones de danger que comporte ce type d'entreprise. Scylla: l'analyse nombrilique incapable de parvenir à la synthèse de l'univers de phénomènes esthétiques qu'elle reflète et ne le voulant d'ailleurs pas. Charybde: le fait de trôner dans les forteresses de plus en plus croulantes de la spéculation pure. Elle ne veut pas dissimuler qu'elle prend ses racines dans l'humus d'une Weltanschauung scientifique et systématique, et elle sait l'allier avec ce que les spécialistes nomment Kunsterfahrung, c'est-à-dire l'observation des comportements de création et de réception.

354

Il serait vain de nier que, jusqu'à ces derniers temps, la
science hongroise s'était montrée incapable d'avancer aucune
entreprise visant à répondre à ce type d'exigence. Dans ce sens,
la synthèse esthétique tardive de György Lukács a constitué une
percée hors du provincialisme de la pensée, et dans le Weltbe-
griff de l'esthétique. Son influence mondiale suffirait à le
démontrer. Mais c'est de manière extraordinaire, sans le moindre
lien avec les modes ou l'actualité manipulée-fétichisée. Et tout
cela à un moment où le dernier cri commence peu à peu à étiqueter
comme dépassée l'exigence même de synthèse, ou commence à pro-
duire en quantité industrielle les succédanés de synthèse. De
nos jours, l'idée selon laquelle vouloir élaborer une esthétique
philosophique serait un rêve irréalisable est en vogue: on prétend que celle-ci voudrait réunir des éléments intérieurement
divergents et, qui plus est, de ceux qui sont déjà utopiques
en soi étant donné la tendance actuelle de la progression de la
science moderne.

On se réfère dans ces cas-là à l'ébranlement subi par l'idée
de la systématisation philosophique, à la percée des théories
systématiques de type nouveau /logiques, mathématiques, cyber-
nétiques, etc./ ou, tout prosaïquement, au vieux topos positiviste: l'inextricabilité des connaissances partielles accumulées.
Nous évoquons un seul symptôme, mais il est caractéristique:
alors qu'à la fin du siècle dernier et au début de ce siècle,
le marché du livre était envahi par les "introductions", nous
sommes parvenus de nos jours à un véritable dumping des frag-
ments. Les Siegfried de l'esthétique actuelle sont incapables
de se forger une épée. Nietzsche écrivait déjà qu'il n'est plus
de moyen d'attraper le Tout au filet de la pensée, car le Tout
lui-même est tombé en pièces. On est bien près de considérer
comme moderne le fait de voir se taire aussi l'esthétique philosophique parce que capable d'être porteuse des conflits de l'é-
poque.

Mais Lukács a toujours parlé avec répugnance, dans sa période
marxiste, du refuge du "the rest is the silence". Il était réellement dans son élément lorsqu'il pouvait prendre la parole,
pour ou contre, même au risque de se tromper. Là aussi, il na-
geait à contre-courant de la modernité postiche. Il n'était bien

entendu pas sans connaître ce courant, et même très bien, car
il avait eu l'expérience personnelle de l'attirance nouvelle
exercée par la pensée fragmentaire. Il ressentit plusieurs fois
au cours de sa carrière ce genre de séductions du confort de
la pensée, et il leur tint tête. Mais il est une chose dont toute
sa carrière fut exempte: la résignation au caractère fragmentaire.
De fait, sa période pré-marxiste prouve déjà qu'il ressentait
comme étroit le cadre de la forme de l'essai. Ses essais, les
meilleurs aussi, constituent des entreprises de reconnaissance
et de travail d'avant-poste qui laissent présager que le gros
du combat n'est pas encore venu. L'une des caractéristiques dé-
terminantes de sa période marxiste est précisément son aspiration à cette intégralité qu'il a apprise de Goethe - dans le
sens que lui confère l'éthique tout autant que la théorie de la
science. Les manuscrits de Lukács écrits entre 1912 et 1917 à
Heidelberg et récemment publiés, qui constituent une ébauche esthétique de jeunesse de grande envergure cloturant la première
période des essais, semblent anticiper sur cette intégralité.
Il suffira ici de faire allusion à un seul de leurs traits, à
savoir une volonté jamais faiblissante d'aller jusqu'au but de
sa pensée. La théorie du roman, célèbre fragment de monographie
s'insérant dans ces Manuscrits, doit également à cet ethos d'a-
voir pu faire école - et pas seulement pour Lucien Goldmann.

Pour en revenir à la synthèse esthétique tardive de La particularité de l'esthétique, commencée dans les années cinquante
et arrêtée en 1962, nous pouvons lire dans la préface que Lukács
ne considérait pas comme réellement complète cette synthèse d'un
volume imposant. Il ne s'était efforcé que d'y fonder philosophiquement et d'une manière générale le Setzungsart esthétique;
de déduire à la manière marxiste, centrée sur la réalité, les
catégories esthétiques de la sphère particulièrement hétérogène
de la pratique humaine quotidienne. Il voulait réserver à une
troisième la mise en lumière complète de la nature sociale et
historique de l'art. On peut sentir derrière ce plan de division
la différenciation très répandue du matérialisme dialectique et
du matérialisme historique, mais aussi le début de la critique
de la séparation rigide de ces deux "disciplines": Lukács a souligné, déjà dans la grande étude préliminaire à cette synthèse,

De la particularité, qu'une telle distinction ne peut être que très relative. Ainsi, il est évident que La particularité de l'esthétique a visé à placer l'esthétique sur une base philosophique homogène. Cela n'empêche pas que le fait demeure: cet opus magnum est resté inachevé, et les deuxième et troisième parties prévues de cette synthèse n'ont pas pu être écrites. Comme il est aisé, dans ce cas, de prononcer le verdict: Lukács marxiste n'a donc pas pu non plus réaliser son rêve de jeunesse d'une esthétique philosophique complète! Et la question se pose à nouveau de savoir si ce rêve est réellement réalisable. Pour en rester dans le domaine des faits, Lukács a en effet entrepris quelque chose de nouveau après avoir achevé le premier tiers de sa synthèse. Et la clef de voûte de son oeuvre entière a finalement été le fruit de cette entreprise, l'Ontologie de l'Etre social, une monographie de vaste envergure qui a été publiée après la mort de son auteur. Beaucoup se laissent induire en erreur par une déclaration dictée à Lukács par une conviction subjective, et selon laquelle cet ouvrage ne constituerait que les prolégomènes d'une éthique marxiste systématique restant encore à écrire. Ceci est vrai dans la mesure ou Lukács, parvenu à sa maturité de penseur, ressentait un profond mépris à l'égard de la mentalité de "mandarin" qui régnait déjà à la fin du siècle dernier dans la vie académique allemande. Lukács, dans ses recherches sur les véritables particularités de l'esthétique /en ne dissimulant d'ailleurs pas les mérites historiques de l'esthétique de Kant/ n'accordait guère de prix à ce genre de "purisme". C'est pourquoi je me risque à supposer que ce nouvel ouvrage, l'Ontologie, a au moins autant été inspiré par le système esthétique lui-même, avec ses ramifications amorcées et ses lois structurales immanentes, imposant un contrôle réitéré de ce qui a été achevé. Il faut aussi accorder une attention toute particulière aux déclarations de Lukács du type: "Chez moi, l'esthétique se transforme en partie organique de l'ontologie de l'Etre social" /Mon chemin vers Marx: préface à l'édition hongroise, 1969/. En bref: on ne peut interpréter avec justesse cette synthèse esthétique de vieillesse, en fonction de la dynamique objective de la structure, qu'en ne s'arrêtant pas à la dernière phrase de La particularité de l'esthétique. Nous

ignorons comment aurait été opérée dans ses détails la transformation projetée du Dôme de Sienne dont l'original, considéré
aujourd'hui encore comme une merveille, n'aurait été que le tran-
sept de l'édifice futur: une épidémie de peste sonna le glas de
ce projet grandiose. Cependant, nous pouvons reconstruire du regard la nouvelle ligne des voûtes et la nouvelle nef en imagination. C'est une voûte reconstituable de ce genre qui embrasse
l'esthétique tardive de Lukács. Avant toute chose, le système
des piliers est en place, et bien solidement. De fait, au plan
de l'intention subjective et de la décision politique, leur place
était déjà prévue en 1918, lorsque le célèbre auteur de La Théorie du Roman, faisant demi-tour au seuil d'une carrière classique
de savant bourgeois, mit sa vie au service du mouvement ouvrier
révolutionnaire. Car Lukács ne fit pas sien le marxisme par un
acte unique, une sorte d'"illumination" à la St-Paul, mais par
une étude constamment renouvelée, comme il le dit lui-même, "en
un mouvement à double sens": en arrière, vers la conception philosophique et esthétique originale de Marx, Engels et Lénine, et
en avant, vers une fouille théorique de plus en plus approfondie
de l'essence conflictuelle du présent, de sa problématique in-
terne - de la problématique de la réalité reflétée également par
l'art.

Je le répète, c'est en marxiste que Lukács aspirait à l'élaboration d'une esthétique philosophique. Pour l'essentiel, c'est
une tradition marxiste ancienne qu'il suit lorsqu'il analyse le
grand art en tant que valeur humanisatrice. C'est ce pilier qui
supporte une partie extrêmement importante du poids de la voûte
théorique. La particularité de l'esthétique, de la préface au
dernier chapitre et aussi dans la suite que l'on peut lui reconstruire, voulait être un témoignage "en faveur de l'art et
contre la religion", comme on peut le lire dans la Préface; en
faveur d'une auto-conscience s'opposant à l'aliénation, et contre
la fausse conscience reproduisant directement ou indirectement
celle-ci, comme le prouve l'oeuvre tout entière. Il s'agit d'une
prise de position décidée et fondée en faveur de la tendance humaniste. Par cela, Lukács donne un poids particulier, entre autres,
aux principes fondamentaux de sa propre conception de l'art que
nous connaissons de plus tôt. Tout en réunissant en une théorie

homogène les éléments de pensée de ses écrits d'émigration à
Berlin et Moscou - notamment sur le caractère anthropomorphe de
la mise en forme artistique et sur sa manière particulière de
refléter la réalité - il examine dès lors également en détail
les lois esthétiques plus générales de l'appropriation artistique de la réalité, capable de saisir l'essentiel. Il met un
accent particulier sur la "mission de défétichisation" qui rend
le grand art apte à contribuer à l'élaboration d'une auto-conscience véritable. Lukács souligne que l'une des caractéristiques
indiscutables de l'art est le fait que sa sphère réelle de réalisation est l'oeuvre d'art, close en un microcosme. Mais quel
est le secret de l'oeuvre en tant que "totalité intensive"? Sa
mise en forme particulière, bien entendu; sa téléologie, qui
reflète dans une mesure importante un problème de forme. Mais
pas uniquement, ni essentiellement. On ne pourrait comprendre
ni la genèse, ni la structure, ni le fonctionnement de l'oeuvre
d'art en tant que totalité intensive si l'on renonçait à un aspect épistémologique généralement approché par la métaphore du
"reflet", et cela depuis Shakespeare et Leibniz, pour ne pas
dire depuis Platon et Aristote. Le premier et l'ultime secret
des oeuvres d'art est leur vérité, leur rapport adéquat a la
réalité, ou plus précisément à l'Etre social.

En effet, souligne Lukács, toute oeuvre d'art porteuse d'une
valeur esthétique véritable fait éclater des fétiches faux, afin
de prendre sous sa protection et d'affirmer la cause de l'humanité, la totalité et l'intégralité humaines. C'est ce que fait
Homère /Lukács citait toujours avec plaisir la grande scène
d'Achille et de Priam/, et c'est également ce qui se passe dans
Le grand voyage de Semprun, dans une situation historique radicalement différente, notamment grâce au personnage du communiste
juif qui, dans l'interprétation de Lukács, prend l'existentialisme
au mot, et choisit, non pas la "mort juive", mais le sort des
héros de la résistance armée. Ce qu'affirme l'art humaniste, ce
sont les valeurs historiquement accumulées et finalement irré-
vocables de la Gattungsmässigkeit. Le grand art constitue toujours une contre-variante historiquement concrète de l'aliénation,
une anticipation de liberté et d'universalité, et cela même dans
les conditions d'aliénation les plus poussées. C'est essentielle-

ment à cela que ces oeuvres doivent être "grandes". Voilà une
vérité partielle dans la conception classicisante de la "perfection" esthétique. Une vérité partielle qui ne se découvre que
grâce à une critique ontologique orientée vers la réalité de
l'harmonie exempte de toute tension. Car les grandes oeuvres sont
"destructives" pour pouvoir construire; elles nient le négatif
pour affirmer l'accumulation des valeurs humaines, le courant
profond de la progression, ce processus qui approche l'individuel et le Gattungsmässige. C'est pour cela qu'elles détruisent
les illusions quotidiennes sur la réalité, les stéréotypes des
conceptions et des idées superficielles et déformées. Leur véritable champ d'action est l'évocation sensible de l'essence
humaine historiquement concrète. Pour cette raison, elles représentent le monde extérieur dès l'abord comme le monde propre
à l'homme, comme le théâtre d'actions et de passions modelant
le destin de l'humanité. Dans une mise en forme artistique de
ce type, l'homme supposé par certains créature divine ou pri-
sonnié du Néant, est à même de révéler sa véritable essence; il
se montre, en effet, l'artisan de son propre destin et en même
temps un "être sociable" dont le noyau intérieur, la substance
humaine sont modelés par son rapport actif à des unités supéri-
eures du genre humain, comme la communauté historiquement donnée,
la classe, la nation, la progression humaine.

   Donner la parole à cette Gattungsmässigkeit par ailleurs "mu-
ette", tel est l'enjeu en art, et Lukács se réfère ici à bon
droit non seulement à Marx, le penseur, mais aussi à Goethe, le
poète des Elégies de Marienbad. C'est le "dieu" de l'art qui le
lui a donné, ainsi qu'à ses compagnons, nous dit Lukács, celui
de l'art qui exprime, dans le langage articulé de l'auto-conscience, ce qui à chaque époque est essentiel pour l'homme, en
montrant de manière sensible les tourments et les joies du monde.
Ce qui resterait "muet" dans la vie de tous les jours, et qui
serait impossible à saisir et à comprendre. En d'autres termes,
ce que la religion /dans ses formes tant traditionnelles que mo-
dernes/ transpose du milieu des rapports d'existence de la tran-
scendance. C'est pour cela que La particularité de l'esthétique
constitue un plaidoyer en faveur de l'art et contre la religion.
L'une des analyses les plus saisissantes est consacrée à la "lutte

pour la libération" des arts: elle constitue d'ailleurs le dernier chapitre, et s'inscrit dans la ligne tracée explicitement
par la synthèse effectivement achevée.

Les thèses proclamant la mission humaniste et défétichisante
resteraient, bien sûr, une déclaration vide si elles n'étaient
soutenues par d'autres piliers de pensée, en l'occurrence tout
un système de nouvelles catégories. Celles-ci ne sont pas toutes
neuves; Lukács avait déjà jeté les bases de la plupart d'entre
elles lors de son émigration à Moscou. Cependant, on en trouve
qui sont re-formulées. En l'occurrence, la particularité de l'art
n'est autre que le fait qu'il fait de cette unité un "médium or-
ganisateur". Il ne s'agit donc pas d'un point, mais d'un champ:
et c'est sur des points extraordinairement variés de ce champ
que les diverses branches artistiques, les genres, les tendances
de l'histoire de l'art, et enfin, les oeuvres concrètes elles-
-mêmes sont situés, qu'ils prennent leur forme définitive entre
ces deux limites extrêmes. Toujours par suite d'une médiation
féconde. L'esthétique n'est donc pas un point unique et authen-
tifié né sous le signe de la particularité - dans cette mesure,
sa sphère est de caractère pluralistique. L'art a toujours trouvé
plusieurs sortes de solution pour se faire le porteur des problèmes épocaux et pour exprimer de manière sensible l'image de
l'homme et l'essence humaine de chaque époque. C'est donc à bon
droit que nous parlons de la variété des branches artistiques et
des oeuvres individuelles, autant que de la coexistence polypho-
nique des mises en forme qui leur sont particulières, à condition
de voir clairement aussi les impasses des interprétations qui
obscurcissent de nos jours le concept du pluralisme esthétique.
C'est le cas d'une part de la régulation normative, quels que
soient les principes sur lesquels elle se base. Les "canons"
restent étrangers à l'esthétique philosophique, si celle-ci ne
veut pas dès l'abord "causer des déceptions". Ils appartiennent
à la sphere de la théologie. Mais la dé-relativisation complète
de la valeur esthétique, actuellement en vogue, ne nous sort pas
davantage des impasses de la normativité. Certains porte-parole
du pluralisme servent des buts tout à fait manipulatifs lorsqu'ils brouillent les limites du grand art et du pseudo-art
/apologétiquement naturaliste ou négativiste/. Lukács n'inter-

prêtait pas le pluralisme de la sphère esthétique en libéral vulgaire. Ce ne furent pas des préjugés ordinaires, mais les particularités objectives de cette sphère qui l'amenèrent à souligner que le champ de mouvement de la particularité, dont nous parlions plus haut, était vaste, mais non sans rivages. S'il s'agit d'un champ de croissance des valeurs, il découle de la notion même qu'il faut que ce soit un champ de mouvement d'émancipation. Tout mode de représentation enchaînant l'oeuvre aux aspects aléatoires du quotidien ou la remplissant d'idoles générales d'apparence scientifique, reste d'une valeur problématique ou même pseudo-esthétique, telle que le naturalisme et l'abstraction appauvrissant la complexité de la vérité à laquelle le grand art est toujours si sensible. Le feu de la création artistique n'est donc pas sans rivages, tant qu'il possède une direction de courant. La particularité ne constitue pas un état statique dans l'oeuvre, ni une réconciliation dénuée de tension et pseudo-harmonique, mais un mouvement oscillant entre l'individuel et le général.

A première vue, cette théorie du particulier peut sembler une construction logique. Un trait de cette synthèse tardive qui n'a pas encore été assez souligné - il est vrai qu'il n'a pas été non plus entièrement explicité - est le mieux à même de démontrer combien ce n'était pas le cas chez Lukács. Eh bien, La particularité de l'esthétique insiste plus fort que son auteur ne l'a jamais fait auparavant sur le problème de la réceptivité esthétique et sur celui de l'efficacité artistique des oeuvres d'art, de l'influence exercée pour elles, et cela sous le signe d'une unité dialectique des valeurs durables et du mode d'existence historique. Lukács donne une réponse à ce qu'il avait déjà posé en question dans ses essais de synthèse de jeunesse, et à quoi Marx trouva une clef méthodologique en analysant l'exemplarité des épopées homériques. Déjà, La particularité de l'esthétique anticipe sur ce discernement:

> La thèse selon laquelle il n'est pas d'objet sans sujet
> peut être purement idéaliste du point de vue épistémo-
> logique, elle n'en est pas moins d'une importance fonda-
> mentale du point de vue du rapport sujet-objet en esthé-
> tique. Naturellement, en soi, tous les objets esthétiques

sont eux aussi indépendants dans une certaine mesure
de la conscience. Mais ainsi, ils n'existent que ma-
tériellement, et non pas esthétiquement. Lorsque leur
projection d'un sujet, puisque /.../ leur particularité
esthétique consiste précisément /.../ dans le fait d'é-
voquer chez le sujet récepteur à l'aide d'une forme particulière du reflet de la réalité objective certaines
choses vécues. /I. p. 515./

Cette efficacité artistique et avec elle le rapport sujet-
-objet est impliquée par la structure articulée de l'oeuvre même.
Sa réalisation ne dépend bien entendu pas seulement de l'oeuvre,
mais aussi du récepteur: ce ne sont pas des gens à la conscience
en "tabula rasa" qui jouissent des oeuvres, s'arrêtent devant
les tableaux, lisent les romans, voient les films. Les tendances
de manipulation et d'aliénation, que recèle la culture de masse
actuelle, nous obligent déjà à compter avec la possibilité de
réactions inadéquates. C'est justement le rapport sujet-objet
qui rend adéquat le mode de réception que Lukács, reprenant un
terme emprunté à la culture grecque antique, nomme catharsis et
élève au rang de catégorie esthétique. Il ne s'agit pas en l'occurrence du principe d'identification ou d'auto-jouissance ob-
jectivée /au sens où l'entend Lipp/, et pas davantage d'identification sentimentale, que soupçonnait et rejetait notamment
Brecht dans ce concept, mais d'un bouleversement, d'une "purification" dont l'essentiel, selon une formule particulièrement
frappante de Lukács, est que le ganzer Mensch peut se transcender
en Menschenganz grâce à l'impression produite par l'oeuvre. En
d'autres termes, le récepteur de la grande oeuvre est libéré de
sa captivité dans la particularité de caractère purement privé
à laquelle le quotidien aliéné le condamnerait sans cela, et se
trouve capable, en vivant intérieurement des destins et des passions "étrangers", de s'identifier aux grands contenus univer-
sels de la classe, de la nation, du genre humain se créant lui-
-même; de continuer à vivre sa propre vie en homme plus complet,
en homme comprenant et transformant activement son propre univers et son époque; de s'élever jusqu'aux hauteurs historiquement
réellement possibles de la Gattungsmässigkeit. C'est par cela
que l'art peut se transformer en chef de file d'une émancipation
réelle et multilatérale, en exemple de la révolte contre des con-

ditions de vie absurdes et dégénérées. C'est par la que cette
totalité intérieure devient gardien et facteur d'enrichissement
des valeurs et de l'intégrité humaines.

Et on se trouve ici devant un nouvel aspect du problème é-
thique de l'intégralité de l'homme, devant une nouvelle explication de ce que nous comprenons par des adjectifs qualificatifs
jusque-là tacitement reliés aux oeuvres d'art: "grand", "parfait",
etc. Il s'agit de toute évidence de l'une des conséquences
esthétiques de la Welthaftigkeit. Dans cette interprétation,
l'oeuvre indique nécessairement un contenu formé; un contenu comme
signification procédant du fait de l'orientation sur la réalité,
et une mise en forme dans le microcosme de l'oeuvre d'art. La
forme "ouverte", si elle exclut conséquemment tous les éléments
de "fermeture", risque d'aboutir à un manque d'articulation de
l'oeuvre-signification. Par contre, si l'on comprend ce caractère clos comme un monade "sans fenêtre", à la Leibniz, ou plus
encore à la Adorno, le principal lien qui rattache l'oeuvre au
sujet et assure sa réception s'atrophie. Les "grandes" oeuvres
d'Homère, de Dante ou de Beethoven ont mérité cette épithète
parce qu'elles sont des évocations mises en forme de destins
humains, et parce qu'elles les reflètent d'une façon efficace
au point de vue de la catharsis.

Et nous voici parvenus à l'un des thèmes les plus anciens
des polémiques suscitées par Lukács et son oeuvre: le réalisme.
Mais, cette fois encore, dans un nouveau contexte. Si Lukács
marxiste a dès le début condamné l'interprétation subjectiviste
de l'appropriation de la réalité dans l'art, en même temps que
l'art décadent de l'apologétique bourgeoise, cette conception
du réalisme est bien entendu allée de pair dès le début avec
une condamnation des méthodes naturalistes. L'approche de ces
problèmes inspirée par l'ontologie sociale approfondit théo-
riquement cette lutte sur deux fronts. En effet, le rapport
sujet-objet ne signifie pas simplement dans l'esthétique tardive de Lukács leur fusion. Dans les grandes oeuvres, ce rapport mène toujours à une élévation à la puissance: le sujet
s'appropriant l'objet /le récepteur tout autant que le créa-
teur/ dépasse sa particularité privée: l'objet, enraciné dans
l'Etre social et tirant sa signification et son efficacité de

364

ses contenus de Gattungsmässigkeit, entre en possession d'un surcroît esthétique en gagnant une objectivité de type social tout empreinte de pratique historique. La synthèse tardive de Lukács n'a pas découvert les principes du fondement ontologique de l'esthétique au prix d'un renoncement à la théorie de la réflexion dans cette discipline /comme dans aucune autre/. S'il fait de la notion-clef d'efficacité adéquate, la catharsis, une catégorie de portée générale, il la considère comme inséparable par principe de la mimésis.

La mimésis, principe d'imitation dans l'esthétique... c'est peut-être là une pierre d'achoppement pour l'idéologie bourgeoise d'aujourd'hui encore plus importante que le réalisme lui--même, qui est discuté depuis le début. Nous avons déjà signalé que les innovations de Lukács concernant les catégories ne sont pas des produits de la mode. Cette fois non plus, ce n'est pas l'approbation des forteresses académiques qu'il vise en élargissant le répertoire des concepts de l'esthétique; il veut cerner, avec l'aide de ces concepts le plus précisément possible des faits objectifs. La théorie lukácsienne de la mimésis n'a rien à voir avec un renouvellement de la théorie de l'imitation mécanique, pas plus qu'elle n'avait à y voir dans la conception antique, d'ailleurs. Lukács considère en principe comme mimétique toute branche artistique "créant un microcosme propre", de la littérature à l'architecture en passant par la musique. Mais il n'est absolument pas question en l'occurrence d'imitation pour ainsi dire "naturaliste", et cela d'autant moins que, selon les raisonnements développés dans La particularité de l'esthétique, la création artistique est dès le départ un mode de projection téléologique - et l'était déjà lorsqu'elle portait encore la gangue des formes de conscience magiques ancestrales. C'est d'ailleurs de cela que découle avec une nécessité esthétique l'unité organique du contenu et de la forme, en même temps que la transformation de l'un dans l'autre. En principe, un chant de travail ancestral a tout autant été structuré "cadenciellement", à partir du but poursuivi, que par exemple la "Neuvième" de Beethoven. Tous deux sont des mimésis de caractère téléologique.

L'idée de l'alliance de la catharsis et de la mimésis fait
également partie du système de piliers de la synthèse tardive
de Lukács dont nous parlions plus haut. Cette alliance colore
également la catégorie du réalisme. Il est intéressant de voir
que La particularité de l'esthétique - après avoir à plusieurs
reprises fait allusion au caractère réaliste de tout art important - n'élabore vraiment explicitement cette nouvelle nuance
qu'en un seul point du texte. Et ce point, celui de la musique,
est précisément l'un des plus névralgiques, car les critiques de
l'oeuvre de Lukács, considérée comme entièrement axée sur la littérature et le roman, voulaient justement y voir un grand contre-
-exemple de réfutation, en discutant la validité générale du réalisme. Ce qui est d'ailleurs déjà en soi caractéristique de la
méthode et du comportement scientifique du penseur désormais âgé.
Toujours est-il qu'il prend ici nettement position en faveur du
réalisme qui peut se manifester en musique, et par-dessus le marché dans la Nouvelle Musique du XXe siècle, soi-disant anti-ré-
aliste a priori. Lukács se réfère à l'art de Béla Bartók.

Il se peut que La particularité de l'esthétique ne traite pas
précisément de la musique sous le meilleur titre général /en
tant que "problème-limite" de la mimésis/. Toujours est-il que,
selon Lukács, on assiste dans les grandes oeuvres musicales à
une "mimésis double": après que la réalité objective se soit
reflétée dans l'intime humain de manière primaire, la musique
transforme ce reflet en un "second" reflet de type spécial, qui
est caractérisé par un langage autonome.

Bref, c'est par toute une série de transmissions que la musique crée l'effet cathartique au sens prégnant du terme. Ainsi,
ce n'est pas la ressemblance avec des phénomènes ou objets con-
crets, ni même la généralité qui caractérise les concepts, qui
confère à la musique son élément d'existence; c'est précisément
pour cela que, dans la sphère de la particularité musicale, l'un-
bestimmte Gegenständlichkeit de la signification des oeuvres
est mise en relief. Dans le cas qui nous occupe, par contre, Lukács ne laisse plus planer aucun doute sur le fait que la musique
n'est pas un art déviant "conmimétique"; ceux qui posent des
questions sur son essence découvrent des choses essentielles,
également du point de vue de l'esthétique. En effet, le réalisme

est, chez le vieux Lukács aussi, une catégorie esthétique générale; plus nous analysons concrètement les branches artistiques,
les genres, et plus clairement apparaît ce qui est commun et général dans les couches profondes des phénomènes. De cette manière,

> le caractère réaliste de l'oeuvre est fonction de la
> profondeur et de la justesse, du caractère synthétique
> et de l'authenticité avec lesquels elle sait reproduire
> et évoquer les problèmes du moment historique où elle a
> vu le jour, et cela à partir de la perspective de la
> signification durable de ces problèmes pour le développe-
> ment de l'humanité... Et c'est dans ce sens diamétralement
> opposé aux vues répandues chez un très grand nombre que
> nous pouvons à bon droit parler de réalisme musical.
> /II. p. 367/

Selon Lukács, dans ce sens, c'est la mise en forme de nos problèmes d'époque s'élevant jusqu'au niveau de la Gattungsmässigkeit qui rend par exemple cathartique et réaliste la Cantata Pro-
fana de Bartók. Nous sommes d'avis que dans le passage qu'il lui
consacre, Lukács dissipe toute une série de légendes, par exemple
celles de la concentration prétendument exclusive de la théorie
lukácsienne du réalisme sur la littérature, ou du "conservatisme
invétéré" de la Kunsterfahrung de Lukács. Ces légendes ne sont
pas sans occasionner beaucoup de trouble chez ceux qui attendent
- avec raison - de l'esthétique philosophique qu'elle ne leur
"cause pas de déception". Pour cette raison, il faut parler en
conclusion d'un aspect fort important de cette synthèse tardive
reconstruite par nous assez schématiquement, à savoir la trans-
-structuration de l'expérience artistique, au sens strict du
terme de Lukács. Pars pro toto: dans sa vieillesse, Lukács écrivit en 1964, sous le titre de In memoriam Hanns Eisler, un texte
très instructif à cet égard. Cet article était un hommage à un
ancien partenaire de discussion, l'adversaire tellement anti-
-Lukács de la grande polémique de l'expressionnisme de la seconde
moitié des années trente, l'antifasciste et communiste allemand.
Dans le même temps, ce texte contient un appel implicite à re-
penser les polémiques d'autrefois, et notamment la célèbre con-
troverse Lukács-Brecht. Le temps qui passe et l'accumulation
d'expériences nouvelles peuvent provoquer des vues modifiées ou
des corrections d'estimation chez ceux qui, indépendamment de

leur âge réel, ne souffrent pas de sclérose de l'esprit. A présent, les lecteurs français peuvent découvrir cet article en
texte intégral, et voir si et dans quel sens se sont modifiées
les estimations de valeur de Lukács. Il apparaît peut-être de
ce petit écrit que ces corrections ne soutiennent pas précisément l'alternative artistique du héros musicien du Doktor Faustus de Thomas Mann, Adrian Leverkühn; les principes ne se ré-
concilient pas chez Lukács, même dans sa vieillesse. Pour cela,
précisément, il vaut la peine de considérer avec attention la
phrase finale:

> Seuls ceux qui cherchent honnêtement trouvent, et seuls
> ceux qui fuient dans la bonne direction trouveront leur
> véritable patrie.

Cette phrase fut écrite par Lukács pour la première fois en
1941 dans une revue hongroise de Moscou, Új Hang /Voix Nouvelle/.
L'article en question portait le titre de "L'actualité et la
fuite devant elle - De la littérature de la guerre", et son auteur vivait alors en émigration, tout comme Eisler, Bartók ou
Thomas Mann. La date n'est pas non plus, ne peut pas être sans
intérêt. Le fascisme tenait alors la moitié de l'Europe sous
sa botte, et se préparait à attaquer l'Union Soviétique. Cet
article ancien nous parle du sens de la quête et de la découverte
de la véritable patrie; sa citation en 1964 est empreinte du
pathos discret de la poursuite de cette recherche et de la re-
-découverte. Verrait-on là uniquement les marques d'un comportement subjectif? Non. A la fin de sa vie aussi, ce sont la recherche et la découverte qui ont été les étoiles-guides de Lukács, et en fin de compte, sa synthèse esthétique a été édifiée
sous ce firmament à l'éclat jamais pâli.